Recommended Bed & Breakfasts™
Mid-Atlantic States

Recommended Bed & Breakfasts™ Series

Recommended Bed & Breakfasts™ Mid-Atlantic States

Delaware · Maryland · New Jersey New York · Pennsylvania · Virginia West Virginia

Suzi Forbes Chase

Old Saybrook, Connecticut

Cover design by Lana Mullen
Cover illustration by Michael Crampton
Illustrations by Mauro Magellan

Library of Congress Cataloging-in-Publication Data

Chase, Suzi Forbes.
      Recommended bed & breakfasts. Mid-Atlantic states / Suzi Forbes Chase
          p.   cm.—(Recommended bed & breakfast series)
      Includes index.
      ISBN 0-7627-0117-X
      1. Bed and breakfast accommodations—Middle Atlantic States —
      Guidebooks. I. Title.   II. Series.
      TX907.3.M53C4747   1997
      647.974'03—dc21
                                   97-30177
                                      CIP

Manufactured in the United States
First Edition/Second Printing

ACKNOWLEDGMENTS

No book is written in a vacuum and this particular book is the product of a marvelous support system. I especially wish to thank Bruce Markot, the former Managing Editor of The Globe Pequot Press, and Laura Strom, the Executive Editor, who had the confidence in me to propose this book in the first place. Laura, in particular, was instrumental in launching it. She ushered it from its initial contract stage through its final production, always exhibiting patience and clear direction. Her support and encouragement have been invaluable. I would also like to thank Paula Brisco, Associate Editor, who handled much of the production scheduling; Mauro Magellan, who is responsible for the engaging line drawings of each B&B; and Trish Charles, the copy editor.

Mostly, however, I would like to thank my husband, Dustin, who accompanies me on my quests for B&Bs whenever his work schedule permits, but who tolerates my frequent absences from home when he cannot go. Without his support and encouragement, I couldn't write the books I write. Often on my lone trips, if the temperature is warm enough, I am chaperoned by my Lhasa apso, Oreo, who willingly spends nights in his car bed and eats meals in village parks—all for the dubious pleasure of traveling with me. Thanks to you too, Oreo.

Help Us Keep This Guide Up to Date

Every effort has been made by the author and editors to make this guide as accurate and useful as possible. However, many things can change after a guide is published—establishments close, phone numbers change, facilities come under new management, etc.

We would love to hear from you concerning your experiences with this guide and how you feel it could be made better and be kept up to date. While we may not be able to respond to all comments and suggestions, we'll take them to heart and we'll also make certain to share them with the author. Please send your comments and suggestions to the following address:

The Globe Pequot Press
Reader Response/Editorial Department
P.O. Box 833
Old Saybrook, CT 06475

Or you may e-mail us at:
editorial@globe-pequot.com

Thanks for your input, and happy travels!

Contents

Introduction

I'll never forget my first visit to a B&B. It was almost thirty years ago and I was charmed by the turreted, gingerbreaded, multidecked Victorian house, as well as by the antique furnishings and the innkeepers. The couple told me about their interest in saving this grand house that was on the verge of collapsing and how, after a trip to Europe, they decided to buy the house, restore it, and then put it to work to pay for itself.

At the time, I was completing my law school education and I had decided to specialize in historic preservation law, so the restoration of historic houses and buildings and their adaptation to today's uses, was extremely appealing to me. Little did I know then that I would one day be privileged to play a role in this great B&B business.

In the 1960s there were probably no more than 200 B&Bs and country inns in America and there was only one guidebook. I've always been an inveterate traveler, so with the guidebook in hand, I made it my mission to stay in a B&B or country inn whenever there was one nearby. Soon, I was writing articles for my local newspaper about B&Bs, country inns, restaurants, and travel—and so my career was launched.

I can't imagine a more rewarding job. The lure of a quiet country road is still irresistible to me, and the joy of discovery when I find a new high-quality B&B never gets old. Today, of course, innkeeping is a highly professional business. The number of B&Bs and country inns has increased over the last thirty years some 750 percent, and the American Bed and Breakfast Association now estimates there are about 30,000 B&Bs and country inns in America.

What Is a B&B?

Perhaps a definition is in order here. Over the years, the terms country inn and bed and breakfast have become blurred, and are sometimes used synonymously. For the purposes of this book, I have tried to be very clear about the difference. Actually, there are three categories of homes in which guests can stay. A home-stay and a guesthouse are terms that generally refer to rooms in a private home where the owner either offers rooms seasonally or where he or she has another full-time job outside the home. These are not included in this guidebook. A B&B is generally a home with from three to fifteen guest rooms. The innkeeper lives on the premises, has licensed his business with the town, operates it as his primary means of income, and offers breakfast as well as a room.

A country inn, on the other hand, generally refers to establishments with more than fifteen rooms and one that has a restaurant offering dinner as well as breakfast. It is also a full-time, licensed business for the innkeepers and in most cases the innkeepers live on the premises. In this book, I have concentrated on B&Bs, but the companion book *Recommended Country Inns of the Mid-Atlantic and Chesapeake Region* describes country inns in the same area.

How Did I Select B&Bs for This Book?

My task is to ferret out the very best B&Bs in the Mid-Atlantic region and to describe them to you in such a way that you can make an informed opinion about where you want to stay. To do that I visited 582 B&Bs and country inns in 1995 and 623 in 1996 and I put more than 7,000 miles on my car each year. Although I have an enormous database in my computer, I learn about new B&Bs from local innkeepers, from other travelers at B&B breakfast tables, from letters sent by readers and innkeepers, and from the numerous newsletters and publications I review. There is seldom a day that goes by that I don't add a new B&B to my list or note a change in an existing one.

On my first visit to a B&B, I arrive unannounced and do a thorough inspection. I take copious notes in hardbound books that I later index, and I add the dates of my inspections and my overall comments to my computer database. This approach has one major drawback: On occasion, there is no one home, and then I must wait to review that B&B on another visit. On the other hand, the approach works because I know I am seeing the B&B just as it will look to paying guests and not spruced up for a visit by a travel writer. If, after my inspection, I believe the B&B warrants inclusion in my book, I usually schedule a return visit to stay there.

To select merely 150 B&Bs from the vast number that are now available, I look for those with the highest standards in each area. I am a stickler for absolute cleanliness, superb maintenance, and friendly on-site innkeepers or managers, so if a B&B is lacking in any of those areas, I generally do not include it. In addition, if a B&B has been in business less than two years, or if there are new owners, I will generally give it time to season.

I believe most travelers today prefer rooms with private baths, so most of the B&Bs in this book have private baths. I also look for B&Bs with comfortable common areas, including verandas, porches, and gardens and those offering something extra—perhaps afternoon tea, or evening wine and cheese, or bicycles to use and maps to follow, or an on-site archeological dig, or an artist in residence. Yet, I also believe I have a responsibility to offer my readers a selection of B&Bs that provide a variety of styles, prices, and amenities and that cover the entire Mid-Atlantic geographic area, although I do concentrate on the most popular tourist destinations.

B&Bs reflect the architectural and decorative styles of the buildings they are located within, as well as the interests of the innkeepers who own them. So whether you're looking for an intimate, romantic retreat with a whirlpool tub and a rose on the pillow at turndown, or an adventure-packed weekend of mountain climbing, you're sure to find what strikes your fancy in these pages. My pledge to you is that each of these B&Bs has been personally inspected by me and, in my opinion, they meet the highest standards of cleanliness, maintenance, decor, and friendliness.

I take my responsibility very seriously and welcome comments from you also. Changes inevitably take place and your personal experiences add to my knowledge about a B&B. You may write to me at The Globe Pequot Press, P.O. Box 833, Old Saybrook, CT 06475.

Happy traveling!

Suzi Forbes Chase

The prices and rates listed in this guidebook were confirmed at press time. We recommend, however, that you call establishments before traveling to obtain current information.

How to Use This B&B Guide

General Information

This guidebook contains more than 150 B&Bs in the seven states that make up the Mid-Atlantic region—Delaware, Maryland, New Jersey, New York, Pennsylvania, Virginia, and West Virginia.

The B&Bs in this guide are alphabetized according to town in each state. You will find a map of the state in front of each chapter. Each B&B is identified by a number on the map, and a legend beside the map indicates the town it's located in. It is usually easiest to decide on your destination and then to read the write-up about each B&B in that area to decide where you want to stay. Several popular geographic areas are listed in the back indexes and the B&Bs in each area are identified here also.

If you are traveling with children, or with a wheelchair-bound person, or with pets, you will also find an index in the back that identifies B&Bs that offer the necessary facilities that best accommodate you.

For the most part, I believe travelers today prefer a room with a private bath, so all the B&Bs in this book, with a few clearly identified exceptions, have rooms with private baths. In addition, at the end of each B&B description, you will find a list of such important details as size, rates, amenities, and policies.

Some Specifics about Rates

The rates in this book are based on double occupancy, and although innkeepers were asked to provide their 1998 rates, you may find slight differences. It is always best to ask for the exact rate when you book—and be sure to ask if the rate includes all taxes, gratuities, and service charges. B&Bs will often require a deposit to hold the room. You should also ask about and understand the B&B's policy about refunds in case you are unable to come when planned.

What's Nearby

To help you plan your trip, I have identified some of the major attractions near each B&B. In some cases, this information is supplemented by details in the write-up about the inn.

Although this data may be helpful when planning your itinerary, be sure to also ask the innkeeper about his or her specific suggestions. In several areas (the Amish/Mennonite section of Pennsylvania and the Gettysburg battlefield area in particular), innkeepers may suggest specific guides to take you on a personalized tour.

Often innkeepers will also be able to direct you to local homes where quilts are made, or to an artist's studio, or they can arrange dinner in a local home, or make special arrangements for you to tour a farm or historic house.

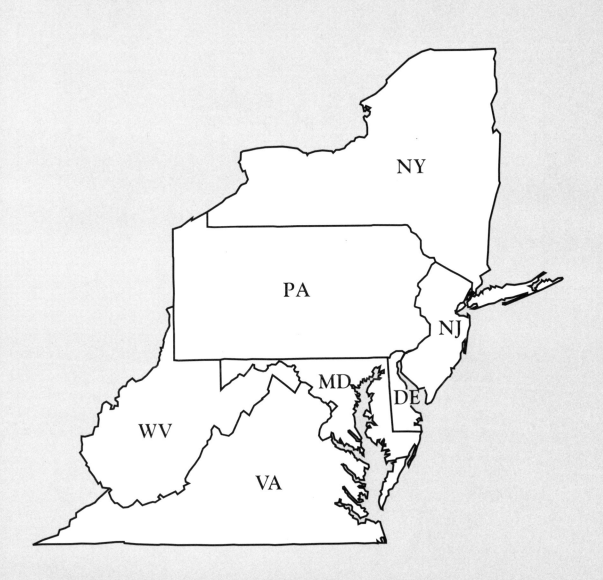

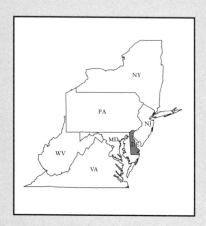

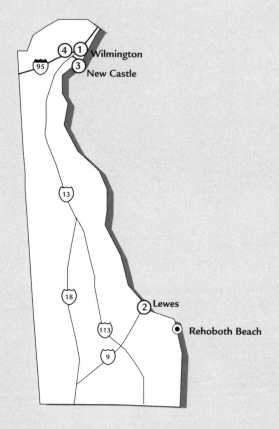

Wilmington

New Castle

Lewes

Rehoboth Beach

N

Delaware

Numbers on map refer to towns numbered below.

Darley Manor Inn
3701 Philadelphia Pike,
Claymont (North Wilmington), DE 19703
(800) 824-4703 or (302) 792-2127;
fax (302) 798-6143;
e-mail: darley@dca.net
website: http://www.dca.net/darley

Innkeepers: Ray and Judith Hester
Rooms: 6, including 4 suites, all with private baths, air conditioning, TVs, VCRs, three telephones, dataports, hair dryers, desks, and robes; 4 with mini-refrigerators, coffee makers, irons, and ironing boards; 2 with fireplaces; 1 with a balcony and a stereo
On the grounds: Garden
Extras: Exercise room; fruit, cookies, tea, coffee, and sodas available in the refreshment room; sherry set out in the front parlor; fax and copier available
Rates: Suites $89–$99, rooms $79–$89, including full breakfast; two-night minimum weekends and holidays in April, May, September, and October
Open: Year-round
Smoking: Permitted outside only
Credit cards accepted: American Express, MasterCard, Visa
How to get there: From Wilmington, take I-95 north. Take exit 10 onto Harvey Road. Turn right onto Harvey Road and proceed about 1 mile to its end. Turn left onto Philadelphia Pike and travel about 1 mile. Turn left onto Darley Road. The B&B is on the corner. Drive in the 1st driveway and park in the parking lot.

In the mid-1800s Claymont was known as a bucolic summer community that offered charming views of the Delaware River, alive with tall ships and sailing vessels. Industrialists and merchants from Philadelphia and Wilmington built grand mansions, and artists came to write and paint. Felix Darley, America's best-known book illustrator, purchased the estate he called "Wren's Nest" in 1859 and lived there until his death in 1888. In his lifetime, he produced more than four thousand illustrations and was espe-cially well known as the illustrator of the books of Edgar Allan Poe, Washington Irving, James Fenimore Cooper, Nathaniel Hawthorne, Henry Wadsworth Longfellow, and Charles Dickens. In fact, there is evidence that in 1867 Charles Dickens spent two weeks at Wren's Nest resting and relaxing during an American tour.

During the 1900s, the countryside surround-ing Wren's Nest and the Delaware River under-went a jarring industrial evolution. Although the clock may never be turned back, the diminished little estate of Wren's Nest is enjoying a renaissance as a delightfully engaging bed and breakfast known as Darley Manor Inn.

Today, thanks to the herculean efforts of Ray and Judith Hester, the B&B is as charming as in Darley's day. The princely public rooms include a foyer with an Empire butler's desk, a front parlor with a magnificent crystal chandelier, a dining room with a baronial table and handcarved 18th-century Chippendale chairs (with another splendid chandelier), as well as a back parlor with a player piano and old books that include Darley illustrations.

The six suites and guest rooms are equally elegant and feature fine antiques throughout. There are canopy and half-canopy beds, Oriental rugs, polished tables and chests, fancy mirrors, woodburning fireplaces, and interesting artwork on the walls. The North-South Writer's Suite has a beamed ceiling and a porch railing from the White House of the Confederacy. The Wren's Nest has both a fireplace and a private balcony.

A full breakfast is served in the dining room by candlelight. Elegant bone china, silver, and fresh flowers adorn the tables. The meal starts with fresh fruit, juice, and hot-from-the-oven baking powder biscuits and finishes with an entrée such as a ham and cheese omelet or pecan pancakes.

The manor house is located on .75 acre and includes an abundant rose garden interspersed with five small bubbling fountains. Every amenity for the comfort of business and pleasure travelers has been considered. There's a fully equipped exercise room, and each room has three telephones (including a dataport), a spacious desk, plus a TV, VCR, hair dryer, robes, and, of course, private tiled bathrooms.

The inn enjoys a location mid-way between Philadelphia and Wilmington and is convenient to the many attractions of the Brandywine Valley, including Winterthur Museum, the Hagley Museum, Longwood Gardens, The Brandywine River Museum, and Nemours Estate.

What's Nearby

Claymont is a northern suburb of Wilmington. Nearby Wilmington attractions include the Hagley Museum, a 240-acre museum that includes the original duPont black powder mill and Eleutherian Mills, the restored and furnished 1803 home of five generations of duPonts. The museum recreates the environment of a nineteenth-century mill village with demonstrations, working machinery, gardens, and restored buildings. (See also Wilmington and the Pennsylvania towns of Chadds Ford, Unionville, and West Chester.)

The Bay Moon Bed & Breakfast

128 Kings Highway
Lewes, DE 19958
(800) 917-2307 (pager) or (302) 644-1802;
fax (302) 644-1802;
e-mail: Baymoon@scsn.net
website: http://www.Lewes.com/BayMoon

Innkeeper: Laura Beth Kelly
Rooms: 6, 4 with private baths, all with air conditioning, cable TV, VCR, radio, and hair dryer; crib available
On the grounds: Gardens, deck, off-street parking
Extras: Evening hors d'oeuvres and wine in bar; telephone and fax available; dog named Aspen
Rates: Summer: $110–$150; Mid-season: $90–$130; Winter: $80-$110, all with full breakfast; two-night minimum summer and holidays.
Credit cards accepted: American Express, MasterCard, Visa
Open: Year-round
Smoking: Outside only
How to get there: From Wilmington, follow Route 13 south to Dover. Then take Route 113 south almost to Milford. North of Milford, take Route 1 south toward Lewes and follow the signs for the Cape May/Lewes Ferry. At the junction with Route 9E (which is Kings Highway) turn right and follow it east for 1 mile. The B&B will be on the left.

Remember when you were a child and your parents pasted glow-in-the-dark stars on the ceiling to keep the Boogie Man away? It's not that you'll be afraid of the dark at The Bay Moon, but you'll appreciate the tranquility of this lovely B&B when you gaze at the constellations on the ceiling of your room.

Due to the happy coincidence of its heritage, this is one of the most impressive inns in Delaware. The first thing you'll notice when you enter the foyer is the abundance of highly polished golden oak found throughout the inn. It's featured in wall paneling, fireplace mantels, flooring, and furniture. Most of the oak was installed by John Paganis, an old-world carpenter who owned the house from 1971 to1995. He salvaged paneling from banks, mantels from old houses, and other architectural pieces wherever he found them and installed them throughout his home. Today we are all able to appreciate the burnished oak graining as well as Mr. Paganis's craftsmanship. The home was purchased by innkeeper Laura Beth Kelly in 1995.

The common rooms are charming. In the living room, a glass-topped coffee table holds a collection of intricate pink and white shells imbedded in sand. A double-sided wood-burning fireplace casts warmth on both the living room and the breakfast room. The den is equipped with games, videos, and books. A TV and VCR are ready to entertain. In the tiny back bar (naturally, of carved oak) evening hors d'oeuvres and local wines are enjoyed as guests become acquainted.

The theme throughout the inn is a celestial one because "it was the moon reflecting over the water" that caused Laura Beth to move here. Guest rooms have such names as Full Moon and Blue Moon, and each has its own private bath, although several are off the common hallway. Blue Moon has an entire wall of oak paneling that serves as backdrop for the bed, but other rooms have handcrafted wrought-iron (made by Laura Beth's husband) or wicker headboards. Fluffy down comforters cover the beds. Each room has a television and VCR.

Laura Beth is a terrific cook (she's also a caterer). You'll awake to the tantalizing aroma of freshly baked muffins or quick breads. On the dining room buffet (oak, of course) you'll find three juices, as well as gourmet coffee, tea, hot chocolate, and fresh fruits. An entreé might consist of lemon-poppyseed flapjacks with a three-berry chutney served with twice-seared tarragon turkey ham. As a finale there will be a tropical pound cake or another sweet confection.

In summer, guests enjoy eating either on the side porch or on the back deck where they can admire Laura Beth's rose, vegetable, herb, and edible-flower gardens. An outdoor grill is particularly appreciated by fishermen, as it can be used to prepare fresh-from-the-sea evening meals.

Lewes (pronounced Lewis) offers an abundance of restaurants and activities. Nearby beaches beckon to summer tourists, and Laura Beth has thoughtfully provided all the equipment: beach chairs, towels, coolers, and even a fully stocked refrigerator from which to fill the cooler. Or you might sit on the back deck in the evening as we did, savoring the scent of the roses and watching the real stars twinkle above.

What's Nearby—Lewes

Lewes was founded in 1631 by the Dutch, and the Zwaanendael Museum offers an interesting excursion into the Dutch era. It's in a building that is a replica of the town hall of Hoorn, Holland, and contains historical exhibits that trace the area from the first colony to the present. The Lewes Historical Complex is a collection of old buildings furnished to reflect the era in which they were built. In addition, the Queen Anne's Railroad, a steam train, offers rides into the countryside, and a number of excursion boats take groups fishing, whale watching, and sightseeing. At Cape Henlopen State Park, you can swim or sit on the sandy beach, picnic, hike, crab, and fish.

Blue Water House

407 East Market Street
Lewes, DE 19958
(800) 493-2080 or (302) 645-7832;
fax (302) 644-0824;
e-mail: bwh@lewes-beach.com

Innkeepers: Chuck and Karen Ulrich
Rooms: 6, all with private baths, air conditioning, radios, and balconies; 4 with televisions; 1 with telephone; crib available
On the grounds: Patios, hammock, picnic table, grill, bicycles, beach chairs, boogie boards
Rates: Mid-May–mid-Sept $120; mid-Sept–mid-Nov $80; mid-Nov–March 31st $60; April 1st–mid-May $80, all including Continental breakfast; two-night minimum summer season; three-night minimum holiday weekends in summer
Credit cards accepted: MasterCard, Visa
Open: Year-round
Smoking: Outside only
How to get there: From Wilmington, follow Route 13 south to Dover. Then take Route 113 south almost to Milford. North of Milford, take Route 1 south toward Lewes and follow the signs for the Cape May/Lewes Ferry. At junction of Routes 1 and 9, follow Route 9 (which becomes Savannah Road) into Lewes. Continue on Savannah Road through the traffic light and across the bridge. Turn left at the first intersection onto Angler's Road. Turn right in 1 block onto East Market Street. The B&B is on the right.

The style of Blue Water House is faintly reminiscent of a lighthouse, perched as it is on stilts above the marsh. The house, which has a weathered shingle exterior trimmed with bright gold and turquoise, is surrounded by reeds that shelter a variety of birds. There are patios with picnic tables and benches and also a pond on the ground level. A bevy of bicycles awaits pedalers.

Chuck and Karen Ulrich built their B&B in 1993, and the guestrooms, which are all on the third floor, are spacious and bright. Chuck is an architect and a charter boat captain, and his love of the sea and of fine craftsmanship are intertwined in the B&B he designed. Wide windows flood the rooms with light (sunrises and sunsets are particularly memorable), and each room has French doors that provide access to the wraparound deck, which is encircled by a picket-fence railing. The spacious rooms are decorated with modern furnishings. You'll find no fancy headboards on the beds here. In fact, there are no headboards at all — merely bright splashes of sherbet colors (one is orange; another is lime) defining the placement of the bed. The baths are finished in white tiles.

The Lookout, an enclosed top-floor deck with wraparound windows, is a favorite guest retreat. There's a big-screen TV up here, a selection of books, and wicker chairs gaily covered in bright fabrics. The panorama of the ocean, which seems to stretch "from sea to shining sea," is particularly impressive. You can see the Cape Henlopen lighthouse and the Cape May ferry approaching and departing. The Ulriches have thoughtfully placed a wet bar and refrigerator up here as well. Guests come here to have wine or a cocktail after returning from the beach (or perhaps from a fishing expedition with Captain Chuck) to discuss local restaurants, to read, or just to talk.

Breakfast is served on the second floor, where the Ulriches and their children, Kayla and Charlie, live. An array of freshly made breads (perhaps a coconut-pineapple or an apricot-almond), fresh fruits, juices, and cereals are laid out on the kitchen counter, and guests may help themselves. This very "child-friendly" inn also has an adjoining children's game room with TV, where kids can watch videos or play games while the adults enjoy a more leisurely breakfast.

The B&B is located across the bridge that spans the Lewes-Rehoboth Canal, a short distance from downtown. Lewes is an interesting little seafaring village with a past. Founded in 1631 by the Dutch, the Zwaanendael Museum offers an interesting excursion into the Dutch era. The collection of shops in town range from those specializing in fine antiques, to clothing, to cafes and bakeries. It's a short bicycle ride to the unspoiled ocean beaches at Cape Henlopen.

This casual, easy-going, bring-the-kids B&B is the ideal place to come when you feel like dressing down instead of up and yet want to enjoy the convenience of modern bedrooms and baths.

What's Nearby
See "What's Nearby Lewes," page 7.

The Inn at Canal Square

122 Market Street
Lewes, DE 19958
(800) 222-7902 or (302) 645-8499;
fax (302) 645-7083;
e-mail: innatcanalsquare@cenet

Innkeeper: Lonnie Brown
Rooms: 23, including 1 apartment and 1 houseboat, all with private baths, air conditioning, TVs, telephones, and radios; 21 with hair dryers; 2 with refrigerators and coffee makers; apartment with VCR and CD player; houseboat with fireplace; crib available
On the grounds: Off-street parking, marina
Rates: $85–$165 rooms and suites, $175–$225 houseboat, all with continental breakfast; two-night minimum summer weekends and holiday weekends; $800–$1,100 per week for apartment
Credit cards accepted: American Express, Diners Club, Discover, MasterCard, Visa
Open: Year-round
Smoking: Permitted in some rooms; designated non-smoking rooms
How to get there: From Wilmington, follow Route 13 south to Dover. Then take Route 113 south almost to Milford. North of Milford, take Route 1 south toward Lewes and follow the signs for the Cape May/Lewes Ferry. At junction of Routes 1 and 9, follow Route 9 east (which becomes Savannah Road) into Lewes. At the traffic light before the bridge, turn left onto Front Street. The B&B will be on the right in 1 block.

Down at the edge of the Lewes-Rehoboth Canal, The Inn at Canal Square offers a nighttime lullaby. The sounds of sailboat rigging faintly slapping against masts and the soft splash of waves against the gently rocking boats in the harbor are haunting and romantic and reassuring, all at the same time. It's as though the call of distant places across the sea has mingled with our familiar surroundings to rock us gently to sleep. In the morning, the rising sun provides a glorious wake-up call.

Larger than most B&Bs, the four-story structure, which has twenty-one rooms, was built in 1988. It has a brown shingle-clad exterior that is in perfect harmony with its nautical setting. A common room, filled with plants and books, has a buffet counter where breakfast is set out every morning. A selection of breakfast breads, fruits, juices, yogurt, and coffee is available. More impersonal than other nearby establishments, this is an excellent choice for those who prefer to eat breakfast alone and who can do without the banter of other guests. You might decide to eat in the common room or to place your food on a tray and take it to your room or, if the day is balmy, you might sit outside at a table on the patio.

The guest rooms are all furnished with Queen Anne reproduction pieces, and they each come with TVs and telephones as well as modern bathrooms. Most of the rooms have private balconies with views of the active little harbor. The ultimate accommodation, however, is the houseboat down in the harbor. It has a fireplace in the living area, a kitchen, TV, and stereo. Walls of windows offer water-level harbor views. On the second floor, there are two bedrooms, each with its own private bath, and there's a sundeck on the roof. In 1996, the owners acquired an apartment next door also that is rented by the week. Although it is open only in the summer, it has a full-sized kitchen—the perfect place for those who wish to have longer-term stays.

The inn is located within the historic district of Lewes—a block from the fine shops and restaurants in the downtown area. There's a bicycle rental nearby for trips to Cape Henlopen State Park or for a meandering jaunt through town to look at the cluster of interesting old homes.

What's Nearby

See "What's Nearby — Lewes," page 7.

Armitage Inn

2 The Strand
New Castle, DE 19720
(302) 328-6618;
fax (302) 324-1163;
e-mail: armitageinn@earthlink.net

Innkeepers: Stephen and Rina Marks
Rooms: 4, all with private baths (1 with shower only) and TVs, telephones with dataports, air conditioning, radios, hair dryers, and desks; 2 with fireplaces.
On the grounds: Walled garden
Extras: 2 rooms with double whirlpools; all with desks; fax available
Rates: $105–$150, including full breakfast; two-night minimum from April through October
Credit cards accepted: American Express, Discover, Mastercard, Visa
Open: Year-round
Smoking: Non-smoking inn
How to get there: Traveling on I-95 take exit 5A (if coming from the south, take I-295 toward New Jersey and take exit 5A) onto Delaware Route 141 south. At the intersection of Routes 9 and 273, turn north onto Route 9 and travel for ¹/2 mile. Bear right to New Castle via Delaware Street. Continue on Delaware Street through the village to The Strand. The inn is on the right.

The Strand, a grassy common bordering the Delaware River, serves as the spacious backyard of Armitage Inn, a handsome brick Federal house with portions that date to the 1600s. Looking much as it did during the American Revolution when owner Zachariah Van Leuvenigh offered hospitality to post riders bringing news from the battle front, the house was converted to a gracious B&B by owners Steve and Rina Marks in 1995.

Guests enter a spacious hallway with polished red-pine floors and a sweeping staircase leading to the second floor. The first-floor common rooms include a parlor with a fireplace, which is furnished in fine period antiques. Beyond, there's a handsome library with floor-to-ceiling bookcases on all four walls. The oldest room in the house, dating to the 1600s and still containing the original cooking fireplace and beehive oven, is used as the office. Doors lead from the library to a screened porch and a walled garden, which contains a quaint little cottage where the owners live. On the opposite side of the hall, there's a formal dining room.

In the four generous bedrooms, guests can enjoy views of the river while snuggled into canopy beds dressed with down pillows and comforters. Televisions are tucked away in period armoires; telephones with modem connections sit beside the beds. Two of the rooms have elegant decorative fireplaces. The private baths (two with oversized whirlpools) are finished with marble and tile. My favorite room is the White Rose Room, which has a nook with windows overlooking The Strand and the Delaware River. I can imagine Mr. Van Leuvenigh watching the river traffic from this spot.

A scrumptious full breakfast is served in the formal dining room each morning. In addition to fresh fruit, juices, and coffee, guests might be treated to an apple-peach crisp or angel cakes (feathery-light little pancakes that incorporate fruit and nuts in the batter and are served with maple syrup) or to maple-cream cheese pastries, a sweet breakfast treat in which a buttery dough is wrapped around a cream cheese mixture, baked, topped with a syrupy maple/brown sugar mixture and baked a bit more.

New Castle is a gift from the past. It was laid out by Peter Stuyvesant in 1651, and William Penn first landed here in 1681. The narrow brick sidewalks are still lighted by flickering street lamps at night. Antiques shops, restaurants, handsome brick public buildings, taverns, and elegant old houses line the streets just as they did in days of yore. The village green, which was once a parade ground, is bordered by an arsenal built during the War of 1812 that now serves as a fine restaurant.

What's Nearby—New Castle

New Castle has several interesting museums to visit. The Amstel House, a 1730s gem, was the home of Governor Van Dyke, while the George Read II House and Garden dates to the 1840s. Both are furnished with lovely period antiques. The Old Court House once served as the meeting place of the Colonial Assembly before the capital was moved to Dover. Its handsome facade, crowned by a cupola, still dominates the center of town. The Dutch House and the Old Library Museum offer glimpses into New Castle's history.

Fox Lodge at Lesley Manor

123 West 7th Street
New Castle, DE 19720
(302) 328-0768

Innkeepers: William and Elaine Class
Rooms: 3, including 1 suite, all with private baths, air conditioning, radios, coffee makers, and desks
On the grounds: Croquet, bocci, gardens
Extras: A Tonkinese cat named Istuan Sändor
Rates: $105–$150, including full breakfast and afternoon snacks; two-night minimum weekends
Credit cards accepted: MasterCard & Visa
Open: Year-round
Smoking: Non-smoking inn
How to get there: Traveling on I-95 take exit 5A (if coming from the south, take I-295 toward New Jersey and take exit 5A) onto Delaware Route 141 south. At the intersection of Routes 9 and 273, turn north onto Route 9 and travel for $1/2$ mile. Bear right to New Castle via Delaware Street. Continue to 7th Street and turn right. The B&B will be at the end of the street in 2 blocks on the left.

The grandest house in New Castle, an 1855 Gothic Revival mansion with thirty-three rooms, was built by the Lesley family and is known locally as "The Castle." Its embellishments include a fanciful turret, gingerbread-trimmed gables, a slate roof, and stained glass. Eventually, its condition deteriorated, and it was deserted and neglected when spied by William and Elaine Class in 1994. It took their vision (William loves architectural history) and Elaine's artistic wizardry (she is an interior designer, artist, and gardener) to transform the magnificent but derelict house into the gracious B&B that they opened in 1996.

It also took a tremendous amount of work. The outside is now painted from top to bottom (a considerable distance) in a honey/buff color with rust trim that highlights the angles and arched windows. Frankly, I have been watching the transformation of the mansion for more than two years, and only on my last visit in early 1997 did I feel it was sufficiently complete to be recommended to readers. Even then, the entry hall and staircase leading to the guest rooms as well as the dining room had not been restored, but I was assured that they soon would be. Istuan Sändor, the house Tonkinese cat, will see to that.

The first floor parlor, which is entered through a massive pair of faux oak pocket doors, has a bay window with louvered wooden shutters at one end, a majestic carved white marble fireplace, walls color-washed in harlequin diamonds and sparkled with gold, and a massive ornate cast bronze chandelier hanging from the 13-foot ceiling. At check-in time a cute piglet may be sitting on the buffet to guard the plate of fruit, meat, cheese, cookies, and wine or beer waiting for her guests.

In the dining room, which has an elaborately carved burled walnut fireplace, the original embossed anaglyphic paper still hangs on the walls. A buffet breakfast of fresh fruit, juice, freshly baked breakfast breads, and cereal is laid out every morning, but if a guest wants a larger breakfast, Elaine might fix a fruit soup, smoked meat or fish, or rice pudding.

The guest rooms and suite are located on the second floor, reached by climbing (there is no elevator) the tall staircase with its elaborate gothic railing. A room-sized landing at the top contains sofas and chairs and a collection of local menus for perusing.

Each of the spacious rooms is artfully designed for comfort as well as serenity. In Jane, there's an elaborate fireplace mantel (alas, it is decorative only) and a headboard that incorporates peeled yucca poles and rope. A birdcage canopy, draped with gauzy fabric, hangs behind. Even on the second floor the ceilings reach to $12^1/_2$ feet, creating rooms that seem even larger than they are. Tall windows flood the rooms with light and also offer views of the various gardens.

Gardens ring the house and include a rose, herb, and vegetable garden as well as a medieval privy garden. There are benches for reading or just for watching the bees and butterflies flit from flower to flower. On the front lawn guests may enjoy a game of croquet or bocci.

The inn is approximately 6 blocks from the downtown shops and restaurants, a pleasant stroll along the water or past village houses.

What's Nearby

See "What's Nearby — New Castle," page 13.

The Boulevard Bed & Breakfast

1909 Baynard Boulevard
Wilmington, DE 19802
(302) 656-9700;
fax (302) 656-9701

Innkeepers: Judy and Charles Powell
Rooms: 6, including 1 suite, 4 with private baths, all with TVs, air conditioning, radios, and desks; 4 with telephones;1 with a whirlpool
On the grounds: Gardens
Extras: Hot mulled cider, iced tea, or lemonade and cookies served in the afternoon
Rates: $65–$85, including full breakfast; two-night minimum on holiday weekends
Credit cards accepted: American Express, MasterCard, Visa
Open: Year-round
Smoking: Permitted on porch only
How to get there: From the south, take I-95 north to exit 8 or Concord Pike (Wilmington 202 South). Proceed to second traffic light and turn right onto Baynard Boulevard. Continue to 1909 Baynard; the B&B is on the right on the corner of 20th Street.

In one of the toniest historic residential neighborhoods of Wilmington—where broad streets are flanked by majestic maple, sycamore, and oak trees and stately mansions speak of wealth and prestige—The Boulevard fits right in. The 1913 brick house has impressive white fluted columns on either side of the entrance and a gracious lawn that slopes down to the sidewalk. Massive trees in the yard shade the interior. After Chuck and Judy Powell retired from the corporate world, they purchased the house and opened it as a B&B.

Inside, the rooms are of noble proportions. To the right of the entry, a formal dining room has a beautiful leaded bay window; to the left, the living room contains a fireplace and comfortable furniture upholstered in ivory. A tile-floored side porch is furnished with an abundance of wicker — the ideal spot to sit and watch the garden grow. French doors lead to the side yard and flower gardens.

The room most enjoyed by guests is the library, a cozy little nook lined with books and encompassing a fireplace with an unusual tile facade. The tiles were apparently created during the Arts and Crafts period in the early 1900s by Herman Mueller, a tile maker in Trenton, New Jersey. They appear to be allegorical, although their meaning is shrouded in mystery, a fact that initiates many lively fireside chats among the guests. In the afternoon, guests congregate here in the winter (and often on the screened porch or the garden in summer) to sample the freshly baked cookies and sip hot mulled wine, iced tea, or lemonade — depending on the season.

As you climb the stairs to the guest rooms, you'll be entranced by the spacious window seat below leaded-glass windows and flanked by 15-foot-tall columns. You'll make a note to return with a good book some rainy afternoon. The guestrooms are furnished eclectically in a combination of family pieces and antiques. The Gold Room, with a lovely brass bed, is the nicest.

Most of the baths include either vintage fixtures or those installed in the 1950s. The Rose Room even has an old whirlpool tub. The rooms on the third floor share a bath.

A full breakfast is served in the dining room during the winter or on the screened-in porch during the summer. The menu is posted on a chalkboard every morning and will include a variety of juices and fruits, muffins or sweet breads, and an entrée such as apple pancakes or cinnamon swirl French toast with bacon or sausage and maple syrup.

There are a multitude of things to do in Wilmington. The B&B is an easy walk from downtown, where a variety of stores entice shoppers. In addition, Longwood Gardens, Winterthur Museum, the Hagley Museum, Nemours Estate, and the Brandywine River Museum are all nearby.

What's Nearby

Wilmington is on the fringe of Pennsylvania's Brandywine Valley. In addition to the better-known attractions of Winterthur Museum and Gardens, the Hagley Museum, Nemours Mansion and Gardens, and Longwood Gardens, visitors will enjoy visiting the Delaware Art Museum, noted for its collection of the illustrations of Howard Pyle, and the Rockwood Museum, a Gothic mansion furnished with exquisite antiques and surrounded by gardens featuring exotic flowers and greenery. The Grand Opera House, a Victorian edifice built in 1871, is home to OperaDelaware and the Delaware Symphony Orchestra. (See also Claymont, DE, and the Pennsylvania towns of Chadds Ford, Unionville, and West Chester.)

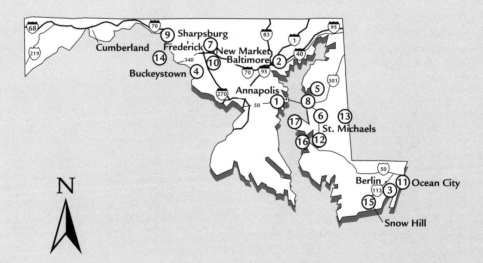

Cumberland

Sharpsburg
Frederick
New Market
Baltimore
Buckeystown
Annapolis
St. Michaels
Berlin
Ocean City
Snow Hill

N

Maryland

Numbers on map refer to towns numbered below.

The Dolls' House Bed & Breakfast

161 Green Street
Annapolis, MD 21401
(410) 626-2028

Innkeepers: Barbara and John Dugan
Rooms: 3, including 1 suite, 1 with a private bath, and 2 with shared bath; all include air conditioning; 1 with TV
On the grounds: Gardens
Extras: Sherry and cookies in the afternoon; chocolates in the room at night; collie named Churchill
Rates: $75 – $150, including full breakfast; two-night minimum for the suite from May to September
Credit cards accepted: None
Open: Year-round except Christmas week
Smoking: On porch or deck only
How to get there: From Route 50, take exit 24 (Rowe Boulevard). Stay on Rowe Blvd. South until it ends at the Maryland State House. Turn right on College Avenue and immediately enter Church Circle. Go around the circle, making a right turn onto Duke of Gloucester Street. Pass Town Hall and then turn left onto Green Street. The Dolls' House is the first house on the left.

Barbara and John Dugan had been collecting antique furniture for years, and Barbara had also assembled an impressive variety of Victorian dolls by the time the couple moved to Annapolis to open their bed and breakfast in 1995. They decorated it in a style they call "Victorian whimsy," using the furniture and dolls.

The house itself is not one of those enormous gabled and turreted showcases, but a more modest house that was built for a Maryland judge in 1901. It stands above the street on a stone foundation and is reached by climbing a staircase past a smiling lion. A broad porch, furnished with wicker and a porch swing and framed by hanging baskets of flowers in the summer, fronts the shingled facade.

When you enter the home, you may be greeted by Churchill, a docile collie who will immediately become your friend. He will show you to the parlor, where you can admire the china cabinet filled with some of Barbara's doll collection. More dolls are standing on Victorian tables and sitting in Victorian chairs. You may decide to stop here to sample the sherry and cookies that have been waiting for your arrival.

Upstairs there are three guest rooms. They include some lovely antiques pieces, and all of them have more dolls to admire. The Victoria Room, for example, has a Jenny Lind bed and Queen Victoria memorabilia, while the Sun Room is decorated with wicker and sunflowers. These rooms share an old-fashioned hall bath with a clawfoot tub and pedestal sink. In the Nutcracker Suite on the third floor, which can sleep six, there are more antiques and dolls. It's rumored that late at night the dolls in this room quietly arise to play and dance together. The bath in this room has both a clawfoot tub and a shower.

A full breakfast is served in the formal dining room. A tiger-oak fireplace mantel dominates one wall (where a fire will glow in winter), and there's an oak buffet on another. Guests sit around an oak dining table. Two elaborate Victorian dollhouses offer endless hours of amusement. Barbara's breakfasts are bountiful. She will start with fresh fruit and juices and freshly made muffins. Her entrée specialties include a French toast cobbler and eggs with cream cheese and chives.

In summer the spacious back deck and garden offer a relaxing retreat from the pace of sightseeing in Annapolis. The garden is Barbara's pride and joy, and it's evident. There are a multitude of colorful blooms from early spring through late fall, and the pretty white iron furniture spaced throughout the grounds provides pleasant refuge from the crowds.

Annapolis has been the state capital of Maryland since the 1700s, and the State House, crowned by a large gold cupola, dominates the town. In addition, the U.S. Naval Academy and the picturesque Annapolis waterfront are easy walks from the B&B.

What's Nearby — Annapolis

The U.S. Naval Academy, covering 30 acres on the banks of the Severn River, was founded in 1845. Visitors can visit the chapel and see where John Paul Jones is buried as well as watch the plebes (new recruits) perform their noontime drill on the quadrangle. In addition, the Maryland State House, which was built in 1772, is the oldest U.S. state capitol building in continuous use in America. It contains a museum devoted to Annapolis history during Colonial times. The William Paca House and Garden, the Hammond-Harwood House, and several other historic homes are open for touring.

Prince George Inn Bed & Breakfast

232 Prince George Street
Annapolis, MD 21401
(410) 263-6418;
fax (410) 626-0009;
e-mail: pginn@annap.infi.net
website: http://www.princegeorgeinn.com

Innkeepers: Janet and Dennis Coughlin
Rooms: 4, 2 with private baths and 2 with shared; all with TVs, VCRs, air conditioning, radios, mini-refrigerators, and CD players
On the grounds: Garden with fountain and gazebo
Extras: Chocolates on the pillow at turndown, fax, e-mail, meeting room
Rates: $95–$120, including a full breakfast; two-night minimum weekends April through December
Credit cards accepted: MasterCard and Visa
Open: Year-round
Smoking: Non-smoking bed and breakfast
How to get there: From Route 50 take exit 24 (Rowe Boulevard). Follow this to its end and turn left onto College Avenue. At King George Street, turn right. Turn right again onto Maryland Avenue and then right again onto Prince George Street. The inn will be on the right.

When Janet and Dennis Coughlin purchased Annapolis's first B&B, the Prince George Inn Bed and Breakfast, in 1996, it was known as a frumpy but kindly old dowager. Originally opened in 1983, the rooms and baths had seen few changes over the years. But that was then, and this is now. Janet, an interior designer, has infused the handsome brick 1884 Victorian townhouse with a new sense of charm and class.

Guests enter a spacious foyer with polished oak floors. To the right, there's a burgundy-painted living room with 11-foot-tall ceilings and a white wooden fireplace mantel. A handsome tall clock resides here next to an Eastlake parlor set and a burgundy leather sofa. The polished wide-plank pine floors gleam. To the side, a sunny glass-enclosed porch has wicker furniture, a cast-iron gas fireplace, a 1928 nickel slot machine embellished with poinsettias, and a treadle sewing machine.

The bright breakfast area overlooks a brick patio and a gracious garden enclosed by brick walls. Brick pathways lead to a tiered fountain, gently splashing its soothing sounds throughout the summer, as well as a gazebo. Wooden benches offer retreats for quiet interludes.

There are four guest rooms upstairs. The two on the second floor have private baths, although these are in the hall. The two on the third floor share a bath. All of the baths have been thoroughly updated and are modern and bright, with tile floors and tile tub surrounds. Each of the rooms is decorated with lovely antiques. One has a walnut dresser with a marble top and a four-poster bed; another, an elaborately carved walnut Victorian headboard. Each of the rooms has a TV, VCR, CD player, and a mini-refrigerator.

Guests gather for breakfast in the glass-enclosed breakfast area, where they may either sit at individual tables overlooking the garden or share a larger table with other guests. In summer, tables are set out on the patio. Janet's breakfasts include juices and fresh fruits, as well as a hot entrée. The specialty of the day may include an enchilada breakfast bake or perhaps French toast stuffed with ham and turkey and served with cranberry-pear sauce.

The Prince George Inn is located in the historic district of Annapolis, within walking distance of shopping, restaurants, and the town's many attractions. The U.S. Naval Academy welcomes visitors to its 30 acres, where they can visit the Preble Hall museum displaying nautical and Navy historical items and also watch the noon-time drill of the first-year cadets (plebes). In the picturesque Annapolis harbor, it's possible to board an excursion boat for a tour or to sail across the Chesapeake Bay to the Eastern Shore of Maryland.

What's Nearby

See "What's Nearby — Annapolis," page 21.

Two-O-One Bed & Breakfast

201 Prince George Street
Annapolis, MD 21401
(410) 268-8053;
fax (410) 263-3007;
e-mail: twoOonebb@aol.com

Innkeepers: Graham W. Gardner and Robert A. Bryant
Rooms: 4, including 1 suite, all with private baths, 27"
TVs, VCRs, air conditioning, mini-refrigerators, robes; 2
with Jacuzzis; 1 with a fireplace
On the grounds: Garden, off-street parking
Extras: Complimentary soft drinks; fresh flowers in
room; ironed sheets; Doberman named Franklin, boxer
named Sailor, cockapoo named Sandy
Rates: $120–$150, including full breakfast; two-night
minimum weekends
Credit cards accepted: American Express, Discover,
MasterCard, Visa
Open: Year-round
Smoking: On patio or in garden only
How to get there: From Route 50 take exit 24 (Rowe
Boulevard). Follow this to its end and turn left onto
College Avenue. At King George Street, turn right. At
Randall Street, turn right and take the next right onto
Prince George Street. The B&B will be on the left.

If you love dogs, you'll feel right at home at 201. If you don't, you probably should stay elsewhere, although then you'd miss the pleasure of staying in Annapolis's most elegant B&B. The dogs, who are sure to greet you when you arrive, include Franklin, a Doberman; Sailor, a boxer; and Sandy, a cockapoo.

Graham Gardner and Robert Bryant purchased this townhouse shaded by maple trees in 1996. Following a top-to-bottom renovation, they opened it in 1997. It is a beauty. The build-ing's architectural features, its decor, and its antique American and English furniture are all of the finest quality.

Guests enter a formal foyer with a dining room to the left and a living room to the right. An elaborate marble fireplace decorates one wall of the seafoam green shadow-striped walls of the dining room, while another carved marble fireplace embellishes the persimmon-colored walls of the living room. In the sunny bay over-looking the street, floor-to-ceiling bookcases offer a wealth of reading material. Gleaming oak floors are topped by elegant Oriental rugs.

Upstairs, three exquisite guest rooms and a suite each have private, thoroughly updated baths that include Italian tile, glass-enclosed showers, sinks in elegant antique tables or chests, and Jacuzzis in several baths. Museum-quality antique armoires or chests-on-chests hold 27" TVs and VCRs, and intricately carved four-poster beds are fluffed with down comforters and pillows. Every detail has been carefully planned. Fresh flowers from the cutting garden in back are placed in each room, and the fine bed linens are lightly starched and ironed.

The Queen Anne Suite is the nicest accommodation. There's a gleaming mahogany canopy bed, a 1760s chest-on-chest hiding the TV and VCR, a tiny kitchen with a mini-refrigerator and wet bar, a sitting room with its own fireplace, and a lovely view of the Capitol dome, which is lighted at night. In the Italian-tiled bath, there's a Jacuzzi and a separate glass-enclosed shower.

The spacious .33-acre walled garden in back includes secluded sitting areas tucked among the flower beds and trees. A fish pond contains koi.

For breakfast, guests gather in the dining room around an antique mahogany pedestal table overseen by an 1870s crystal chandelier. Fine silverware, Irish linen napkins in silver napkin rings, and silver accessories enhance the ambience. In addition to fresh fruit, juice, and croissants, Robert may have prepared a quiche, a frittata, or his "Sunday best" French toast with orange juice and triple sec.

Annapolis offers numerous museums to visit. The 1763 William Paca House and Garden was the home of one of the signers of the Declaration of Independence. It has thirty-seven rooms decorated in period furnishings and a particularly noteworthy garden. The Hammond-Harwood House, built in 1774, offers a showcase of Georgian architecture and decorative ornamentation.

What's Nearby

See "What's Nearby — Annapolis," page 21.

William Page Inn
8 Martin Street
Annapolis, MD 21401
(800) 364-4160 or (410) 626-1506;
fax (410) 263-4841;
e-mail: wmpageinn@aol.com

Innkeeper: Robert L. Zuchelli
Rooms: 5, including 1 suite; 3 with private baths; all with air conditioning, radios, hair dryers, and irons and ironing boards; 1 with TV; 2 with whirlpool tubs
On the grounds: Parking
Extras: Chocolates and port in room at turndown, whirlpools, fax, copier, laundry available; dog named Chancellor
Rates: $95–$195, including full breakfast; two-night minimum weekends mid-March through November
Credit cards accepted: MasterCard & Visa
Open: Year-round
Smoking: Non-smoking bed and breakfast
How to get there: From Route 50, take exit 24 (Rowe Boulevard). Stay on Rowe Blvd. south until it ends at the Maryland State House. Turn left onto College Avenue and continue to the traffic light. Turn right onto King George Street and continue almost to the Visitor's Gate of the U. S. Naval Academy. Turn right onto East Street. Go 1 block and turn right onto Martin Street. The B&B is on the corner.

The William Page Inn, setting a high standard in Annapolis since it opened in 1987, is in a 1908 brown shingle-style house occupying a quiet corner near the U.S. Naval Academy. For more than fifty years it served as the headquarters for the Democratic Club in Annapolis. This is the closest B&B to the Naval Academy, an easy walk through the gates to view the daily noontime drill of the "plebes" in the quadrangle or to visit the chapel where John Paul Jones is buried.

A modest house from the outside, guests enter a tiled foyer with paneled walls. A Victorian crystal chandelier dominates the stairway. In the adjacent living room, a fire may be crackling in the fireplace in winter. Carpeted in beige and with vanilla walls, the living room boasts sofas and chairs upholstered in ivory damask as well as wing chairs in peach. Elegant drapes frame the windows. A lustrous cherry sideboard stands on one wall, while a beautiful antique Chippendale desk with a divided pediment graces another. A wet bar is built into the wall, ready to be put into service for cocktails before dinner.

The guest rooms are named for characters in *Charlotte's Web* by E. B. White. Why? "Because I liked the whimsy," explained innkeeper Robert Zuchelli. One, the Fern Room, which is located on the first floor, has a unique antique Victorian curvilinear bed and an antique Victorian dresser with a marble top. There's a private bath and direct access to a side porch. Three other guest rooms are on the second floor. Each has a carved four-poster bed as well as antique armoires and marble-topped Victorian night stands. Templeton has its own private bath with a whirlpool tub, while Wilbur and Charlotte share a hall bath.

The Marilyn Suite (a name not from *Charlotte's Web*) on the third floor is the most spacious accommodation. There are dormer windows with window seats and a skylight to cast a beam of sunlight across the handsome sleigh bed in the morning. This is the only room with a television. A two-room bath includes a whirlpool tub and a shower.

Breakfast is placed on the buffet in the living room every morning. In addition to fresh fruits, juices, breakfast breads, and a cheese plate, a hot entrée (perhaps a quiche) will be available. Small tables can accommodate one or two people in the living room, or, on warm summer days, guests often take their plates out to the porch.

Do you remember Charlotte's children saying, "We take to the breeze; we go as we please?" And so do we. But our breezes are bound to bring us back to the William Page Inn soon.

What's Nearby

See "What's Nearby — Annapolis," page 21.

Abacrombie Badger Bed & Breakfast

58 West Biddle Street
Baltimore, MD 21201-5502
(410) 244-7227;
fax (410) 244-8415

Innkeepers: Paul Bragaw and Collin Clarke
Rooms: 12, all with private baths, air conditioning, TVs, telephones with private lines, radios, desks, and hair dryers; 1 with decorative fireplace; 1 with CD player
On the grounds: Parking
Extras: Turndown with chocolates, private telephone lines, fax available
Rates: $79 – $135, including continental breakfast; two-night minimum on weekends
Credit cards accepted: American Express, Discover, MasterCard, Visa
Open: Year-round
Smoking: Non-smoking B&B
How to get there: From I-83, take exit 6 (North Avenue/Mt. Royal Avenue). Continue straight ahead (south) on Mt. Royal Avenue for 1/2 mile. After crossing the light rail tracks, bear right onto Cathedral Street. Go 2 blocks to the stoplight at Biddle Street. The B&B is on the left.

Most of us think of Baltimore as a city of steel and glass and row after row of brick townhouses. But actually, there's a woodland hidden away in the brick forest. In addition to squirrels, raccoons, and a multitude of birds, it seems there is also at least one badger and one mole. Mr. Mole (Bed & Breakfast) has been residing in a handsome brick townhouse in the Bolton Hill Historic District since 1992, but ever since he told his friend Abacrombie Badger about his place, Badger has been eager to have a dwelling of his own. In 1995 his dream was realized.

Abacrombie Badger resides in the heart of Baltimore's cultural area, in an 1890s brick townhouse across from Meyerhoff Symphony Hall, home of the Baltimore Symphony. He's much larger than his friend Mr. Mole, but equally elegant. His friends Paul Bragaw and Collin Clarke saw to that.

The parlor, which is on the first floor, is decorated with Victorian furnishings. There are oil portraits on the walls and a gleaming 1815 Sheraton sideboard.

The twelve guest rooms, each with its own distinctive theme, are located on the second and third floors. The Green Garden Room has a forest green carpet and a four-poster canopy bed draped with floral chintz. An antique mahogany dresser has a harp-shaped mirror, and the walls contain framed floral needlepoint pictures. The bath has a stained-glass window. Mrs. Biddle's Attic is particularly engaging. Although it would appeal to a little girl, there is nothing frilly or fussy about it. There's a quilted headboard and a quilt on the bed. Doll houses, doll furniture, and dolls constitute the decor.

Mr. Badger fixes a breakfast similar to Mr. Mole's, which is composed of sliced meats and cheeses, fresh fruits, and freshly made sweet breads and cakes. Guests are seated in the spacious breakfast room on the first floor, where they often exchange opinions about restaurants and cultural events. Mr. Badger leased out the basement to a friend who installed a smart Italian restaurant called La Tessa Tana (the Badger's Den). It has its own private entrance, so guests may choose to eat there themselves or to ignore it altogether.

If you love music, there's no finer place to stay in Baltimore. The Meyerhoff Symphony Hall, the Lyric Opera House, the Theater Project, and Baltimore's Antique Row are just outside the door. The light rail is only 1 block away, and the subway is merely 2 blocks.

What's Nearby — Baltimore

The Joseph Meyerhoff Symphony Hall is home to the Baltimore Symphony Orchestra and the Baltimore Chorale Arts Society. Harborplace—a collection of restaurants, shops, and boutiques—is a magnet for tourists, while Baltimore's City Life Museums include numerous historic sites and houses, including the Peale Museum, which contains a collection of paintings by the noted early nineteenth-century painter Rembrandt Peale. Visitors should plan to visit the Baltimore Museum of Art, which holds more than 120,000 paintings. Sports enthusiasts will want to attend a game in Oriole Park, the home of the Baltimore Orioles, and also go to Pimlico Race Course.

Innkeepers: Joanne and Andrew Mazurek
Rooms: 4, including 2 suites, all with air conditioning and radios; 3 with fireplaces
On the grounds: Garden
Extras: Chocolates at turndown
Rates: $85 – $110, including full breakfast; two-night minimum holiday weekends
Credit cards accepted: None
Open: Year-round
Smoking: Non-smoking bed and breakfast
How to get there: From Pratt Street in downtown Baltimore, proceed east and turn right onto President Street. Turn left onto Fleet Street and right onto Ann Street. The B&B is on the right just before Thames Street — a brick building with twin doors, next to Robert Long Museum.

Ann Street Bed & Breakfast
804 South Ann Street
Baltimore, MD 21231
(410) 342-5883

The first shipbuilding facility was established in Baltimore's historic Fells Point area in 1730, and by 1800 there were sixteen shipyards operating along its docks. The handsome pair of brick townhouses occupied by Ann Street Bed and Breakfast were built here in the 1790s, and their history has been intertwined with that of the Mazurek family for many generations. Andrew Mazurek's great grandmother once owned them, and then in 1945, his mother bought them, but she was forced to sell when they were condemned for a proposed highway.

The highway never materialized, but the buildings were boarded up, vandalized, and stripped. In 1978, Andrew and Joanne were allowed to purchase them, but it took five years of painstaking renovation before they were livable. Now, however, they are exquisitely restored to the 1790s era.

The four-story buildings are notable for their symmetry. Individually, they are merely 14 feet wide, but they have lovely mullioned windows, twin paneled doors, and fourth-floor dormers. Inside there are twelve working fireplaces and handsome hardwood floors.

The Mazureks have decorated their B&B with antiques and period eighteenth-century reproductions. In the parlor, Windsor and wing-back chairs offer places to sit before the fireplace. Oil portraits and hunt scenes from the late 1700s hang on the walls, and bouquets of fresh flowers sit on tables. In summer, guests love to sit in the brick-walled garden in back, which is filled with a cornucopia of flowers from early April to late October.

The B&B has two suites and two bedrooms, and only one does not include a fireplace in the bedroom. The rooms all have either full tester beds or antique rope beds (to remain authentic to the eighteenth-century period, all beds are double-sized). There are lustrous cherry custom-made Windsor chairs, wing-back chairs, blanket chests, and fresh flowers on the tables. Each of the rooms has its own private bath.

A full breakfast is served in the dining room-kitchen, which has a woodstove and a bay window overlooking the gardens. Joanne sets individual tables with fresh flowers, country checked placemats, and candles. A typical meal will include fresh juices and fruits (maybe a grapefruit broiled with brown sugar) and fresh blueberry muffins, followed by a German pancake served with powdered sugar, lemon, and maple syrup.

Fells Point is alive with activity throughout the year. In summer, tall ships berth here, street musicians play, and vendors sell everything from balloons to T-shirts. Little Italy is an easy walk and Baltimore's Inner Harbor is about a mile away. Guests especially enjoy visits to the Aquarium, and the American Visionary Art Museum, which specializes in outsider art.

What's Nearby

See "What's Nearby — Baltimore," page 29.

Celie's Waterfront Bed & Breakfast

1714 Thames Street
Baltimore, MD 21231
(800) 432-0184 or (410) 522-2323;
fax (410) 522-2324;
e-mail: celies@aol.com

Innkeeper: Celie Ives
Rooms: 7, including 1 suite, all with private baths, air conditioning, TVs, telephones, radios, dataports, desks, mini-refrigerators, robes, irons, and ironing boards; 6 rooms with coffee makers; 4 rooms with whirlpool tubs; 2 with woodburning fireplaces; 2 with balconies; 1 room with wheelchair access
On the grounds: Courtyard garden; rooftop view deck
Extras: Fresh flowers in room; whirlpool tubs; spacious desks; dataports
Rates: $100 – $200, including Continental breakfast; two- or three-night minimum holiday and special event weekends
Credit cards accepted: American Express, Discover, MasterCard, Visa
Open: Year-round
Smoking: Permitted outside only.
How to get there: From Pratt Street in downtown Baltimore, proceed east and turn right onto President Street. Turn left onto Fleet Street and right onto Ann Street. At Thames Street, turn right again. The B&B is in the middle of the block — a gray building with rose trim.

To visit Baltimore's historic Fell's Point harborside district is to step back in time — to a time in the 1700s when it was a bustling ship-building hub. It was here that sleek clipper ships, schooners, and the first U.S. Navy frigate, the *Constellation*, were built. As you walk along the cobblestone streets past the rows of brick townhouses, you almost feel as if you're back in the eighteenth century.

Until you walk into Celie's Waterfront Bed and Breakfast, that is. Tucked into a row of townhouses, the tiny entrance and the long brick passageway offer little preparation for the warm contemporary accommodations lying beyond. But when you enter the living room with its fireplace and polished pine floors, you will see the bright brick courtyard with its gentle fountain and iron tables and chairs beyond, and you'll immediately feel at home.

Your guest room will be painted a creamy ivory and enhanced by a bouquet of fresh flowers. If you are staying in #1 or #2, you will enjoy views of the harbor from your window seat and a woodburning fireplace. There will be a whirlpool tub in your spotless and bright bathroom. In a little alcove, a mini-refrigerator, coffee maker, and a microwave will speed your morning journey. If, instead, you have chosen either room #5 or #6, you will have a private balcony with window boxes overflowing with flowers and a table and chairs overlooking the garden courtyard. In your bath, you'll have a whirlpool tub.

The favorite retreat in this B&B, however, is the rooftop deck, where the panoramic view of the harbor and its multitude of boats can be mesmerizing. We came up here one warm night to watch the sun dip beyond the horizon, outlining the masts of the historic ships in the harbor in orange and pink. The sounds of rigging slapping against masts mingled with the call of seagulls as we luxuriated in the serenity and beauty of the night. Celie has thoughtfully furnished her rooms in crisp pine and wicker furniture. There are TVs, and VCRs (in several rooms), telephones with private lines, dataports, answering machines, spacious desks, and coffee makers.

A help-yourself breakfast is set out each morning on the pine sideboard in the breakfast area. Guests may select breakfast breads, juices, yogurt, granola, and coffee or tea. Then they must make the difficult choice about where to eat it. Will it be on the pine table in the breakfast room or on the rooftop deck or in the courtyard garden or on their private balcony?

From this convenient location, it's possible to walk to excellent restaurants and shops, to take a self-guided walking tour of the Fell's Point Historic District, or to ride a water taxi to the Baltimore Convention Center or to Oriole Park to watch the Baltimore Oriole's in action.

What's Nearby
See "What's Nearby — Baltimore," page 29.

Mr. Mole Bed & Breakfast

1601 Bolton Street
Baltimore, MD 21217
(410) 728-1179;
fax (410) 728-3379

Innkeepers: Collin Clarke and Paul Bragaw
Rooms: 5, including 2 suites, all with private baths, air conditioning, telephones with private lines, radios, hair dryers, desks, and robes
On the grounds: Garage parking with door-opener
Extras: Turndown with chocolates; desk and telephones with private line in room; fax available
Rates: $97 – $155, including continental breakfast; two-night minimum weekends
Credit cards accepted: American Express, Master-Card, Visa
Open: Year-round
Smoking: Non-smoking bed and breakfast
How to get there: From I-95, take exit 53 to I-395. Bear right onto Martin Luther King, Jr. Blvd and follow it for 2 miles. Turn left onto Eutaw Street and continue .6 mile, turning right at the fourth traffic light onto McMechen Street. Bolton Street is the next intersection. Mr. Mole is diagonally across the intersection from the stop sign.

Houses in the Bolton Hill Historic District of Baltimore were built by wealthy merchants in the mid-1800s. The quiet, tree-lined streets with their brick row houses retain the air of a genteel suburb even though it is now surrounded by the bustle of Baltimore. Mr. Mole (a character the innkeepers Collin Clarke and Paul Bragaw have adopted to speak for them — a reflection of their droll sense of humor and whimsy and a name taken from *Wind in the Willows*) occupies a handsome 1870s house that was converted to a B&B in 1992.

Mr. Mole's home is a gracious and elegant mansion, reflecting a lifestyle that was fashionable when the house was built. In the most elegant B&B in Baltimore, eighteenth- and nineteenth-century English and American antiques decorate the common rooms as well as the suites. One enters a charming vestibule where the 14-foot ceilings create a sense of spaciousness. The first floor has a living room, a breakfast room, and a drawing room, all painted daffodil yellow. The striking color scheme is complemented by an abundance of large Oriental blue and white porcelain pieces. Handsome oil portraits hang beside etchings from the 1830s — all enhanced by bay windows and creamy marble fireplaces.

The guest rooms are equally sumptuous. The London Suite, for example, is as large as many Manhattan apartments. It has two bedrooms and in the sitting room bottle-green wainscotting is spiced with cardinal red walls and softened by white accents. The four-poster bed is lacquered red and swagged with red, green, and white plaids and the sofas and chairs are upholstered in the same manner. The Garden Suite on the third floor has an overhanging garden porch and antique white wicker furniture. The bed is covered with a coverlet and swagged in a soft buttery linen.

One of the treats when staying with Mr. Mole is to become acquainted with Collin and Paul. They are conversant on a variety of topics and will describe Baltimore's museums, theatrical events, and restaurants, as well as their many travels around the world. They are especially eager to introduce guests to Mr. Mole's friend Abacrombie Badger, who has just opened a new bed and breakfast across the street from the Meyerhoff Symphony Hall.

A Continental breakfast that includes a variety of sliced meats and cheeses, fresh fruit and juices, freshly baked breakfast breads, cakes, pies, and pastries as well as coffee and tea is served at little tables discreetly dispersed throughout the common rooms. Guests can therefore be as sociable or as reclusive as they wish.

What's Nearby

See "What's Nearby — Baltimore," page 29.

Innkeeper: W. Kirk Burbage; manager, Todd Durand
Rooms: 8, including 1 suite; 6 with private baths; all with air conditioning; 1 with Jacuzzi
On the grounds: 18 acres of gardens, parking
Extras: Lemonade or tea in the afternoon
Rates: $150 – $175 mid-May to mid-October; $95 – $125 mid-October to mid-May; includes full breakfast; two-night minimum weekends from mid-May to mid-October
Credit cards accepted: MasterCard and Visa
Open: Year-round
Smoking: Permitted outside only
How to get there: From Washington, DC, take Route 50 across the Chesapeake Bay Bridge and continue east to Berlin. In Berlin take the exit for Route 113 south and go 2.5 miles to the B&B, which will be on the right side of the road.

Merry Sherwood Plantation

8909 Worcester Highway (Route 113)
Berlin, MD 21811
(800) 660-0358 or (410) 641-2112;
fax (410) 641-9528

The countryside on the southern Eastern Shore of Maryland is rural and sparsely settled. Mostly it is a patchwork of farmland, so the appearance of this magnificent 1859 seafoam green mansion, dripping with gingerbread from its squared-off wraparound porch, as well as from its overhanging eaves and its cupola, comes as a surprise. You will drive through the ornate gates and along the maple-shaded drive in awe as you admire the lovely home. The meticulous restoration of the 27-room, 8,500-square-foot mansion was the two-year project of local businessman Kirk Burbage, whose family has lived near Berlin for more than 200 years.

Inside, the main-floor rooms are furnished with elegant taste. The ballroom has twin ivory marble fireplaces, an ornate square grand piano, and an unusual carved wooden chair somewhat reminiscent of a throne. It has carved lion's head arms and a brass portrait of Queen Victoria, and it's rumored to have been made for an anticipated visit by the queen. Lace curtains filter light at the windows, and damask and tapestry-covered antique Victorian sofas, loveseats, and chairs are welcoming. Also available for guests to use are a small parlor, a formal dining room with a spectacular brass chandelier and a carved walnut sideboard, and a library filled with rare books and secret closets. A sunporch overlooks the gardens. When we arrived, afternoon tea and lemonade were waiting, so we relaxed on the porch, letting the pressures of the drive melt away.

The bedrooms, which are on the second and third floors, are furnished with museum-quality antiques, including a canopy bed in the Johnson Room, a bed with beehive-finials in the Chase Room, and a Gothic Revival bed in the Harrison Room. Six of the rooms have private baths with marble floors and showers, vintage fixtures such as pedestal sinks and clawfoot tubs, and brass hardware. Each room and bath has Victorian light fixtures as well. The Honey-moon Suite also has a Jacuzzi.

Breakfast is served in the dining room, where we feasted on fresh fruit, homemade muffins, juices, and a ham and broccoli strata. The meal is served on linen cloths with silver flatware and fine china around a handsome mahogany table.

The broad wraparound porch of the house is bordered by paneled columns joined by arches. There are comfortable rockers and wicker tables. Ferns and flowers hang in baskets from the arches. The 18 acres of gardens at Merry Sherwood Plantation are noted for their broad variety of rare specimens. *Southern Living* magazine has been helping with their restoration.

Nearby attractions include the Assateague Island Wildlife Preserve and the beaches at Ocean City, as well as the Globe Theatre in Berlin.

What's Nearby

The Assateague Island National Seashore offers miles of beaches and marshland that provide protected homes for waterbirds and wildlife. Hiking, camping, swimming, and fishing along this coastal wilderness are popular pastimes. Berlin is a fetching Victorian town that has antiques shops and restaurants located in historic buildings. Be sure to see the old Globe Theatre, which has an art gallery upstairs and a bookstore, gift shop, and cafe downstairs. Entertainment ranging from folk performers to puppet shows for children takes place year-round. Golfers will appreciate that there are several courses in or near Berlin. (See also Ocean City and Snow Hill.)

Catoctin Inn

3613 Buckeystown Pike
(mailing address: Box 243)
Buckeystown, MD 21717
(800) 730-5550 or (301) 874-5555;
fax (301) 874-2026;
e-mail: catoctin@bigdog.fred.net
website: http://www.catoctininn.com

Innkeepers: Terry and Sarah MacGillivray
Rooms: 16, including 8 suites, all with private baths, air conditioning, TVs, telephones with dataports, radios, hair dryers, robes, irons, and ironing boards; 13 with mini-refrigerators and fireplaces; 12 with whirlpool tubs and desks; 11 with coffee makers; 1 with wheelchair access; cribs available
On the grounds: Parking; gardens with gazebo
Extras: Afternoon tea; bicycles to use
Rates: $85 – $150, including full breakfast
Credit cards accepted: American Express, Master-Card, Visa
Open: Year-round
Smoking: Permitted outside only; one guest room designated for smokers.
How to get there: Traveling west on I-70, take exit 54. Turn right at the light onto Route 85. At the second light, stay to the right and continue on Route 85. The inn is 5 miles farther on the left before you go down the hill into Buckeystown.

When Terry and Sarah MacGillivray first opened their gleaming white clapboard 1780s house as a bed and breakfast in 1991, they also operated their antiques business out of the immense 1890s brick carriage house down the hill. They offered five guest rooms, all decorated with a variety of antiques ranging in style from American Country to Victorian. The house is located on 4 park-like acres that, in addition to the carriage house, include three cottages, a lawn with dogwood and magnolia trees, and a gazebo. From the wraparound porch, there are glorious views of the Catoctin Mountains.

In 1995, the couple renovated the cottages and turned them into guest accommodations also, adding gas fireplaces and whirlpool tubs. By now, they realized that although there were other bed and breakfasts in the area, there were none that catered to the special needs of business travelers. Therefore, they added telephones with dataports and voice mail, as well as TVs and VCRs to all their rooms. Then, in 1996, they renovated a brick stable-hand's quarters behind the carriage house to create eight more spacious guest rooms. Half are furnished with an eclectic mix of older furniture and the other half have a Southwestern theme, with heavy pine furniture and crackle-painted chests and tables. Each room is complete with modern marble baths with whirlpool tubs, gas fireplaces, coffee makers, irons, ironing boards, and mini-refrigerators. They have a fax machine, an IBM-compatible computer, and a laser jet printer for their guests to use, and they offer a flexible time for breakfast, provide dry-cleaning service, and will arrange airport transportation. Meetings and small conferences can take place in the carriage house.

In the main house the lovely common rooms provide guests with the comfort and style of a gracious home. There's a library with a cathedral ceiling, two marble fireplaces, pine-paneled pocket doors, and a multitude of books. Two notable items are found here.

There's a chestnut Federal dresser with a marble top that came from Robert E. Lee's estate and an autographed picture of Babe Ruth, whose interesting origin Terry will tell you all about. Afternoon tea is served here.

Guests eat breakfast in the dining room, which has another fireplace. Tables that can accommodate from two to six people offer flexibility in seating. The MacGillivrays offer a full breakfast that may include French toast with apples and maple syrup or perhaps blueberry pancakes. These are accompanied by country sausage or bacon, fresh fruit and juices, and breakfast breads.

There are numerous attractions near Buckeystown. The town itself offers interesting historic buildings housing antiques shops. A bicycle path traces the boundary of the C & O Canal for 244 miles from Washington, DC, to Cumberland, Maryland, and passes about 8 miles from Buckeystown. The B&B has bicycles for guests to use. The Appalachian Trail is nearby also.

What's Nearby

The Appalachian Trail, which extends from Maine to Georgia, passes through Maryland close to Buckeystown. For bicyclists, the C & O Canal National Historic Park, a 184-mile trail stretching from Washington to Cumberland, Maryland, offers miles of scenic cycling on a trail that borders the Potomac River. It passes about 8 miles from Buckeystown. The Monacacy National Battlefield is nearby as well.

Brampton Inn
25227 Chestertown Road (Route 20 South)
Chestertown, MD 21620
(410) 778-1860;
fax (410) 778-1805;
e-mail: brampton@friend.ly.net

Innkeepers: Michael and Danielle Hanscom; manager, Terry Suzi
Rooms: 10, including 2 suites, all with private baths, air conditioning, and desks; 8 with fireplaces; 7 with TVs; 3 with coffee makers; 2 with whirlpool tubs and patios; 1 room with wheelchair access: crib available
On the grounds: Garden
Extras: Afternoon tea, complimentary beverages; fax, copier, and dataport available; dog named Penny, several cats
Rates: $95 – $175, including full breakfast and afternoon tea; two-night minimum April through December if stay includes Saturday night
Credit cards accepted: American Express, MasterCard, and Visa
Open: Year-round
Smoking: Permitted outside only
How to get there: From Washington, DC, take Route 50, cross the Chesapeake Bay Bridge and continue on Route 301/50 until it splits. Take Route 301 north for 5 miles to Route 213 north. Follow Route 213 through Centreville and into Chestertown. At the traffic light follow Spring Avenue to High Street (Route 20). Continue on Route 20 through town. The B&B is located about 1 mile SW of town on Route 20.

Brampton has evolved. When Michael and Danielle Hanscom first opened their impressive brick mansion as a bed and breakfast in 1987, there were only two guest rooms. On a visit in 1993, the number of guest rooms had grown to seven but they were still awaiting the arrival of the handsome Sheraton-style sofas they had ordered from a local craftsman for their front parlor. (It took five years.)

By 1996, the number of guest rooms had increased to ten, and the gorgeous sofas were now in place. Covered in a rich lemon-yellow damask, they sit before the fireplace in the parlor that now serves as the heart of the inn. Oriental rugs cover glowing pine floors and bookcases reach to the 12-foot ceilings. The windows on all the floors reach from floor to ceiling, flooding the rooms with light and sun.

The seven guest rooms within the main building are spacious and each has a private bath. My favorite is the Fairy Hill Suite, which occupies the former kitchen. You enter a sitting room that has a large woodburning fireplace and a sofa covered in French Provincial fabric. The bedroom is upstairs, where a queen-sized cherry four-poster bed is covered with a hand-made quilt, and a modern bath has cobalt blue tiles on the floor.

The Smokehouse, a little cottage in back, contains another room with beamed ceilings, a woodstove, and a four-poster bed, but the nicest rooms are the newest ones. These are located in the Garden Cottage, a short walk across the fields. Both spacious and very private suites have woodburning fireplaces, private patios, cherry floors topped with Oriental rugs, and baths with double whirlpool tubs and separate showers.

In the back parlor guests can watch movies on the TV or enjoy the colorful flower garden beyond. In the afternoon freshly baked cookies, tea, and sherry are savored by the guests, often in one of the swings on the spacious front porch.

Danielle is Swiss, and the breakfasts she prepares reflect her heritage. You will feast on fresh muffins or scones and perhaps puffed pancakes with poached pears or cottage cheese waffles with maple syrup as well as fruits, juices, and meats. It's served at individual tables in the formal dining room, which has another fireplace and a 1940s Waterford crystal chandelier.

The tranquil setting, sublimely situated on 35 acres, seems so peaceful that it's hard to believe you are only 1 mile from Chestertown. Yet, within five minutes, excellent restaurants, shops, art galleries, and museums may be visited.

What's Nearby — Chestertown

Chestertown is a charming and historic town whose historic district includes several interesting buildings that are open to the public. Concerts, films, lectures, art exhibits, and live theater take place on the campus of Washington College. St. Paul's Church was erected in 1713 and is one of the oldest continuously operating churches in Maryland. The Waterman's Museum in nearby Rock Hall provides a unique perspective into the life of baymen and watermen. Especially during the migratory season, Eastern Neck Natural Wildlife Refuge is heavily populated with waterfowl.

Great Oak Manor Bed & Breakfast

10568 Cliff Road
Chestertown, MD 21620
(800) 504-3098 or (410) 778-5943;
fax (410) 778-5943;
e-mail: doncantor@friend.ly.net

Innkeepers: Don and Dianne Cantor
Rooms: 11, including 1 suite, all with private baths, air conditioning, telephones, radios, and desks; 5 with fireplaces; 2 with TVs and dataports
On the grounds: Private beach, bicycle rentals, yard games, gardens, benches with bay views. Nearby: dock, tennis, swimming pool, golf course
Extras: Coffee, tea, soft drinks, and snacks in the afternoon; port and sherry in evening; yellow lab named Beau
Rates: $75 – $145, including Continental breakfast
Credit cards accepted: MasterCard and Visa
Open: April - mid-February
Smoking: Permitted outside only
How to get there: From Washington, DC, take Route 50 across the Chesapeake Bay Bridge and continue on Route 301/50 until it splits. Take Route 301 north for 5 miles to Route 213 north. Follow Route 213 through Centreville and into Chestertown. Pass Washington College and turn left at the traffic light onto Route 291 (Morgnec Road). When it dead ends, turn right onto Route 20. Turn right onto Route 514. After crossing Route 298, continue on Route 514 for another 1.8 miles. Turn left onto Great Oak Landing Road. Pass silos, go through first set of brick pillars, continue past golf course, continue straight ahead through second set of brick pillars to large brick manor house.

Great Oak Manor is naughty but nice. One can imagine the wild nights of cognac, cigars, and cash that changed hands at the estate bordering the Chesapeake Bay in the 1950s when it welcomed celebrities such as Arthur Godfrey and Guy Lombardo. They would fly, undetected, into the private airport and then spend a few daytime hours shooting ducks or geese and many after-dark hours playing roulette, blackjack, and poker in the exclusive gaming hall. Those days are long gone, but guests still revel in the stories.

The grand brick 25-room Federal-style manor house was built in 1938 by Russell D'Oench, a W. R. Grace heir. It sat on a 1,700-acre point of land that projected into the Chesa-

Chesapeake Bay. Today, although the estate has dwindled to 12 acres, it still offers marvelous views of the Chesapeake Bay and Fairlee Creek from its bluff-top perch. Inside, the detailed moldings and rich paneling illustrate the craftsmanship that was lavished on this gem.

Dianne and Don Cantor were boating along the East Coast when they fell in love with Chestertown. A realtor told them about a derelict manor house on the water that was for sale. " 'Water' was the operative word," admitted Dianne. "We didn't even hear 'derelict.'" Don had just sold his California computer company to A. T. & T. They purchased the property in 1993 and began the work of restoring the mansion and converting it to a B&B.

Today we admire the carved icons over the doors and fireplace mantels, the rich paneling, and the sweeping stairway that rises from the massive front-to-back entrance hall. In the Gun Room, a map of the original 1,700-acre estate is hand-painted on a panel that pulls down to hide the bar. In the evening guests gather here to watch movies on the large-screen TV.

The guest rooms are furnished with antiques, and five have working fireplaces. One of the most interesting is Russell, which is located in the former gambling hall. It has pine paneling, a stone fireplace, and a cathedral ceiling. D'Oench has a fireplace and a view across the manicured lawns to the bay.

The grounds include flower gardens and a boxwood garden with benches placed in private bowers. More benches line the lip of the bluff, offering wonderful views across the water, especially at sunset.

A Continental breakfast of fruits, yogurts, cereals, homemade muffins and quick breads, coffee, and tea is served every morning in the dining room. Guests may help themselves and eat at the common table, on the brick terrace, or on a bench overlooking the water.

At the little club next door, there's a golf course as well as tennis courts, a swimming pool, a private beach, and a dock — allowing guests to arrive by boat as well as by car. The quiet country lanes are ideal for bicycling. Excellent restaurants will be found in the nearby village of Chestertown as well as numerous antiques shops and art galleries.

What's Nearby

See "What's Nearby — Chestertown," page 41.

The White Swan Tavern

231 High Street
Chestertown, MD 21620
(410) 778-2300;
fax (410) 778-4543

Innkeeper: Mary Susan Maisel
Rooms: 6, including 2 suites, all with private baths, air conditioning, mini-refrigerators, hair dryers, desks; 1 with patio; 2 rooms with wheelchair access; crib available
On the grounds: Off-street parking, gardens
Extras: Afternoon tea; evening wine and sherry; turn-down service with mints and sherry; exercise room with Nordic Track; pets occasionally permitted if prior arrangements made
Rates: $100 – $150, including Continental breakfast
Credit cards accepted: None
Open: Year-round
Smoking: In 1 guest room only
How to get there: From Washington, DC, take Route 50 across the Chesapeake Bay Bridge and continue on Route 301/50 until it splits. Take Route 301 north for 5 miles to Route 213 north. Follow Route 213 through Centreville and into Chestertown. At the traffic light follow Spring Avenue to High Street (Route 20). Turn left onto High Street. The B&B will be on the right.

Chestertown's White Swan Tavern is a living history museum as well as a bed and breakfast — one of the few places where guests can truly immerse themselves in a historical era. The original tavern dates to 1733, but through meticulous research and archaeological excavations it has been fully restored. Returning it to its 1793 roots, the center hall now contains paneling that was original to the period, while the Nicholson Room and the Issac Cannell Room incorporate period cornices, window and door trims, baseboards, paneling, light fixtures, and fireplace mantels.

There are six guest rooms in the tavern, each with its own private bath. A favorite is located in the original kitchen on the first floor. The Lovegrove Kitchen includes huge posts and beams, stucco walls, a brick floor, a private patio, and a massive kitchen fireplace. There are polished wood tables and a low four-poster bed. The Thomas Peacock Room and the Wilmer Room have reproduction canopy beds, while the Sterling Suite has a queen canopy bed, a fireplace, and lovely burnished wood tables and chests. Oil paintings hang on the walls. Unfortunately, the guest room fireplaces cannot be used, but those in the common rooms often are lighted in cool weather.

An afternoon tea of "White Swan" cookies, hot mulled cider, and perhaps scones, lemon cake, or carrot cake, and the establishment's signature tea, is offered in the Cannell Room or on the terrace every day from 3 to 5 P.M. People drive from miles around to have tea and look at the artifacts found during the excavations that are displayed in the glass case.

In addition to the common room where tourists often mingle with bed and breakfast guests for afternoon tea, there is a small sitting room with a fireplace and a TV for guests to use.

Board games, jigsaw puzzles, books, and a stereo offer additional amusements. In the late afternoon wine and sherry are available to guests, who often retreat to the back of the B&B to sit at the tables and chairs on the brick terrace overlooking the pretty flower-filled garden.

A Continental breakfast, consisting of freshly squeezed juices, fruits, homemade breads, and coffee or tea, is served in a basket, where it may be eaten either on the terrace, in the Cannell Room, or in the room.

The White Swan is located in Chestertown's historic district, across from a fine restaurant and adjacent to numerous antiques shops, art galleries, restaurants, and shops. The charming village provides maps and directions to the local attractions as well as suggestions for bicycling and walking tours.

What's Nearby

See "What's Nearby — Chestertown," page 41.

Ashby 1663

27448 Ashby Drive
Easton, MD 21601
(800) 458-3622 or
(410) 822-4235;
fax (410) 822-9288

Innkeepers: Cliff Meredith and Jeanie Wagner
Rooms: 13, including 5 suites and 3 cottages, all with private baths, TVs, air conditioning, telephones, and robes; 12 with desks; 8 with balconies or patios and whirlpool tubs; 7 with fireplaces
On the grounds: Swimming pool; lighted tennis court; dock; gardens
Extras: Exercise room; afternoon tea; complimentary cocktails in the evening; turndown with bedside cookies
Rates: $195 – $595, including full breakfast, afternoon tea, cocktails; two-night minimum if stay includes Saturday night
Credit cards accepted: American Express, Master-Card, Visa
Open: Year-round
Smoking: Non-smoking bed and breakfast
How to get there: From Washington, DC, take Route 50 across the Chesapeake Bay Bridge and follow it to Easton. At Airport Road turn right and travel to the stop sign. Turn right again onto Goldsborough Neck Road and bear left at the fork, traveling past the "No outlet" sign. Turn left again at the sign that reads "Ashby 1663." Continue on the paved road for .75 mile to the B&B.

It's true that the foundation of this grand white clapboard mansion with its Greek Revival entrance dates to 1663, but its style harks to its 1858 period. When Cliff Meredith and Jeanie Wagner purchased the abandoned estate on 30 acres bordering the Miles River, it was in such disrepair that it was in danger of falling down. Cliff, a realtor and contractor, thoroughly updated the mechanical systems and then rebuilt major portions of the house. There's now a wall of Palladian-style windows in the sun room offering vistas of the Miles River and French doors that provide access to the freeform pool. There's a fireplace at each end and polished antique chests and tables. From the entrance hall, a sweeping stairway leads to the second and third floors. Guests often enter the house through the spectacular kitchen.

The guest rooms are so palatial that you may decide to stay for weeks. The main house includes four rooms and a suite. The Robert Goldsborough Suite has a canopy bed swagged and draped in peach and green. It sits in front of a fireplace and has a view of the river. A dressing room leads to a private porch. The marble bath is positively stunning and utterly romantic. A two-person whirlpool tub sits on a raised platform offering sweeping views of the river. It faces a second fireplace, which casts a seductive glow across the room.

There are additional accommodations in the George Goldsborough House and the Mary Trippe Place. A new building at the edge of the river was completed in 1996. It contains four more rooms. Each of these has a view of the river, light oak floors, a fireplace, a kitchen, and a sparkling tile bath with a Jacuzzi.

Breakfast is served in the formal dining room or on the screened porch. Guests will enjoy freshly baked muffins and breads, fruits, juices, and cereals, as well as such delicious entrées as asparagus in crêpes with hollandaise sauce and baked French toast with bananas and walnuts topped with maple syrup. Tea and freshly baked cookies are available in the afternoon. In the evening, guests become acquainted while sampling complimentary cocktails and light hors d'oeuvres.

There are few reasons to leave the grounds of Ashby 1663. There's a dock by which many guests arrive and where canoes and paddleboats are found. A pool and lighted tennis court offer outdoor diversions, while an exercise room has numerous machines. The quiet country lanes surrounding Ashby 1663 are ideal for walking or bicycling. In nearby Easton, the Academy of the Arts, the Chesapeake Bay Maritime Museum, the Historic Avalon Theatre, and the Historical Society of Talbot County provide cultural outlets.

What's Nearby

The activities available on Eastern Shore Maryland are astounding. The Chesapeake Bay Maritime Museum has a variety of exhibits, while the Talbot County Historical Society includes exhibits in a collection of eight historical buildings. The Academy of the Arts is a regional arts center offering changing exhibits as well as concerts, while the Historic Avalon Theatre is home to performing arts programs that range from a chamber music festival to a waterfowl festival. (See also Oxford and St. Michaels.)

Tyler-Spite Inn
112 West Church Street
Frederick, MD 21701
(301) 831-4455

Innkeepers: Bill and Andrea Myer
Rooms: 9, including 4 suites; 4 with private baths; all with air conditioning, woodburning fireplaces, robes, hair dryers, irons, ironing boards; one room with wheelchair access; telephones available for guest rooms, otherwise telephone at B&B check-in desk
On the grounds: Swimming pool; garden with fountain
Extras: Parking on premises; afternoon high tea; decanters of sherry in the room; standard poodle named Mitzi
Rates: $180 – $250 weekends, $100 – $150 weekdays, including full breakfast and high tea; two-night minimum major holidays
Credit cards accepted: American Express, MasterCard, Visa
Open: Year-round except first two weeks of January
Smoking: Non-smoking bed and breakfast
How to get there: From any freeway, follow signs for Frederick National Historic District. Continue to Church Street in the center of town. The B&B will be on the right opposite the old Court House.

In addition to being an innovative doctor (he performed the first cataract operation in America), Dr. John Tyler was a provocative character. When the town decided to cut a road through his vacant property, he hired a crew who worked throughout the night laying a foundation for this grand house. The next morning, when the road crew arrived, they found Dr. Tyler rocking in his favorite chair on his foundation. Town law prohibited seizure of land if there was a significant structure being built.

The three-story Federal-style stucco Tyler-Spite Inn certainly is a significant structure.

Inside it has elaborate ceiling moldings surrounding the 13-foot-high walls as well as elaborate columns, arches, chandeliers, and fireplace mantels. The calico marble mantel in the library is matched by the room's burnt red color and there are carved marble mantels in the music room, dining room, and parlor that are also noteworthy. Historically furnished by owners Bill and Andrea Myer, you will see priceless oil paintings, Oriental rugs on polished pine floors, and the mahogany campaign desk on which General Douglas MacArthur signed the peace treaty in Manila.

The spacious guest rooms are equally dramatic, with fireplaces in many, canopy featherbeds, and windows lavishly draped in silk. The walls are dramatically painted in navy or brushed with peach. The Nelson House next door is also part of the inn. It has elegant common rooms (including a terrific back porch overlooking the gardens) and guest rooms furnished in a similar manner. Of the nine rooms, four have private baths; the rest share. The Nelson Suite in the Nelson House has a marble bath with a whirlpool in an alcove and a separate marble shower entered through fluted columns. For those who prefer a less elegant setting, the Myers Suite in the Nelson House is a garret suite with a painted floor, painted furniture, and a patriotic flag theme. It has a private bath with a double whirlpool.

The lovely formal walled gardens, which have a fountain, are splendidly alive with color in the summer, and there's a brick patio and a swimming pool tucked away in back. A full breakfast is either served formally in the dining room or informally on the patio. Fine linens, china, and silver are used. In addition to fresh fruit, juice, and breakfast breads, there will be a hot entrée of perhaps baked apple dumplings, Belgian waffles, a soufflé, or fried green tomatoes. On special occasions, a treat called "kinklings" will be prepared. These are made with a shortbread dough that is deep fried and dipped in powdered sugar. A formal afternoon tea is served on weekends. There will be lemonade, tea, wine, tea sandwiches, specialty cakes, strawberries, cheese, and crackers. Decanters of sherry are placed in the rooms for a nightcap.

Historic and architecturally important, Frederick is worth a stopover of several days. Take a walking tour of the city to learn about the dramatic events that brought George Washington to town in the eighteenth century and Abraham Lincoln in the nineteenth century.

What's Nearby

The Frederick National Historic District includes 33 blocks of buildings of historic and architectural significance. Stop at the visitor center for walking maps. Local museums open for visits include the Francis Scott Key Museum, the Barbara Fritchie House & Museum, the National Museum of Civil War Medicine, and the Schifferstadt Architectural Museum. The Rose Hill Manor Children's Museum, located in a 1790s Georgian mansion that was the home of Maryland's first governor, is a hands-on living museum where children can learn to quilt, comb wool, weave, make soap and candles, and participate in other activities.

Lands End Manor
on the Bay

232 Prospect Bay Drive
Grasonville, MD 21638
(410) 827-6284

Innkeeper: Elaine Johnson Wheatley
Rooms: 2, both with private baths and air conditioning, TVs, telephones, radios, hair dryers, desks, robes, and CD player; 1 with fireplace; crib available
On the grounds: Swimming pool; dock, rowboat, canoe, paddleboat; bicycles
Extras: Afternoon tea; evening drinks; turndown with homemade cookies, fruit, and sherry; pets permitted with prior permission; resident dog named Hobo
Rates: $150, including full breakfast, afternoon tea, evening drinks; two-night minimum preferred
Credit cards accepted: MasterCard and Visa
Open: Year-round
Smoking: Permitted in solarium only
How to get there: From Washington, DC, take Route 50 across the Chesapeake Bay Bridge (Route 50/301 to exit 45B (Nesbit Road). Turn right onto Nesbit Road and follow it to the stop sign. Turn left onto Route 18 and continue to the first intersection (Bennett Point Road). Turn right and continue to Perry Corner Road. Turn right again and go to the next intersection (Prospect Bay Road). Turn left and continue to the Prospect Bay Lighthouse. Turn right at the lighthouse and continue to the stop sign. Turn right onto Prospect Bay Drive and continue for 2 miles to Lands End Manor, which will be on the left. You will see a mailbox marked "Lands End" and "#232." The property is surrounded by a split-rail fence.

The rural countryside of Maryland's Eastern Shore is dotted with promontories, inlets, creeks, and rivers that create its jagged coastline. Grasonville, a tiny spot merely fifteen minutes from the Chesapeake Bay Bridge, has yet to be discovered by tourists and therefore offers the ultimate peaceful getaway. Originally called Prospect Plantation, Lands End Manor is located on a 17-acre point surrounded by peaceful vistas of Eastern and Prospect Bays and of Greenwood Creek. St. Michael's, Maryland, can be seen across the water on a clear night. Waterfowl nest in the marshes, and the fishing is legendary. That's why, for many years, the manor house served as a private hunting lodge.

Today, it is the home of Charles and Elaine

Wheatley and a delightful bed and breakfast run by Elaine, who is an architectural interior designer and a charming innkeeper. One enters a formal entry hall. There's a little library filled with books and a solarium with a flagstone floor and a wall of windows overlooking the gardens. A formal living room has another fireplace and an elaborate molded ceiling. Bouquets of flowers from the garden add splashes of color throughout.

The impressive great room, once the nucleus of the hunting lodge, has oak floors, pine-paneled walls, beamed ceilings with an antler chandelier, and a massive fireplace with eighteenth-century Delft tiles in the surround. There are leather sofas here where guests can sit to enjoy the view, and a large-screen TV for watching videos. The Gun Room has a Tudor feeling with dark beams and stucco walls, another fireplace, a terra cotta tile floor, and racks of guns.

There are two spacious guest rooms on the second floor. Both have private baths and views of the water. The Heron Room has a feather bed with an upholstered headboard and a wood-burning fireplace. In the Swan Room, there's a pencil-post tiger-maple canopy bed and a gorgeous tiger maple chest with twisted spindles. A third bedroom is occasionally used, but it has a bath downstairs.

Elaine is the perfect pampering hostess. She serves canapés and desserts with afternoon tea. Wine, sherry, and drinks are available prior to going out in the evening. Turndown service includes homemade cookies, sherry, and fresh fruit. A full breakfast is served in the dining room or on the patio. It will include fresh fruit and juice, a homemade coffee cake or other bread, and an entrée of perhaps eggs rellenos or an apple pancake puff as well as bacon, ham, or sausage.

In a very private setting, concealed from the house by trees, there's a swimming pool. At the private dock, guests may arrive by boat, and there are rowboats, canoes, and paddleboats for guests' enjoyment. Bicycles are available for back-road jaunts. Benches are located by the water, offering an ideal spot for a private picnic.

What's Nearby

In this rural setting near the Eastern Shore end of the Bay Bridge, boating, fishing, and bicycling are pleasant recreational activities. There are miles of untraveled roads to explore. Wye Mills, a nearby restored village, was first settled in the 1600s. It contains an operating grist mill and the restored Wye Church, which dates to 1721 and has its original hanging pulpit and high box pews. The Wye Oak is a venerable 450-year-old specimen that resides in its own 250-acre park.

Innkeepers: John and Barbara Dreisch
Rooms: 5, all with private baths, air conditioning, fire-places, balconies, garden tubs, and hair dryers; telephones are available for guest rooms, if requested
On the grounds: Hiking and walking trails through the woods
Extras: Complimentary tea, sodas, coffee, wine, and cordials; cocker spaniel named Max
Rates: $115 –$160, including full breakfast; two-night minimum on weekends
Credit cards accepted: American Express, Diners Club, MasterCard, Visa
Open: Year-round
Smoking: Non-smoking bed and breakfast
How to get there: Call for directions. Near Sharpsburg and Boonsboro, Maryland, and Shepherdstown, West Virginia

Antietam Overlook Farm
Bed & Breakfast
P.O. Box 30
Keedysville, MD 21756
(800) 878-4241 or (301) 432-4200

From this eagle's-nest perch high in the Blue Ridge Mountains, with a four-state view and overlooking the Civil War's Antietam National Battlefield, the serenity is almost palpable. Deer graze in the adjacent fields, wild turkeys feed on grain, and migratory birds stop to spend a few days before continuing on their journey. The seclusion and serenity is so zealously guarded that there's an electrically operated gate at the entrance. Once guests reach this 95-acre aerie, their lives change, at least during their stay. The relaxed pace becomes habit-forming — there's no place to rush off to.

Originally, this was the private retreat of John and Barbara Dreisch, and their own home is right next door. The guest portion was newly constructed in 1990. The friendliness and hospitality of the Dreisch's — and of their cocker spaniel, Max — and the privacy of the setting have brought guests to their doorstep who return again and again.

The building is constructed of stone and

pine. There are rough-sawn yellow pine walls, hand-hewn beams, and posts. The massive stone fireplace in the Country Room is the focal point throughout the winter, while the screened-in porch with its panoramic views is the summer retreat. The decor includes a wagon-wheel chandelier, comfortable sofas and chairs, braided rugs on pine floors, shelves filled with books and magazines, quilts and folk art on the wall, and Civil War memorabilia. There's a wet bar; a full refrigerator stocked with sodas and wine; tea, coffee, an instant hot water tap; and a cabinet filled with cordials and liqueurs. Board games, jigsaw puzzles, and lively conversation take the place of a television.

The guest rooms are unique. Each has its own gas remote-controlled fireplace, a screened-in porch with a top-of-the-world view, fantastically comfortable beds, and a deep, private soaking tub tucked into an alcove that's surrounded by plants and has a view of the val-ley and of the flickering flames in the fireplace. The Dreisch's call this a "garden tub. " There's also a shower in each of the baths. One of the advantages of new construction is that central air, thorough soundproofing between walls, and soundless carpeting can be installed. Here, guests feel as if they're in a private cocoon.

A full breakfast is prepared every morning and served at communal tables in the Country Room. On a typical morning, it will include such local fare as fresh fruit; country ham baked with fresh pineapple and cinnamon sugar; fried tomatoes; a three-cheese fluffy egg casserole; battered and fried cranberry nut bread; fresh juices; and homemade jams, curds, and chutneys.

Nearby attractions, in addition to Antietam, include Harpers Ferry National Park, hiking on the Appalachian Trail or on the inn trails, and bicycling on the C. & O. Canal Path. Fine restaurants are nearby, as are antiques and gift shops.

What's Nearby

From this perch high above the Antietam National Battlefield, it's possible to imagine the scene that took place below in September 1862 when 23,000 troops were killed or wounded during the battle following the first Southern invasion of Northern soil in the Civil War. The Appalachian Trail meanders across the nearby mountains, offering interesting day hikes or longer ones. (See also Sharpsburg, Maryland, as well as Charles Town, Harpers Ferry, and Shepherdstown, West Virginia.)

National Pike Inn

9 West Main Street
(mailing address: P.O. Box 299)
New Market, MD 21774
(301) 865-5055; website:
http://www.newmarketmd.com/natpike.htm

Innkeepers: Tom and Terry Rimel
Rooms: 6, including 1 suite; 4 with private baths; 2 that share; all with air conditioning; telephone available in entrance hall
On the grounds: Gardens; parking
Extras: Freshly baked cookies on secretary in entrance hall
Rates: $75 – $160, including full breakfast; two-night minimum in September and on local special-event weekends
Credit cards accepted: MasterCard and Visa
Open: Year-round except Thanksgiving and Christmas
Smoking: Permitted outside only
How to get there: From I-70, take exit 62 to Route 75 and go north for 1 block to Main Street. Turn left onto Main Street (Route 144) and continue for about 3 blocks to the inn, which is in the center of town.

Ask innkeeper Terry Rimel about her garden, and her eyes light up. In fact, you may want to retire to this lovely oasis as soon as you arrive to nibble on a chocolate chip—oatmeal or a peanut butter butterscotch krispie cookie from the jar at the entrance. The .5-acre garden contains iron benches tucked away among an abundance of flowers that include tulips, roses, peonies, and annuals and more than 200 azalea bushes. There's a brick courtyard, a brick smokehouse, and brick pathways leading past gurgling fountains, bird baths, and bird feeders. It's a peaceful start to a relaxing visit.

The National Pike Inn is a homey and casual bed and breakfast in a historic brick building in a town that calls itself "the antiques capital of Maryland." More than thirty shops are within an easy walk or ride of the B&B. The entire downtown section of the town is a National Historic District. Named for the first federally financed turnpike in the United States, the building saw horse-drawn carriages and stagecoaches pass its doors before the advent of the horseless carriage.

The National Pike Inn was built in three stages. The oldest portion, which is in the rear, dates to 1796, while the buildings that front the street date from 1802 and 1804. The juxtaposition of these three buildings creates interesting twists to the interior hallways and stairways, adding to the inn's charm.

There is a living room just off the entrance hall with period reproduction tables, a brass chandelier, and an Oriental rug covering wide-plank floors. The Colonial ambience is so authentic you feel as if you're visiting the early seventeenth century. On the left, a small sitting room contains a TV directly from the twentieth

century. The dining room is located in the 1796 part of the house. Here, under its brass chandelier and on a lace tablecloth, Terry serves cold cereals and fruit, fresh juice, homemade bread or muffins (perhaps a chocolate chip-banana bread), an egg dish, and a breakfast meat.

The guest rooms are decorated in a simple, country style. There are brass beds, oak headboards, and small baths. Several rooms share baths. The nicest room is the Colonial Room, which has a burgundy rug, a canopy bed with a deep bedskirt, and an updated bath.

There's an excellent restaurant across the street. In addition to antiquing, there are free community concerts on Sundays in summer, and hiking trails lace nearby parks.

What's Nearby

The entire downtown section of New Market is a National Historic District. Noted as the "Antiques Capital of Maryland," there are more than thirty shops in town. A walking tour of the town identifies the historic buildings. Wine tastings and tours take place at nearby Linganore Wine Cellars in Mt. Airy, and you can cross-country ski on the property in winter.

The Lighthouse Club Hotel

56th Street
Ocean City, MD 21842
(800) 767-6060 or (410) 524-5400;
fax (410) 524-9327;
e-mail: island@dmv.com
website: http://www.oceancity.com/fagers.htm

Innkeeper: Angela Reynolds
Rooms: 23, including 8 suites, all with air conditioning, TVs, VCRs, 3 telephones, mini-refrigerators, coffee makers, hair dryers, desks, balconies, robes, and whirlpool tubs; 8 with fireplaces; fax, cribs, irons, and ironing boards available
On the grounds: Parking
Extras: Turndown service with mints; complimentary split of champagne
Rates: $89 – $259, including Continental breakfast; two-night minimum mid-April to mid-November
Credit cards accepted: American Express, Carte Blanche, Diners Club, Discover, MasterCard, Visa
Open: Year-round
Smoking: Allowed in all rooms
How to get there: From Washington, DC, take Route 50 across the Chesapeake Bay Bridge and continue east past Salisbury. Take Route 90 toward North Ocean City. At the junction of Route 90 and Coastal Highway, turn right onto Coastal Highway. Turn right at 56th Street Bayside. The Lighthouse Club is directly ahead.

Rising like a mirage from the surrounding marshlands and overlooking a very private stretch of wetland on Isle of Wight Bay, this circular white clapboard lighthouse was built to house a restaurant in 1978. Modeled after the Thomas Point Lighthouse, located near Annapolis, it has a lookout on top and dormer windows piercing the sloping red roof on the third floor. Owner John Fager converted it to a luxury bed and breakfast in 1988. It's as different from the nearby tacky strip motels and high-rise

hotels as it can be. In location, style, and comfort, the inn offers the best of all worlds.

One enters a small vestibule with a tasteful reception desk and a corner library containing floor-to-ceiling shelves of books. A library ladder helps guests reach the top shelves.

The guest rooms are on the two top floors, which project out over the base of the lighthouse. The fifteen rooms on the second floor are slightly smaller than the eight enormous units on the third, but all rooms have private decks, and those on the bay side have breathtaking views of the water.

The decor is primarily white and beige, complimenting the hues of the bay and marsh. Queen-sized mattresses rest on bamboo platforms, and tables have glass tops. Each room has a refrigerator with an ice maker, and a wet bar. Sodas and a split of champagne are complimentary. There are TVs and VCRs in armoires, and every room and suite has three telephones and a built-in stereo system. The suites all have gas fireplaces.

As luxurious as the rooms are, however, the baths are even more so. They are finished in white marble and mirrors, and all have whirlpool tubs.

Unlike most bed and breakfasts, a Continental breakfast is delivered to each room in the evening when the beds are turned down. It will consist of a slice of fruit, a loaf of breakfast bread such as cranberry nut or banana, and orange juice. Coffee makers are located in each guest room. When guests arise in the morning, they can enjoy breakfast in the room or on their private deck.

Guests can walk across the marsh on a wooden walkway to Fager's Island Restaurant and Bar, a bayside restaurant with spacious decks offering panoramic water and sunset views. A swimming pool, located at a nearby sister hotel, is available for guests staying at The Lighthouse.

What's Nearby

Ocean City is a premier resort town located on 10 miles of white sandy beaches. There's a 3-mile boardwalk that includes a handsome restored carousel with hand-carved and painted horses and a multitude of restaurants, shops, and nighttime entertainment activities. Charter boats take tourists fishing and sightseeing, or people can watch as the daily catch is brought in at the nearby West Ocean City Harbor. At the Ocean City Life-Saving Station Museum, visitors learn about the hurricanes and storms that have devastated the region in the past, and they can also visit a saltwater aquarium.

Combsberry

4837 Evergreen Road
Oxford, MD 21654
(410) 226-5353;
fax (410) 228-1453;
website: http://www.combsberry.com or
through Yahoo! under B&Bs

Innkeepers: Dr. Mahmood and Ann Shariff; manager, Catherine Magrogan
Rooms: 6, including 1 suite and 1 cottage, all with private baths, air conditioning, robes, and hair dryers; 4 with whirlpools, fireplaces, balconies or patios; 3 with kitchens; portable telephones for guests to use
On the grounds: Formal gardens; dock, fishing, crabbing, canoeing, paddleboating
Extras: Wine, tea, and cheese on arrival; chocolates at turndown; whirlpool tubs; access to fax; Jack Russell terrier named Katie
Rates: $140 – $175 December to April; $250 – $395 April to December, including full breakfast; two-night minimum weekends preferred
Credit cards accepted: MasterCard and Visa
Open: Year-round except Thanksgiving and Christmas Day
Smoking: Permitted outside only
How to get there: From Washington, DC, take Route 50 across the Chesapeake Bay Bridge. Stay on Route 50 to Route 322 south, the Easton Parkway. Then take Route 333 south toward Oxford for 6.8 miles and turn left onto Evergreen Road. Turn left again at the second driveway through the brick pillars. Drive down a long dirt driveway to the inn.

Were I to choose my favorite spot at Combsberry, I believe it would be the brick patio surrounded by the flower garden and enclosed by a picket fence behind the Oxford Cottage. From this vantage point, I could watch the herons and egrets and swans on Island Creek. My special friend would have picked a magnolia blossom from the nearby tree for my hair, and we would sit here while the sun sank behind the horizon to watch the pink and gold sky fade away. We would be enchanted as the inn's gardens and pathways were illuminated by moonbeams. Can any other place offer such tranquility — such sublime harmony with nature?

The history of Combsberry Plantation actually began in 1649, when 100 acres were awarded to Josias Cooper. In 1718 the property passed to John Oldham, who began construction of the fine brick manor house that has now been converted to a B&B. The house's history is far from over. Now in the caring hands of Dr. Mahmood and Ann Shariff, the elegant house has been fully restored to the gracious style it knew under the Oldhams. The brick manor house sits on 9.5 acres, and it contains some unusual architectural features. Stairs do not rise from a center hall, but within a stair tower, and there are six fireplaces with arched brick openings. The living room has elegant antique furnishings, polished wide-plank pine floors (original to the house) topped with Oriental rugs, and English chintz fabric draped across the windows. Through an archway, hand-painted with flowers, there's a green paneled library with a woodburning fireplace and walls lined with books. In front, a tile-floored sun room offers a stunning view of the river, and French doors lead to a brick-walled garden.

There's a formal dining room where breakfast may be served, but most people prefer to eat in the casual atmosphere of the striking kitchen. The huge space has brick walls, tile floors, and an open island. On the river side, a bay of windows provides views to guests seated at little cafe tables. Breakfast will include fresh breads, fruits, and juices as well as perhaps a ham and broccoli strata or a quiche.

There are six guest accommodations — all with spectacular views of the water. The Magnolia Suite is in shades of pink and green and includes a canopy bed, a woodburning fireplace, a dresser with flowers hand-painted on it, a private deck, and an elegant bath with a double whirlpool and a tiled shower. The charming Victoria Garden Room is in blue and white and furnished with wicker furniture and a wrought iron bed. It has a private stairway to the English garden, which is softly illuminated at night. Two additional rooms in a building, built in 1997, are equally enchanting. These two share a great-room and a kitchen.

There's a dock, which provides access to boaters who wish to arrive by water. A canoe and paddleboat are available, and guests can fish and crab off the pier.

What's Nearby

Oxford was the first port of entry on the Eastern Shore in 1694, and it's still possible to walk its quiet streets to admire the historic old buildings. Take the Historic Oxford-Bellevue Ferry across the Tred Avon River; visit the Oxford Customs House, an exact replica of the first one; and the Oxford Museum, where you can learn more about the history of the town. (See also Easton and St. Michaels.)

Tarr House B&B
109 Green Street
(mailing address: P.O. Box 1152)
St. Michaels, MD 21663
(410) 745-2175

Innkeeper: Bonnie Baseman
Rooms: 2, with private baths, air conditioning, and hair dryers; 1 with a fireplace
On the grounds: Gardens
Rates: $125 – $135 weekdays; $135 – $145 weekends, including Continental breakfast; two-night minimum weekends
Credit cards accepted: None
Open: Year-round
Smoking: Permitted outside only
How to get there: From Washington, DC, cross the Bay Bridge and take Route 50 east. Before Easton, take Route 322/Easton Bypass to Route 33 and follow it into St. Michaels. You will be on Talbot Street. Turn right at Christ Church onto Willow Street, which becomes Green Street in 1 block. The B & B will be in 1 block on the left.

Charming, engaging, captivating, and delightful are all adjectives that come to mind when describing Tarr House B&B. From a little doll's house of brick (circa 1667, making it one of the oldest houses in St. Michaels) that has a new clapboard extension merely 200 years old, innkeeper Bonnie Baseman, an interior designer, has fashioned an enchanting and sweet little B&B. There are green shutters on the windows and window boxes with a cute bunny and rose design that overflow with geraniums in summer. Tucked away on a quiet side street in this village that buzzes with tourists throughout the summer, her sanctuary provides ample space to escape. If you are fortunate enough to have booked one of her two rooms, you'll congratulate yourself throughout your visit.

There are three common rooms for guests to use. Both the living room and the library have woodburning fireplaces, white paneled walls, wide-plank heart pine floors, and English chintz-covered chairs and windows. Floor-to-ceiling bookcases hold a variety of interesting books. The library also contains the house television and a desk with a telephone and fax. At the back of the house, Bonnie added a tile-floored solarium with French doors that open to the spacious terrace and a garden filled with an ever-changing kaleidoscope of color from early tulips and iris to daisies and mums. A small natural pond, surrounded with rocks, holds koi.

The dining room, where Bonnie serves an extraordinary Continental breakfast, has another fireplace; there's a sideboard laden with silver; and a glass-topped table set with linen placemats, sterling flatware, and Lenox china. A swan chandelier oversees the bounty. She starts the meal with a plate of fresh fruit (perhaps bananas, kiwi, and melon) decorated with seasonal flowers. This is followed by an array of breakfast breads, from croissants to melt-in-your-mouth blueberry muffins.

The two guest rooms are on the second floor, and they both have private baths. One has a cathedral ceiling, a king-sized bed with a headboard upholstered in a brilliant Clarence House fabric, an antique French walnut armoire, an antique French ladies' writing desk, and a wood-burning fireplace. The small bath has a shower. The other room has a queen-sized bed with a headboard upholstered in a wisteria pattern, an antique German armoire, and a bath with a clawfoot tub and a hand-held shower. A decanter of sherry sits on an antique table in each room.

The B&B is only a few steps from the harbor and an easy walk to the Chesapeake Bay Maritime Museum. Cove Park is across the street. Restaurants, a variety of antiques stores and gift shops, and art galleries are nearby.

What's Nearby — St. Michaels

St. Michaels is the hub of activity in this section of Eastern Shore Maryland. There are numerous shops, boutiques, and restaurants along the pretty main street. (Don't miss a visit to one of the crab houses that overlook the Miles River.) The Chesapeake Bay Maritime Museum consists of a group of eighteen historic buildings that include an authentic 1880s lighthouse, an aquarium, and a boat restoration shop. There's no better way to learn about the seafaring life of the Chesapeake Bay. Charter boats take visitors on fishing excursions, and there's also a narrated sightseeing cruise. (See also Easton, Oxford, Tilghman Island, and Wittman.)

Victoriana Inn

205 Cherry Street
(mailing address: P.O. Box 449)
St. Michaels, MD 21663
(410) 745-3368

Innkeeper: Janet Bernstein
Rooms: 5, 2 with private baths; 3 that share two baths; all with air conditioning; 2 with fireplaces
On the grounds: Gardens; parking
Extras: Afternoon tea, fruit, lemonade, cookies, port; mints and port in rooms; golden retriever
Rates: $125 – $175, including full breakfast; two-night minimum on weekends
Credit cards accepted: MasterCard and Visa
Open: Year-round
Smoking: Permitted outside only
How to get there: From Washington, DC, take Route 50 across the Chesapeake Bay Bridge and take Route 50 east. Before Easton, take Route 322/Easton Bypass to Route 33. Follow that into St. Michaels, where it becomes Talbot Street. Turn right onto Mill Street and look for the parking lot, which will be on the right.

Verdant lawns slope gently down to the harbor from the tidy white Victorian inn with its mansard roof. A broad covered porch across the back of the house holds white wicker furniture, and there are Adirondack chairs on the lawn — all for contemplating the parade of boats in the water.

The inn is a gem. Innkeeper Janet Bernstein converted the house to a B&B in 1987, and unlike many Victorians, it has been decorated with elegance rather than frills and lace. From the entry hall, with its Second Empire-style cherry credenza and heart pine floors, guests gravitate toward the parlor, which is furnished with plush sofas before a fireplace and a coffee table piled with books and magazines. A solarium is down a half step flanked by columns, and it offers the perfect harbor vantage point, which is particularly lovely at sunset.

The two favorite rooms are located on the first floor. Tilghman Island has a canopy bed draped in black and rose fabric, a working fireplace, and a beautiful armoire. The tile bath has a pedestal sink. The Sharp Room has a canopy bed swagged with purple fabric, another fireplace, and a private bath. There are three more bedrooms on the second floor. These have sinks in the rooms but they share two hall baths. The antique French Victorian bedroom suite in Poplar Island is particularly impressive, as it is inlaid with twelve different kinds of woods.

Janet serves a full breakfast in the parlor and solarium. By cleverly expanding the end tables and coffee tables, she creates breakfast tables for the morning meal. They will be set with linen napkins, silver, crystal, and flowered Victorian china. She will serve fresh fruit, homemade breads (her cinnamon buns are especially popular) or cakes such as her lemon cream cake, and an entrée — perhaps eggs Benedict or fruit pancakes or a frittata.

Among the B&B's other attributes: there's a wonderful garden filled with old-fashioned annuals that Janet changes three times a season. The garden includes such old-time favorites as cosmos and hollyhocks as well as a butterfly garden and a cutting garden. There's a private parking lot in back — a real plus in this town that teems with tourists in the summer; tea, fresh fruit, lemonade, freshly baked cookies, and port are set out in the afternoon. There are board games, jigsaw puzzles, lots of books, and a TV for guests to use.

The inn is in the heart of the historic district and a short walk from the Chesapeake Bay Maritime Museum and from excursion boats that ply the Miles River. There are numerous bicycle adventures in store for bicyclists along the miles of flat picturesque roads.

What's Nearby

See "What's Nearby — St. Michaels," page 61.

The Inn at Antietam

220 East Main Street
(mailing address: P.O. Box 119)
Sharpsburg, MD 21782
(301) 432-6601;
fax (301) 432-5981

Innkeepers: Betty and Cal Fairbourn
Rooms: 4 suites, all with private baths, air condition-
ing, and radios; 1 with a TV; 1 with a fireplace
On the grounds: Gardens; parking
Extras: Decanter of sherry in the parlor, cookies in the
sun room; dog named Tucker, cat named Rebok
Rates: $95 weekdays, $105 weekends, including full
breakfast; two-night minimum weekends and holidays
Credit cards accepted: American Express
Open: Mid-February to mid-December
Smoking: Non-smoking bed and breakfast
How to get there: From I-70 or I-270, go to Frederick.
Continue west on I-70 to exit 49 (Braddock Heights).
Turn left onto Alt. Route 40 west and follow this
through Middletown and Boonsboro. In Boonsboro
turn left onto Route 34 and follow this for 6 miles to
Sharpsburg. As you approach Sharpsburg, you will see
the Antietam National Cemetery on the left. The inn is
beside it, also on the left.

The trim white 1908 clapboard Victorian sits high above the road on 7.5 acres next to the Antietam Cemetery. From a swing or rocker on the wraparound porch, you can contemplate the tragic events of September 17, 1862, when 23,000 Confederate and Union men lost their lives or were wounded in the Battle of Antietam. Or you can read about them in one of the innkeepers' many Civil War books.

Today the roar of muskets and the thunder of cannons have been replaced by the peaceful sounds of birds chirping. Betty and Cal Fairbourn (he was formerly a vice president of General Motors Acceptance Corporation) restored the house in 1984 and have created a lovely haven for their guests.

Guests park at the rear of the house so the flower-filled gardens and the brick patio with its white wicker and iron furniture are the first view they receive of this fine inn. A bowl of fruit and freshly baked cookies will be waiting in the sun room, where a magnificent hibiscus tree blooms next to antique wicker furniture. You will surely want to take a cup of tea or a glass of wine to the patio to admire the flowers and the view of the Blue Ridge Mountains beyond. On cooler days, you might sit in the parlor, which is furnished with antique Victorian furniture and has a piano. On a marble-topped Victorian table, there's a decanter of sherry.

The four guest rooms are spacious enough to include sitting areas, and each has a thoroughly updated bath. Each room is decorated with antiques. In the rustic Smoke House, there's a massive brick fireplace, beamed ceilings, barnwood walls, and a large wrought iron bed in a loft. In the Master Suite, there's a four-poster crown canopy bed dressed in a peach floral fabric that matches the wallpaper, and lace curtains on the windows. The Blue Bird Suite has a white iron bed and whimsical flop-eared

bunnies. The Queen Suite has a sleigh bed.

Breakfast is served every morning in the formal dining room, which has elegant pale blue walls. Betty sets the table with a lace tablecloth and her fine silver and china. Candles add a romantic air. She often starts the meal with fresh juice and fruit. Although she may fix coddled eggs or baked apples or poached pears, her specialties are Belgian waffles, blueberry pancakes, and blueberry blintzes.

Many of the Fairbourn's guests are Civil War buffs who come to immerse themselves in Civil War history. They will find many interesting books in the collection at the inn, and they will spend hours walking through the Antietam Cemetery, reading the inscriptions on the marble, bronze, and granite monuments. You can also drive an 8-mile, self-guided audio tour of the site.

What's Nearby

A visit to the Antietam National Battlefield should begin at the visitor center, where historical exhibits and an audiovisual program will lay the groundwork for an understanding of the events that took place here. A walk through the Antietam National Cemetery, located next door to the B&B, will have a profound impact. (See also Keedysville, Maryland, as well as Charles Town, Harpers Ferry, and Shepherdstown, West Virginia.)

Chanceford Hall Bed & Breakfast Inn

209 West Federal Street
Snow Hill, MD 21863
(410) 632-2231

Innkeepers: Michael and Thelma Driscoll
Rooms: 5, including 1 suite, all with private baths and air conditioning; 4 with working fireplaces; 2 with desks; the telephone is located near the entrance, although there are portable telephones should guests prefer to talk in the privacy of their room
On the grounds: Parking; lap pool; gardens
Extras: Wine and hors d'oeuvres in the evening
Rates: $115 – $135, including full breakfast
Credit cards accepted: None
Open: Year-round
Smoking: The smoking policy is flexible
How to get there: From Washington, DC, take Route 50 across the Chesapeake Bay Bridge. Continue on Route 50 east to Salisbury and then take Route 13 bypass toward Norfolk. In 2.5 miles, take Route 12 and continue for 16 miles to Snow Hill. Go over the bridge and continue for 1 block past the light. Turn right onto Federal Street. The inn is 2 blocks farther on the left.

The pretty, peaceful little village of Snow Hill on the Pocomoke River was a delightful surprise to me on my first visit. I was unprepared for the wide streets lined with flowering Bradford pear trees, the brick sidewalks, and the stately mansions centered on manicured lawns. Snow Hill was founded in 1642, and it soon became an active shipping port, with schooners, and later steamboats, tieing up at the docks and shipping goods throughout the world.

Chanceford Hall, a magnificent brick Greek Revival mansion, was built in three stages between 1759 and 1780. It sits back from the road on 1.25 acres that include a spacious front lawn and a lovely back garden that contains the third-oldest walnut tree in Maryland.

The house itself is a jewel, impeccably restored by Michael and Thelma Driscoll and opened as a bed and breakfast in 1988. Michael, an extraordinary cabinetmaker and designer of historic custom furniture, brought the intricate hand-carved mantels (the house has ten working fireplaces), stair railings, spindles, and random-width yellow pine floors back to life. He and Thelma filled the rooms with richly hued Oriental rugs and with wonderful reproductions of English and American antiques. If they couldn't find the perfect piece, Michael made one that is so perfectly detailed you would have difficulty distinguishing it from an original. In addition to the formal living room, there's a sun room with another fireplace and a TV and VCR for nighttime entertainment.

The five spacious guest rooms (the smallest is 16 x 16 feet) are furnished with as much care as the common rooms. Each has a 10^1/$_2$-foot ceiling and private bath. The Chanceford Room has a queen-sized canopy bed, a woodburning fireplace, and a gleaming highboy. The largest room, the Carrington Suite, has a queen pencil-post canopy bed as well as a single cannon ball bed. There's a working fireplace and another highboy. Only the Cliveden Room does not have a working fireplace. Although all rooms have private baths, one has a bath just outside the bedroom door, and another has a bath across the hall.

Thelma and Michael are among the most accommodating innkeepers you'll find. There will be wine and hors d'oeuvres waiting every afternoon, which you may enjoy on the patio, in the sun room, in the living room, or in your guest room. In the morning, Thelma will fix a sumptuous breakfast, which she's happy to serve at your convenience anytime between 7 and 11 A.M. It's served at the dining room table, where guests can relax in complete comfort. The full repast will include homemade muffins (maybe apple raisin) as well as perhaps a cheese and mushroom omelet or French toast. There will also be a variety of fresh fruits and juices.

The pretty backyard and gardens are secluded from the street. There's a deck as well as a patio and also a lap pool with its own patio. Tables shaded by umbrellas offer a quiet place to spend an afternoon reading. On the other hand, the Driscolls have bicycles for their guests to use, and they will also be happy to provide a guide for a walking tour of the town. Don't pass up the opportunity to learn more about this fascinating town. I didn't.

What's Nearby — Snow Hill

Take a walking tour of historic Snow Hill, board a sightseeing boat for a cruise along the Pocomoke River, or rent a canoe for your own excursion. Visit the Julia A. Purnell Museum to see the exhibits of art and objects related to Worcester County. At Shad Landing State Park you can picnic, boat, or swim in a pool, or you can bask in the sun on the sandy ocean beaches in nearby Assateague State Park. (See also Berlin, Maryland, and Chincoteague, Virginia.)

The River House Inn

201 East Market Street
Snow Hill, MD 21863
(410) 632-2722;
fax (410) 632-2866;
e-mail: riverinn@shore.intercom.net
website: http://www.bbonline.com/md/
riverhouse or http://www.1sttravelerschoice.
virtualcities

Innkeepers: Larry and Susanne Knudsen
Rooms: 8, including 1 suite and 1 cottage, all with private baths, air conditioning, and radios; 6 with fireplaces; 4 with balconies or patios; 3 with TVs, mini-refrigerators, desks, and coffee makers; 2 with hair dryers, irons, and ironing boards; 2 rooms with wheelchair access; cribs available
On the grounds: Lawns and gardens down to Pocomoke River
Extras: Wine and snacks in afternoon; soft drinks, coffee, and tea always available; fax available; pets occasionally permitted; two resident standard poodles named Belle and Winner
Rates: $100 – $160, including full breakfast; two-night minimum weekends July–September
Credit cards accepted: American Express, Discover, MasterCard, Visa
Open: Year-round
Smoking: Permitted outside only
How to get there: From Washington, DC, take Route 50 across the Chesapeake Bay Bridge. Continue on Route 50 east to Salisbury and then take Route 13 bypass toward Norfolk. In 2.5 miles, take Route 12 and continue for 16 miles to Snow Hill. Go over the bridge and continue to the light. Turn left onto Market Street and go 1 block. Turn left onto Green Street and then right into the driveway of the B&B.

Although the elaborate white clapboard Victorian sits just off the main street of town, its 2 acres of lawns and gardens slope down to the edge of the Pocomoke River. Built between 1860 and 1890, it is a confection of dripping gingerbread from multiple gables. There's also an overhanging wraparound porch supported by boxed columns, lacy black wrought iron trim reminiscent of New Orleans buildings, fancy keyhole trim in the gables, and black shutters.

Larry and Susanne Knudsen opened the house to guests in 1991 and have been adding new rooms and buildings ever since. In addition to the main house, which has four guest rooms and one suite, there's also River Cottage, an 1890s carriage barn that has been converted to a deluxe guest room with private porch and tiny kitchen fireplace, and Riverview Hideaway, a new building on the banks of the river with two rooms offering whirlpool tubs and fireplaces as well as sweeping river views from private 28-foot porches.

The River House is still the heart of the B&B. In the entry hall the striking stairway newel is made of lustrous burled walnut. The twin parlors, which are painted cardinal red, have forest green accents in the fireplace surrounds, the carpets, and the upholstered pieces. Guests gather here on winter evenings before the fireplace or on either the upper or lower porch in summer to sip coffee, tea, or wine and nibble on snacks in the afternoon while admiring the view of the river. There's also a TV and VCR and a video library as well as a variety of books and board games.

The guest rooms are furnished with either antiques or period reproductions. The River Room, for example, has a magnificent antique French bedroom suite; the West Room has an early mahogany Chippendale-style bedroom suite with carved phoenixes; and the East Room has a gas fireplace. The rooms in the Riverview Hideaway are equally luxurious. The Colonial Room has a Queen Anne-style canopy bed, while the Garden Room has an iron canopy bed.

A full breakfast is served in either the formal dining room or in the breakfast room, where guests sit at individual tables. There will be placemats and linen napkins, silver, and china. The meal will include fruits, juice, and perhaps Susanne's River House eggs — a combination of eggs shirred in cream and topped with herbs and cheese — or her yummy croissant French toast with dried fruits, as well as bacon or sausage.

Were I to plan the perfect day in Snow Hill, I would arise early and walk to the nearby boat rental for a canoe outing on the Pocomoke River, a state-designated wild and scenic river. I would return in time for Susanne's excellent breakfast, and then I'd set out on a walking tour of Snow Hill, or I'd borrow one of the inn bicycles for an afternoon of cycling about the countryside. Larry is also a riverboat captain, and he takes people for tours of the river on his pontoon boat, the *Otter,* so — All aboard!

What's Nearby
See "What's Nearby — Snow Hill," page 67.

The Lazyjack Inn

5907 Tilghman Island Road
(mailing address: P.O. Box 248)
Tilghman Island, MD 21671
(800) 690-5080 or (410) 886-2215;
fax (410) 886-2635;
e-mail: mrichards@skipjack.bluecrab.org
website: http://www.bluecrab.org
/members/mrichards

Innkeepers: Mike and Carol Richards
Rooms: 4, including 1 suite, all with private baths, air conditioning, clock radios, and hair dryers; 2 with fireplaces, whirlpool tubs, and robes; 1 with a desk
On the grounds: Sailing yacht
Extras: Afternoon tea and snacks; chocolates, bottled water, and sherry in guest rooms; three outside cats
Rates: $130 – $200 May to mid-November; $110 – $175 mid-November to April; two-night minimum weekends April to mid-November and holidays
Credit cards accepted: MasterCard & Visa
Open: Year-round
Smoking: Permitted outside only
How to get there: From Washington, DC, take Route 50 across the Chesapeake Bay Bridge and continue east on Route 50. Before Easton, take Route 322/Easton Bypass to Route 33. Continue on Route 33 through St. Michaels for another 11 miles to Tilghman Island. The B&B will be on the left.

Languid little Tilghman Island enjoys one of the longest histories in America. It was charted by Captain John Smith in 1608, and it is now the home of the last remaining fleet of skipjacks, historic flat-bottomed sailboats used for dredging oysters. The lore of the watermen who skipper these craft is laced with romance and adventure — a real life chapter from James Michener's *Chesapeake*.

The Lazyjack Inn is run by Mike and Carol Richards, who are seafarers and restoration spe-
cialists themselves. Not only have they lovingly restored the little house that became their bed and breakfast, but they also restored the *Lady Patty* yacht, a splendid 45-foot bronze and teak bay ketch built in 1935. Captain Richards takes travelers on two-hour cruises by advance reservations. The champagne sunset sails are particularly popular.

The inn is as bright and pretty as a new penny. Originally a waterman's house built sometime prior to 1855, it has a driveway of crushed oyster shells. The white clapboard house is fronted by a veranda painted pink and filled with white wicker and Adirondack chairs. In the Harbor Room, with its wall of windows offering wonderful views of the interesting old boats in Dogwood Harbor, there's a gas fireplace. The library has an extensive collection of maritime books as well as another fireplace.

The guest rooms are spacious and eclectic. The grandest is the Nellie Byrd Suite, which has a magnificent brass bed, a late 1800s Victorian love seat, and lots of duck decoys. The bath has an enclosed whirlpool tub and a sink placed in a marvelous old carved dresser. The stunning view reaches up the Choptank River and across Dogwood Harbor. The East Room has exposed beams and heart pine floors covered by a lovely Oriental rug as well as sunrise views. The bedroom suite is particularly interesting. A complete set of Waterfall furniture with half-shell handles dates from the 1930s. There's a striking handmade quilt on the bed. The tiled bath is small but well-designed and

includes a glass-enclosed shower. A brand new Garden Room, also with a whirlpool and a private porch, was added in the spring of 1997.

Afternoon tea is offered daily, and a decanter of sherry is provided in each room. At bedtime you'll find a bottle of water beside your bed and a chocolate on your pillow.

For breakfast Carol and Mike may start with a baked French tart garnished with frozen yogurt and freshly baked bran muffins. A hot dish—perhaps a portobello mushroom omelet with cubed red potatoes and sweet red peppers—will follow. This will be accompanied by freshly baked Scottish scones served with homemade strawberry jam.

Just like the residents, you should spend your time on Tilghman Island on the water. There are nature expeditions through the marshes, a trip on a skipjack, and fishing boats to charter as well as the *Lady Patty*. Several restaurants specializing in seafood are located on the island.

What's Nearby

Tilghman Island is a laid-back unconventional island reached by bridge across Knapps Narrows and about 15 miles from St. Michaels. Fishing and shellfishing remain the primary activities, and numerous charter and excursion boats offer fishing and sightseeing trips, including a trip on an authentic skipjack. You can watch the watermen bring in their catch of oysters in the evening, rent a canoe or a kayak, or traverse the island by bicycle. The Blackwater National Wildlife Refuge is nearby. Come for the Tilghman Island Seafood Festival in June or the Tilghman Island Jazz Festival, an outdoor concert, in September. (See also St. Michaels and Wittman.)

The Inn at Christmas Farm

8873 Tilghman Island Road
Wittman, MD 21676
(800) 987-8436 or (410) 745-5312;
fax (410) 745-5618

Innkeepers: David and Beatrice Lee; managers, Paul Curtis and Susan Rockwell
Rooms: 5, including 4 suites, all with private baths, air conditioning, and radios; 4 with patios; 2 with mini-refrigerators, wet bars, coffee makers, and whirlpool tubs
On the grounds: 50 acres of waterfront on Cummings Creek; pond, gardens, and farm animals, including sheep, chickens, peacocks, horses
Extras: Wine and sodas on arrival; three dogs and one cat
Rates: $155 – $175 weekends, two-night minimum; $155 1st night, 50% off 2nd night, 3rd night complimentary, Sundays - Thursdays, including full breakfast
Credit cards accepted: MasterCard & Visa
Open: February - December
Smoking: Permitted outside only
How to get there: From Washington, DC, take Route 50 across the Chesapeake Bay Bridge. Continue on Route 50 east to Route 322/Easton Bypass and turn right. Turn right again onto Route 33 and follow signs for St. Michaels. Continue on Route 33 past St. Michaels for approximately 6.7 miles (just after the Wittman Market) and turn left into the driveway of Christmas Farm.

Tucked away on 50 acres down an unassuming little gravel road, Christmas Farm is a combination of working farm, wildfowl refuge, and elegant B&B. You will see snowy egrets, swans, and blue herons feeding in the marsh grasses and sheep, chickens, pygmy goats, horses, and haughty peacocks with their multicolored tails fanned on the farmland.

This is no ordinary B&B. In addition to the stately manor house, which contains one suite and one room, there are two suites in a charm-

ing 1893 chapel and one more carved out of an 1890s waterman's cottage. The latter two buildings were moved to the property specifically to house guests.

We were charmed by the inn from the moment we walked in. There are enormous happy plants sitting beside red and white checked sofas in the entry. There's a sun porch filled with rustic farm tables where breakfast is served. Beyond the broad windows, there's a swimming pond surrounded by tables and chairs for sunny weather lounging. When we arrived, a cool glass of wine was waiting, and we welcomed the opportunity to relax by the swimming pond to unwind after our journey. The seclusion is intoxicating. The loudest noise we heard was the crow of a rooster in the morning, the cry of the peacocks, the occasional bleating of a sheep, and the distant clang of a buoy in the harbor.

The fetching accommodations at Christmas Farm are decorated with beguiling appeal. The Bell Tower Suite in the 1893 St. James Chapel, which was moved to the farm in 1992, is entered through arched double church doors. There's an iron canopy bed and polished pine floors covered with Oriental carpets as well as a wet bar and a refrigerator. Uncle's Room, a new addition to the main house in 1997, has a two-person Jacuzzi on a platform that oversees the spectacular view from a picture window.

Of all the rooms, however, the Christmas Cottage is our favorite. This little two-story gem was formerly a waterman's cottage. We entered the cottage through double Dutch doors. The sitting room has a tile floor with a Jacuzzi tucked behind a screen. The bedroom is upstairs, where a windowed tower fills the room with light.

A farm breakfast is served on the sun porch in the morning. It will include fresh fruits, or perhaps poached pears, and maybe stuffed French toast or an egg soufflé — all served on flowered china. The tables will have either red or green or yellow checked tablecloths and napkins, and there will be a huge bowl of fruit in the center.

The narrow peninsula south of nearby St. Michaels is a prime bicycling area with flat roads and exquisite scenery. The inn is next door to a gladioli farm where visitors may purchase bunches of fresh flowers in season as well as bulbs to take home. Canoeing and kayaking in the marshy inlets and bays produce glimpses of waterfowl, animals, birds, fish, and shellfish. St. Michaels is filled with excellent restaurants and shops, as is Tilghman Island, where skipjacks continue to harvest oysters.

What's Nearby

Wittman is located between St. Michaels and Tilghman Island, offering all the activities and amenities of both. Visit the next-door gladiola farm, charter a fishing boat on Tilghman Island, or go swimming across the street at Wittman Beach. (See also St. Michaels and Tilghman Island.)

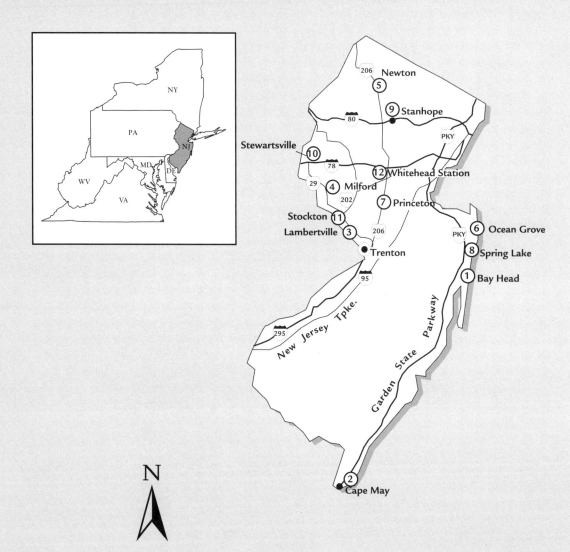

N

New Jersey

Numbers on map refer to towns numbered below.

Innkeepers: Don Haurie and Ed Laubusch
Rooms: 11, all with private baths, air conditioning, telephones, and radios; 3 with balconies; 1 with a fireplace (electric)
Extras: Parking on premise
Rates: $95 – $195, including full breakfast; two-night minimum weekends, three-night minimum holidays
Credit cards accepted: American Express, Discover, MasterCard, Visa
Open: Mid-March to December
Smoking: Non-smoking bed and breakfast
How to get there: From the Garden State Parkway, take exit 98 to Route 34. At the second traffic circle, take Route 35 south through Point Pleasant to Bay Head. The B&B is on the right as you come into town.

Bay Head Gables
Bed & Breakfast

200 Main Avenue
Bay Head, NJ 08742
(800) 984-9536 or (732) 899-9844;
fax (732) 295-2196

Bay Head is a sleepy little Jersey Shore town that was developed in the late nineteenth century by folks from Princeton and Philadelphia. Handsome shingle-style cottages and Victorian houses line the narrow streets, and the beach is unencumbered by high-rise hotels or shops selling saltwater taffy and T-shirts. Most of the bed and breakfast establishments are within a block of the beach, making it a pleasant walking town, although Route 35, which is called Main Avenue in Bay Head, can become quite busy in the summer.

Bay Head Gables occupies one of the most distinctive houses in Bay Head, reputedly designed by the firm of McKim, Mead, and White and built in 1914. This wedding present for a young bride has a natural shingle exterior with white columns and railings as well as an expansive wraparound porch and a gabled roof. With such a traditional summer "cottage," one expects a conventional interior, but that is far from the case.

Don Haurie and Ed Laubusch have decorated their inn in a variety of styles, ranging from art deco to Oriental. The living room, a composition in Art-Deco style, has glass tables; mirrors; chairs with voluptuous curves; and a black, grey, and white color scheme with zesty teal accents. There's a window seat in the bay window and a gas fireplace. The dining room, however, is as traditional as the house in style, with a spectacular crystal chandelier. Even here there are notable exceptions, however. The walls are navy blue, and a fireplace mantel is overflowing with the owners' collection of pigs.

A breakfast room was created by enclosing a corner of the wraparound porch in glass. It contains individual tables that offer glimpses of the ocean a block away. The five-course breakfast will please the hungriest of guests. It begins with a selection of juices. This will be followed by a fruit dish such as poached spiced pears or a fruit compote and a breakfast bread such as banana bread or coffee cake. An entrée of per-

haps an apple/cheddar strata or an omelet or fruited pancakes will follow.

The guest rooms are as eclectically designed as the common rooms. They range in style from Room #2, which has a Southwestern theme that includes a picture of a steer's skull, a canopy bed, artificial cactus plants, and a carved rooster in the bathroom to Room #4, a contemporary black and white room on the front of the inn with a covered porch offering an ocean view. One of the B&Bs most distinctive features is the work space incorporated into some of the rooms. The Oriental Room (Room #5), for example, has a pull-out computer shelf, and all rooms have telephones.

East Street, which parallels the ocean, stretches for $2^1/_2$ miles, offering an excellent place to bicycle (the B&B has bicycles for guests to use), roller blade, jog, and walk. For sunbathers, beach passes, towels, and chairs are provided.

What's Nearby — Bay Head

Bay Head has a marvelous uncrowded ocean beach, and although it's private, most B&Bs provide beach passes. Nearby Point Pleasant has an old-fashioned boardwalk, as does Seaside Heights, and Point Pleasant also has an aquarium. Fishing boats can be chartered here. Other nearby attractions include the Garden State Arts Center, the Red Oak Theatre, and the Strand Theater in Lakewood where the New Jersey Ballet performs.

Conover's Bay Head Inn

646 Main Avenue
Bay Head, NJ 08742
(800) 956-9099 or (732) 892-4664;
fax (732) 892-8748
website: http//www.combbianj/Conovers

Innkeepers: Carl, Beverly, and Timothy Conover
Rooms: 12, including 1 cottage, all with private baths, air conditioning, telephones, TVs, VCRs, and radios; 1 with porch and fireplace.
On the grounds: Garden, croquet, lawn games; parking
Extras: Package of candies at turndown; snacks and Arizona Tea always available
Rates: $120 – $210, including full breakfast; two-night minimum weekends; three-night minimum summer weekends; four-night minimum holiday weekends
Credit cards accepted: American Express, Master-Card, Visa
Open: Year-round
Smoking: Non-smoking bed and breakfast
How to get there: From the Garden State Parkway, take exit 98 to Route 34. At the second traffic circle, take Route 35 south through Point Pleasant to Bay Head. The inn is 7 blocks ahead on the right after reaching Bay Head.

Carl and Beverly Conover opened Conover's Bay Head Inn more than twenty-five years ago. Their longevity is remarkable in itself, but what's even more remarkable is that their inn looks and feels as fresh today as it must have when it opened. Furthermore, so do the Conovers. They are as friendly and as refreshing as new innkeepers, exhibiting none of the burnout that you might expect. What's their secret? They truly love what they're doing.

The house is a pretty shingled cottage with white trim. In summer, awnings shield the front windows from the sun, and you walk through an arched trellis covered with pink roses to reach the front door. A picket fence borders the sidewalk and defines the abundant flower gardens, which are in bloom from early spring through late fall. On the porch, there are white painted tables, a white wicker sofa, and white rocking chairs.

The B&B has a cozy sitting room with a plum-colored floral carpet and a white stone fireplace. Just beyond, the breakfast room has a lovely oak hutch. Guests eat breakfast on individual glass-topped tables. They might start the day with eggs baked with herbs and accompanied by Canadian bacon, or perhaps French toast with cream cheese. In winter, the Conovers receive citrus fruit directly from Florida, but fresh fruit is served throughout the year. Beverly is noted for the breakfast breads she bakes. She may prepare cheddar cheese biscuits or walnut orange cake or piña colada muffins, and, of course, there will be a selection of juices, coffee, and tea. A little refrigerator in the breakfast room is stocked with a selection of Arizona Tea (Carl is a distributor) — always a welcome treat when returning from the beach. A cabinet here also holds videos for viewing on the VCRs in the rooms.

The guest rooms are spacious, and all have private baths. Room #2, a soothing space in beige tones, has a gas fireplace and a private porch. The bath has a clawfoot tub and a shower as well as a pretty antique wicker vanity dressed with a silver Victorian comb and brush set. Many of the rooms have iron and brass beds, and Beverly has painted some beautiful stencils on the walls and ceilings.

In addition to a large parking area, the B&B is blessed with a spacious side yard shielded from the street by a dense privet hedge. Games of croquet take place here, and lawn chairs offer secluded spots to read, sip an Arizona Tea, or talk. Beach passes, towels, and chairs are available for guests to use. An excellent sports equipment rental is located nearby, where bicycles, wind surfing equipment, and roller blades are especially popular.

Nearby Point Pleasant has an active fishing port where it's possible to charter a fishing boat and to watch commercial fishermen bring in the catch of the day. Naturally, there are also some excellent seafood restaurants overlooking Manasquan Inlet. The kind of broad boardwalk that made the Jersey Shore famous still exists here also, offering miles of bicycling, jogging, walking, and roller blading.

What's Nearby

See "What's Nearby — Bay Head," page 77.

Fairthorne Bed & Breakfast

111 Ocean Street
(mailing address: P.O. Box 2381)
Cape May, NJ 08204
(800) 438-8742 or (609) 884-8791; fax
(609) 884-1902; e-mail: wehfair@aol.com
website: http://www.bbianj.com/fairthorne

Innkeepers: Diane and Ed Hutchinson
Rooms: 6, including 1 suite, all with private baths, air conditioning, TVs, radios, and robes; 3 with mini-refrigerators
On the grounds: Gardens
Extras: Afternoon tea with cheese and crackers, sherry, homemade cookies; fax and dataport available; cat named Alley Cat
Rates: $110– $190, including full breakfast and afternoon tea; two-night minimum weekends; three-night minimum July and August
Credit cards accepted: American Express, Discover, MasterCard, Visa
Open: Year-round
Smoking: Non-smoking bed and breakfast
How to get there: From the end of the Garden State Parkway or the Lewes Ferry, take Route 109 south into Cape May. After crossing the bridge and passing the marina, you will be on Lafayette Street. Turn left at the second traffic light onto Ocean Street. The bed and breakfast will be in 3 more blocks on the left.

If you love Victoriana, then you must come to Cape May. This lovely seaside Victorian village somehow escaped the wave of modernization that swept so many towns in the early 1900s. There are still more than 600 Victorian buildings within the town's National Historic District. The Victorian ambience is so complete that you feel as if you should be wearing a long rustling skirt and a bonnet.

The Fairthorne Inn, a natural shingled house with white trim and a broad wraparound porch, has an utterly romantic but welcoming look. Perhaps it's the garden in front, filled with an array of flowers, that you can't help but stop to admire, making you long to sit in the wicker chairs or big rockers on the veranda in the afternoon to watch the butterflies and bees flit from one to the next.

The Colonial Revival-style house was built in 1892 by a whaling captain. There are elaborate stained-glass and leaded windows throughout. Diane and Ed Hutchinson, who were both raised in Cape May County and who retired from Bell Atlantic, purchased it in 1991 and have turned it into a stunning bed and breakfast. In addition to the terrific stained glass, each room is decorated with striking antiques.

Patricia's Mini-Suite is one of the most popular rooms. It has a private entrance off the veranda, a fireplace with a painted mantel, and a lovely Eastlake Victorian sideboard. Emma Kate's Suite has a Victorian dresser and a separate sitting room with a view of the water. Each of the bedrooms has its own private bath.

Breakfast is served in the dining room in winter or on the porch in summer. In the dining room, guests will sit at a common table set with a lace tablecloth, linen napkins, fine china, and silver. The meal will start with fresh fruit and juice. In addition, Diane may prepare a spinach soufflé with bacon and homemade mocha walnut muffins, or perhaps she will fix baked blueberry French toast with country sausage accompanied by cranberry scones. Regardless of the daily fare, it will be delicious and bountiful.

A self-guided walking tour of the village Victorians should be on every list, or you may prefer to tour by trolley. The village abounds in antiques shops and art galleries. Or, it's a pleasant bicycle ride out to the restored 1859 Cape May Lighthouse. This is one of the oldest continuously operating lighthouses in the United States, and the panoramic views from its top are breathtaking.

What's Nearby — Cape May

Cape May has an extensive boardwalk bordering its miles of white sandy beaches. Most B&Bs provide beach passes, and it's possible to rent beach chairs and umbrellas from one of the many stands. Before or after a day at the beach, be sure to take a walking tour or a horse-drawn carriage tour of this very Victorian town, where time seems to be frozen in the late nineteenth century. Fantastic Victorian houses will be seen on every block (there are almost 700 in all). You may tour the Emlen Physick House and Estate, an eighteen-room Victorian mansion designed by Frank Furness. Festivals and special town and house tours take place throughout the year, and many people time their visits to coincide with their favorite. You can obtain a schedule from the Mid-Atlantic Center for the Arts in Cape May.

The Humphrey Hughes House

29 Ocean Street
Cape May, NJ 08204
(800) 582-3634 or (609) 884-4428;
fax (609) 884-3138

Innkeepers: Lorraine and Terry Schmidt
Rooms: 11, including 4 suites, all with private baths, air conditioning, radios, hair dryers, irons, and ironing boards; 6 with TVs; 2 with telephones, coffee makers, mini-refrigerators, and robes; 1 suite with wheelchair access
On the grounds: Gardens, patio, veranda
Extras: Afternoon tea; cookies and tea in sun room
Rates: $120 – $215 throughout July and August and weekends in June and September; $80 –$155 rest of year, including full breakfast; three-night minimum on weekends, May - October
Credit cards accepted: MasterCard and Visa
Open: Year-round
Smoking: Non-smoking bed and breakfast
How to get there: From the end of the Garden State Parkway or the Lewes Ferry, take Route 109 south into Cape May. After crossing the bridge and passing the marina, you will be on Lafayette Street. Turn left at the second traffic light onto Ocean Street. The B&B will be on the left on the corner of Ocean and Columbia Streets.

Captain Humphrey Hughes arrived in Cape May in 1692 to become one of the town's original landholders. The Humphrey Hughes house was built by a descendant in 1903 on a portion of his property, and it remained a Hughes residence until the death in 1980 of Dr. Harold Hughes. Although there are many fine homes in Cape May, this is one of the most stately. Sitting high above the street, the wide covered veranda projects across the front on both sides, offering a variety of places to sit on wicker chairs to enjoy the cooling sea breezes.

Lorraine and Terry Schmidt have retained the historical characteristics of their B&B while updating it. Guests enter a living room flanked by carved fluted chestnut columns and admire the ornate grandfather clock that once belonged to Dr. Hughes. The living room has a square grand piano and a fireplace. The dining room has another fireplace, and an elaborate Oriental rug covers the oak floors. An ornate Victorian walnut buffet stands along one wall, and there's a lovely crystal chandelier hanging from a ceiling medallion.

One of the favorite spots in the house to relax is the sun room, located off the dining room. It's filled with plants and white wicker furniture festively dressed with pink and red cushions. Hot and cold tea, coffee, chocolate, and the overflowing cookie jar are located here.

Every afternoon an elaborate tea is set out for the guests. It will include little tea sandwiches such as cucumber or tomato, cream scones with strawberry butter, and at least two sweets such as Lorraine's chocolate cake with mocha frosting.

The guest rooms have equally beautiful antique Victorian furnishings. In the Rose Room, there's an elaborate Victorian bed with a carved headboard, a lamp with a fringed shade, and a fainting couch. The tiled bath is well designed and spotless. The Ocean View Room has a bay window and an unusual tub in the bathroom that includes a separate footbath in its design. Even though Le Petit is the smallest, it is one of the most charming, with forest green walls and a white iron bed

In the morning guests look forward to a bountiful breakfast served around the mahogany dining room table. It's set with placemats and fine china. Guests receive a copy of a printed menu the night before. A typical breakfast might include a toasted bagel with scrambled eggs and cheese sauce accompanied by potato latkes and homemade English muffins.

For a unique trip back in time, it's interesting to visit Cold Spring Village, a 22-acre living history museum. In this restoration of a nineteenth-century farm community, visitors can talk to "locals" dressed in bonnets and long skirts, see bread being kneaded and then baked in a brick oven, watch a flyer being printed, see a spinner twist wool into yarn, and iron being shaped at a forge.

What's Nearby
See "What's Nearby — Cape May," page 81.

The Mainstay Inn

635 Columbia Avenue
Cape May, NJ 08204
(609) 884-8690;
website: http://www.bbianj.com.mainstayinn

Innkeepers: Tom and Sue Carroll; manager, Kathleen Moore
Rooms: 16, including 6 suites, all with private baths; 10 with air conditioning and desks; 6 with private balconies; 4 with telephones, TVs, VCRs, radios, mini-refrigerators, coffee makers, fireplaces, irons, ironing boards, and whirlpool tubs; 1 room with wheelchair access
On the grounds: Gardens
Extras: Parking for 13 cars; afternoon high tea; outdoor cats named Boots and Baby
Rates: $95 – $255, including full breakfast and afternoon tea; three-night minimum weekends in summer
Credit cards accepted: None
Open: Officers' Quarters open year-round; Mainstay and Cottage open mid-March to December
Smoking: Non-smoking bed and breakfast
How to get there: From the end of the Garden State Parkway or the Lewes Ferry, take Route 109 south into Cape May. After crossing the bridge and passing the marina, you will be on Lafayette Street. At the first traffic light, turn left onto Madison Street. Proceed 3 blocks and turn right onto Columbia Avenue. You will see the B&B in 3 blocks on the right.

When Tom and Sue Carroll opened the first B&B in Cape May in the early 1970s, they started a phenomenon that has now spawned more than 100 accommodations in Cape May. They also were in the forefront of a business that has now swept the United States.

The Carrolls have never looked back. They sold that first B&B when they purchased The Mainstay, and eventually they also bought the gracious Victorian cottage next door as well as a building across the street known as The Officers' Quarters. The entire complex is a restoration of the highest caliber, making it the finest place to stay in Cape May.

The original Mainstay Inn, an elaborate Italianate villa with intricate gingerbread trim, was built as an exclusive gambling hall in 1872. The main floor rooms have 14-foot ceilings embellished with lustrous Bradbury and Bradbury wallpapers and furnished with gorgeous

Victorian antiques, many of which are original to the building. Across the front of both the Mainstay and the Cottage, there are broad verandas filled with green chairs for afternoons at leisure. And there is also the belvedere on top of The Mainstay, where the sound of sea breezes rustling through the sycamore trees mingles with the clip-clop of passing horsedrawn carriages to re-create the sounds of early Cape May.

The guest rooms are as romantic and as elegant as the common rooms. In Henry Clay, for example, there's a magnificent Victorian walnut headboard, an elaborate Victorian chandelier, and a lovely private bath. In the Grant Suite, there's a brass bed and a sitting room furnished with antique wicker. In the Officers' Quarters, the huge suites contain either one or two bedrooms decorated in country pine or country Victorian furniture, living rooms with gas fireplaces, two TVs and VCRs, snack kitchens, telephones, private decks, and large modern baths with whirlpool tubs and separate showers. Stained-glass windows are backlighted for an utterly romantic ambience. These are the only rooms that are open all winter.

Breakfast is a wonderful affair at The Mainstay. Sue may prepare her blintz soufflé with angel biscuits or perhaps her hash brown quiche with baked ham and poppyseed coffee cake. Generally, it's served in formal splendor around the gleaming walnut dining room table, but in the height of the summer a hearty Continental breakfast may be served on the veranda.

The afternoon high tea at The Mainstay is an event that should not be missed. A tour of the main-floor rooms of the house is offered to those not staying at the B&B. This is followed by tea served on the veranda in summer or in the dining room in winter. There will be a selection of tea sandwiches, cheese daisies, and sweets such as almond cake squares and fattening frosted brownies.

What's Nearby
See "What's Nearby — Cape May," page 81.

Innkeepers: Nancy and Tom McDonald
Rooms: 10, including 1 suite, all with private baths, air conditioning, hair dryers, robes, irons, and ironing boards; 1 with TV and whirlpool tub
On the grounds: Garden
Extras: Afternoon tea, sherry, and baked snacks; cookies in the evening; one dog, Beebe, a keeshond, in garden at times
Rates: $85 – $215, including full breakfast and afternoon tea; two-night minimum all weekends; three-night minimum throughout July and August
Credit cards accepted: Discover, MasterCard, Visa
Open: February - December
Smoking: Permitted outside only
How to get there: From the end of the Garden State Parkway or the Lewes Ferry, take Route 109 south into Cape May. After crossing the bridge and passing the marina, you will be on Lafayette Street. Continue for 8 blocks and then turn left onto Franklin Street. Go 2 blocks and turn right onto Hughes. The B&B will be in the second block on the left.

Manor House Inn

612 Hughes Street
Cape May, NJ 08204
(609) 884-4710; fax (609) 898-0471

Tom and Nancy McDonald purchased their dream B&B in 1994. It's tucked down a small side street and has a particularly pretty little back garden. There are brick pathways and abundant flowers (more than 150 varieties of tulips bloom in the spring) and herbs (used in the inn breakfasts and afternoon snacks), and it offers a quieter retreat than many of the nearby bed and breakfasts. It's not as grand as some of its neighbors either, but in many ways that makes it more comfortable.

As you enter the spacious foyer, you will notice the polished oak and chestnut floors, woodwork, and stairway. There's an oak window seat on the stair landing and a lovely stained-glass window above. The front parlor has a piano, while the back parlor has a fireplace and an abundance of jigsaw puzzles, games, and books.

In the dining room, which has a lovely breakfront with a marble top, breakfast is served on a table set with placemats, linen napkins, and fine silver. Nancy is a gourmet cook, and so her breakfasts reflect her love of food. She may prepare an apple cheddar omelet, or a "Wild and Crazy" waffle with wild rice and pecans, or a tomato and oregano frittata, or maybe a corny egg pie. Each entrée will be accompanied by a variety of fruit, juices, and a meat dish such as bacon or sausage. In addition, Nancy always fixes "Mary's sticky buns," a recipe from her predecessor that everyone loves.

This is one inn where you certainly won't leave hungry. In the afternoon, Nancy prepares at least three sweet and savory treats. There may be gourmet pretzels, canapés, pound cake, and pecan bars as well as coffee, tea, lemonade, port, and sherry. In the evening a bowl is filled with cookies straight from Nancy's kitchen that are bound to assure her guests of sweet dreams.

The rooms are continuously being upgraded. All guest rooms now have their own private bath. Room #6, which stretches across the front of the house, has a pretty wicker loveseat and chairs. In the bath, which has a painted floor, there's a whirlpool tub. Room #8 has red walls and a beautiful antique Victorian marble-topped dresser.

Visitors to Cape May often like to time their trip to coincide with one of the special Victorian weekends. The month of December is always a special time as numerous houses are open for tours, and events such as a community wassail party and a gingerbread workshop take place. Other special events are scheduled on weekends in April, May, and October. Regardless of the time of year, a visit to the Emlen Physick Estate, a restored 18-room Victorian gem, offers interesting insights into early Cape May life.

What's Nearby

See "What's Nearby — Cape May," page 81.

The Queen Victoria

102 Ocean Street
Cape May, NJ 08204
(609) 884-8702

Innkeepers: Dane and Joan Wells
Rooms: 23, including 6 suites and 2 cottages, all with private baths, air conditioning, radios, and mini-refrigerators in every room; 14 with whirlpool tubs; 9 with private balconies or porches; 8 with TVs and desks, 4 with fireplaces and telephones; one with wheelchair access; cribs available
Extras: Afternoon tea and savories; turndown with chocolates; breakfast in bed available; desks in some rooms; two cats, in owner's quarters only, named Spats and Mugsy
Rates: $80 – $275, including full breakfast and afternoon tea; three-night minimum weekends from April - October and in December and on holidays; four-night minimum some weekends mid-summer
Credit cards accepted: Personal checks preferred
Open: Year-round
Smoking: Non-smoking bed and breakfast
How to get there: From the end of the Garden State Parkway or the Lewes Ferry, take Route 109 south into Cape May. After crossing the bridge and passing the marina, you will be on Lafayette Street. At the second traffic light, turn left onto Ocean Street. The B&B will be on the right in 3 blocks.

It's hard to imagine how any innkeepers could be better suited to their jobs. Before becoming innkeepers, Joan was the Director of the Victorian Society in America, and Dane was Manager of Philadelphia's Neighborhood Commercial Revitalization Program. But in 1980 they decided to open their own B&B in America's most Victorian town, and this amazing, energetic couple has been adding to it ever since. They started with The Queen Victoria, a majestic 1881 Victorian house, but soon they added the Prince Albert, and now their enclave includes three houses, a carriage house, a little cottage, and a small hotel. In addition, they have been instrumental in organizing Victorian Weeks in Cape May, Christmas in Cape May, and a three-day extravaganza of Dickens events.

The Queen Victoria, her prince consort, and ladies in waiting are not of the frilly and fussy Victorian variety as so many in Cape May are.

Rather, they are a reflection of the Arts and Crafts period, when straight lines and solid oak tables were the fashion. Each is decorated with elaborate Bradbury and Bradbury papers on the walls and contain some excellent pieces of signed Stickley and Roycroft furniture. Joan has a wonderful collection of Van Briggle pottery in the china cabinet in the dining room. Each of the buildings has its own little pantry stocked with juices and a snack basket, and there are selections of books and games.

All rooms in the Prince Albert building have whirlpool tubs as well as Victorian furnishings that frequently include beds with carved walnut headboards and marble-topped dressers. A tiny little private cottage called Regents Park is tucked next to the Prince Albert. Nightly turn-down service includes a custom-made chocolate. Rooms in the Queens Hotel are smaller and well-suited to business travelers who desire a desk on which to work or to travelers who prefer to get breakfast on their own in the morning.

B&B guests are invited to the Queen Victoria's dining room for a variety of sweets and savories in the afternoon. It's a chance to meet and greet one another and to obtain suggestions from Dane and Joan for dinner destinations and activities. In the morning, breakfast is served in both the Queen Victoria and Prince Albert buildings. It is an elaborate affair that is generally self-serve from a buffet. There will be a variety of juices, cereals, fruits, yogurt, and breads as well as a hot entrée — perhaps Aunt Ruth's baked eggs and cheese served with savory sausage patties or a hash brown potato bake with crisp bacon slices.

The Wellses will offer an array of suggestions for activities while you're in town, and they have a bevy of bicycles available to get you there. If your destination is the beach, they provide beach tags, towels, and an outside shower.

What's Nearby

See "What's Nearby — Cape May," page 81.

The Southern Mansion
(The George Allen Estate)

720 Washington Street
Cape May, NJ 08204
(800) 381-3888 or (609) 884-7171;
fax (609) 898-0492;
e-mail: mansion@jerseycape
website: http://www.capenet.com/cape-
may/allen

Innkeepers: Richard and Barbara Wilde; manager, Denise Cortina
Rooms: 25, including private baths, air conditioning, TVs, telephones with dataports, radios, mini-refrigerators, hair dryers, and robes; 20 with desks; 10 with private balconies; 2 with fireplaces
On the grounds: Parking, swimming pool (planned for 1997), gardens
Extras: Afternoon cookies and tea or lemonade, fax, copier, audio-visual equipment, meeting and conference rooms
Rates: $185 – $350, including full breakfast and afternoon refreshments; two-night minimum weekends September - April (longer holiday weekends); three-night minimum weekends May - September (longer holiday weekends)
Credit cards accepted: American Express, Master-Card, Visa
Open: Year-round
Smoking: Non-smoking bed and breakfast
How to get there: From the end of the Garden State Parkway or the Lewes Ferry, take Route 109 south into Cape May. After crossing the bridge and passing the marina, you will be on Lafayette Street. Continue on Lafayette Street through the first traffic light. Turn left at the second street, which is Jefferson. Go 2 blocks. The B&B will be straight ahead on the corner of Washington Street.

For many years visitors and residents of Cape May had shaken their heads sadly when they looked at the George Allen house. Cape May's largest and most elaborate Victorian mansion, a 14,000-square-foot Italianate villa built in the 1850s, had deteriorated into a dismal state by the time Rick and Barbara Wilde spotted the

gem in 1994. Rick is a contractor, however, so the couple knew just what to do. They completed the first phase of the renovation in time to have their own wedding there.

Today the B&B probably looks better than when it was new. Ornate crystal chandeliers hang from 15-foot ceilings in the parlor, the elaborate cornice moldings and ceiling medallions have been restored, the twin carved ivory mantels in the parlor are repaired, and the walnut, mahogany, and red tulip floor with its center bird's eye maple star has been cleaned and polished to reveal its luster. Now the parlor walls are painted a teal blue, and the elaborate medallions stand out against a gold ceiling. Bouquets of perfect roses sit on oak tables perfuming the room with their sweetness, and in the afternoon cookies, iced tea, wine, and lemonade await arriving guests on a marble-topped Victorian sideboard.

The guest rooms are massive. The smallest is 300 square feet. On the second floor, there are broad hallways (filled with interesting pictures of old Cape May), and the ceilings reach to 13 feet, giving the rooms a baronial spaciousness and allowing the Wildes to decorate with panache. Rooms are painted in brilliant hues — one in vermillion, another in sapphire. They all have museum-quality Victorian antiques, many of which are original to the mansion. Every room has its own bath, with hand-painted tiles decorating the showers. Sinks are placed in the guest rooms in ornate armoires.

Among my favorites is Room #6, which has sapphire blue walls, gold brocade covering the bed and pillows, and a spectacular Victorian chandelier hanging in the center. In the bath, a peacock is painted on the tiles in the shower. Room #8 has a four-poster bed and marble-topped dressers against butterscotch walls.

From the rooftop cupola, there's a sensational view of the harbor and town. Guests love to come here to watch the sunset in the evening. For an utterly romantic evening, the staff will serve a five-course dinner up here, complete with wine or champagne.

A new wing was completed late in 1996 that matches the original house in grandeur. There are ten additional rooms, all with private balconies or porches, as well as conference and meeting space. There's a broad wraparound porch across the front of the main house filled with rockers, and a side yard where a pool is scheduled to go.

Breakfast is served in the parlor. A selection of breakfast breads, juices, and fruits are laid out on the sideboard. An entrée of perhaps eggs Benedict or French toast is served at the table.

The B&B is located in the heart of the residential area. One of Cape May's finest restaurants is across the street, and the beach is just three blocks away.

What's Nearby

See "What's Nearby — Cape May," page 81.

Chimney Hill Bed and Breakfast

207 Goat Hill Road
Lambertville, NJ 08530
(609) 397-1516; fax (609) 397-9353

Innkeepers: Terry Ann and Richard Anderson
Rooms: 8, all with private baths and air conditioning; 4 with fireplaces; portable telephones available
On the grounds: Gardens
Extras: Pantry with snacks, cookies, sherry, and port; fax, copier, dataport, telephone available
Rates: $130– $175, weekends with full breakfast; $85 – $105, weekdays with Continental breakfast
Credit cards accepted: American Express, Master-Card, Visa
Open: Year-round except Christmas
Smoking: Non-smoking bed and breakfast
How to get there: From New York take the New Jersey Turnpike south to exit 14 and follow I-78 west to exit 29. Follow I-287 south to Route 202 south. Follow Route 202 for approximately 20 miles to Route 179 south. Stay on Route 179 until you reach a traffic light. Route 179 turns right here, but you go straight ahead. Take the second left onto Swan Street. Turn right onto Studdiford Street, which will change to Goat Hill Road. The B&B is at the top of the hill on the left.

The grand stone manor house began as a humble farmhouse but was expanded in 1927 to its present proportions. It sits on 8¹/₂ acres where deer, rabbits, and wild turkeys will frequently be seen.

The original farmhouse, with its low-beamed ceiling and massive fireplace, now serves as the dining room for the inn. A full breakfast of fresh fruits, sweet breads, and perhaps oven-baked French toast with apples and brown sugar is served on weekends; during the week a Continental breakfast is set out on the mahogany table in the bay window that over-looks a little side courtyard with a pretty fountain. Individual tables are set with placemats and silver candelabra.

The magnificent living room has wide-plank pine floors topped by exquisite Oriental rugs. A fireplace graces one wall, and sofas and chairs are upholstered in wine-colored tapestry. A multitude of books fill cases, and a baby grand piano sits at one end. The adjacent Stone

Room, aptly named because of its stone floor and stone fireplace, is a favorite retreat. Splashy floral chintz covers the chairs, beautiful English oil paintings hang on the walls, and French doors lead to the gardens.

In 1988 the house was host to a decorator showhouse, and many of the wall treatments and light fixtures date from that period. Terry and Rich Anderson acquired the house in 1994. One of the grandest guest rooms is in the home's original Library on the main floor. The shelves are still lined with books in this large room, and there's a canopy bed and a huge fireplace with a wooden mantel. The walls are covered with a grey and white toile. A lovely tiled bath is in the hallway.

The remaining rooms are upstairs. In the Hunt Room a splashy red fabric with green trees is festooned across the windows, table skirt, and bed canopy and skirt. There's a lovely antique dresser with spiraled arms holding the mirror. The bath has oxblood walls and elaborate tasseled stenciling. Every room has its own private tiled bath, but some are located in the hallway. To provide additional rooms with fireplaces, the Andersons have installed units with gorgeous mahogany mantels that use cans of Sterno for flame.

There's a nice butler's pantry off the breakfast room with a mini-refrigerator. Port and cream sherry are available as well as a selection of teas, coffee, and home-baked cookies. A basket of snacks and the inn's only telephone are here as well, although portable telephones are also available.

The gardens are spectacular, offering lovely secluded spots for reading and relaxing. Hushed classical music is piped outside in the summer. In addition, there are excellent restaurants in Lambertville and New Hope, Pennsylvania, just across the river. The Bucks County Playhouse, where theatrical productions are offered most of the year, is also in New Hope.

What's Nearby

Although located in New Jersey, Lambertville is just across the Delaware River from New Hope, Pennsylvania, the shopping and cultural center of Pennsylvania's Bucks County. The Lambertville Chamber of Commerce has prepared a walking tour of the historic sites and buildings along the village streets, and there are marvelous shops and restaurants in town. In addition, there are picnic sites and other activities in New Jersey's longest park, the Delaware and Raritan Canal State Park, which borders the Delaware River. (See also Stockton, New Jersey, and New Hope, Pennsylvania.)

Chestnut Hill on the Delaware

63 Church Street (mailing address: P.O. Box N)
Milford, NJ 08848
(908) 995-9761; fax (908) 995-4200;
e-mail: chhillinn@aol.com

Innkeepers: Linda and Rob Castagna
Rooms: 6, including 1 suite and 1 cottage; 4 with private baths; all with air conditioning, radios, and robes; 5 with telephones; 4 with TVs; 3 with hair dryers; 2 with balconies or porches; 1 with whirlpool tub; cottage with fireplace; 1 room with wheelchair access
On the grounds: Gardens, patio with picnic tables; parking
Extras: Afternoon tea with homemade snacks; fax available
Rates: $90 - $140, including full breakfast; two-night minimum weekends
Credit cards accepted: None
Open: Year-round
Smoking: Permitted outside only
How to get there: From I-78, take exit 11 (Pattenburg). Follow Route 614 for 8 miles south to Spring Hill. Turn left onto Route 519 and travel 3 miles south to Milford. In Milford turn right onto Bridge Street and then right onto Church Street. At the end of Church Street turn left; the inn's parking lot is straight ahead.

The first thing you'll notice when you drive up to Chestnut Hill is the spectacular view of the Delaware River. The next will be the lovely 1860s Victorian house handsomely painted in shades of green to highlight its numerous gables and gingerbread. There's an elaborate grapevine wrought iron trim that parades across the porch and down the columns. You may find the collection of antique rockers on the porch so inviting—they offer views of the river over the abundant rhododendron bushes—that you will forego your trip inside until you have relaxed here with a glass of iced tea that Linda will bring to you.

When you eventually venture inside, you will be welcomed by a mannequin dressed in a nineteenth-century dress. The drawing room to the left of the entrance is furnished with a pump organ and an upright piano. An ornately carved walnut fireplace mantel is overseen by Bradbury and Bradbury wallpaper borders. Along one wall, there's a black walnut apothecary cabinet filled with Linda's unique gift shop. She has an artist's eye for exquisite craft items: wooden boxes painted to look like charming English cottages that hold tissues and intricate hair clips she purchased from an artist in Costa Rica. Linda also sells some of the jewelry she makes.

The guest rooms are decorated with Victorian flair — each with its own theme. In the Rose Garden, there's a window seat offering a terrific view of the river, rose motif paper on the wall, and a bath with lovely tile work and a whirlpool tub. Teddy's Place on the third floor has a brass and iron bed, a TV, a telephone, and a bath with a sink in a Victorian chest. There are more than 150 teddy bears marching up the stairs and enjoying the spacious room with the guests. The Country Cottage by the River, located next door, has its own private porch (complete with a carousel horse) and a fireplace in the bedroom. When guests return to the inn after dinner, they'll find a good-night note waiting on the stair newel and chocolates and warm cookies in their rooms.

Linda prepares an elegant gourmet breakfast and serves it in her formal dining room, which has a magnificent crystal chandelier. She sets her black walnut table with fine china, crystal, silver, and candles. Linda will start with a fresh fruit cup and freshly baked breads. This will be followed by an entrée such as macadamia/banana pancakes with fruit or maple syrup.

To allow their guests to enjoy the river even more, Rob is building a riverwalk. At present, there are benches for watching the river up close to see the ospreys, swans, and otters. There are an array of flea markets, antiques auctions, and art galleries nearby as well as fine restaurants.

What's Nearby

Milford has the small-town ambience of an earlier time. Its shops and restaurants are refined and upbeat but not as utterly sophisticated as those across the river. Popular activities in this section of the Delaware River Valley include canoeing and rafting on the Delaware River and walking along the towpath that borders it. (See also Erwinna, Kintnersville, Ottsville, and Upper Black Eddy, Pennsylvania.)

The Wooden Duck Bed & Breakfast

140 Goodale Road
Newton, NJ 07860
(973) 300-0395

Innkeepers: Bob and Barbara Hadden
Rooms: 5, including 1 suite, all with private baths, air conditioning, TVs, VCRs, telephones with dataports, radios, desks, robes, irons, and ironing boards
On the grounds: Gardens, swimming pool surrounded by brick patios, horseshoes, hiking, cross-country skiing
Extras: Parking; tea, fruit drinks, snacks, and chocolate chip cookies available 24 hours
Rates: $100 – $120 double; $85 – $90 single, including full breakfast; two-night minimum holiday weekends
Credit cards accepted: American Express, Discover, MasterCard, Visa
Open: Year-round
Smoking: Permitted outside only
How to get there: From I-80 eastbound, take exit 19 to Route 517 north and travel for 6.3 miles to Andover Center. From I-80 westbound, take exit 25 to Route 206 north and travel for 6.2 miles to Andover Center. Continue on Route 206 for 1.6 miles to Goodale Road. Turn right (at Lakeland Rescue Squad) and travel for 1.5 miles. The Wooden Duck is on the left.

New Jersey is known as the "Garden State," and when you reach northern New Jersey, you understand how the state got its moniker. Here there are still fields of pumpkins and strawberries, forests, horse farms, and houses with spacious lawns and gardens of flowers.

When Bob and Barbara Hadden retired from the corporate world, they began a search for a smaller retirement house with a little land. But when they saw this huge house, their plans changed.

The Wooden Duck is located on 17 acres of utter serenity. The first thing you're likely to see in the morning is deer feeding in a field or wild turkeys foraging for seeds or cardinals, woodpeckers, and hummingbirds feeding at the numerous feeders.

The gracious rooms of the manor house have tall ceilings. The massive entry has a double-sided fireplace that can be enjoyed in the Game Room also. The living room, which has a beamed ceiling and bay window, flows into the

Dining Room. The Game Room has a selection of jigsaw puzzles, games, bumper pool, and a video library. An 1860s map of the United States covers one whole wall.

Each of the guest rooms is named for a type of duck. There are three in the main house and two in the carriage house, and they all have sitting areas with TVs and VCRs tucked into armoires, as well as telephones with dataports. Ruddy Duck is decorated in cheerful yellows with pine furniture, including a high four-poster bed. Mallard is in hunter green and has cherry furniture, including a heavy cherry homestead bed. One of the favorites is Pintail, which is located in the carriage house. It has knotty pine walls with built-ins, pine furniture, and a huge picture window that looks out on the fields.

Guest often awake to see deer grazing nearby.

Breakfast is served in the formal dining room on fine china with sterling silver and crystal glassware. Barbara is a marvelous cook. She starts the meal with freshly squeezed orange juice and perhaps a warm apple crisp, along with maybe applesauce/oatmeal muffins or banana bread. She may fix pancakes with bananas or with fresh strawberries for an entrée.

There are a variety of things to do near Newton. The bed and breakfast adjoins the Kittatinny Valley State Park, where hiking and cross-country ski trails offer hours of summer and winter recreation. At the nearby Lafayette Mill Antiques Center, there are forty dealers in four historic 1800s mill buildings. Dealers offer antiques that range from furniture to dolls.

What's Nearby

The Delaware Water Gap National Recreation Area is located near Newton. The Appalachian Trail runs its length, and there are places to take rafting and canoeing expeditions. The New Jersey Cardinals are headquartered in Newton, and fans can watch a baseball game. (See also Stanhope.)

Ocean Plaza

18 Ocean Pathway
Ocean Grove, NJ 07756
(888) 891-9442 or (732) 774-6552

Innkeepers: Valerie and Jack Green; manager, Laurett Gannon
Rooms: 18, including 2 suites, all with private baths, air conditioning, TVs, VCRs, telephones, and radios; 2 have private porches, mini-refrigerators, and coffee makers; 5 rooms with wheelchair access
On the grounds: Vegetable garden
Extras: Mints on the pillow at night; afternoon tea and coffee; cat named Stubby
Rates: $79 – $165 July through September, two-night minimum weekends; $65 – $135 October through June, except Memorial Day weekend, all including Continental breakfast
Credit cards accepted: MasterCard and Visa
Open: Year-round
Smoking: Permitted outside only
How to get there: From the Garden State Parkway south, take exit 100B; from the Garden State Parkway north, take exit 100. Follow Route 33 east to Ocean Grove. At the end of Route 33, take a left, then take the second right onto Main Avenue and go east. Turn left onto Beach Avenue, which is 1 block before the ocean. Travel 4 blocks. The B&B is on the corner of Beach Avenue and Ocean Parkway.

Ocean Grove is a lovely secret treasure — a village still immersed in the traditions by which it was founded. During the last half of the nineteenth century, the Methodist Episcopal Church established communities throughout the United States where open-air religious revivals were held in seaside or woodland settings. Cottages and houses were built in the elaborate Victorian style of the day. Although several other communities have survived, no other is as complete as Ocean Grove, which harks back to 1869. Many of the original cottages with their tent-like projections have been handed down from generation to generation. The entire town is listed on the National Register of Historic Places.

Camp Meeting Week is still held here every summer — in 1998 it enjoys its 129th season. Throughout July and August, there are Bible hours, band and organ recitals, family picnics, and a variety of events ranging from craft shows to concerts by popular artists to revivals led by recognized evangelists — all interspersed with walks along the beach and bicycle and roller blading jaunts along the boardwalk.

The Ocean Plaza Hotel was built in 1870 by one of the founders of the Ocean Grove Camp Meeting Association, and it served as a summer boarding house for many years. The building has a distinctive facade that includes fanciful railings enclosing broad porches. When purchased by Jack and Valerie Green in 1993, the hotel had thirty-five tiny rooms and six bathrooms. Jack had summered in Ocean Grove as a child, and when he and Valerie married shortly after college, they became summer tenters. Jack owns a construction company, so the task of restoring the big old building was not overly daunting. It opened as a classy B&B in 1996.

There are Tennessee rockers on the first-level wraparound porch. Inside, a sunny common room has an Oriental rug on a polished oak floor, wing chairs covered in bright yellow floral chintz, and flowers painted above the windows. Pretty watercolors of local scenes, such as the restored Asbury Park carousel, grace the walls, and happy ferns wave from pedestal stands.

The guest rooms are equally bright, with floral spreads, wicker chairs, pine armoires holding TVs and VCRs, and carpeted floors. Each of the rooms has a private bath in black and white tiles, and both the guest rooms and the baths have ivy and flowers hand-painted on the walls. Several rooms have private porches. The two suites on the top floor are especially spacious, and they each have a private porch with a lovely ocean view.

A Continental breakfast is served on the second-floor porch, which is outfitted with wicker tables and chairs. The B&B is merely a block from the ocean.

What's Nearby

Especially in July and August when the Ocean Grove Camp Meeting Weeks take place, there are many things to do for the entire family. There are spiritual hours; band and organ concerts and recitals; events ranging from craft shows to revivals led by recognized evangelists; and concerts by big-name performers. No matter what time of the year you come, however, the pristine white sandy beach bordered by a boardwalk is an inviting place to walk, bicycle, rollerblade, or just to sit and contemplate the ocean's vastness. (See also Spring Lake.)

Red Maple Farm

203 Raymond Road
(mailing address: RD4)
Princeton, NJ 08540
(908) 329-3821

Innkeepers: Roberta and Lindsey Churchill
Rooms: 3, all with shared baths and air conditioning; 1 with fireplace
On the grounds: Swimming pool, gardens, orchard
Extras: tea, espresso, cookies on sideboard all day
Rates: $48 – $78, including full breakfast; $10 supplement for one-night stay on weekends
Credit cards accepted: American Express, Diners, Discover, MasterCard, Visa
Open: Year-round
Smoking: Permitted outside only
How to get there: From Route 1 north of Princeton (Route 1 is a Princeton bypass that runs east of the city) watch for Stouts Lane. After Stouts Lane, take the next left onto Raymond Road. The B&B will be on the left. Look for "Red Maple Farm" on the mailbox.

Princeton is one of the most sophisticated university towns in America, yet there are few country inns or bed and breakfast establishments nearby. Red Maple Farm is the exception. Located on a back road about 4 miles from the university, the 2¹/2-acre property is made up of a white clapboard farm house, an 1850s barn/carriage house, a smokehouse, a chicken house, and a pool house (this was once a playhouse). There's an orchard, an organic vegetable garden, and a berry garden. A swimming pool is sequestered behind the pool house. The historic house and property are on the National Register of Historic Places, and a secret room and tunnel to the barn suggest that it may have been a stop on the Underground Railway.

Both Lindsey and Roberta Churchill are academics, and their collection of books is impressive to say the least, but the eclectic decor of their inn reflects their worldwide travels and interest in folk art as well. Peruvian, Navaho, and Finnish rugs hang on the walls and lie on the wide-plank floors in the parlor. A needlepoint picture from Georgia (in the former USSR) adds additional interest. There's a fireplace in the parlor as well as in the small room where the inn's only TV and VCR are located.

There are three guest rooms, and none of them has a private bath. Each of the bedrooms opens off a large center hall that Roberta stenciled with cascades of ivy. The Strawberry Room has a huge fireplace and a lovely pine cupboard. There's a brass bed with a pretty quilt and a braided rug on the polished pumpkin-colored pine floor. Next door, the Flower Room is done in shades of green. These two rooms have separate entrances to a charming bath with a green tile floor and pretty hand-painted stenciling on the walls. The Blue Room has a four-poster bed with pineapple finials. The occupants of this room share a bath with the owners.

The pine sideboard in the Dining Room is set with coffee, tea, and homemade cookies so that guests may help themselves in the afternoon. Roberta was formerly the chef of a Princeton restaurant that *The New York Times* critic acclaimed as one of the five best in New Jersey. As one might imagine her breakfasts are terrific. Guests sit at the huge pine table that will be set with the Churchill's lovely Limoges or Noritake china and fine silver. A Tiffany-style lamp hangs overhead. In winter, the fireplace will be glowing. Roberta may offer a cheese and bread pudding, homemade muffins or breads, perhaps bacon or sausage, and a crumble made with fruits of the season.

The Churchill's have bicycles for their guests to use. The grounds include glorious beds of flowers — some in the stone circle where the farm's massive red maple tree used to reside.

What's Nearby

Sophisticated and urbane, Princeton has lovely shops and innovative restaurants. Princeton University offers a wealth of cultural events throughout the year ranging from lectures to concerts. The Westminster Choir College performs during the year also. Nearby Washington Crossing State Park on the Delaware River has picnicking, hiking trails, and historic exhibits.

Hollycroft Inn

506 North Boulevard, South Belmer
(mailing address: P.O. Box 448)
Spring Lake, NJ 07762
(800) 679-2254 or (732) 681-2254;
fax (732) 280-8145

Innkeepers: Linda and Mark Fessler
Rooms: 8, including 1 suite, all with private baths and air conditioning; 3 with fireplaces; 2 with porches; 1 with TV, radio, mini-refrigerator, coffee maker, hair dryer, desk, and Jacuzzi
On the grounds: Hammock for two
Extras: Sherry in living room; Perrier and imported chocolates in room; two cats named Bouncer and Pip
Rates: $95 – $275, including full breakfast; two-night minimum weekends mid-May through September
Credit cards accepted: American Express
Open: Year-round
Smoking: Permitted outside only
How to get there: From the Garden State Parkway, take exit 98 onto Route 34 south. At the traffic circle go $3/4$ of the way around and exit onto Route 524 east (Allaire Road). Go 3.3 miles to the 3rd traffic light and turn left onto Route 71. Make an immediate right onto Church Street and continue for $1/2$ mile to Third Avenue. Turn left and go 2 blocks. Turn right at the lake onto North Blvd. Go $2^1/2$ blocks and you will see the Hollycroft sign on the right. Drive up the driveway. The B&B is the house on the left. Proceed around the house to the parking area.

W hat do you do if you want a cottage by the sea but your wife longs for the smell of evergreens in the mountains? You find the highest point near the ocean, plant it with pine and oak trees, rhododendrons, holly trees, azaleas, and mountain laurel, and build a log and stone Adirondack-style mountain lodge overlooking a lake. Surprisingly, this solution worked beautifully for the owners, and it works for us, too.

The first floor and the chimneys are made of local ironstone, which is turning a lovely reddish color with age, while the second story is of half-timber and stucco construction. The house was purchased in 1985 by Mark and Linda Fessler from descendants of the original owners. Mark is an architect, and Linda is an expert artist and crafts person. Together they have preserved the unique characteristics of the house, while creating a charming and comfortable getaway.

You enter a living room with yellow pine floors and a massive fireplace and chimney made of jagged pieces of ironstone. An extension of the living room has a brick floor and a view of Lake Como. A decanter of sherry sits on a table as encouragement for winding down to enjoy this special place. Throughout this floor, there are massive cedar log beams and pine-paneled walls. Beyond the living room, French doors lead to an enclosed sun room with a brick floor, a wall of stone, and a lattice ceiling.

The guest rooms are equally distinctive. Ambleside has a pine canopy bed and a private balcony with a view of the lake. Although all the rooms have private baths, several are located across the hall.

The Lord of the Manor Suite is stunning. The small sitting room includes a wet bar and refrigerator hidden in a corner cupboard charmingly hand-painted by Linda. A massive ironstone fireplace casts a glow across the iron canopy featherbed. The walls are sponged in pale yellow, and the ceiling in a pale blue that creates the illusion of clouds. A large private porch offers views of the lake. The bathroom, however, is the tour de force. A double Jacuzzi sits by a picture window, offering tree-top views of the lake.

Linda sets out a buffet-style breakfast in the dining room, which has another ironstone fireplace. There will be juice, fresh fruit such as bananas and oranges layered with honey, freshly baked nut bread and Irish soda bread, an entrée such as a sweet pepper and caramelized onion frittata with sage sausage patties, and also a dessert such as a four-berry crumble served with chantilly cream.

Perhaps a relaxing day at the beach with a book will beckon, or maybe the hammock in back will call. If you seek other diversions, follow the advise on the Hollycroft brochure. "You can swing a fishing rod, a golf club, or a tennis racket. You can ride a wave or a trolley, a horse, or a ferris wheel."

What's Nearby—Spring Lake

Pretty Spring Lake has a shopping street lined with antiques shops and interior design studios. Do not miss Vitale and Vitale, specialists in antique clocks. Its magnificent collection of clocks is as much a museum of horology as a salesroom. At the PNC/Garden State Arts Center there are concerts year-round, while the Spring Lake Historical Museum offers interesting historical exhibits. Spring Lake has a lovely boardwalk that's perfect for walking, rollerblading, and bicycling and there's a jogging/walking trail around the lake. (See also Ocean Grove.)

La Maison—A B&B and Gallery

404 Jersey Avenue
Spring Lake, NJ 07762
(800) 276-2088 or (732) 449-0969;
fax (732) 449-4860

Innkeepers: Barbara Furdyna and Peter Oliver; manager, Paula Jordan
Rooms: 8, including 2 suites and 1 cottage, all with private baths, air conditioning, TVs, and telephones with dataports; 1 with whirlpool tub; 1 with mini-refrigerator, coffee maker, iron, and ironing board; 1 room with wheelchair access; crib available
On the grounds: Side garden
Extras: Fresh flowers in the room; afternoon "happy hour" with wine, cheese, and hors d'oeuvres
Rates: $120 – $270, including full breakfast and afternoon "happy hour"; three-night minimum weekends July and August; two-night minimum weekends rest of year
Credit cards accepted: American Express, Diners, Discover, MasterCard, Visa
Open: February - December
Smoking: Permitted outside only
How to get there: From the Garden State Parkway, take exit 98 onto Route 34 south. Follow Route 34 to the traffic circle and then take Route 524 east to Spring Lake. After crossing the railroad tracks, take the second right onto Fourth Avenue. Proceed for 5 blocks and turn right onto Jersey Avenue. La Maison is the second house on the right.

Spring Lake is home to scores of distinctive artists. Peter Oliver, one of the innkeepers, is a fine watercolorist, and Paula Jordan, the assistant innkeeper, paints in watercolors and oils. Barbara Furdyna, the vivacious owner/innkeeper, is a superb artist as well. Not only has she created a unique art gallery (all the artwork is for sale) on the first floor and stairway of her B&B, she has decorated it with exceptional taste and style.

Barbara is an acknowledged Francophile. She was a French major in college and lived in France, where she studied at the Sorbonne, and she never really left France spiritually. Therefore, her B&B is infused with a French mood that includes French antiques, champagne buckets filled with fresh flowers, and French music playing in the background. The cozy parlor has a fireplace, a lovely Persian rug, shelves filled with books about France, French chairs and tables, and a huge painting of poppy fields in Provence. Every afternoon cheeses, pâtés, fruits, wine, and sherry are set out on an antique desk.

You'll find light, airy, and utterly romantic guest rooms with French sleigh beds, carved armoires, iron beds, ornate French iron chairs, and fresh flowers. There are colorful balloon shades on the windows, and white duvets on the beds. The baths are bright and modern. I especially like the King Juan Carlos Room, with its sexy bath that contains a two-person whirlpool and a skylight in the cathedral ceiling, through which we could view a full moon. A wonderful little cottage in back, with its own private garden, is open in the summer.

Breakfast is served in the formal dining room, which has a pine trestle table overseen by two brass and crystal chandeliers. Red walls and ladderback chairs give it a French country appeal. The relaxed en famille atmosphere begins with glasses of mimosas. Barbara may serve a menu of poached pears in orange sauce followed by crème brûlée French toast and a dish of fresh fruit, all accompanied by oversized cups of coffee, tea, or cappuccino.

Spring Lake is a peaceful and charming seaside Victorian village unaffected by the fast-food emporiums and honky-tonk dives that characterize other sections of the New Jersey shore. Stately mansions with broad lawns line the well-kept wide streets, and the village has an impressive collection of antiques shops, decorator showrooms, and cafes. Vitale and Vitale, specialists in antique clocks, is located here, and its magnificent collection is as much a museum of horology as a salesroom.

Barbara offers complimentary beach, pool, and tennis passes to her guests (chairs and umbrellas, too) as well as membership in a full-service health club. She also has bicycles for her guests to use.

What's Nearby

See "What's Nearby — Spring Lake," page 103.

Normandy Inn

21 Tuttle Avenue
Spring Lake, NJ 07762
(800) 449-1888 or (732) 449-7172;
fax (732) 449-1070

Innkeepers: Michael and Susan Ingino; managers, Michael and Jeri Robertson
Rooms: 19, including 2 suites, all with private baths, air conditioning, radios, and telephones; 5 with fireplaces; 2 with whirlpool tubs; 1 with private porch; cribs available
On the grounds: Parking for one-half of guest cars
Extras: Afternoon snacks; one sheltie named Samantha
Rates: $101 – $190 for rooms; $215 – $300 for suites, including full breakfast and afternoon snacks
Credit cards accepted: American Express, Diners, Discover, MasterCard, Visa
Open: Year-round
Smoking: Permitted outside only
How to get there: From the Garden State Parkway, take exit 98 onto Route 34 south. Follow Route 34 to the traffic circle and then take Route 524 east to Ocean Avenue in Spring Lake. Turn right. Go 1 block and turn right again onto Tuttle Avenue. The B&B will be on the left in 1 block.

The tangy smell of salt air in Spring Lake always reminds me of childhood afternoons spent playing in the surf. Beaches are still my favorite destinations, and this white-sand beach stretches for miles. Spring Lake's boardwalk is alive on sunny days with bicyclists, joggers, in-line skaters, and walkers.

The Normandy Inn, an 1888 Italianate villa, was built as a five-bedroom rental house. Early ads told of a parlor, a library, and an entire fourth floor tower reserved for trunks. It rented for $1,200 per season. Located originally at First Avenue and Passaic, it was moved to the present location in 1909, where it continued to operate as a boarding house.

Now a B&B, the house has an elaborate olive, jade, burgundy, and terra cotta paint scheme, embellished with gold. There are arched windows and a multitude of porches, including a huge wraparound porch across the front filled with wicker furniture.

Inside, two rose-colored parlors are furnished with lavish antiques. A Rococo Revival parlor set, an ornate bronze chandelier, a grand piano, and an elaborate tall-case clock are characteristic. To the side, a porch is reserved for casual relaxation. There's a refrigerator where guests can store their drinks, a TV, and stacks of magazines and local newspapers. In the afternoon, cookies, iced tea, and lemonade are available here. Even though it is decorated with high-Victoriana, it is a casual, laid-back B&B. Because of the B&Bs size, however, it is more impersonal than others in the area.

The guest rooms are furnished with gorgeous antique beds. Room #101 has a full-tester canopy bed with gold bed drapes, a gas fireplace, and a terrific new bath with a granite floor. Other rooms have burled walnut or iron and brass beds, and gas fireplaces have been added to several. Although all rooms have private baths, work is continuously underway to improve them.

The dining room, which is as big as some restaurants, has individual tables, and the service is similar to a restaurant. A menu is presented that offers guests a selection of juices; cereals; eggs fixed as you like them, including a variety of six omelets; four varieties of pancakes; and even French toast made with two different breads. Bacon, ham, pork roll, or link sausage are also available.

After such a hefty breakfast, many guests head out on one of the B&Bs bicycles for a ride along the boardwalk or borrow beach passes, chairs, and towels and go to the beach (there is a slight charge for all).

What's Nearby

See "What's Nearby — Spring Lake," page 103.

Sea Crest by the Sea

19 Tuttle Avenue
Spring Lake, NJ 07762
(800) 803-9031 or (732) 449-9031;
fax (732) 974-0403;
e-mail: johnrkirby@msn.com
website: http://www.bbianj./com/seacrest

Innkeepers: John and Carol Kirby; manager, Terri Thomson
Rooms: 12, including 2 suites, all with private baths, air conditioning, TVs, VCRs, telephones, hair dryers, and robes; 8 with gas fireplaces; 1 with whirlpool tub; 1 with large soaking tub
On the grounds: Parking
Extras: Afternoon tea and desserts; chocolates at night; one dog named Daisy, 2 cats named Princess and Sneakers
Rates: $159 – $259 mid-May through September; $145-$245 October to mid-May, including full breakfast and afternoon tea; three-night minimum weekends and two-night minimum weekdays from June through September, two-night minimum weekends from October through May
Credit cards accepted: American Express, MasterCard, Visa
Open: Year-round
Smoking: Permitted outside only
How to get there: From the Garden State Parkway, take exit 98 onto Route 34 south. Follow Route 34 to the traffic circle and then take Route 524 east to Ocean Avenue in Spring Lake. Turn right. Go 1 block and turn right again onto Tuttle Avenue. The B&B will be on the left in 1 block.

We love the turrets and gingerbread, the bay windows, ornate fireplace mantels, and the broad porches of fine Victorian homes. So naturally, we love Sea Crest, a Victorian gem that has furnishings as Victorian as its architecture.

John and Carol Kirby fled corporate life for innkeeping in 1989, purchasing this 1885 home that has been welcoming guests for more than 100 years. We walked across the wraparound porch to the ornate front door and were immediately immersed in the spell of the late 1800s. Tea and freshly baked cookies and cakes (it was a white chocolate cheese cake when we last visited) were waiting in the dining room when we arrived, and we relaxed while John told us about the history of Spring Lake.

The guest rooms are fantasy retreats designed for adults who are seeking a romantic escape.

Take the Casablanca room, for example. You will enter through a bead curtain, sleep on a rattan bed, and be surrounded by lamps and artifacts that John collected in Africa when he was an officer in the Merchant Marines. A trench coat hangs behind the door, and "the" movie is available in the video library to watch on the VCR in your room. The Queen Victoria Suite has a four-poster canopy featherbed, pictures of the Queen, a sitting room with a fireplace, and a Jacuzzi. Several of the baths are small, but adequate.

Individual touches abound at this inn that is infused with the personalities of the creative innkeepers. There's a wonderful gift corner just inside the entrance where unusual jewelry, paintings, and craft items are sold. Also, when guests return from dinner they will be greeted by "James the Butler," a charming wooden gent who will be standing on the stairway holding a tray of delectable homemade chocolates.

Breakfast is an elaborate affair that is served in the formal dining room and also in a cozy addition that boasts a woodstove. We started with breads, including freshly baked buttermilk scones, juices, and cereals that we selected ourselves from a corner cupboard. This was followed by Carol's popular featherbed eggs, a baked soufflé of eggs and bread, spiced with her seasonings of choice. She might use ham and cheese, or spicy peppers and herbs for a Mexican flavor. A side dish of fresh fruit is included as well as freshly roasted and ground coffee that guests rave about. It's all served on pretty china on placemats.

Although guests are often reluctant to leave the lively table conversations that begin around John and Carol's table, John might suggest a spritely walk along the 2-mile boardwalk, which he claims "is guaranteed to use up at least 400 calories." Or, there is a fleet of English 3-speed bicycles for guests to use. One stop all guests should make along the pretty little shopping streets is at Vitale and Vitale, the outstanding antique clock emporium.

What's Nearby

See "What's Nearby — Spring Lake," page 103.

Whistling Swan Inn

110 Main Street
Stanhope, NJ 07874
(973) 347-6369;
fax (973) 347-3391;
e-mail: wswan@worldnet.att.net
website: http//bbianj.com/whistlingswan

Innkeepers: Joe and Paula Williams Mulay; manager, Carol Regts
Rooms: 10, including 1 suite, all with private baths, air conditioning, telephones with dataports, radios, hair dryers, irons, and ironing boards; 6 with desks; 4 with whirlpool tubs; 1 with TV and mini-refrigerator; TVs available for other rooms
On the grounds: Parking, side yard with swings, picnic table, hammocks, gardens
Extras: Afternoon refreshments, including lemonade and freshly baked cookies; fax, copier, light typing available
Rates: $90 – $140, including full breakfast and afternoon snacks; two-night minimum holiday weekends and all weekends in September and October
Credit cards accepted: American Express, Discover, MasterCard, Visa
Open: Year-round
Smoking: Permitted outside only
How to get there: From I-80 take exit 25 eastbound or exit 27B westbound and follow Route 206 until it becomes Route 183. Continue on Route 183 to the Hess gasoline station in Stanhope. Turn left onto Main Street. The B&B will be on the left.

When the Erie Canal opened in 1825, it linked the huge population on the East Coast with the industrial products and the agricultural produce made further west. Soon feeder canals were built as well. The Morris Canal, a link between the Hudson and Delaware Rivers, was of primary importance, and Stanhope became a major stop along this great canal. Eventually, Stanhope blossomed into an industrial town itself.

Joe and Paula Mulay decided to leave the corporate world of A.T.& T. when they realized they saw more of each other in airports than at home. Operating a B&B was something they considered, so when they found a Whistling Swan sign in an antiques store, they bought it and looked for a house to hang it on. The swan and this house are symbolic. Swans mate for life and are elegant, both elements that apply here as well.

The Whistling Swan sits on a stone foundation that creates a wide wraparound porch across the front and side. It's filled with wicker chairs and rockers and a wicker porch swing. Inside, there's a fireplace in both the foyer and one of the parlors. Red walls create a rich backdrop for the warm tiger oak floors, columns, fretwork, and fireplace mantel. Some interesting antique pieces furnish the rooms, much of it from Paula's grandmother's home. In one parlor, there's a player piano and an old Victrola as well as a TV, VCR, a movie library, games, and jigsaw puzzles. In the dining room, there's a tiger oak china closet with dolphin handles.

There are ten guest rooms in this spacious house, and each is enhanced by a working antique radio and a colorful afghan made by Joe's mother. Waterloo Village is one of our favorites. It has a bed with a lace canopy and an oak wardrobe. The bath is seductively painted in red and has a clawfoot tub, pedestal sink, and brass fixtures. On the third floor there's a magnificent 7-foot stained-glass window at the end of the hall and an oak halltree with twisted spindles on the landing.

The most unique room, however, is not a guest room at all, but a bathroom. All rooms on the second floor have showers in the baths, but off the second floor hallway, there's a separate bath with twin clawfoot tubs painted blue to match the walls. Joe and Paula call this their Victorian Jacuzzi.

Breakfast is served in the formal dining room. The meal will start with freshly baked breakfast breads and a cold soup, perhaps a peach soup made with tapioca or yogurt. The main course might be a quiche or perhaps a potato-apple dish with turkey sausage.

This rural northwest region of Sussex County, New Jersey, is called "the Skylands" because of its low-lying mountains and abundance of rivers, streams, and lakes. Lake Hopatcong and the Allamuchy Mountain Preserve are both nearby. At Waterloo Village, visitors can see what life was like during the heyday of the Morris Canal.

What's Nearby

Historic Waterloo Village is a charming complex of restored eighteenth-century stone buildings, boat locks, and mills in a peaceful setting on the Morris Canal in Allamuchy Mountain State Park, just west of Stanhope. During the summer months, there are craft demonstrations as well as craft, antiques, and art exhibits and concerts. In addition, guests can go horseback riding or hiking or visit a local winery. (See also Newton.)

Innkeeper: Lynne McGarry
Rooms: 7, including 2 suites, all with private baths, air conditioning, TVs, telephones, radios, and desks; 6 with mini-refrigerators; 2 with fireplaces; 1 with a whirlpool tub
On the grounds: Parking, swimming pool, gardens
Extras: Homemade cookies; fax, copier available; laundry and dry cleaning
Rates: $95 – $135, including full breakfast
Credit cards accepted: American Express, Master-Card, Visa
Open: Year-round
Smoking: Non-smoking bed and breakfast
How to get there: Traveling on I-78, take exit 4 and turn right. The inn is .2 mile on the left.

Stewart Inn

708 South Main Street
(mailing address: P.O. Box 6)
Stewartsville, NJ 08886
(908) 479-6060;
fax (908) 479-4211

Stewartsville is a tiny village off I-78, located almost on the Pennsylvania border. The area is rural and serene, a patchwork of fields neatly defined by fences and dotted with farms. An occasional church steeple or silo will reach to the sky, but otherwise the land undulates in hills and valleys, cut by streams and rock outcroppings.

The Stewart Inn occupies 16 acres in this tranquil setting, and the property includes a grand fieldstone manor house, a stately barn, and numerous outbuildings. The manor house was originally the home of a miller, and it's a beauty. There are mullioned windows with shutters bracketing them and numerous chimneys rising above the slate roof. At one time the house was owned by Ann Harding, an actress, and her husband. They operated an acclaimed restaurant in the old mill across the street, and their home often provided overnight lodging to stars such as Clark Gable, Jean Harlow, and Ralph Bellamy.

Lynne greets her guests in a foyer, which has pegged oak floors. The spacious living room has a big sofa and gracious wing chairs in which to enjoy a fire in the large fireplace as well as a view of the grounds and gardens from the grand windows. Her collection of tiny tea sets are enchanting. There's a library with an arched corner fireplace for guests to enjoy as well.

The spacious guest rooms have TVs, telephones, and private baths. Each room has numerous happy and healthy plants. Room #4 has a fireplace and a woven rug on a pegged oak floor, room #8 has a four-poster bed on a green carpet and a comfortable chaise lounge, and room #2 has another four-poster bed on pegged oak floors and a sunken tub in the bath. Room #3 has a whirlpool tub.

Breakfast is served in the formal dining room, which has another fireplace. Lynne will prepare whatever her guests want, including pancakes and omelets.

The atmosphere at Stewart Inn is much more relaxed now than when it was a country haven for stars. Today, it's a refuge for animals. Lynne cares for injured rabbits, raccoons, and birds, and she has sheep, lambs, geese, ducks, peacocks, cats, and rabbits on the property. You will also get to know Abigail, Lynne's border collie.

In addition to visiting the animals in the barn, you will probably want to spend time on the patio or walking along the stone pathways through the gardens or swimming in the free-form pool. If you are a fly fisherperson, you will undoubtedly be familiar with the Pohatcong Creek that runs through the property. It is noted for its fine fishing, and there are hiking trails along its banks as well.

What's Nearby

Guests come from miles around to fly fish on the Pohatcong Creek on the B&B's property. It's also a short drive to the Delaware River, where you can canoe and raft. The nearby Clinton Historical Museum Village includes the Old Red Mill, built in the 1700s; a log cabin; a springhouse; a blacksmith shop; and a multitude of exhibits relating to early American life. The Hunterdon Art Center in Clinton is housed in a nineteenth-century stone gristmill.

The Woolverton Inn

6 Woolverton Road
Stockton, NJ 08559
(888) AN INN 4U or (609) 397-0802;
fax (609) 397-4936; e-mail:
woolbandb@aol.com

Innkeepers: Elizabeth and Michael Palmer
Rooms: 10, including 2 suites, all with private baths, air conditioning, radios, and robes; 2 with fireplaces; 2 with whirlpool tubs; 1 with private porch
On the grounds: Parking, gardens, croquet lawn, horseshoes pit, pastures with sheep named Babs and Sally
Extras: Afternoon refreshments; dog named Jake, cat named Willie
Rates: $90 – $190, including full breakfast and afternoon refreshments; two-night minimum weekends; three-night minimum some holiday weekends
Credit cards accepted: American Express, MasterCard, Visa
Open: Year-round
Smoking: Permitted outside only
How to get there: From New York take the New Jersey Turnpike south to exit 14 and follow I-78 west to exit 29. Follow I-287 south to Route 202 south. Stay on Route 202 to the second Lambertville exit. Then take Route 29, traveling north to Stockton. Travel through the village to the fork. Turn right onto Route 523 and go .2 mile. Turn left onto Woolverton Road. The inn is

The Woolverton Inn is one of my favorite bed and breakfasts. The setting on 10 pastoral acres high above the Delaware River is so serene that cares seem to melt away. The magnificent eighteenth-century stone manor house, with its lacy porch railings and wrought iron roof crest, is impressive but welcoming at the same time. Sheep graze in the meadow, and sweeping lawns encompass stands of apple and oak trees, flower gardens, and a pretty pergola.

Although the bed and breakfast has been welcoming guests since 1980, Elizabeth and Michael Palmer purchased the inn in 1993 and have worked continuously to create the special retreat we enjoy today. Private baths were added to every guest room, and in two rooms, there are two-person whirlpool tubs. There are canopy beds, lush fabrics, fireplaces in two rooms, and walls charmingly handpainted with flowers or pastoral scenes.

My favorite room is Amelia's Garden, which

has a four-poster cherry bed with a fishnet canopy, a pretty sitting room, and an elegant bath with pink walls and a walnut dresser outfitted with a sink. In Letitia's Repose, a pink and green confection with a fireplace, the bath has a dreamy mural on the wall beside the Jacuzzi tub. The Stockton Quay Suite has a twig bed and chair and a bath with a corner Jacuzzi tub and a woodland scene painted on the ceiling. Caroline's Balustrade has its own private second-floor porch, and although the bath is across the hall, it's the most charming of all. It has a garden scene, complete with abundant flowers cascading along a stone wall.

Every afternoon Elizabeth prepares light refreshments that will include hot and cold drinks and a fruit and cheese tray, or perhaps crudités and a dip, as well as freshly baked cookies.

Breakfast is served in the formal dining room, which has another fireplace, or on one of the porches or the veranda in summer. Elizabeth may prepare cinnamon sticky buns, a special juice such as strawberry/orange, fresh fruit, eggs Benedict with pan-fried potatoes, and brandied raisin bread pudding with caramel sauce or it may be zucchini and pineapple muffins, fresh fruit, yogurt crêpes with cider sauce, and a peach and blueberry cobbler.

There are a stone spring house, a picturesque barn that may one day contain additional rooms, and a carriage house with two guest rooms. Hiking trails meander about, and there's a croquet lawn and a horseshoes pit.

Walking along the old tow path that borders the Delaware River is a popular nearby activity, as is rafting and canoeing. The Bucks County Playhouse offers theatrical productions year-round and there are a plethora of antiques shops nearby. Several excellent restaurants are located in Stockton.

What's Nearby

Stockton, located on the Delaware River, is near Point Pleasant, Pennsylvania, where you can rent canoes and rafts for trips down the river. The Bull's Island park section of the Delaware & Raritan Canal State Park has campsites and picnic areas. Stockton has several interesting shops and restaurants, including Phillip's Fine Wines, one of the best wine shops in the state with about 5,000 labels and stocking about 200,000 bottles. The Mt. Airy ski area is located nearby. (See also Lambertville, New Jersey, and New Hope, Pennsylvania.)

Holly Thorn House
143 Readington Road
Whitehouse Station, NJ 08889
(908) 534-1616;
fax (908) 534-9017

Innkeepers: Anne and Joe Fosbre
Rooms: 5, all with private baths, air conditioning, telephones with dataports, radios, hair dryers, and desks; 1 room with wheelchair access
On the grounds: Parking, swimming pool with cabana, herb garden
Extras: Snacks, wine, soft drinks, coffee, and cookies; fax, telephones with modems; cat named Lilly
Rates: $100 weekdays, $115 – $145 weekends, including full breakfast
Credit cards accepted: American Express, Discover, MasterCard, Visa
Open: Year-round
Smoking: Non-smoking bed and breakfast
How to get there: From I-78, take exit 26 and turn left onto Lamington Road. At the T, turn left and go 700 yards; turn right onto Orr Drive and follow this across Route 22. You are now on Readington Road. Follow Readington Road south for 3 miles to its end. Turn right at the church and go 300 yards. The Holly Thorn House is on the left.

It's hard to imagine that this elegant rambling beige stucco bed and breakfast began life as a cow barn, but the exposed beams and grand first-floor open space continue to give it a distinctive character. Anne and Joe Fosbre raised their children in this unique structure that they redesigned to replicate an English manor house. When the children were grown, they converted it to a bed and breakfast.

One enters a great room encircled by a balcony and encompassing several comfortable sitting areas with fireplaces. There's a darkly paneled billiards room with plaid carpeting. A wet bar and a refrigerator stocked with soft drinks are located here. Up the spiral stairs and at the end of the second-floor hall, a library contains a gas fireplace and a TV and VCR as well as an extensive video library and a multitude of books and games. Overstuffed chairs welcome relaxation, and the snack bar is stocked with snacks, coffee, fruit, and a filled cookie jar. Another refrigerator holds soft drinks. A fax machine keeps you in touch, if you must.

The open kitchen becomes a gathering spot, especially in the morning. Guests may eat breakfast at a table in front of a fireplace while admiring Anne's collection of more than 125 monks. They are found on steins, carved wooden statues, and glassware. Breakfast will consist of juice and fruit, perhaps blueberry pancakes with sausage, and homemade scones.

The guest rooms are sophisticated and unique, and each has a private bath. The suite has black and white French toile on the walls, a gas fireplace with a magnificent carved mantel, and a tall carved headboard. The Hunt Room has a masculine feel with large hunting prints on brown walls, a massive armoire, and an antique four-poster bed.

The 3 acres of the property include a fragrant "herbary walk," where guests may pick samples; a pool with a poolhouse and changing room; and sunny lawns and patios.

The inn is in a rural setting, yet there are numerous activities nearby. There's an indoor ice skating arena, antiquing, wineries, and hot air ballooning. Golf is just 2 miles away.

What's Nearby

For sports enthusiasts, there are several golf courses in the area, while for adventurers, hot air balloon expeditions can be arranged. History buffs will want to visit Washington's winter headquarters during the Revolutionary War in 1778–1779, which was located in nearby Somerville. Those with a green thumb can visit Wallace House as well as Duke Gardens, a group of eleven gardens enclosed in a glass conservatory.

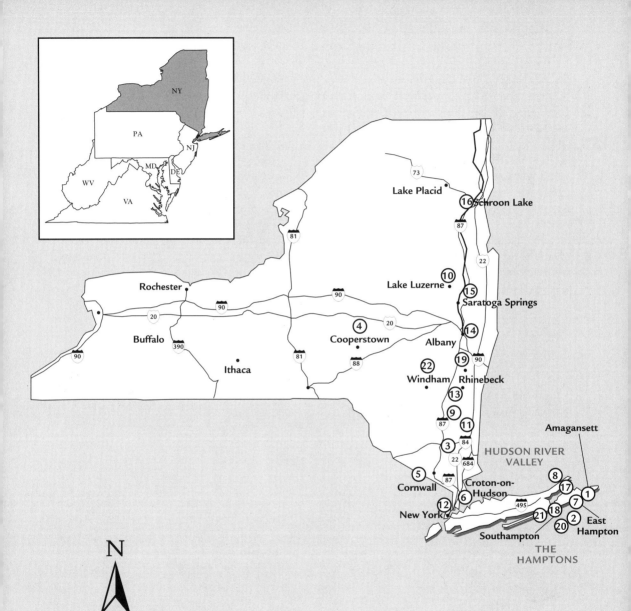

NY

PA

NJ

MD

DE

WV

VA

73

Lake Placid

16 Schroon Lake

87

22

81

10 Lake Luzerne

15

Saratoga Springs

Rochester

90

90

20

20

4

Buffalo

390

Cooperstown

Albany

14

19

90

Ithaca

81

22 Windham

Rhinebeck

88

13

9

87

11

Amagansett

3

84

22

684

HUDSON RIVER
VALLEY

5

8

Cornwall

87

17

Croton-on-
Hudson

7

1

6

495

2

12

21

18

New York

20

East
Hampton

Southampton

THE
HAMPTONS

N

New York

Numbers on map refer to towns numbered below.

Innkeepers: John J. Pakulek III and Clement M. Thompson
Rooms: 4, all with private baths and air conditioning
On the grounds: Parking, gardens
Rates: $210 – $230, including Continental breakfast; three-night minimum weekends, four-night minimum major holiday weekends
Credit cards accepted: American Express, Master-Card, Visa
Open: Memorial Day - Labor Day
Smoking: Non-smoking bed and breakfast
How to get there: From New York City, take I-495 (the Long Island Expressway) to exit 70 (Manorville) and follow Route 111 south to Highway 27 (Sunrise Highway). Follow Highway 27 (which becomes the Montauk Highway) east to Amagansett. Continue through the village of Amagansett and turn right onto Atlantic Avenue (just before the fire station). Proceed 2 blocks. The B&B is on the right, on the corner of Atlantic Avenue and Bluff Road.

Bluff Cottage

266 Bluff Road
(mailing address: P.O. Box 428)
Amagansett, NY 11930
(516) 267-6172

We love Bluff Cottage. The handsome shingled house with its neat white trim sits high enough on its corner lot to capture an unobstructed view of the ocean about three blocks away. We can walk to Atlantic Beach, and we don't have to worry about parking the car. We can sit in the pretty wicker chairs on the wide porch, which is shielded from the street by a high privet hedge, and sip a glass of wine before dinner in total privacy. Or, we can sit on the smaller second-level porch to watch the sun come up across the ocean. But best of all, we appreciate the friendliness of the innkeepers, Clem and John, who make us feel as if we've come to stay with friends.

Bluff Cottage was built in 1892 by Dr. Rossiter Johnson, an editor at Funk and Wagnalls, a New York publishing firm. The Dutch Colonial has a hip roof and shingles that have weathered naturally to a soft grey patina. Clem and John have owned it since 1971, but they turned it into a bed and breakfast only in 1992.

The inside is furnished with lovely French and English antiques the pair have collected on their travels. Most notable are the ornately carved mahogany partners desk in the den and the 8-foot-tall carved French fruitwood confessional in a corner of the living room. On arrival, Clem might sit in the living room with you (before the fireplace, if the weather is chilly) to see if he can help you plan your stay. He'll have excellent suggestions about restaurants.

Bluff Cottage has four dramatically furnished guest rooms — two with ocean views — all with private baths. The Green Room has a masculine feel with its forest green carpeting, plaid silk duvet, and carved four-poster rice bed, whereas the Peach Bisque Room is — peach. It has a canopy bed, an English fruitwood armoire, and an antique marble-topped bombé chest. Clem and John proudly proclaim, "Our guests have told us they come here to get away from TVs and telephones." Therefore, this is one B&B that has no TV or VCR, and the only telephone is in the den.

For breakfast, either Clem or John will pop up the street to the Amagansett Farmers' Market to pick up some fresh fruit and freshly baked croissants, muffins, scones, or sticky buns. They will set it out buffet-style in the formal dining room where guests can eat at their leisure by the fireplace, or they may wish to take their meal out to the porch. Either way, they will certainly admire the collection of rose medallion Chinese export china in the dining room.

The B&B is across the street from the East Hampton Town Marine Museum, which contains a fascinating history of whaling, fishing, and boating in the Hamptons. Just up the street, the village of Amagansett has numerous antiques shops, art galleries, and boutiques as well as a collection of factory outlet shops located in a low-key village setting.

What's Nearby

Bluff Cottage is across the street from a gorgeous beach that includes an excellent snack bar and a parking lot (although why drive when you can walk or bicycle?). Bluff Road is one of the favorite cycling and rollerblading streets also, as it is a relatively quiet road that parallels both Montauk Highway and the ocean. The East Hampton Town Marine Museum, just across the street from the B&B on a bluff overlooking the ocean, contains fascinating exhibits depicting the life of local baymen and the boats and equipment they use to catch fish and shellfish. Don't miss the Stephen Talkhouse, a nightclub where top-name entertainers perform year-round, and where you might see Paul McCartney, Paul Simon, or Jimmy Buffet sit in for a set. (See also East Hampton.)

Bridgehampton Inn

2266 Main Street
(mailing address: P.O. Box 1342)
Bridgehampton, NY 11932
(516) 537-3660

Innkeepers: Anna and Detlef Pump; managers, Marion and Maureen
Rooms: 8, including 1 suite, all with private baths, air conditioning, TVs, and telephones; cribs available
On the grounds: Parking, gardens
Extras: Wine offered in the afternoon; fresh flowers throughout; breakfast in bed available; beach towels provided
Rates: $185 – $290 mid-May to mid-October; $145–$250 mid-October to mid-May, including Continental breakfast, full breakfast offered at supplemental rate ranging from $3 to $12.50; two-night minimum mid-May to mid-October; three-night minimum holiday weekends
Credit cards accepted: American Express, MasterCard, Visa
Open: Year-round
Smoking: Non-smoking bed and breakfast
How to get there: From New York City take I-495 (the Long Island Expressway) to exit 70 (Manorville) and follow Route 111 south to Highway 27 (Sunrise Highway). Follow Highway 27 (which becomes the Montauk Highway) east. It becomes Main Street as it reaches Bridgehampton. The B&B is on the left 1/2 mile beyond the traffic light at the entrance to Bridgehampton Common shopping center and before reaching the village of Bridgehampton.

The Bridgehampton Inn sits on the edge of this fashionable village, where it enjoys the best of all worlds. It's close to wonderful shops and restaurants and yet is far enough from the bustle of pedestrian traffic to offer a peaceful country feeling. The mansion was built in 1795 and served as the Boxwood Inn for many years, but when Detlef and Anna Pump purchased it in 1993, it needed considerable attention. Detlef is a builder, however, and he appreciates a challenge. Today, the inn is a reflection of its historic past and of the Scandinavian heritage of its owners.

The large white clapboard house has a handsome facade. There's a gabled roof in the center portion and wings projecting from both sides. It sits on an acre behind a picket fence surrounded by gardens. Inside, the style is crisp but warm. There are Oriental rugs on polished oak floors. The reception area has a fireplace. The living room, which has French doors to the back garden and to a side patio, has a Victorian sofa upholstered in forest-green velvet and a fireplace where a fire will be glowing in winter. A glass bowl of fresh fruit sits on an antique table and a pitcher of fresh flowers graces the mantel.

Anna is the owner of one of the Hamptons premier catering firms, Loaves and Fishes, so on occasion guests find a tray of cheeses or perhaps some hors d'oeuvres to accompany the carafes of wine waiting in the afternoon in the bright breakfast room, which has a third fireplace. A Continental breakfast is served here featuring homemade blueberry (or another variety) muffins, scones, and croissants, fresh juice, and fruit. This can be supplemented by an egg dish accompanied perhaps by smoked salmon or ham for an additional charge.

The guest rooms are unique— all are decorated in a warm European country ambience, and each is furnished with a custom-crafted four-poster bed and elegant antiques. There's wall-to-wall carpeting, burnished antique chests and tables, and a serene and restful atmosphere. The most alluring room is Number 6, a suite that is furnished with an extraordinary, eight-piece antique Biedermeier bedroom ensemble that includes a bed, chests, dressers, and tables. The gray marble baths have deep European sinks with wide countertops. The glass showers are big enough for two and have the practical European feature of a center shower head — something one sees frequently in Anna and Detlef's native Denmark.

Some of the Hamptons finest restaurants are located right here in Bridgehampton, so there's no need to travel far for dinner.

What's Nearby

If you're coming for a weekend stay in the summer, be sure to arrive before 5:00 P.M. on a Friday night so you can go to the Friday Live author readings and receptions at the Hampton Library in Bridgehampton. The town is a terrific place to bicycle. Take the back roads (ask for a map) to Sagg Main Beach (there's plenty of bike parking) or pedal down Ocean Road to the W. Scott Cameron Beach (plenty of parking here, also). The Corwith House, an 1820s beauty, contains period furnishings and exhibits describing Bridgehampton's history. If you love historic old cars, come for the Old Car Road Rally, which is held in Bridgehampton every summer. (See also East Hampton, Southampton, and Water Mill.)

Pig Hill Inn

73 Main Street
Cold Spring-on-Hudson, NY 10516
(914) 265-9247;
fax (914) 265-4614

Innkeepers: Wendy and Daniel O'Brien; manager, Christine Bertha
Rooms: 8, including 4 with private baths and 4 sharing 2 baths; all with air conditioning; cribs available; telephones available
On the grounds: Parking for 4 cars, garden
Extras: Afternoon tea or cider, plus homemade breads and cookies; breakfast available in guest rooms; fax available
Rates: $100 –$150, including full breakfast; two-night minimum weekends mid-May to October; three-night minimum holiday weekends May to November
Credit cards accepted: American Express, MasterCard, Transmedia, Visa
Open: Year-round
Smoking: Non-smoking bed and breakfast
How to get there: From New York City, cross the George Washington Bridge and travel north on the Palisades Parkway. Cross the Hudson River again on the Bear Mountain Bridge, making the first left after crossing the bridge onto Route 9D. Follow Route 9D north to the light at the corner of Route 9D and Route 301 (Cold Spring's Main Street). Turn left onto Main Street. The B&B will be on the left in 2 blocks.

Main Street in Cold Spring is as quaint and "country" as an upscale Hudson River town can be. Boutiques, bookstores, cafes, and restaurants share space with classy antiques shops — including Wendy's Pig Hill. But Wendy has put an interesting spin on hers. Her antiques shop occupies most of the first floor of her brick building, and she uses her antique beds, tables, and dressers to furnish the eight guest rooms of her B&B, located on the second and third floors. Not only that, but each of the rooms is decorated in a distinctive style, ranging from Southwestern to Chinoiserie, and most have fireplaces. On the night stand beside each bed there's a description of each antique and collectible in the room and its price.

Why name a B&B "Pig Hill"? Wendy grew up on a farm where her family raised pigs, and her collection of pigs is extensive. You'll see numerous pigs lurking about the antiques shop. So, the name seemed a natural extension to her.

The hallways of Wendy's B&B are bright and sunny, thanks to a large window wall in the stairwell and a balcony at the top of the stairs. The walls and door frames were stenciled with cascades of ivy by a local artist. Room #1 has an eclectic Western feeling. There's an adobe kiva-style fireplace in the corner, American Indian blankets and rugs, and birch branch furniture. The headboard is made from wooden fence posts. The room overlooks the garden. Room #6 is Victorian in style. It has a four-poster Victorian bed with lace draped above, sage colored walls, yellow Chinese-patterned chintz on the windows and custom-made spreads, and a large taupe enameled woodstove. On each floor, two guest rooms have private bathrooms, and the two remaining guest rooms share one bath.

There's a pretty two-tiered garden with a brick and stone courtyard in back. Somehow, although merely steps from the street, a calm pervades these little spaces. Enclosed by trees and flowers, guests enjoy lounging on the white garden and twig furniture.

Breakfast is served either in the guest's room, the garden, or downstairs in the dining room every morning. Typically, it will include fresh fruit and freshly baked breads such as blueberry muffins, spice cake, or herb biscuits. This is followed by a hot dish, such as asparagus soufflé, and bacon.

Cold Spring's Main Street ends at the Hudson River with a little park filled with benches. We love to sit here to watch the tugs, barges, sailboats, and yachts slip by. The area is rich with history, however, and numerous museums and historic houses offer interesting diversions. The Foundry School Museum tells a history of the West Point Foundry and of the Hudson River. West Point, home of the United State Military Academy, is just across the river. You can visit its museum, which contains a collection of military art and artifacts, or watch a cadet parade or listen to a concert.

What's Nearby

Get a glimpse of how the wealthy lived in a bygone era by visiting the numerous historic mansions in the area, including Boscobel, an exquisite nineteenth-century jewel in nearby Garrison. The Foundry School Museum has a collection of Hudson River paintings and a re-created country store. West Point, home of the United State Military Academy, is just across the river. You can visit the museum, which contains a collection of military art and artifacts, or watch a cadet parade or listen to a concert. (See also Croton-on-Hudson and Hopewell Junction.)

Innkeepers: Angelo and Laura Zuccotti
Rooms: 8, including 3 suites; 4 with private baths; all with robes; 2 with air conditioning, irons, ironing boards, and whirlpool tubs; 1 with a fireplace
On the grounds: Parking, gardens
Extras: Cookies and port at turndown; afternoon tea and pastries; box of pastries and mineral water on departure
Rates: $85 – $225, including full breakfast; two-night minimum weekends, three-night minimum certain holiday weekends
Credit cards accepted: American Express, Master-Card, Visa
Open: May - December
Smoking: Non-smoking bed and breakfast
How to get there: Cooperstown is 70 miles west of Albany. From I-90 or I-87, take I-88 west toward Oneonta. At the junction with Route 28, follow that north to Cooperstown (about 20 miles). Route 28 becomes Chestnut Street. Proceed to #63, which is in the village.

The J.P. Sill House

63 Chestnut Street
Cooperstown, NY 13326
(607) 547-2633

The J.P. Sill House is one of the finest Victorian restorations on the East Coast. There are elaborate custom-crafted, hand-screened Bradbury and Bradbury wallpapers used lavishly throughout the B&B — on the ceiling and walls of the parlor, for example, there are as many as nine different patterns used.

Even if it weren't embellished with such extravagance, the house would be unique. Built in 1864 for the president of the Bank of Cooperstown, it has tiger oak floors, carved moldings, and feather-grained doors. Incredibly, a considerable amount of the original furniture and fixtures have remained in the house through the years. There are carved marble fireplace mantels with lustrous gilt mirrors over them, Victorian light fixtures with etched shades, and elaborate pieces of furniture.

The B&B is made even more interesting by Angelo and Laura Zuccotti — the creative innkeepers who oversaw the house's transformation. Angelo had formerly been part owner and manager (he was there for fifty-six years) of the renowned Manhattan restaurant and nightclub El Morocco, and Laura worked there for twenty-three years. They fascinate their guests with stories about the famous and infamous they've known, and it's interesting to see an original menu from the restaurant framed on the wall in the dining room.

The Bridal Suite, located on the first floor, is the most lavish guest room. The walls and ceiling are covered with intricate wallpapers, and there's a Bokhara carpet on the floor. There's an iron and brass bed, and robin's egg blue Chinese silk draperies that once hung in El Morocco hang from draft rods. The large bath has a double whirlpool and a pine armoire. There are four beautiful rooms upstairs, all decorated with more wallpaper and elaborate antiques. These share two baths.

The carriage house was recently renovated into several suites. These have a quieter, cheerful, country-elegant tone. There are yellow walls, iron and brass beds, lace curtains at the windows, and pretty Laura Ashley fabrics used throughout. Each has a full kitchen, an iron and ironing board, and even a washer and dryer.

As one might imagine, when breakfast is prepared by a former restaurant owner and graduate of the Cordon Bleu, it's memorable. Guests are seated in the formal dining room, where the table is set with a lace cloth, fine china, crystal, and silver. There will always be fresh juice and fruit. In addition, Laura may serve a crêpe filled with fruit or a three-cheese soufflé, as well as freshly baked coconut bread and scones. Furthermore, tea or lemonade and pastries are served in the afternoon, and when guests depart, they receive a box of pastries and a bottle of mineral water.

The bed and breakfast is on 2 acres of peaceful flower gardens and spacious lawns, all presided over by century-old maple trees. There are benches and chairs for quiet afternoon talks with your favorite person or for reading.

The charming town of Cooperstown, on the banks of Otsego Lake, was founded by Judge William Cooper, the father of James Fenimore Cooper, who immortalized his home town and the surrounding area in his *Leatherstocking Tales*.

What's Nearby

Cooperstown is noted as the home of the National Baseball Hall of Fame and Museum and the town where Abner Doubleday devised the original rules for the game that became "America's Pastime." Don't miss the museum. It's packed with interesting exhibits and ephemera. The Farmers Museum and Village Crossroads is a collection of salvaged and restored buildings where various farming demonstrations such as shoeing horses, spinning thread, baking bread, etc., are performed. The Glimmerglass Opera has an excellent and widespread reputation for its fine productions.

Cromwell Manor Inn
Angola Road
Cornwall, NY 12518
(914) 534-7136;
fax (914) 534-3709

Innkeepers: Dale and Barbara O'Hara
Rooms: 13, including 2 suites, all with private baths, air conditioning, and radios; 6 with fireplaces; 1 with a private balcony and a whirlpool tub; 1 with wheelchair access
On the grounds: Parking, gardens
Rates: $120 – $250, including full breakfast; two-night minimum summer weekends
Credit cards accepted: MasterCard and Visa
Open: Year-round
Smoking: Non-smoking bed and breakfast
How to get there: From New York City, cross the George Washington Bridge and follow the Palisades Parkway north. Stay on the Palisades Parkway to its end at Bear Mountain. At the traffic circle, take 9W north for 11.25 miles to the Angola Road (Cornwall) exit. At the end of the exit ramp, turn left onto Angola Road and continue for .3 miles. The B&B will be on the right.

No, Oliver Cromwell did not stay here, but his descendant, David, did. David Cromwell built Cromwell Manor, a brick Greek Revival mansion with massive white boxed columns across the front, in 1820. The majestic house sits on 7 serene acres that include formal gardens, a croquet lawn, a pond, and an even earlier cottage built in 1764. It's directly across the street from the 4,000-acre Black Rock Forest and adjacent to the Museum of the Hudson

Highlands, which includes an additional 200 acres.

Innkeepers are the most fascinating people I know. They must be risk-takers, caretakers, and astute business people. In this case, Dale O'Hara was driving along a back country road in 1984 when he spotted a crumbling mansion with a FOR SALE sign out front. The next day he owned it. Just like that. Over the next six years, he scraped, painted, fixed, repaired, and got married. Eventually, the couple decided to become innkeepers, and that required another two years to get the necessary permits and to put in thirteen new bathrooms. But in 1993 they opened the doors.

This grand manor house is perfect in every detail. The elegant formal parlor has a fireplace with a marble mantel. There's a bronze chandelier, an antique coffee table with a lyre base, and an antique secretary with a roll-top desk. The chrysanthemum yellow walls provide a stunning background for the white on white Empire sofas and chairs.

The guest rooms are filled with antiques as well. The Darby Room has a sleigh bed and a bath with vibrant raspberry tile. The Cromwell Suite has a canopy bed and a marble fireplace mantel. The bath is enormous. It has a bidet, a double whirlpool tub, and two pedestal sinks. The Wellington Room is in the former parlor, and it has another fireplace with a marble mantel. There are yellow walls and a bed covered in green tapestry as well as a Federal couch and dresser. The Canterbury Room is in the former dining room. It has floor-to-ceiling windows and a fireplace. There are four additional rooms in the cottage.

Breakfast is served in the country breakfast room, which was formerly the kitchen. It has a relaxed, cozy feeling highlighted by a collection of intricate models of square-rigged galleons that sit atop the natural wood cabinets. There are various-sized individual tables for guests to use. Breakfast will include yogurt and apples or baked apples, perhaps French toast or a zucchini quiche, and a crumb cake or mini cheese cakes.

There are numerous things to do locally. The Museum of the Hudson Highlands, located in a rustic building, has natural history and art exhibits as well as live animals and nature trails. There are wineries nearby to visit, and the Jones Farm Country Store is just down the road. Locally made jams, preserves, maple syrup, cider, baskets, and craft items are displayed in an old barn.

What's Nearby

Visitors to Orange County should not miss Storm King Art Center in Mountainville. This 200-acre sculpture park includes work by Nevelson, Noguchi, and Calder. There are hiking trails and swimming possibilities in nearby Harriman State Park as well as in Bear Mountain State Park, where in winter there are also facilities for ice skating and ski jumping. The Appalachian Trail bisects nearby Bear Mountain.

Alexander Hamilton House
49 Van Wyck Street
Croton-on-Hudson, NY 10520
(914) 271-6737;
fax (914) 271-3927;
e-mail: alexhmlths@aol.com

Innkeeper: Barbara Notarius; manager, Brenda Barta
Rooms: 7, including 4 suites, all with private baths, air conditioning, TVs, radios, telephones with dataports, robes, and hair dryers; 5 with fireplaces; 3 with mini-refrigerators and VCRs; 2 with whirlpool tubs, CD players, and desks
On the grounds: Swimming pool, gardens, parking
Extras: Cookies, candy, and fruit available all day; also cheese and crackers in the afternoon; answering machine available
Rates: $95–$250 double; $75–$175 single (plus 9.75% tax and 10% gratuity), including full breakfast; two-night minimum weekends
Credit cards accepted: American Express, Diners Club, Discover, MasterCard, Visa
Open: Year-round
Smoking: Non-smoking bed and breakfast
How to get there: From Manhattan take the Saw Mill River Parkway north to Route 9A. Continue north on Route 9A for approximately 10 miles to Route 9 and continue to Croton-on-Hudson. Exit Route 9 at Route 129 and go east to the traffic light on Riverside Avenue. Turn left onto Riverside and go 1 block. Turn right onto Grand Street and go 1 block. Turn left onto Hamilton, which will intersect with Van Wyck in front of the B&B.

When Barbara Notarius decided to buy a house, she knew specifically what she wanted. It had to be big, with multiple fireplaces, and it had to have a view and a pool. She got all she wanted — and more. The 1889, 7,000-square-foot Victorian has ten bedrooms, eight bathrooms, seven fireplaces, and much of its original woodwork and moldings. She scraped, painted, and repaired the giant and soon realized she would have to put the house to work. When she opened her B&B in 1982,

there was just one room, but she quickly added the rest. As with other things this energetic, enthusiastic woman does, she soon was totally immersed in her new occupation. She became the manager of a bed and breakfast reservation service, and then she wrote a book describing how to open and operate a B&B. Although she no longer runs the reservation service, her book is now in its third printing.

Today, her B&B occupies all her time, especially since she never stops working on the house. It seems she's forever adding a new bathroom, upgrading an old one, or adding a new fireplace (five rooms now have their own).

The parlor has a mix of antique furnishings that range from a carved French rococo baby grand piano to a Victorian platform rocker. There's a creamy striped paper on the walls. In the adjoining dining room, which has a Queen Anne-style table and chairs, the color scheme is peach tones. Breakfast is served on the sun porch, which has an eclectic mix of oak and wicker furniture. A TV and VCR are here also.

The guest rooms are furnished primarily with floral fabrics, white and brass iron beds, or beds in verdigris wrought iron. The Master Suite is extraordinary. It has a green marble fireplace mantel, silk Oriental rugs on hardwood floors, a private entertainment center, and a view of the river. The bath includes a two-person whirlpool tub and a huge stained-glass window that is back-lighted for the ultimate in romantic impact. The most requested room, however, is the stunning Bridal Chamber, located on the third floor. It has an iron and brass bed,

Victorian furnishings on wall-to-wall carpeting, and a marble-fronted fireplace — all overseen by multiple skylights. It has its own entertainment center also, and in the bath there's a two-person whirlpool tub.

Breakfast is a formal event in the dining room, where Barbara may prepare her popular apple blintzes with sour cream and a hot fruit compote, along with juices, fresh fruit, and freshly baked muffins such as chocolate chip or blueberry. Throughout the day she has fresh fruit, coffee, tea, cookies, and candy available, and in the afternoon, she also offers cheese and crackers.

The grounds contain informal vegetable plots and formal flower gardens as well as a swimming pool with sun decks surrounding it. The patio has a barbecue area.

The village of Croton-on-Hudson is 45 minutes from Grand Central Station on Metro North. Union Church of Pocantico Hills, which contains stained glass by Marc Chagall and Henri Matisse, is nearby, as is Caramoor estate, which is noted for its outstanding summer concert series.

What's Nearby

Historic Croton-on-Hudson offers several fine museum house restorations, including Van Cortlandt Manor, Philipsburg Manor, and Sunnyside (once the home of author Washington Irving). Lyndhurst, which is also nearby, is a National Trust property. The latest historic home to be opened to the public is Kykuit, the former Rockefeller compound, established by John D. Rockefeller. The Hudson River Museum of Westchester County includes a nineteenth-century mansion and a planetarium. (See also Cold Spring-on-Hudson.)

Innkeepers: David A. Oxford and Harry Chancey, Jr.; manager, Bernadette Meade
Rooms: 6, including 1 cottage rented by the week only, all with private baths, air conditioning, TVs, VCRs, telephones, hair dryers, and robes; 2 with fireplaces; 1 with private deck; crib available
On the grounds: Swimming pool, gardens, parking
Extras: Soft drinks, bottled water, snacks, port, and sherry; one Lhasa apso, Edwinna, on premise; exercise equipment; beach passes, beach towels, and chairs available; fax, copy machine, business services available
Rates: $200 – $375 mid-May to mid-October; $150 – $195 mid-October to mid-May, including full breakfast; two-night minimum weekends in spring and autumn; three-night minimum weekends in summer; longer minimum stays holiday weekends
Credit cards accepted: MasterCard and Visa
Open: Year-round
Smoking: Non-smoking bed and breakfast
How to get there: From New York City take I-495 (the Long Island Expressway) to exit 70 (Manorville) and follow Route 111 south to Highway 27 (Sunrise Highway). Follow Highway 27 (which becomes the Montauk Highway) east for another 32 miles to East Hampton. The B&B is on the right, just before the light at the intersection of Main Street and the Montauk Highway. (If you pass Town Pond, you have gone too far.)

Centennial House

13 Woods Lane
East Hampton, NY 11937
(516) 324-9414;
fax (516) 324-0493;
e-mail: centhouse@hamptons.com

As David Oxford and Harry Chancey were renovating their classic Hamptons shingle-style cottage, they found a board with an inscription dating to 1876 — and this became the inspiration for their B&B's name. It's perfect. A century isn't that old in a village that was founded in 1648, yet it signifies a house that has character and longevity.

The house sits well back from the road on 1.5 acres. A large porch runs across the front, but most guests retreat to the backyard, where the spacious lawns are studded with abundant flower beds and there's a pool that is surrounded by roses and day lilies. The property is completed by a cottage and a barn that contains an exercise room.

We think Centennial House perfectly captures the country elegance of the Hamptons without being overdone. David and Harry, the ideal hosts, have seen to it that everything is flawless. The living room has twin crystal chandeliers and European oil paintings on the walls. There's a piano at one end and a tall case clock. At the other, a fireplace is flanked by sofas and chairs covered in damask or chintz.

Upstairs in the hallway, there's a refrigerator filled with bottled waters, soft drinks, and ice. A marble counter holds stemmed glasses and a decanter of sherry. A basket of snacks is available for guests — a tempting nibble while they watch a video from the inn's collection on their in-room VCR.

The guest rooms are as elegant as the main floor. The Bay Room holds an antique four-poster carved rice bed in a bay window overlooking the side gardens. A fireplace provides a cozy warmth, and an Oriental rug covers the wide-plank pine floors. Beside the French provincial secretary, the exposed board reading "April 22, 1876, T.E.B." has been carefully preserved. The step-down bath is huge. It has a claw foot tub, a sink in an antique pine pulpit, an antique vanity table, and a glass-enclosed shower. The Lincoln Room, done in shades of green and burgundy, has an ornate Victorian bed similar to the one in which Abraham Lincoln died, as well as a matching armoire. The bath has a marble sink with brass legs.

Breakfast is served on gilt-edged china in the elegant formal dining room. The lovely Italian dining room table has floral marquetry inlays. In one corner, sage green bookshelves reach to the ceiling filled with interesting books for guests to read.

Breakfast is an event. The guests and innkeepers carry on a spirited banter while eating fresh fruits and juices, and an entrée of perhaps eggs Benedict or pancakes and ham as well as homemade biscuits and other breads.

The B&B is equidistant from East Hampton's Main Beach and the downtown shops and restaurants. It's a pleasant bicycle ride or walk in either direction. In addition, a nice restaurant (open in the summer only) is just across the street.

What's Nearby — East Hampton

East Hampton has one of the prettiest ocean beaches of any town, and it also is endowed with the most amenities. There's an excellent snack bar; you can buy suntan lotion and sunglasses; you can rent beach chairs or umbrellas; there are changing rooms and restrooms; and there's plenty of bicycle and auto parking (although you must pay for the latter). In addition, the village has wonderful shops and restaurants as well as cultural activities that range from the movie theater to the John Drew Theatre and Guild Hall, where name entertainers perform throughout the year. Historic attractions include the Mulford Farm, Home Sweet Home, and the historic Hook Windmill. (See also Amagansett and Bridgehampton.)

The J. Harper Poor Cottage

181 Main Street
East Hampton, NY 11937
(516) 324-4081; fax (516) 329-5931

Innkeepers: Gary and Rita Reiswig
Rooms: 5, all with private baths, air conditioning, TVs, VCRs, two or three telephones with dataports, and robes; 4 with fireplaces and desks; 3 with whirlpool tubs; 1 with private balcony
On the grounds: Parking, parterre garden, wisteria arbor
Extras: Turndown with chocolates; cheeses, fruits, crudités, or little pizzas, and wine (small additional charge) in the afternoon; one dog named Ashley; beach passes, beach towels, and chairs available
Rates: $195 – $375, including full breakfast; two-night minimum weekends throughout the year, except in July and August, when there's a one-week minimum
Credit cards accepted: American Express, MasterCard, Visa
Open: Year-round
Smoking: Non-smoking bed and breakfast
How to get there: From New York City take I-495 (the Long Island Expressway) to exit 70 (Manorville) and follow Route 111 south to Highway 27 (Sunrise Highway). Follow Highway 27 (which becomes the Montauk Highway) east for another 32 miles to East Hampton. At the traffic light, turn left. You will now be on Main Street; continue to #181, which will be on the left.

Hidden away behind a stucco wall lies one of the secret treasures of East Hampton. This lovely mansion, a medley of rich woods, multiple fireplaces, and William Morris-inspired furniture and decor, was transformed into the Hampton's finest B&B in 1996. Experienced inn-keepers/owners Gary and Rita Reiswig owned the Maidstone Arms for many years, but their latest venture tops anything else in the Hamptons.

The "cottage," said to incorporate the oldest continually occupied structure in East Hampton, has a distinctly Arts and Crafts design due to a renovation that took place in 1910. It boasts Elizabethan gables, mullioned windows, and a soft buff stucco exterior made especially charming by the guardian angels that oversee the front door.

There's a large entry hall with comfortable

seating areas and a library filled with interesting books. In the breakfast room, the low beamed ceilings are from the house's earliest era. A woodstove offers warmth and a cozy country ambience. In the living room, the molded patterned plaster ceiling and massive tiled fireplace are examples of William Morris, as are the patterned fabrics on the chairs and sofas and the frieze atop the wall. Mullioned windows on both sides create a light and bright space for reading, conversation, or playing the piano.

The guest rooms are spacious and sophisticated. One room combines floral and plaid fabrics in yellow and green with pine furniture. The bath is lavish in its use of patterned tile, and there's an elegant whirlpool tub as well as a glassed-in shower. Another room has paneled walls, a fireplace (with a cache of wood ready to be put to use), an iron bed, and beamed ceilings. A private balcony overlooks Main Street, and there is a tiled bath (all the tilework was expertly laid by Gary's son). Every room has not only a TV and VCR but at least two telephones with dataports. The two largest rooms each have three telephones.

Guests enter the B&B, not through the front door, but through a lovely carved wooden door in the solid stucco wall behind the B&B, which hides an acre of courtyards and gardens. A purple wisteria is a cascade of blooms in May, and the courtyard offers both secluded and open spaces. A sunken parterre garden is lush and tranquil. Beyond the garden, there's plenty of parking space, a scarce commodity in East Hampton.

A full breakfast is prepared every morning. It is served in either the breakfast room or in the courtyard, depending on the weather. Guests start with freshly baked breads, juices, and fruits. Entrées will include perhaps a salmon and scallion frittata or cinnamon swirl French toast. In addition, there will be a fruit salad or a fruit dish such as apples with custard.

Away from the crowds, and yet close enough to encourage a walk to town, the B&B is near the John Drew Theatre and Guild Hall. Art exhibits, classes, and exhibitions take place throughout the year here, as well as lectures, theatrical productions, and concerts. The B&B is also within walking distance of the beach.

What's Nearby

See "What's Nearby — East Hampton," page 133.

Lysander House

132 Main Street
East Hampton, NY 11937
(516) 329-9025

Innkeepers: Larry and Leslie Tell Hillel
Rooms: 3, including 1 suite, all with private baths, air conditioning, radios, and hair dryers; a private telephone may be connected in the suite
On the grounds: Parking, gardens
Extras: Tea or cider and cookies in afternoon; bag of fresh cookies on departure; one cat named Persie in owners quarters; beach passes, beach towels, and chairs available
Rates: $165 – $275 May to October; $110 – $180 October to May, including full breakfast; two-night minimum weekends spring and fall; three-night minimum weekends from July 4th to Labor Day
Credit cards accepted: None
Open: Year-round
Smoking: Permitted outside only
How to get there: From New York City take I-495 (the Long Island Expressway) to exit 70 (Manorville) and follow Route 111 south to Highway 27 (Sunrise Highway). Follow Highway 27 (which becomes the Montauk Highway) east for another 32 miles to East Hampton. At the traffic light, turn left. You will now be on Main Street; continue to #132, which will be on the right.

The one thing you learn when writing about B&Bs and country inns is that each one is a wonderful reflection of the creativity and imagination of its innkeepers. The outside may be identical to that of its neighbors, but inside you'll find Early American, Country French, or an eclectic combination of styles and patterns that are so unique and yet blend together so harmoniously, that you are eager to meet the people who chose these items and placed them so perfectly.

That's what you feel when you see Lysander House. The Hamptons are filled with houses sheathed in weathered shingles and trimmed in white. Most of them have porches across the front (Larry and Leslie added one to theirs), and they reach to two or three stories. This one, a rather unremarkable Victorian farmhouse, was built in 1885 on land that was used for growing flax during the Civil War. Larry (formerly a banker) and Leslie (formerly a school teacher) Hillel had lived in Mexico and Japan prior to migrating to the Hamptons, so their furnishings include an unusual blend of three distinctive cultures. But it's more the style in which they're used than the pieces themselves that give this B&B its character.

The couple painted and repaired and fixed and decorated their house after purchasing it in 1995. All the floors are white. In the parlor there are masks from Mexico and Japan, mixed with an engaging New England folk art scene painted on a plank that hangs over the fireplace. There's a TV and VCR here. Leslie has mixed interesting antique furniture with old painted or sponged tables and chairs. The spacious sitting/dining room, painted a sunny yellow with white trim and white shutters on the windows, provides a comfortable area with lots of books. The most unusual item in the house is a Japanese step *tansu,* a clever devise that served as a movable set of stairs and also as storage space, as there's a drawer under each stair.

Each of the three guest rooms is unique. Liza's Suite is the largest. It has an iron headboard and a pine bookcase and dresser. On one of the pale pink walls of the bedroom hangs a contemporary watercolor, but in the sitting room, there's another folk art painting. Alexander's Master Bedroom is painted a buttercup yellow, and it includes an iron and brass bed, a pine wardrobe, and several more folk art paintings. Everyone raves about the mattresses here, and it's no wonder. They've been imported from Sweden and are the Rolls Royce of the field. Each room has its own bath, although several are quite small. There are no telephones in the guest rooms, but guests may use one in the kitchen.

Leslie and Larry serve a full breakfast that will include homemade scones and breads and perhaps orange French toast or oatmeal/yogurt pancakes as well as fresh fruits, juices, cakes, and cookies. The meal is served in the sitting/dining room, where guests eat at a common table. The Hillels also serve tea or cider and cookies in late afternoon (after guests return from the beach), and Leslie provides a bag of biscotti or cookies for guests to enjoy on the trip home.

The house sits on 1.5 acres in the heart of the historic district of the village. Gardens surround the house, and the lawns stretching behind the house lead to two individual cottages that are rented year-round to long-term tenants.

The B&B is close to town. It's near Guild Hall and the John Drew Theatre and only three blocks from downtown. The Hillels have storage space for guests' bicycles and in-line skates. Excellent golf courses are nearby as well as tennis courts and cross-country skiing.

What's Nearby

See "What's Nearby — East Hampton," page 133.

Mill House Inn

33 North Main Street
East Hampton, NY 11937
(516) 324-9766;
fax (516) 324-9793;
e-mail: millhouse@worldnet.att.net

Innkeepers: Dan and Katherine Hartnett; manager, Robin Goldfarb

Rooms: 8, with private baths, air conditioning, TVs, telephones, radios, and hair dryers; 6 with fireplaces; 4 with whirlpool tubs; 2 with desks and 2 with robes; 1 room with wheelchair access; cribs available

On the grounds: Parking, garden

Extras: Afternoon snack; fax, voice mail, and small conference area available; beach passes, beach towels, and chairs available

Rates: $200 – $315 mid-May to October; $125 – $225 November to mid-May, including full breakfast and afternoon snacks; three-night minimum weekends June-August; four-night minimum holiday weekends

Credit cards accepted: MasterCard and Visa

Open: Year-round

Smoking: Non-smoking bed and breakfast

How to get there: From New York City take I-495 (the Long Island Expressway) to exit 70 (Manorville) and follow Route 111 south to Highway 27 (Sunrise Highway). Follow Highway 27 (which becomes the Montauk Highway) east for another 32 miles to East Hampton. At the traffic light, turn left. You will now be on Main Street; continue through town and straight ahead at the next traffic light. Approximately 150 feet beyond the light, bear left onto North Main Street, traveling left of the Hook Windmill. The B&B is the fifth house on the left.

Resting on a knoll that overlooks East Hampton's famed Hook Windmill, the Mill House Inn has been welcoming guests since 1973, but it has virtually been rebuilt since Dan and Katherine Hartnett purchased it in 1994. The enclosed front porch with its cool tile floor is inviting for afternoon relaxation (and views of the windmill). Wonderful white rockers with cutwork and spindles beg you to sit, and the exterior of the house sports a fresh layer of shingles.

The inn's decor, previously in the folksy and homey category, now has a country sophistication. The living and dining rooms have exposed beams, and the living room also has a fireplace. In the parlor there's a tall case clock that formerly belonged to an early East Hampton family.

My favorite room is the Hampton Holiday on the third floor. It's done in shades of green and plum. A Mission-style sleigh bed faces the fireplace, and in the large bath, there's a skylight over the whirlpool tub and a separate tiled shower. Emerald green carpet and French toile wallpaper decorate the Patrick Lynch Room, which has an oak dresser and an antique bed with acorn posts. The Rose Room has rose carpeting, an iron bed, a pine wardrobe, and a gas fireplace. In the sparkling new bath, there's another whirlpool tub.

Behind the B&B, there's plenty of parking space for guests' cars as well as a lawn with Adirondack chairs and tables.

Katherine used to be a chef at the Pierre Hotel in New York, and one of the first things the couple did was to install a commercial kitchen. Obviously, the breakfasts are terrific. A sample menu includes a potato, cheddar, and onion frittata as well as several breads — such as an Irish soda bread and peasant bread — and also a cranberry/apple crisp. All the baking is done right here, so guests can also look forward to chocolate chip cookies or lemon bar squares with their afternoon tea or lemonade.

The B&B is located in the North Main section of East Hampton, where several of the village's premiere restaurants, such as Nick and Toni's and Della Femina, are located. From the B&B it's also an easy walk to other restaurants and the shopping area in the heart of town. It should be noted that a train infrequently rumbles past the backyard. Those who want a quieter night's repose should ask for a room on the street side.

What's Nearby

See "What's Nearby — East Hampton," page 133.

The Pink House

26 James Lane
East Hampton, NY 11937
(516) 324-3400;
fax (516) 324-5254

Innkeeper: Ron Steinhilber
Rooms: 6, including 1 suite, all with private baths, air conditioning, TVs, telephones, hair dryers, and robes; 1 with a patio, and 1 with a whirlpool tub; 1 room with wheelchair access
On the grounds: Parking, swimming pool, gardens
Extras: Chocolates at turndown; fax available; bar with beer and wine; three dogs named Katie, Rosey, and Ginger; beach passes and beach towels available
Rates: $154 – $325, including full breakfast; three - five-night minimum Memorial Day - Labor Day; two-night minimum weekends rest of year
Credit cards accepted: American Express, Diners Club, Discover, MasterCard, Visa
Open: Year-round
Smoking: Non-smoking bed and breakfast
How to get there: From New York City take I-495 (the Long Island Expressway) to exit 70 (Manorville) and follow Route 111 south to Highway 27 (Sunrise Highway). Follow Highway 27 (which becomes the Montauk Highway) east for another 32 miles to East Hampton. At the traffic light turn left and drive past Town Pond, which will be on the right. Turn right at the first street, and the B&B's driveway will be directly ahead across James Lane.

Yes, it is pink — not a shocking bright pink, but a subdued cotton candy pink — pretty enough to eat. It's trimmed in white, and a flock of white wicker chairs rest on the front porch interspersed with planters of pink geraniums, hydrangeas, and impatiens. The entire effect is charming. Ron Steinhilber, an architect and builder, renovated the 1850s house in 1990 and opened it to guests. It's located on 1.5 acres on a quiet side street across from Town Pond and beside the spacious lawns of St. Luke's Episco-

pal Church. But even if this didn't assure its quiet repose, the tall privet hedge and fences surrounding it give it a feeling of utter seclusion and privacy.

The living room and dining room are low key and Country Hamptons in feel, but spiced with some unusual pieces. You may spend hours studying the lively watercolors painted by Walter Steinhilber, Ron's grandfather. He was a peripatetic traveler who chronicled his journeys in his paintings, capturing wonderful details that make each one come to life. Also note the lamp in the living room made from a street lamp Ron rescued when Brooklyn's Myrtle Avenue El was being demolished. Both the living room and dining room have fireplaces.

There are six guest rooms — four on the second floor, a suite on the top floor, and a room on the ground floor. All have private baths. The roomy Blue Room has a pencil-post pine canopy bed and a window seat offering views of Town Pond. The bath has a marble shower. The Garden Room, which is located on the first floor, has a four-poster bed and its own private patio with pots of flowers — a welcome hideaway. The most-requested room, however, is the spacious Elk Room on the top floor. It has a distinctive look that includes a moose head and cowboy hats on the wall, a TV and VCR, and a bath with a whirlpool tub.

Surrounded by a tall hedge and a wide slate terrace, the pool in the backyard — with its abundance of chaise lounges, chairs, and umbrella-shaded tables—is a popular retreat. Frosty cold soft drinks, beer, and wine stock a refrigerator, and guests frequently relax here after a day at the beach, spent shopping in town, or at the Hamptons Classic Horse Show.

Ron prepares a full breakfast every morning, which he serves in the dining room in cool weather or on the back porch when it's warm. If guests are lucky, he may prepare his popular batter-dipped sourdough French toast. Homemade granola will always be available, and if it isn't a French toast day, he may prepare Belgian waffles or a frittata.

The B&B is within a block's walk of Mulford Farm, Home Sweet Home, and fine restaurants. The East Hampton Library is also nearby. Bicycling, in-line skating, golfing, and tennis are all popular and nearby.

What's Nearby

See "What's Nearby — East Hampton," page 133.

The Plover's Nest

199 Main Street
East Hampton, NY 11937
telephone/fax (516) 329-1120

Innkeepers: Fred and Adele Filasky
Rooms: 4, including 1 suite, all with private baths, air conditioning, and TVs; 3 with desks; 2 with fireplaces
On the grounds: Gardens, parking
Extras: Wine and hors d'oeuvres in the afternoon; chocolates at turndown; bicycles and helmets available, as well as beach passes and towels; a boxer named Baran and a dachshund named Ginger in owner's quarters
Rates: $225 – $250 Memorial Day to Labor Day, $135–$200 rest of year, including Continental breakfast; two-night minimum weekends Memorial Day to Labor Day; three-night minimum holiday weekends
Credit cards accepted: American Express, MasterCard, Visa
Open: Year-round
Smoking: Permitted outside only
How to get there: From New York City take I-495 (the Long Island Expressway) to exit 70 (Manorville) and follow Route 111 south to Highway 27 (Sunrise Highway). Follow Highway 27 (which becomes the Montauk Highway) east for another 32 miles to East Hampton. At the traffic light, turn left. You will now be on Main Street; continue to #199, which will be on the left.

Fred and Adele Filasky have been renovating old houses for some time, so when they bought this beauty, they were prepared to make the improvements it needed. Thankfully, they retained its interesting character in the process. Although the weathered shingle house was built in 1774, its foundation dates to 1650, merely two years after East Hampton was first settled.

It's shielded from Main Street by a tall privet hedge.

The house still feels and looks as it might have during Colonial times. It has low, hand-hewn beamed ceilings and a multitude of fireplaces. In the living room, where hors d'oeuvres and wine are set out every afternoon, there are raspberry-colored walls and a wooden fireplace mantel with a marble face. Sisal rugs cover the random-width pine floors. Down-filled chairs covered in red damask and a down-filled sofa in a bright chintz are so comfortable you may snuggle in for the evening. The Filaskys have thoughtfully outfitted a guest office with a desk, telephone (there are none in the rooms), and a fax for those who need these items.

For travelers who are tired of the fuss and frills of many B&Bs, this is the antidote. The guest rooms are charming but uncluttered. They have wide-plank pine floors covered with sisal or Oriental rugs and simple, well-designed furniture. The Blue Room has its own fireplace and a sleigh bed. The Green Room has a four-poster bed and another fireplace. My favorite, however, is the Raspberry Room, which has a beamed ceiling, an antique white iron and brass bed, and green wicker furniture. It's cozy and utterly romantic. All the baths are fresh and sparkling with new tilework, and all the baths are in the guest rooms except the one for the Blue Room, which is in the hall.

Breakfast is served buffet style in the gra-cious dining room, and there's a brick fireplace here as well. There's an English-style wallpaper in yellow and blue on the walls and a blue wash on the paneling. Guests are seated at individual tables before the fireplace in winter. In nice weather, guests often choose to eat on the brick patio, which is under the canopy of a magnificent old beech tree. Dutch doors lead there from a little anteroom just off the dining room. The B&B is on an acre of land, and beyond the patio and parking area, there's a private, lush lawn enclosed by forsythia. Here wait Adirondack chairs and an iron table that provide a restful place for relaxing with a good book.

Breakfast will consist of homemade fruit scones, muffins, or perhaps hot cross buns as well as fresh fruit, juices, berries in season, and cereals.

The B&B is located across from Town Pond and near fine restaurants. Mulford Farm, Home Sweet Home, Guild Hall, and the John Drew Theatre are nearby. There are bicycles and helmets for guests to use.

What's Nearby

See "What's Nearby — East Hampton," page 133.

Innkeeper: Jacqueline Smith
Rooms: 3, all with private baths; 2 with air conditioning; telephone available
On the grounds: Gardens, parking
Rates: $75 – $105, including full breakfast; two-night minimum weekends from May to October
Credit cards accepted: MasterCard & Visa
Open: February to December
Smoking: Non-smoking bed and breakfast
How to get there: From New York City take I-495 (the Long Island Expressway) to exit 73, where it terminates. Follow County Road 58 east to Route 25, then follow Route 25 for about 30 miles to Greenport. Follow Route 25 (which becomes Front Street) through the village. At the traffic light turn left onto Main Street and continue for another .5 mile. Fordham House will be on the left.

Fordham House Bed & Breakfast

817 Main Street
Greenport, NY 11944
(516) 477-8419

Are you the sort who likes to sit on the front porch of a Victorian house and close your eyes to imagine you hear horses approaching or the bells of sailing ships in the harbor? If so, this is your B&B. Time has been kind to Greenport. It has changed insignificantly since its Victorian days. Victorian reveries seem to come alive on the porch of Fordham House.

When both New York and Boston were adolescents (in the mid-1700s and 1800s), steamers regularly made overnight voyages from Greenport to Boston, shortening the journey from New York by days and eliminating travel obstacles. George Washington took this route in 1757 on his way from Virginia to Massachusetts to secure a com-

mission to lead the Virginia troops in battle against the British. By avoiding the overland passage through Connecticut, he bypassed eighteen rivers and streams during a blustery winter. Greenport, then, was not only an important transportation hub, but also a leader in shipping and shipbuilding. Sailing ships from around the world brought their cargo to Greenport.

The pristine white exterior of this 1901 Victorian inn has a combination of fishscale shingles and clapboards on its top level. It sits in a residential neighborhood on upper Main Street, flanked by other gracious houses. Sitting well back from the street on spacious lawns, it is fronted by a wide wraparound porch filled with wicker chairs, tables, and a hanging porch swing for two. Behind the B&B, there are pretty flower gardens and park benches.

The inside includes a delightful array of darkly stained American white oak fretwork in a medley of balls, arches, and spindles that laces over the doorways, and there are elaborate stained-glass windows that cast shafts of red, blue, and green reflections across the oak floors. Built by shipbuilder H. Fletcher Fordham, the house is a showcase of turn-of-the-century construction. A painted wooden mantel surmounts the living room fireplace (alas it doesn't work), and a bay window floods the living room with light. A pretty sunroom is home to a profusion of happy plants who bask in the sun that streams through the tall windows.

Jacqueline Smith has lived on the East End for more than twenty years, and she renovated this house into a B&B in 1994. Each of the guest rooms has been furnished with fine antiques, including one with a four-poster bed. Another room has a pine queen-sized bed and an Eastlake rocker. All baths ingeniously combine modern comfort with an old-world charm that includes pedestal sinks, hexagonal-tile floors, pull-chain toilets, stained-glass windows, and wainscotted walls. Each of the baths has a spacious shower.

Breakfast is served in the dining room on a lace-covered table. Jacqueline uses her collection of English dishes, Depression glass, and silver. Fresh flowers decorate the table. The full breakfast may include French toast with sausage or blueberry pancakes with Canadian bacon as well as fresh fruit with yogurt, juice, and coffee.

What's Nearby

The North Fork of Long Island is noted for its fine wines and expansive farms. You can visit sixteen wineries along the narrow strip of land that stretches from Aquebogue to Southold. Greenport has several interesting museums, including the East End Seaport Maritime Museum, the Railroad Museum of Long Island, Stirling Historical Society Museum, and the Regina Maris, a three-masted, square-rigged barkentine, built in 1908. In addition, you may visit Orient Beach State Park, located at the end of the North Fork on a lovely 4-mile stretch of rather pebbly beach.

Bykenhulle House 1841 B&B

21 Bykenhulle Road
Hopewell Junction, NY 12533
(914) 221-4182; fax (914) 227-6805

Innkeepers: Bill and Florence Beausoleil
Rooms: 5, all with private baths, air conditioning, TVs, telephones, and radios; 2 with fireplaces; 2 with whirlpool tubs,
On the grounds: Swimming pool, parking, gazebo
Extras: Turndown with chocolates; fax, dataport, CD player, coffee maker, iron and ironing board available
Rates: $125 – $145, including full breakfast; two-night minimum in October
Credit cards accepted: American Express, Discover, MasterCard, Visa
Open: Year-round
Smoking: Non-smoking bed and breakfast
How to get there: From New York City take the Henry Hudson Parkway north to the Saw Mill River Parkway. Follow the Saw Mill River Parkway north to the Taconic Parkway. Traveling north on the Taconic, go 3 miles past I-84 and turn right onto Carpenter Road (at the Muscoot Restaurant). Take the first left, which is Bykenhulle Road. The B&B is on the left in .5 mile.

This handsome 1841 Georgian manor house sits on a quiet country road behind a brick wall, its spacious grounds drifting away into fields on either side. Built by Peter Adriance, a Dutch silversmith, it's been home to Bill and Florence Beausoleil since 1972. (What a friendly name for innkeepers! It means "beautiful sun" in French.) Bill is an engineer with IBM, and he explains that they "raised six children in a seven-bath, seven-bedroom, seven-fireplace home."

But in 1987 they put the house to work by converting it to a bed and breakfast.

The house was a gem when the Beausoleils bought it. The fabric on the walls of the dining room, for example, dates to the 1920s. The Beausoleils traveled extensively in Europe with IBM before settling here, and the fine antique furnishings and Persian rugs were acquired during their sojourns. Every piece is in pristine condition, as is the house. There are a 1790s chest in the hall and a magnificent pier mirror. Florence collects Heisey glass, and it's displayed on shelves in the hallway. To the left of the entrance, twin parlors have oak floors topped with Persian rugs, handsome fireplaces, and sparkling crystal chandeliers. The walls are painted a soft pink, and the woodwork a bright white. Beyond is a wicker-filled sun room overlooking the lovely flower garden, a gazebo, and a swimming pool. A glassed-in pavilion, with French doors leading to a brick terrace, was added in 1996 to accommodate wedding receptions, parties, and small meetings.

Upstairs, the guest rooms contain additional fine antiques; several have four-poster or canopy beds. Valerie's Room is lovely, with a four-poster bed, woodburning fireplace, and a pretty bath. Two suites on the third floor, the Raspberry Room and the Almond Room, are extraordinarily spacious, with window seats beneath bay windows overlooking the grounds. Each has a two-person Jacuzzi in a private nook in the room as well as an impressive full bath.

Florence has attended the nearby Culinary Institute of America, and her breakfasts reflect the accomplishments of a gourmet cook. We had freshly baked muffins one morning, followed by French toast crusted with crushed corn flakes and then sautéed, accompanied by maple syrup and sausage. The entrée might also include apple sugar babies (a combination of a pancake and a popover) or apple crêpes laced with golden raisins and slivered almonds. Breakfast is served on fine china in the formal dining room, where the innkeepers liberally share information about the area.

The inn, which is ideally located for touring the Hudson River Valley, is on 6 acres. There are several excellent restaurants nearby, and West Point is just across the river. Hyde Park is about 10 miles north, and Boscobel Restoration, one of the finest estate restorations in the area, is just to the south. But perhaps you'll decide to stay right here, resting and relaxing and letting Bill and Florence pamper you into forgetting there's another world beyond the gentle tempo of their bed and breakfast. This is an inn for lazing by the pool or cozily sitting before a fireplace and dreaming of never returning to a faster-paced life.

What's Nearby

Hopewell Junction is near Poughkeepsie, the home of Vassar College. There are art exhibitions, concerts, lectures, and seminars year-round. Poughkeepsie is also the home of Bardavon 1869 Opera House, a National Historic Landmark and New York's oldest opera house. Events and tours take place from September through July.

The Lamplight Inn Bed & Breakfast

231 Lake Avenue
(mailing address: P.O. Box 70)
Lake Luzerne, NY 12846
(800) 262-4668 or (518) 696-5294;
e-mail: lampinfo@adirondack.net

Innkeepers: Linda and Gene Merlino
Rooms: 17, all with private baths, air conditioning, telephones, and radios; 12 with fireplaces; 7 with TVs; 4 with whirlpool tubs and private porches
On the grounds: Parking; walking and hiking trails, cross-country ski trails; gardens
Extras: Fax available; a husky/shepherd named Toto
Rates: $89 – $165, including full breakfast; two-night minimum weekends; three-night minimum holidays and special event weekends
Credit cards accepted: American Express, Master-Card, Visa
Open: Year-round except December 24th and 25th
Smoking: Non-smoking bed and breakfast
How to get there: From I-87, take exit 21 (Lake Luzerne/Lake George). At the end of the ramp bear left onto Route 9N south. Follow 9N for 10 miles. The B&B will be on the right.

It sits serenely on a hill just outside the small village of Lake Luzerne, and its daffodil yellow clapboard facade with white trim is as welcoming as a sunny smile. But so are the friendly innkeepers. Warm and outgoing, Linda and Gene Merlino are the ideal innkeepers. Gene was the manager of a textile engraving plant for twenty years, and Linda was a textile artist and fashion illustrator. They bought the 1890s Victorian in 1985 and immediately began the creation of their bed and breakfast by painstakingly renovating the dilapidated house. And they just never stopped. In 1996, Gene built a new car-riage house that has five luxury rooms with fire-places, private porches, and whirlpool tubs. The new carriage house allows the bed and breakfast to appeal to two very different types of guests.

For those who enjoy Victoriana, the main inn is literally stuffed with Victorian furniture and decorative items, all embraced by warm chestnut and oak paneling and floors. There are 12-foot beamed ceilings and fireplaces in both the great room and in one of the parlors. Several of Linda's collections are on view here. Her doll collection, which includes a number of Madame Alexander dolls, is located in cabinets and on tables throughout the entrance and the huge 20- x 40-foot great room as well as in the three large sitting areas. A large gift shop offers soaps, dolls, stationery, and gift items for sale. A small service bar is nearby where guests may purchase wine and beer. There's also a wraparound porch with porch swings, rockers, and wicker furniture.

The guest rooms in the main inn are as Victorian as the common rooms. They have canopy or white iron beds, oak dressers, and small private baths. Victorian lamps, quilts on the beds, Victorian pillows, lace curtains at the windows — all add to the Victorian ambience. The rooms here tend to be small, and the baths could use some upgrading.

For guests who prefer more privacy and a less fussy Victorian decor, the Brookside Cottage, which was originally the caretaker's cottage, and the new Carriage House offer modern rooms furnished with wicker, and all have gas fireplaces. The Carriage House also has whirlpool tubs in the rooms and private decks surrounded by trees. They are crisp, clean, and spacious rather than luxurious.

Breakfast is served in the large oak-floored dining room, which has a sunny exposure. Linda decorates the room seasonally with abundant plants and fresh flowers. Guests are seated at individual glass-topped tables, where they are presented with a daily menu. They help themselves to a buffet of fresh fruit, breads, coffee cakes, juices, and Linda's homemade granola. Gene then prepares the main course. It may consist of an omelette — perhaps with cheddar, Swiss, and American cheese or with peppers, onion, ham, and cheese. On the side, he serves spicy home-fried potatoes and bacon or sausage.

The bed and breakfast is located on 10 acres in the Adirondack Mountains, 10 miles from Lake George and 18 miles from Saratoga Springs. The village of Lake Luzerne is tucked between the Hudson River and pretty Lake Luzerne. Scenic Rockwell Falls, the narrowest point on the Hudson, is located in town, and the lake has been an Adirondack summer resort since the nineteenth century. In summer, there's boating, swimming, fishing, and golfing; in winter, there's plenty of snowmobiling and cross-country skiing. Summer concerts, museums to explore, and a championship rodeo that attracts rodeo stars and country singers offer alternative activities.

What's Nearby

Lake Luzerne is located on the southern fringe of the Adirondack State Park. You can visit the Frances Garner Kinnear Museum of Local History, the Pulp Mill Museum, and the School House Museum to see interesting exhibits. At Bennett's Riding Stables you can take guided trail rides for varying lengths of time. Visitors also can boat, golf, and cross-country ski nearby.

The Mill at Bloomvale Falls

Route 82
Millbrook, NY 12545
(mailing address: P.O. Box 155A,
Salt Point, New York 12578)
(914) 266-4234; fax (914) 266-4061

Innkeepers: Frieda Gattine and Don Salvato
Rooms: 4, sharing 2¹/2 baths; 1 with woodstove; portable telephones available
On the grounds: Parking, swimming hole, suspension bridge over falls, gazebo; 3 sheep, chickens, ducks
Extras: Tea, coffee, or cold drinks plus cookies or pastry in afternoon; border collie named Muffy, dachshund named Bruno, Persian cat named Sugar; guest pets by prior permission
Rates: $95 – $125, including full breakfast and afternoon refreshments; two-night minimum weekends Memorial Day through October and on holiday weekends
Credit cards accepted: American Express, MasterCard, Visa
Open: Year-round
Smoking: Smoking outside only preferred.
How to get there: From New York City take the Henry Hudson Parkway north to the Saw Mill River Parkway and then go north to the Taconic Parkway. Follow the Taconic Parkway north to the Route 44 (Millbrook/Poughkeepsie) exit. Travel east on Route 44 for 1 mile. Turn left onto Route 82 north and go for 1.33 miles. You will see the B&B sign on the right at the intersection of Route 13.

This eclectic and unusual B&B may not suit everyone. For those who require a private bathroom, for example, this B&B will not do at all. For travelers looking for an unparalleled setting in an unusual building, however, amid a wide array of original art, few B&Bs can match it.

Don Salvato, an artist with an impressive talent, has owned the picturesque stone cider mill for some thirty years. It's said that applejack was produced here during Prohibition. The mill sits on 24 acres beside a tumultuous waterfall on Wappingers Creek that crashes from a rocky ledge. Another rushing torrent, the remains of the original mill raceway, continues to cut a swath that seems to course directly beneath the building. Ghostly stone walls from a much earlier mill enclose a pretty courtyard and fountain. A pathway leads across a suspended bridge to the opposite banks, where a gazebo made from locust branches awaits you. Just below, guests can splash in the pool at the base of the falls. Another path leads even higher along the cliff to Don's new multilevel studio.

To reach the entrance of the B&B, we climbed

a series of stairs to a mid-level point, where a covered rock patio leads to a doorway. Except for the cars parked below, the mill appeared to be deserted. Inside, however, the old building is alive. Stone walls glow with art that ranges from Picasso-like abstracts to large bold florals to realistic contemporary pieces. A grand piano waits in the great room for players, a multitude of books fill shelves, and comfortable sofas and chairs are oriented toward the stone fireplace and a view of the falls. There are corner cupboards and hutches holding brightly colored pottery and an abundance of collectibles. Healthy plants abound. The house telephone is located just off the great room.

The guest rooms are located up a steep stairway. Don is also an architect, and the rooms are cozy and snug. Several have impressive views of the falls, and the soft hiss of the water is sure to ensure a deep sleep. The Garden Room is in the most private setting off an upstairs terrace. It has an iron bed and its own woodstove. My favorite, however, is the Red Room, so named for the brilliant acrylic painting featuring a stand of red poppies that graces one stone wall. The room has a view of the falls, warm oak floors covered with hooked rugs, and an 1850s rope bed. The B&B has one common bath off the hallway, another in Don and Frieda's room (which guests are free to use), and a half bath downstairs.

Frieda, an ex-banker, prepares a full breakfast daily. A typical menu will include fresh fruit and juices, homemade muffins and breads, an entrée such as fruit pancakes or a quiche or frittata, and a dessert such as a cobbler or a fruit parfait.

Wappinger's Creek is noted for its trout fly-fishing, and many guests of the B&B bring their fishing poles. Should they forget, Don does have a few extras. And should they land a catch, Don may pan fry it that night or perhaps smoke it. There are hiking and walking trails throughout the property. Millbrook is a charming, elegant village of boutiques, restaurants, and antiques shops. It is in the heart of New York's horse country, and several nearby facilities offer horseback riding.

What's Nearby

Millbrook Vineyards and Winery, which makes excellent wines, is worth a visit. It has a modern tasting room on a hilltop with lovely views of the valley below. Cascade Mountain Winery in nearby Amenia also makes excellent wines. It has a restaurant where splendid meals are served either inside by a woodstove or outside on a deck, depending on the weather. The Institute of Ecosystem Studies at Mary Flager Cary Arboretum includes nature trails, perennial gardens, and an outdoor science center, while Innisfree Garden is a lovely but little-known garden with a lake and natural, uncontrived plantings. (See also Rhinebeck.)

Bed & Breakfast on the Park

113 Prospect Park West
New York (Brooklyn), NY 11215
(718) 499-6115; fax (718) 499-1385

Innkeepers: Liana and Jonna Paolella
Rooms: 9, including 4 suites, 7 with private baths, all with air conditioning, TVs, telephones, mini-refrigerators, coffee makers, hair dryers, irons, and ironing boards; 2 with fireplaces; 1 with two-tiered deck
On the grounds: Garden
Extras: Cookies beside bed; Silva, a shepherd, and Nani-Nani, a parakeet, on premises; fresh flowers in rooms
Rates: $100 – $375, including full breakfast; two-night minimum
Credit cards accepted: MasterCard and Visa
Open: Year-round
Smoking: Non-smoking bed and breakfast
How to get there: From Manhattan, take the Brooklyn Bridge. After crossing the bridge, turn left onto Atlantic Avenue at the Mobil Station. Turn right onto 4th Avenue and continue for about 1 mile. At 5th Street, turn left and continue to its end. Turn right onto Prospect Park West. Go 2 blocks to #113.

Liana Paolella was an antiques dealer when she purchased this grand limestone townhouse in 1985. It needed a tremendous amount of work, but she knew what to do. Stripping the paneled walls, doors, stair railings, detailed fretwork, and window frames, she converted a Victorian derelict into a rare emerald. She then filled it with antiques that might have been used when George Brickelmeier, a liquor merchant, built the house in 1892.

There are fringed sofas and chairs and an elaborate floor lamp with a beaded fringe in one parlor. In the front parlor, there are massive oil paintings (one that is exceptionally fine was painted by Liana's step-father, William Earl Singer) and a Pairpoint lamp (it has a blown-glass shade that is reverse-painted with poppies). The rich African mahogany woodwork stands out against the frothy lace curtains that shield the windows from the street. More paintings line the stairway, and the oak-lined foyer hides a lovely powder room behind paneling.

The guest rooms are elegant and refined, just as Victorian boudoirs should be. My favorite is the Park Suite, a jewel that overlooks Prospect Park. It has a bed with an antique Brussels lace crown canopy that cascades down the wall and a crocheted coverlet. Handmade Brussels lace curtains hang at the windows, and there's a spectacular stained-glass window. The dressing room is fully paneled with bird's eye maple and includes mirrored doors and even a built-in vanity. The Lady Liberty Suite has a canopy bed and ornately carved marble-topped dressers as well as French doors leading to a private deck. Another set of stairs leads even higher to a rooftop perch offering a view that stretches from the Empire State Building to Lady Liberty herself.

Breakfast is served in the most Victorian room in the house. The dining room has a bay of stained-glass windows defined by Victorian fretwork, and the walls are lined with china cabinets filled with elaborate Victorian silver and china. Liana sets her table with a lace tablecloth, sterling silver flatware, cut glass crystal, and gold-rimmed china. Silver teapots and other serving pieces grace the table. The setting is as Victorian as a scene from a Merchant and Ivory period movie. I always feel as if I should be attired in a long, flowing dress. Breakfast will include fresh fruits and cereals, homemade muffins and breads, and an entrée such as German pancakes or a frittata with a sweet potato crust.

Liana and Jonna, her daughter and assistant innkeeper, have just created two more fantastic suites in a nearby townhouse as well. The Palazzo Venezia Suite is an elaborate fantasyland of half-paneled walls with dreamy murals above, elaborate crystal chandeliers, and elegant fireplaces. These new suites are the ultimate in romantic retreats.

Park Slope is a lovely section of Brooklyn. Tree-lined streets are faced with elegant townhouses and brownstones, and there are fine restaurants nearby.

What's Nearby

Directly across the street from the B&B is Brooklyn's crown jewel, the 526-acre Prospect Park, created by Frederick Law Olmsted and Calvert Vaux, designers of Manhattan's Central Park. You can ride on a restored carousel, visit the excellent Brooklyn Museum, or walk through the Brooklyn Botanic Gardens —all within its confines. Just around the corner, the Brooklyn Academy of Music offers a potpourri of music, dance, and theater year-round.

The Inn at Irving Place
54 Irving Place
New York (Manhattan), NY 10003
(800) 685-1447 or (212) 533-4000;
fax (212) 533-4611;
e-mail: irving56@aol.com
website: http://www.slh.com

Innkeeper: John Simoudis; proprietor, Naomi Blumenthal
Rooms: 12, all with private baths, air conditioning, TVs, VCRs, telephones with dataports, desks, stereos, mini-refrigerators, CD players, and non-functioning fireplaces
Extras: Afternoon tea, bar service available (there is a charge); fresh flowers in the rooms; fax, laptop computers with internet access, cellular telephones, and pagers available
Rates: $300 – $400, including Continental breakfast
Credit cards accepted: American Express, Diners Club, MasterCard, Visa
Open: Year-round
Smoking: Smoking permitted; some rooms designated non-smoking
How to get there: Irving Place is an extension of Lexington Avenue, separated from it by Gramercy Park. The B&B is between East 17th and East 18th Streets.

Like a page from *Time and Again,* The Inn at Irving Place seems to have emerged from an earlier era. It's possible to imagine Elsie de Wolfe arriving at her house across the street by horse-drawn carriage to prepare for one of her salons or O. Henry scurrying along in the chilly winter air to reach the warm, convivial atmosphere of Pete's Tavern to finish writing "Gift of the Magi." The street has changed little over the years, and the two townhouses where this sumptuous bed and breakfast are located retain their original stoops, wrought-iron balustrades, and elegant entrances. The inn is so discreet that there isn't even a sign outside announcing its presence.

An earlier time pervades the inside as well. Imagine walking up the stairs, pressing the bell, and then being escorted into a gracious parlor filled with antique sofas, chairs, and tables. A fire glows in the fireplace; oil paintings hang on the walls. There is no reception desk or visible sign that this is not someone's home. John Simoudis, the innkeeper, warmly greets you and offers you tea. You relax, knowing you're in good hands, and feeling as if you've left the brisk pace of New York far behind.

The guest rooms, which are named for well-known Victorian personalities, are as refined and urbane as the parlor. Although each is furnished with fine antiques, they are all decorated with a restrained dignity that is the antithesis of the fussy Victorian homes of its age. Yet we're sure Elsie would smile approvingly. The room named for Stanford White (who certainly trod this street) has a carved walnut bed, elaborate ceiling moldings, an inlaid floor, and a magnificent armoire. Washington Irving's room has a bed and matching armoire inlaid with a musical instrument motif, while the O. Henry room has a brass bed and a carved armoire. Each of the rooms has a private bath with a black and white tile floor, pedestal sink, and a tub or shower (or sometimes both).

The parlor in one of the townhouses is now Lady Mendl's Tearoom (née Elsie de Wolfe). Afternoon tea, evening drinks, and Continental breakfast are served here. Reminiscent of a French salon de thé, the tiny boîte is furnished with Victorian cast-iron tables and colorful chairs. Wooden shutters cover the windows. Although there is a restaurant on the ground floor, it is under different management and not connected to the B&B.

A Continental breakfast of fresh fruit, freshly baked pastries, and coffee is either delivered to guests' rooms, or guests may eat in Lady Mendl's Tearoom or in the Parlor.

Irving Place is the business street of the Gramercy Park neighborhood. The park, from which the neighborhood takes its name, is encircled by a high wrought-iron fence. Keys for the gate are available to full-time residents only. Pete's Tavern is still as busy today as in O. Henry's time, and it even looks the same. There are numerous other restaurants on the block as well as shops and boutiques.

What's Nearby

The Inn at Irving Place is in the Gramercy Park section of Manhattan, close to Greenwich Village, Soho, and Tribeca. The Theodore Roosevelt Birthplace, a rebuilt townhouse that duplicates the home in which the president was born, is nearby, as is the Pierpont Morgan Library, an interesting library and museum in an elegant and historic building.

Inn New York City
266 West 71st Street
New York (Manhattan), NY 10023
(212) 580-1900; fax (212) 580-4437

Innkeepers: Ruth Mensch and Elyn Mensch
Rooms: 4 suites, all with private baths, air conditioning, TVs, VCRs, telephones with dataports, CD players, kitchens; 2 with fireplaces and 2 with whirlpool tubs; 1 with a balcony.
Extras: Chocolates by the bed; soft drinks, bottled waters, wine, quiche, cheeses in refrigerators; basket of snacks, candy bars, fresh fruit, port, and sherry in hallway
Rates: $225 – $395, including Continental breakfast; two-night minimum
Credit cards accepted: American Express, MasterCard, Visa
Open: Year-round
Smoking: Non-smoking bed and breakfast
How to get there: The B&B is located on the south side of West 71st Street, between Broadway and West End Avenue.

When a guest calls the innkeeper in the morning and says "Ah, this was a night in Paradise," the innkeeper knows she's doing things right.

Located on a charming side street of townhouses and brownstones on Manhattan's Upper West side, Inn New York City is a unique treasure. It's a little bit of "country" in the heart of the city — an easy walk from Lincoln Center, Central Park, and Riverside Park, and near the upscale Upper Broadway shopping area. Ruth Mensch and her daughter Elyn converted this townhouse to a four-suite bed and breakfast in 1989, and it's seldom had a vacancy ever since.

The four-story brownstone, which has an ornate wrought-iron door flanked by sandstone pillars, has such an archetypal New York ambience that guests feel right at home — so much so, in fact, that some make it their home-away-from-home for extended visits. Broadway and Lincoln Center performers have found the ambience and the location ideal.

The vestibule and front parlor of the B&B are charming. They have high ceilings, inlaid hardwood floors, elaborate moldings, carved cabinetry, and crystal chandeliers — all evocative of the nineteenth century. Guests often invite friends over to have a drink in the parlor before departing for a local restaurant or a concert at Lincoln Center.

The suites are spacious and alluring. Ruth is a genius at salvaging discarded architectural treasures and turning them into striking pieces of furniture. Her creativity is found throughout the B&B. The Spa Suite, for example, on the top floor, has a king-sized bed with a headboard set into an antique chestnut armoire. The sybaritic bath, however, is the pièce de résistance. It has a double Jacuzzi on a platform in the center of the room, a fireplace with a carved mantel, an old barber chair, a cast-iron foot bath, a Victorian dresser with a sink set into its marble top, a sauna for two, and a glassed-in shower.

The Parlor Suite has an 18-foot living room with a 12-foot-high ceiling. The foyer has a stained-glass ceiling, and there's a Baldwin grand piano in the living room. The bedroom has a balcony, a fireplace, and a queen-sized bed with a headboard containing cabinets with stained-glass doors. Every room has a small kitchen and such personal touches as private libraries, fresh flowers, and fluffy robes.

Every evening after guests leave for dinner, Ruth or Elyn stock their refrigerators with morning food, such as freshly baked muffins or other treats, coffee, fruit, and juice. A copy of *The New York Times* is left at the door every morning.

The B&B is close to Lincoln Center and Riverside Park. It's an easy walk to Central Park, to the Upper Broadway shopping area, and to numerous fine restaurants.

What's Nearby

Lincoln Center for the Performing Arts— home of the New York Philharmonic, the Metropolitan Opera, the American Ballet Theatre, the New York City Opera, Juilliard School, and so much more—is within walking distance of this B&B. Riverside Park is virtually across the street, and the Museum of Natural History and the New York Historical Society are also nearby.

Innkeeper: Chuck Atkins
Rooms: 4, 2 with private baths, 2 with shared baths; all with air conditioning; 2 with telephones and 2 with robes
On the grounds: Parking, swimming pool, gardens
Extras: Three Norwich terriers named Pip, Max, and Clara
Rates: $110 – $250, including full breakfast; two-night minimum weekends
Credit cards accepted: None
Open: Year-round
Smoking: Non-smoking bed and breakfast
How to get there: From New York City, take the Hudson River Parkway north to the Saw Mill River Parkway north and then the Taconic Parkway north. Take the exit marked Red Hook/Pine Plains/Route 199 and follow Route 199 west. At the traffic light, continue straight ahead onto Route 308 west. Continue on Route 308 for approximately 4 miles to the sign for the B&B, which will be on the left. The carriage house is about a quarter mile down the driveway.

Stanford White's Carriage House

252 Route 308
Rhinebeck, NY 12572
telephone/fax (914) 876-7257

In a secluded glen far from even a hint of traffic noise, this brick carriage house with its peaked dormers offers a classic retreat. Yes, Stanford White did design the carriage house. It was part of an estate he designed for Philip Schuyler (scion of an old New York Dutch family) in 1892 called The Grove. Among other things, Schuyler was the brother-in-law of Alexander Hamilton. The grand proportions of the building are typical of White's work. Restored in 1995 by innkeeper Chuck Atkins, a former TV executive, the inn is surrounded by 6 acres of manicured lawns and formal gardens. An extravagant floral display ranges from daffodils and tulips in spring to lilies, clematis, and potted geraniums in the summer. The rear garden is ablaze in white flowers throughout the growing season. Beyond, there's a secluded swimming pool surrounded by a terrace and enclosed by a brick wall.

The impressive 1,000-square-foot living room is smartly furnished with down-filled sofas and chairs, all in pristine white. It's ultra-sophisticated. A fireplace warms one end, oak floors gleam with polish, and a wall of windows and French doors bathe the room in light.

The guest rooms, all on the second floor, are equally svelte. They are all white from the walls to the painted floors and the white down-filled duvets covering the beds. Even the luxe baths are done in white marble. Rooms A and B share a hall bath; the bath for Room C is also across the hall. It's the Studio that's the pièce de résistance, however. This grand suite (also in white) has a cathedral ceiling and contains a palatial living room, a full kitchen, and a luxurious bedroom overseen by a giant fan window offering views of the gardens and pool. This is the ultimate romantic retreat — the perfect honeymoon hideaway. From this perch you can look out on the lawns to see deer grazing at dusk and dawn.

Breakfast is served in a pretty kitchen that's embellished with colorful tiles or, in the summer, outside on the terrace. It might include blueberry pancakes or scrambled eggs with Canadian bacon, fresh muffins, and seasonal fruit.

A concert grand piano in the living room entices amateur and professional performers, but soothing classical music plays throughout the day. There are board games and books for enjoyment as well.

There are a myriad of museum houses to visit near Rhinebeck. The very Victorian Wilderstein is nearby, as is Montgomery Place, a former Livingston estate.

What's Nearby — Rhinebeck

The Hudson River Valley is a treasure trove of places to see and things to do. Near Rhinebeck you can visit a number of historic homes: Clermont, Vanderbilt Mansion, Mills Mansion, and Wilderstein as well as the Roosevelt home and library in Hyde Park. The Culinary Institute of America also is located in Hyde Park. Visit the kitchens in this training ground for America's finest chefs and then stay to sample the food in one of the on-site restaurants (but be sure to make reservations because they are often booked months in advance). (See also Millbrook and Stanfordville.)

Veranda House Bed & Breakfast

82 Montgomery Street
Rhinebeck, NY 12572
(914) 876-4133; fax (914) 876-6218;
e-mail: veranda@pojonews.infi.net
website: http://www.pojonews.com/veranda

Innkeepers: Linda and Ward Stanley
Rooms: 4, all with private baths and air conditioning
On the grounds: Parking
Extras: Decanter of sherry on sideboard in dining room; chocolates in room; Sat. night reception with appetizers and non-alcoholic beverages; one calico cat named Katerine in owner's quarters only
Rates: $85 – $120, including full breakfast; two-night minimum weekends May - October
Credit cards accepted: None
Open: Year-round
Smoking: Non-smoking bed and breakfast
How to get there: From New York City, take the Hudson River Parkway north to the Saw Mill River Parkway north and then follow the Taconic Parkway north. Take the exit marked Red Hook/Pine Plains/Route 199 and follow Route 199 west. At the traffic light, continue straight ahead onto Route 308 west. Continue on Route 308 for approximately 6 miles to the traffic light in Rhinebeck. Turn right onto Route 9 north (Montgomery Street). Go 3 blocks and turn left onto Locust Grove Road. Turn right at the first driveway into the B&B parking area.

Named for the broad veranda across the front that's filled with wicker furniture in the summer, the house was built in 1845 as a humble farmhouse. It later served as the parsonage for the Episcopal Church of the Messiah for some ninety years. It was probably during this period that the elaborate brackets under the eaves and the front veranda were added. It was purchased by the Stanleys in 1993, and they converted it to a bed and breakfast.

The house has several interesting architec-

tural features that were of particular interest to Ward, a former college professor of art and architectural history. The doorways are topped by elaborate cornice brackets, there are unusually pretty oak parquet floors with mahogany border inserts, and there is a unique bay window with faceted glass.

The gracious living room has a painted wood mantel over the fireplace and comfortable sofas and chairs. The adjoining library, where the B&B's TV and VCR are located, has floor-to-ceiling shelves filled with art, history, and architectural tomes (and, of course, Ward loves to tell guests about local history and architecture as well), and numerous happy plants basking in the light that streams in the windows. There are French doors here that lead to a bluestone patio where breakfast is often served in the summer. The dining room also has a parquet floor covered by an Oriental rug, a crystal chandelier, and another set of French doors to the patio. There are several handsome oak hutches and chests here also.

The guest rooms are simple and comfortable, and they all have private baths. One room has predominantly green colors with a cherry pencil post four-poster bed, a window seat, and a Victorian marble-topped dresser. The small bath has wainscotted walls. Another room is decorated in blue and white gingham and has built-in bookcases. This room has a bath that was original to the house and includes a handsome sink with a marble countertop and twisted nickel-plated legs.

Breakfast is served in the dining room unless the weather is nice enough to eat on the terrace. Ward and Linda added a professional kitchen to the house in 1996, and Linda prides herself on her three-course breakfasts. Guests will begin the meal with a fresh fruit plate such as pear slices with kiwi and raspberries, as well as homemade breads. Among the favorites are French fruit braid, maple walnut coffee cake, and orange date muffins. For an entrée, she may serve crêpes filled with feta cheese and sautéed zucchini in a light cream sauce and topped with a pesto sauce, or orange yogurt pancakes.

The lawns of Veranda House slope away from the house in back, and there are stately trees and overflowing flower beds. The house is merely a three-block walk from the center of town and close to several historic Hudson River mansions, including Montgomery Place, a 434-acre former Livingston family estate with a 23-room restored mansion. Visitors are encouraged to come during apple harvest time to pick their own apples.

What's Nearby

See "What's Nearby — Rhinebeck," page 159.

WhistleWood Farm

11 Pells Road
(mailing address: RD 1, Box 109)
Rhinebeck, NY 12572
(914) 876-6838;
fax (914) 876-5513;
website: http://www.whistlewood.com

Innkeeper: Maggie Myer
Rooms: 4, plus 2 cottages; all with private baths and air conditioning, cottages with fireplaces and porches; 1 room with porch; 1 with whirlpool tub; 1 room with wheelchair access; cribs available
On the grounds: Gardens, stables and horses
Extras: Baked treats, fruit, and drinks available all day; pets allowed with prior permission for an additional charge of $15 per night
Rates: $125 – $175, including full breakfast and day-long treats
Credit cards accepted: American Express
Open: Year-round
Smoking: Non-smoking bed and breakfast
How to get there: From New York City, take the Hudson River Parkway north to the Saw Mill River Parkway north and then follow the Taconic Parkway north. Take the exit marked Red Hook/Pine Plains/Route 199 and follow Route 199 west for four miles. At the traffic light, continue straight ahead onto Route 308 west. Continue on Route 308 for approximately 3 miles. At the crossroads, turn left onto Pells Road. The B&B is the fifth driveway on the right.

And now for something completely different! If all the upscale, city-sophisticate–B&Bs in and near Rhinebeck make you feel as if you must play dress-up, trade your city shoes for cowboy boots, don your jeans, and come to real country. WhistleWood Farm is a working breeding and boarding horse farm. The warm welcome of innkeeper Maggie Myer and the incredible array of food that she prepares every day, remind you that this is what B&Bs used to be all about. I can think of few places more conducive to a family getaway. The farm is on 13¹/₂ acres, and kids can run free to play with the friendly dogs and to pet the horses.

You'll approach the rambling ranch house after passing the barns and paddocks. Off the entry hall, there's a sunken living room with a cathedral ceiling. The walls are covered with saddles, farm implements, a buffalo head, deer antlers, and handmade quilts. Braided rugs cover wide-plank pine floors. A denim-covered sofa sits before a fieldstone fireplace, which perfumes the room with its heady scent in winter. But it's the smells wafting from the kitchen that persuade you to move on. There, every afternoon, guests find enough baked goods to satisfy a bunch of hungry ranch hands. On a recent visit, the harvest table contained a lemon poppyseed cake, muffins, a blueberry cobbler, chocolate chip cookies, oatmeal cookies, and fruit. It's a big, friendly kitchen with tables for eating, a player piano presided over by a huge horse mural, a TV tucked into a bookcase loaded with books, and an atrium sunporch off the back for gazing at the gardens.

The rooms are country fresh and comfortable, simply furnished with nice old pieces. When you arrive, you'll find your name on the door. The Wyoming Room contains a four-poster pine bed that Maggie made herself. There's a wooden canoe suspended from the ceiling and antique quilts and Indian blankets on the walls. The bath has a whirlpool tub. The Juniper Room has a pencil-post bed and a private deck surrounded by rose and lilac bushes. In 1996, Maggie converted a barn into a pretty cottage she calls the Corral Cottage. The charming accommodation has hooked rugs on pine floors, barnwood walls, and cheerful yellow gingham curtains. There's a great room with a woodstove and sliding doors to a private patio. The bedroom has a Shaker-style four-poster bed. Another cottage (Maggie calls it Lake Cliff Cottage at Beaver Point) is located in a village about 13 miles away.

A full country breakfast is served every morning and set up on an old Hoosier in the kitchen. Maggie will make several breads and muffins, and she may prepare eggs with home fries and bacon and buttermilk pancakes with maple syrup. There will be several kinds of fresh fruits and berries as well as juices. No one goes away hungry!

Guests often help Maggie feed the horses or they may play tennis at the private club at the end of the driveway. Maggie may suggest a winery tour, or a sail on the Hudson River, or a trip to several of her favorite antiques shops.

What's Nearby

See "What's Nearby — Rhinebeck," page 159.

The Mansion Inn
801 Route 29
(mailing address: P.O. Box 77)
Rock City Falls, NY 12863
telephone/fax (518) 885-1607

Innkeepers: Tom Clark and Alan Churchill
Rooms: 7, all with private baths and air conditioning; 3 with fireplaces
On the grounds: Parking, gardens, swimming pool, croquet, nature area
Extras: Afternoon tea and refreshments; turndown with chocolates, cookies, and port; two dogs named Salsa and Sable, a cat named Brandy, sheep named Silver and Sheeba
Rates: $95 – $185, including full breakfast and afternoon tea; two-night minimum weekends May - October
Credit cards accepted: None
Open: Year-round
Smoking: Permitted outside only
How to get there: From I-87 take exit 13 and follow Route 9 (Broadway) north to Route 29. Turn left (west) onto Route 29 and proceed 7 miles to the B&B, which will be on the right.

When I arrived one sunny fall day, the leaves were turning to brilliant reds, golds, oranges, and yellows. The B&B was as vibrant as the leaves, its stark white clapboard exterior etched against the brilliant blue sky.

The majestic and fanciful house was built in 1866 by "The Paper Bag King," George West, an industrialist and inventor of the folded paper bag. He owned six paper mills, two woolen factories, and three cotton factories on the Kayaderosseras Creek in Rock City Falls, and this house, across from his Excelsior Mill, which he built at the point of a 25-foot waterfall, was his summer home — designed for grand events.

The thirty-room mansion was built in the style of a Venetian villa with a fanciful cupola on top and an exterior that was embellished with a virtual catalog of Victorian gingerbread. Inside, the moldings and doors are of chestnut and walnut, and the ceilings reach to 14 feet.

There are two magnificent parlors — one furnished with Empire-style antiques and the other with Eastlake treasures. In the entrance hall, there's a wonderful Tiffany chandelier with wooden arms and etched glass balls, while in the double parlors, entered through magnificent arched doors from the hallway and with ceiling-high pocket doors between, there are beautiful marble fireplaces and a stunning collection of American Impressionist paintings. A mahogany statue of St. Francis is a focal point. The library is also entered through massive arched doors. It has walls surrounded by books in chestnut cases with walnut trim. There are Victorian couches and a wide variety of books for guests to read. Extending along one side of the house for 60 feet is a Victorian porch filled with antique wicker that's fronted by grand pillars interspersed with planter boxes overflowing with flowers — the ideal place to rest with a good book from the library and to gaze at the waterfall across the way.

In the Guest Suite on the first floor, the floors are a medley of oak, maple, and rosewood inlaid in intricate patterns. Notable details include a cherry sleigh bed, a marble fireplace, and a bath with a pink marble sink. In the sitting room, there's a Victorian couch that was rescued from Saratoga's old Grand Union Hotel. On the second floor, reached by a grand stairway, a sitting room furnished with bentwood rockers offers a view of the mills and waterfall across the road. Each of the remaining guest rooms has either a four-poster or a high oak bed, and several have fireplaces. They all have lovely bathrooms — finished either in marble or tile.

Breakfast is served in the formal dining room, which has an extraordinary fireplace topped by an 8-foot carved mirror. Guests are seated at individual tables that are set with Royal Doulton china, pink and lime tablecloths, fresh flowers, silver, and fine crystal. The menu includes freshly squeezed orange juice and three or four other juices, fresh fruit, warm freshly baked breads, and an option of perhaps scrambled eggs with fine herbs, a cheese or mushroom omelet, or Grand Marnier French toast with maple syrup.

The B&B is located on 4 acres that include gardens, a little private cottage that is also rented in the summer, a swimming pool, lawns for croquet, and a nature area that is a haven for birds and grazing sheep.

What's Nearby

Rock City Falls has a nice collection of antiques shops. In addition, the Saratoga National Battlefield Park is in nearby Stillwater, and the General Philip Schuyler Mansion is in Schuylerville. The numerous attractions of Saratoga Springs are just 7 miles east. (See also Saratoga Springs.)

The Batcheller Mansion Inn

20 Circular Street
Saratoga Springs, NY 12866
(800) 616-7012 or (518) 584-7012;
fax (518) 581-7746

Innkeeper: Janet Coon; president of management company, Frank Burns, Jr.; proprietor, Bruce Levinsky
Rooms: 9, all with private baths, air conditioning, TVs, telephones, radios, mini-refrigerators, hair dryers, desks, irons, ironing boards, and robes; 4 with fireplaces; 3 with whirlpool tubs; 1 with a balcony
On the grounds: Parking, gardens
Extras: Turndown service with chocolates; tea and cookies in afternoon during racing season
Rates: $115 – $230 from May to mid-July; $200 – $360 from mid-July through August; $115 – $230 September and October; $80 – $180 November through April; two-night minimum weekends April - October; four-night minimum during racing season from late July through Labor Day weekend
Credit cards accepted: American Express, MasterCard, Visa
Open: Year-round
Smoking: Permitted outside only
How to get there: From I-87 (the Northway) take exit 14. At the end of the ramp, turn right onto Union Avenue (Route 9P). Traveling west for 2 miles, follow Union Avenue to its end. Turn left onto Circular Street. The B&B is located straight ahead after one long block.

This twenty-eight-room High Victorian Gothic mansion narrowly escaped the wrecker's ball when it was abandoned in 1966 and then condemned by the city in 1972. Fortunately, it was purchased in 1973, and a twenty-year restoration began that concluded in 1994. Today this mélange of minarets, towers, and turrets takes its place once again as the showplace of Saratoga Springs — an opulent and extravagant B&B.

The house was built by George Sherman Batcheller, a Brigadier General in the Union Army and Ambassador to Portugal, among other things. He spared no cost when he built his summer "House of Pleasure" in 1873. Today the outside is painted a creamy ivory with grey-green and burgundy trim.

In the foyer there are magnificent walnut and tiger maple inlaid floors and a grand stairway leading to the second floor. The living room has an 1800s Czechoslovakian chandelier with milky-blue glass arms that hangs from the 12-foot-tall ceiling. Massive oil paintings by Stuart Williams, a copy artist and a former owner of the B&B, cover the walls. There's also a baby grand piano and a fireplace with a marble mantel. Ingenious Victorian double-hung windows rise to create a doorway to the porch. The Library has parquet floors and paneled bookshelves that have intricately carved details. Here guests will find a huge library table in a turret, wine velvet sofas and chairs, and a large-screen TV. Classical music plays in the background.

There are nine guest rooms on the second and third floors of the house. Even on the second floor the ceilings reach 12 feet. The Katrina Trask Room is often used as a bridal chamber. It has a lacy canopy bed, a blue carpet, a marble fireplace mantel, a marble-topped dresser, and a private balcony with wicker tables and chairs entered by way of a double hung window. The bath has a pedestal sink and paneling painted blue. The most incredible room, however, is Diamond Jim Brady. This 18- x 28-foot room has a king-sized canopy bed and a sitting area with a full-sized pool table. In the bath, there's a Jacuzzi tub.

The kitchen is fantastic. It has 26-foot-tall ceilings and a tile floor. One entire wall above the countertops is composed of a massive glass window salvaged from the Shawmut Bank in Boston. On the opposite wall, paintings by Williams climb to the ceiling. Breakfast is prepared here and served to guests seated in the dining room or on the porch. Individual tables are set with fine linen, Royal Doulton china, silver, and fine crystal.

During the week a Continental breakfast is offered consisting of fresh fruit, freshly baked pastries, juice, and coffee. On weekends, guests may also have their choice of an egg or pancake entrée.

Behind the house, there's a lovely and very private garden overseen by a back porch. The house is across the street from Congress Park, a park that contains Saratoga's famed brick casino building. The famous and the infamous gathered there in the late nineteenth and early twentieth century to gamble the night away amid opulent splendor. It is said that solitaire originated here and that the club sandwich was first made in the casino kitchens. Today, a gift shop, an art gallery, and a museum are open to the public.

What's Nearby — Saratoga Springs

Saratoga Springs is noted for the Saratoga Flat Track, where thoroughbred racing takes place in August and other racing events are scheduled throughout the rest of the summer. In addition, it is the home of the Saratoga Performing Arts Center, which is the summer home of the Philadelphia Orchestra and the New York City Ballet. The Saratoga Spa State Park includes soothing therapy at bath houses that have attracted the famous for years, while the National Museum of Racing and Hall of Fame is located across Union Avenue from the racetrack. (See also Rock City Falls.)

Union Gables Bed & Breakfast

55 Union Avenue
Saratoga Springs, NY 12866
(800) 398-1558 or (518) 584-1558;
fax (518) 583-0649;
e-mail: 73752.645@compuserve.com

Innkeepers: Jody and Tom Roohan
Rooms: 10, including 1 suite, all with private baths, air conditioning, TVs, telephones, large desks, and mini-refrigerators; 2 with balconies; cribs available
On the grounds: Parking, tennis court, hot tub, gardens, hammock
Extras: Exercise room; fax, modem, copier, small meeting space available; one dog named Max, one cat named Oreo; guest pets allowed
Rates: $95 – $240, including Continental breakfast
Credit cards accepted: American Express, Discover, MasterCard, Visa
Open: Year-round
Smoking: Non-smoking bed and breakfast
How to get there: From I-87 (the Northway) take exit 14. At the end of the ramp, turn right onto Union Avenue (Route 9P). Union Gables is about a mile farther on the right.

When Skidmore College decided they no longer needed to use Furness House as a dormitory, Tom Roohan, a local realtor, saw the perfect opportunity. It had all the makings of an elegant bed and breakfast. Massive renovation was necessary to create spacious rooms with a private bath in each, but in 1992, when the construction was complete, Tom and his wife Jody opened the house to local designers for a Decorator Showhouse, and the B&B was appropriately launched.

The grand 1901 Victorian is located on Saratoga Spring's finest street—a broad tree-lined esplanade with stately mansions on both sides. The house features gables, turrets, fanciful gingerbread trim, and a huge wraparound porch. It's set on spacious lawns bordered by overflowing flower beds.

One enters a wide foyer with boxed beams and a fireplace flanked by oak paneling and benches. One of the most unique features of the house is visible in the turret room that the

Roohans use as an office. The room is paneled in curly maple with bamboo trim, and the living room is fully trimmed with curly maple also. There's another fireplace in the living room as well as a baby grand piano and a chess set on a table in the turret.

The guest rooms are spacious and dramatic, and each has a TV, telephone, and a mini-refrigerator stocked with the area's famed Saratoga Springs water. Cindy (all the rooms are named for family members), a suite, has inlaid oak floors and navy blue walls with white trim. There's a massive pine cannonball bed in the main room and another room with twin beds — an ideal arrangement for families. The bath is tiled, and there's a private screened-in porch overlooking the back. Kate has a horsy theme with plaid walls and bedspread, a hand-painted chest of drawers featuring the Victorian houses of Saratoga, and a clever bath that has a mirror over the sink that's framed in a massive leather horse yoke.

A Continental breakfast is served in the dining room, which has another fireplace with a wonderful carved mahogany mantel, a bay window, and lincresta ceiling trim. Guests sit at the large dining room table, but they eat whenever they are ready. Breakfast will include a variety of bakery rolls, fresh fruit, and juices.

The house has one of the largest wraparound porches you'll ever see, which is furnished with wicker tables and chairs interspersed with verdigris metal pieces. The B&B has bicycles for guests to use, a tennis court, an outdoor hot tub, and an exercise room.

Saratoga Springs, known as the "Queen of Spas," was once the most fashionable of summer resorts. The 1940 WPA guide speaks nostalgically about the 1890s, when the resort was in its prime. "It stirs with anticipation in June, swings into preparatory activity in July, and rushes headlong into the full tumult of its summer season in August." There were grand hotels where glamorous balls and dinners took place, and the casino was filled with the notables and the notorious. Saratoga Springs is still a beehive of activity in the summer, especially from late July through Labor Day weekend when the thoroughbreds race at the Saratoga Flat Track. But Saratoga Springs is also the summer home of the Philadelphia Orchestra and the New York City Ballet, who perform, along with popular artists, at the Saratoga Performing Arts Center.

What's Nearby

See "What's Nearby — Saratoga Springs," page 167.

Schroon Lake Bed & Breakfast

Route 9 (mailing address: RD1, Box 274)
Schroon Lake, NY 12870
(518) 532-7042;
fax (518) 532-9820;
e-mail: schroonbb@worldnet.att.net
website: http://www.lakeplacid.com

Innkeepers: Rita and Bob Skojec
Rooms: 5, including 1 suite, 3 with private baths, 2 share a bath, all with air conditioning and robes
On the grounds: Parking, gardens
Extras: Complimentary sodas and juices; computer access and fax available
Rates: $75 – $90, including full breakfast; two-night minimum July - October
Credit cards accepted: Discover, MasterCard, Visa
Open: Year-round
Smoking: Non-smoking bed and breakfast
How to get there: From I-87 (the Northway) take exit 28. At the end of the ramp turn right and go .2 mile to the flashing red light. Turn right onto Route 9 south. The B&B is on the right just a few yards down the road.

Schroon Lake is a beautiful 9-mile-long mountain lake in the vast 6¹/₂-million-acre Adirondack State Park. It was a particularly popular summer resort in the early 1900s. At one point there were hotels and tourist homes lining the main street of the village and leading down to the lake that stretched for 2 miles. Few of these structures remain today, but the lake is as beautiful and as unspoiled as ever.

The neat beige clapboard house with white trim that's now known as Schroon Lake Bed & Breakfast was built in the 1920s, and it's rumored that Dutch Schultz once stayed here. A fire totally destroyed the house in the 1930s, but remnants of bootlegger bounty have been found in the brick foundation. The modest house was rebuilt in the 1930s. It was then a boarding house and later a private residence until it was converted to a B&B in the late 1980s. Bob and Rita purchased the B&B in 1995 and completed a top-to-bottom renovation before re-opening it to guests. Bob is a retired systems analyst with IBM, and Rita was a New York-based food writer and stylist (at one time she was a columnist with

House Beautiful).

The pretty house is fronted by a porch set with white wicker rockers and chairs. Ivy geraniums hang from the middle of each of the eleven arches created by the Victorian gingerbread surrounding the porch. The house sits on a knoll offering views of the mountains beyond Schroon Lake.

In the gracious living room, there are hardwood floors, Oriental rugs, a puffy sofa before a fieldstone fireplace, and Tiffany-style lamps. Upstairs, there's a den where books, magazines, board games, jigsaw puzzles, and a TV/VCR are available for guests to use.

The guest rooms include Yellow Iris, a large room with a king-sized bed topped by an enormous painting of yellow and blue iris, an antique armoire, and Oriental rugs on polished oak floors. Sea Mist has an antique brass queen-sized bed and an antique curly maple dresser. The largest room is Monaco, which has an antique black iron and brass queen-sized bed, a

brocade settee in the sitting area, and a view of the Pharaoh Wilderness area. Each of these rooms has a sparkling new tiled private bath. The remaining two rooms share a bath.

Breakfast is served in the Victorian dining room, which is filled with antiques, or on the porch in summer. A food writer must know how to cook, and Rita has perfected her craft. She may prepare apple-walnut French toast with "burst of berries" fruit sauce or orange Belgian waffles with whipped cream and fresh raspberries, or perhaps Adirondack eggs Benedict, a light dish resembling little soufflés that she tops with hollandaise sauce.

Activities abound in all seasons. In the summer, lakeside beaches beckon as well as sailing and canoeing on Schroon Lake. In the fall, the brilliant foliage captures our romantic fancy, and its images fill the pages of photographers' scrapbooks. In winter, there are cross-country and snowmobile trails as well as downhill skiing at Whiteface and Gore Mountains.

What's Nearby — Schroon Lake

The Adirondack Museum in Blue Mountain Lake is housed in 20 different buildings. There are logging, mining, and transportation exhibits as well as an art museum and displays relating to the history of the Adirondacks. Fort Ticonderoga is nearby as well, where there is a military museum and the restored 1755 fort. During the summer, there are fife and drum parades, cannon and mortar drills, and much more. There's a Balloon Festival in Glens Falls in the early fall, and the Adirondack Marathon is held in Schroon Lake in September. The Siegal Colony for Performing Arts, a musical performance training center, is located in Schroon Lake.

Innkeepers: Phyllis and Clifford Rogers
Rooms: 8, all with private baths, 4 with small kitchens, whirlpool tubs, and coffee makers; 2 rooms with wheelchair access
On the grounds: Parking, gardens, gazebo, yard games, hiking trails
Extras: Turndown with chocolates; tea, coffee, cheeses, and cookies available; telephone, fax, computer, dataport, office area available; one chocolate lab named Lilly, one calico cat named Shacka
Rates: $80 – $99, including full breakfast; two-night minimum holiday weekends
Credit cards accepted: MasterCard, Visa
Open: Year-round
Smoking: Non-smoking bed and breakfast
How to get there: Take I-87 (the Northway) to exit 28. At the end of the ramp turn right and go .2 mile to the flashing red light. Turn left onto Route 9 north. The B&B will be on the left in 1.8 miles.

Silver Spruce Inn Bed & Breakfast

Route 9
Schroon Lake, NY 12870
telephone/fax (518) 532-7031

Unique, fascinating, and an American original, the earliest portion of the Silver Spruce Inn, a 8,200-square-foot clapboard house built of post and beam construction, dates to 1846. After Mrs. Sallie Smith purchased it in 1926, however, it took on a whole new persona.

Mrs. Smith was the owner of Randolph and Clowes Foundry in Waterbury, Connecticut, which eventually became the American Standard company. She purchased the house as an executive retreat for her employees. It already had six bedrooms and eight bathrooms when she bought it, but she added seventeen rooms and some fascinating architectural features. One room, for example, that was used for square dances could quickly be divided into three separate rooms by lowering hinged walls from the ceiling. A bookcase rolls back to reveal the liquor cabinet (this was during the reckless Flapper days of Prohibition). Down a set of thick plank stairs, which are revealed by raising a hinged section of the living room floor, there's a Tavern with a quarry-stone floor and walls, a massive stone fireplace, and beamed ceilings. A handsome bar, which was rescued from New York's old 34th Street Waldorf Astoria (where the Empire State Building now stands), is located here. The house must have been a showplace of Victorian furnishings and decor. After Mrs. Smith died, they were auctioned off by Sotheby's in 1954 in a sale that took an entire week to conduct.

The restoration of the house and grounds has been the passion of the current owners, Cliff and Phyllis Rogers, since 1981. They opened it as a B&B in 1994. The clapboard house is painted a creamy white, and it has black shutters and a slate roof. Across the front, there's a quarry stone porch filled with pretty antique wicker furniture. The walls of the living room are cedar, and there's a huge stone fireplace. In the dining room, the walls are sandblasted pine, and there's another huge stone fireplace as well as a woodstove. Phyllis is a quilter and weaver, and her artistry is found throughout.

There are eight guest rooms, all with private baths and each charmingly decorated with quilts. The four rooms in the main house have cedar walls and fir plank floors topped by braided or woven rugs. The furnishings are of oak, mostly from the Arts and Crafts period. In room #2, for example, there's a walnut headboard on the bed, an oak Morris reclining chair, and a pretty oak desk. The baths have cast-iron tubs with stenciled surrounds. Room #5, which is the largest, however, has a heated water bed with a half canopy, a combination not often seen in a B&B. Four new rooms were created in 1997 in the former carriage house. They each have gas fireplaces or corner stoves, sitting areas, king-sized beds, and whirlpool tubs in the fresh new baths.

Breakfast is served in the dining room, where Phyllis brings out her fine silver, crystal, and china. The meal will include fresh fruits and juices, freshly baked muffins such as blueberry or raspberry, and an egg dish or maybe French toast served with New York State maple syrup.

The B&B sits on 16 acres in the heart of the 6¹/₂-million-acre Adirondack State Park. There are hiking and cross-country ski trails and trout fishing on the Schroon River.

What's Nearby

See "What's Nearby — Schroon Lake," page 171.

Stearns Point House

7 Stearns Point Road
Shelter Island Heights
(Shelter Island), NY 11965
(516) 749-4162

Innkeeper: Jan Carlson
Rooms: 4, all with private baths
On the grounds: Parking
Extras: Telephone available
Rates: $85 – $125, including Continental breakfast; two-night minimum weekends May - October, three-night minimum holiday weekends
Credit cards accepted: None
Open: Year-round
Smoking: Permitted in common room only
How to get there: From New York City take I-495 (the Long Island Expressway) to exit 73, where it terminates. Follow County Road 58 east to Route 25, then follow Route 25 for about 30 miles to Greenport. Once in Greenport, follow the signs for the Shelter Island Ferry. After exiting the ferry on Shelter Island, you will be on Route 114, which becomes Grand Avenue. Stay on Grand, which then becomes New York Avenue. At the end of the golf course, turn right onto West Neck Road and go up the hill. At the intersection with Shore Road, turn right onto Shore Road. Take the second left onto Stearns Point Road, and the B&B will be the first building on the left.

Shelter Island, reached by ferry from either the North or the South Fork of Eastern Long Island, is such a quiet, remote spot that it's seldom discussed in the same breath as its swank neighbor to the south, the Hamptons, or its up-and-coming wine country neighbor to the north. It lies in stark contrast to both, offering more sophisticated accommodations than the North Fork and a more relaxed pace than the Hamptons—a laid-back hideaway where the rich and famous and the rest of us can find a total escape.

Shelter Island Heights, a steeply hilled section on the northern bluff of the island, was developed in the 1870s when the Methodist Episcopal Church established the Grove and Camp Meeting Association here. Handsome Victorian houses welcomed the prominent lecturers and orators of the day, and many of these remain today.

Stearns Point House was built in Shelter Island Heights in the 1920s. The owners started taking in boarders in the 1930s, and in the 1950s, the house was moved to the quiet country lane on which it sits today. Jan Carlson, who was an English instructor and dean at Nassau Community College, had summered on Shelter Island for many years. She had rented several rooms in her beach-front house, and she eventually purchased and renovated the old boarding house to create Stearns Point House.

The building is a handsome one — a white clapboard farmhouse with a porch across the front that rests in the center of $^3/_4$ acre of spacious lawns bordered by flower beds. A split-rail fence surrounds the property, and a parking area offers space for cars in back. The common room is furnished with painted tables and chairs. A buffet breakfast is set up here, and guests are free to eat in their rooms or to take their meal to the porch in summer. Jan prepares fresh muffins every day as well as platters of fresh fruit, juice, cereals, coffee, and tea. A guest refrigerator is available should guests wish to stock up on wine or soft drinks.

The rooms are crisp and charming, and the location ensures a quiet stay. They have either half-canopy beds with draperies that hang from the ceiling or canopy beds. Wicker chairs are covered with flowered chintz cushions. Each bedroom has its own private bath, but otherwise there are no amenities. One telephone is located in a phone booth near the common room.

Although not located in the village, the B&B has an excellent restaurant and country inn next door. Crescent Beach, the primary public swimming beach on Shelter Island, is an easy walk away.

What's Nearby

Shelter Island is cradled between the North and South Forks on the eastern end of Long Island and offers numerous watery pleasures, including swimming, boating, fishing, and canoeing. In addition, Shelter Island is home to Mashomack Preserve, a 2,000-acre expanse of marshes, freshwater ponds, tidal creeks, and forests owned by The Nature Conservancy. There are hiking trails throughout the property. Shelter Island has numerous paved roads ideal for bicycling.

Evergreen on Pine Bed & Breakfast

89 Pine Street
Southampton, NY 19968
telephone/fax (516) 283-0564

Innkeepers: Peter and JoAnn Rogoski
Rooms: 5, including 1 suite, all with private baths, air conditioning, telephone, radio, robes
On the grounds: Parking, gardens
Extras: Telephone with dataport and modem; one Maltese named Michelle
Rates: $145–$195 from May to October; $116 – $156 from October to May; two-night minimum April–August
Credit cards accepted: American Express, Diner's Club, Discover, MasterCard, Visa
Open: Year-round
Smoking: Non-smoking bed and breakfast
How to get there: From New York City take I-495 (the Long Island Expressway) to exit 70 (Manorville) and follow Route 111 south to Highway 27 (Sunrise Highway). Follow Highway 27 (which becomes County Road 39) east to Southampton. Turn right onto North Sea Road, which becomes Main Street. Follow Main Street through the shopping area of the village and turn left at the traffic light onto Meeting House Lane. Go 2 blocks and turn left onto Pine Street. The first driveway on the left leads to the parking area for the B&B, which is on the corner of Meeting House Lane and Pine Street.

Settled in 1640, Southampton is the oldest English settlement in New York State, yet today its shops, restaurants, and boutiques are the essence of twentieth-century chic. Evergreen on Pine is within a short two-block walk of the fashionable shops of Main Street and Jobs Lane and almost next door to the Southampton Historical Museum, where guests can learn about Southampton's interesting history. The museum consists of twelve buildings and thirty-five separate exhibits, ranging from an old New York schoolhouse to a collection of artifacts relating to the Shinnecock Indians.

The white shingled B&B is 250 years younger than the town. Built in 1887 and thoroughly updated by Peter and JoAnn Rogoski in 1996 (who moved here from Darien, Connecticut, for a lifestyle change), it's a modest Victorian with a front porch outfitted with wicker. A tall privet hedge surrounds the property, except for an arch cut to accommodate the gate, which leads to the flower-bordered sidewalk. A parking area is located in back, and to the side, a tiled patio is surrounded by lawns and more flower beds. White iron chairs and tables with umbrellas repose here, a welcoming spot to sip a glass of wine and nibble the fresh fruit acquired at one of the local farm stands.

Inside, there's a handsome living room with Oriental rugs on oak floors, a white wooden fireplace mantel with scrollwork, and an antique camelback sofa. The decor is tied together in an English country theme.

There are two guest rooms on the main floor, and three upstairs. One room on the first floor has an elaborate high brass bed, a fireplace mantel (although the fireplace does not work), and a dressing table with a sculptured beveled mirror. There are oak floors and a paisley spread in gold, green, and rust on the bed.

The other downstairs room is furnished with a sleigh bed that's covered with a green Laura Ashley fabric. The rooms upstairs are equally charming. A sunny corner room, furnished with white wicker and a pretty Laura Ashley fabric in yellows and blues, is a favorite. Although all the rooms have private baths, two of the rooms upstairs have baths off the hallway instead of in the room.

A Continental breakfast of fresh fruit, homemade muffins, croissants, and juice is served buffet-style in the dining room, which has another fireplace. The decor is light and fun. JoAnn covers the dining room table with a runner decorated with country animals and placemats featuring bunnies. She uses a white on white china, as well as crystal and silver. In nice weather guests often take their breakfast out to the patio.

What's Nearby

Ocean and bay beaches beckon visitors throughout the summer, but there are many things to do here year-round. The Parrish Art Museum has an excellent collection of paintings by artists who lived and painted in the Hamptons, while the Southampton Historical Museum, which is housed in numerous buildings in a village setting, has a re-created country store with a post office, a blacksmith shop, and much more. Southampton College of Long Island University, located in Southampton, has a Fine Art Museum and offers a wide array of cultural activities year-round. (See also Bridgehampton, Water Mill, and Westhampton Beach.)

Fields of Dreams

276 Majors Path
(mailing address: P.O. Box 2481)
Southampton, NY 11969
(516) 283-4691

Innkeeper: Monika Heitmeyer
Rooms: 5, 3 with private baths, 2 share one bath, all with air conditioning, hair dryers, and balconies or patios; 1 with a fireplace, TV, and radio; telephones, irons, and ironing boards available for all rooms on request; 2 rooms with wheelchair access
On the grounds: Pool, spacious gardens
Extras: Fresh flowers, fruit, and bottled water in every room
Rates: $185–$245 weekends; $165–$215 weekdays, including full breakfast; three-day minimum weekends
Credit cards accepted: None
Open: May - October
Smoking: Non-smoking bed and breakfast
How to get there: From New York City take I-495 (the Long Island Expressway) to exit 70 (Manorville) and follow Route 111 south to Highway 27 (Sunrise Highway). Follow Highway 27 (which becomes County Road 39) east to Southampton. At the traffic light by the 7-Eleven, turn left onto North Sea Road and immediately take the right fork onto Majors Path. Follow this for .5 mile to #276, which will be on the right. Drive along the private road past the horse pastures to the locked gate. An appointment is necessary to go beyond the gated entry.

The driveway leads past pastoral fields of grazing horses; there's a barn in the distance. The handsome natural shingled house with white trim seems to emerge like a flower in full bloom from the fields of poppies, daisies, coneflowers, cosmos, and lavender that surround it. A natural, rock-lined pool reflects the array of colors on its silvery surface.

If you were designing a B&B specifically to grace the pages of Architectural Digest, this would be your model. The house is merely seven years old, so everything is in premier condition, but it has a dignity and spaciousness well beyond its years. The common rooms are expansive and light, and the guest rooms and bathrooms are large and furnished with exquisite antiques. Each has either a balcony overlooking the fields of flowers or a patio.

Being a guest at Fields of Dreams is more like coming to the country to stay with a friend than staying in a typical B&B; Monika Heitmeyer is a vivacious, enthusiastic, and gracious hostess. You will be pampered and cared for, and yet you will have plenty of "space." As Monika says, "I love people. As a former Pan Am stewardess, I traveled the world and liked it most when I stayed in homes with friends. That's the feeling I want to create here."

The five rooms are very large. The biggest has an iron-and-brass bed, a fireplace, a painted leather screen, and an armoire. In another, a collection of antique coffee pots is on display, and there's a private herbal garden with chairs for afternoon book reading while enjoying the heady smell of mint. French doors in all the rooms lead to broad decks or patios. The spectacular European baths have footed tubs, pedestal sinks, hardwood floors, and needlepoint rugs. There are antique linens on the beds. The two newest rooms are located in a charming addition and include wainscotted walls. One room has an antique French cherry sleigh bed and a table with a white marble top on a sewing machine base. The other room features an English mahogany canopy bed and old photographs on the wall that give it a vintage Ralph Lauren look.

Breakfast is served either in the dining room or on an outside deck overlooking the gardens. Monika is a gourmet cook, and her breakfasts are memorable. She serves fresh juice and several fresh fruits every day and lavishly decorates the plates with flowers, perhaps a showy pink hibiscus will rest beside watermelon, grapes, papaya, and berries. For an entrée she may serve eggs with fresh herbs, white asparagus, and a grilled tomato; German pancakes with smoked salmon; or apple pancakes. She uses a variety of decorator dishes to create a frame around each composition.

Set on 4 acres, the property abounds in flowers gardens. A perennial garden surrounds the pool; in addition, there are an herb garden, a white flower garden, and a huge wildflower garden.

What's Nearby

See "What's Nearby — Southampton," page 177.

Mainstay

579 Hill Street
Southampton, NY 11968
(516) 283-4375; fax (516) 287-6240

Innkeeper: Elizabeth Main
Rooms: 8, including 1 suite, 5 with private baths and 3 sharing one bath; 5 with robes; 3 with TVs; 1 with a fireplace
On the grounds: Parking, swimming pool, gardens
Extras: Decanter of sherry in guestroom; one cat named Daisy
Rates: $125 – $300, including full or Continental breakfast; two-night minimum May -October
Credit cards accepted: American Express, Master-Card, Visa
Open: Year-round
Smoking: Non-smoking bed and breakfast
How to get there: From New York City take I-495 (the Long Island Expressway) to exit 70 (Manorville) and follow Route 111 south to Highway 27 (Sunrise Highway). Follow Highway 27 (which becomes County Road 39) east to Southampton University. At Tucka-hoe Road, turn right and continue to Old Montauk Highway (Route 27A and Hill Street). Continue for .5 mile to the B&B, which will be on the left.

Although the shingled house on the outskirts of Southampton has been a B&B since 1985, it wasn't until Elizabeth Main began adding her clever and artistic wizardry in 1992 that it took on its alluring appeal. The house itself is an 1870s Colonial with a weathered-shingle exterior and white trim. Previously a country store for many years, it sits well back from the street behind a picket fence on an acre of land that's alive with flower gardens punctu-ated by secluded bowers with benches.

Elizabeth is a potter and artist who formerly was a photo stylist in New York. She has cleverly taken a simple house with narrow hallways and transformed it into a cute and hospitable B&B. This is not an elegant and fancy B&B, but one that is very comfortable and welcoming — the sort of place where you might sit with a cup of tea in the afternoon and curl up before the fire in the parlor or use it as a base for a weekend bicycle ride. When you enter the foyer of the house, you'll see sponge-painted walls in spring green and flowers fancifully climbing the door frames. Over the entrance to the front parlor, there's an arrangement of dried flowers. The front parlor has bead board ceilings and a fireplace. In the country dining room, one side is dominated by a huge old woodstove, while another has a pine country cupboard displaying a colorful collection of Elizabeth's pottery. The walls here are sponged an ochre color, and there are grapes, apples, and pears painted across the walls above the wainscotting.

Guests are welcome to enter the bright, open, and light country kitchen at any time, and it would be a shame if they didn't. Painted across one wall is a marvelous mural of English climbing roses. In a little pantry off the kitchen, shelves hold stacks of Elizabeth's cups, saucers, bowls, and plates, ready to be used for breakfast or afternoon snacks.

The guest rooms are equally artistic. Room #5, the large master suite, has its own wood-burning fireplace, a king-sized iron bed, and a pine armoire. There are built-in shelves of books and in the bath, a clawfoot tub. In Room #6, there's an iron and brass bed and a pine armoire

amid walls painted all over with climbing hydrangeas. The bath is modern and charming with bead board walls and ceiling and a clawfoot tub. Room #8 is the newest creation. In what was formerly the attic, Elizabeth has built a two-room suite. It has slanted ceilings, walls sponge-painted in yellow and gold, antique iron beds, lace curtains, and a skylight. One room has a cloud-filled sky on the ceiling. It has a terrific bath with wainscot walls. Other rooms have mirrors with wild dots, squiggles, and dashes splashed on the frame. Of the eight guest rooms, five have private baths, and the other three share one bath.

A Continental breakfast is served buffet-style. Cereals, fruits, and juices are set out on a sideboard and on the huge pine table in the center of the room. On weekends, Elizabeth prepares a waffle batter that she sets on the old woodstove so that guests may prepare waffles at their leisure.

There's a swimming pool behind the house surrounded by a tall fence. The front porch holds wicker chairs, and there's plenty of parking for guest cars.

What's Nearby

See "What's Nearby — Southampton," page 177.

The 1708 House
126 Main Street
Southampton, N Y 11968
(516) 287-1708

Innkeepers: Skip and Lorraine Ralph; manager, Pete Reyer
Rooms: 12, including 3 suites and 3 cottages, all with private baths and air conditioning, TVs, telephones, and desks; 4 with porches; cottages with mini-refrigerators, VCRs, and coffee makers
On the grounds: Parking
Extras: Cheese and wine in afternoon
Rates: $165 – $275, including Continental or full breakfast; two-night minimum weekends Memorial Day - Labor Day; 15% premium charged for weekends in July and August; three-night minimum holidays
Credit cards accepted: American Express, MasterCard, Visa
Open: Year-round
Smoking: Non-smoking bed and breakfast
How to get there: From New York City take I-495 (the Long Island Expressway) to exit 70 (Manorville) and follow Route 111 south to Highway 27 (Sunrise Highway). Follow Highway 27 (which becomes County Road 39) east to Southampton. Turn right onto North Sea Road, which becomes Main Street, and proceed to #126, which will be on the left.

Antiques and historic houses go together, so antiques dealers who open B&Bs have definitely found their calling. Skip and Lorraine Ralph owned a bed and breakfast in Pittsburgh (where Skip was raised). Since they had also lived on Long Island for some time and had often spent summers in the Hamptons, they decided to open a B&B there for their next venture. Was it an uncanny instinct or fate that led them to their discovery of the rambling old house on Main Street?

The 1708 House is one of the most historic in Southampton, yet in 1993 it was in such disastrous shape that it didn't look as if it could possibly see 1994. There were squatters living in the cottages in back, the weeds were as high as a sly fox's eye, the foundation was crumbling, and the roof was falling in. Yet, Skip and Lorraine Ralph saw possibilities, particularly since it was on the village's premiere street and next door to a Saks Fifth Avenue store.

Thanks to the Ralphs' foresight and perseverance (it took three years to obtain the necessary permits for the B&B), they are now proprietors of a classy new B&B in a historic old shell. From top to bottom, the B&B shines.

In the living room, there are polished pine floors, an oak mantel over the woodburning fireplace, and tapestry-covered wing chairs. The library has pine floors, exposed hand-hewn oak beams, and a wood-burning fireplace. The dining room has hand-hewn beams and a ceiling of exposed floorboards. French doors lead to a spacious patio. Individual tables are used for games of cards in the evening and for breakfast in the morning. All the antiques are supplied from the couple's antiques shop around the corner, and everything is for sale.

Each of the nine guest rooms and three cottages is spacious and luxurious. The South Wing is on two levels and has a huge private deck. There's a beautiful Ralph Lauren plaid paired with checked fabric that is lavishly used on the bed. Room #2 has fabulous antique beds, an armoire, bead board walls, and a pine floor. There are three restored cottages in back, each with an eat-in kitchen.

Downstairs, the utterly romantic wine cellar features brick walls, a terrific brick fireplace, and a tile floor. Old hand-hewn beams are supported by peeled locust posts. At one end, a bar is set up, and classical music gently plays while wine and cheese are served every afternoon.

On weekday mornings, guests may help themselves to croissants, bagels, juices, fruits, and coffee or tea. On Saturday and Sunday mornings, the Continental breakfast is supplemented by a hot entrée such as a crab meat omelet with béarnaise sauce or challah French toast or quiche Lorraine (in honor of the innkeeper).

Besides offering shopping in the nearby excellent boutiques, galleries, shops, and ateliers, the B&B is close to ocean beaches and to Agawam Park, where concerts take place throughout the summer. The Parrish Art Museum has a fine collection of American Impressionist paintings, many of which were painted in the Hamptons.

What's Nearby

See "What's Nearby — Southampton," page 177.

Lakehouse Inn

Shelley Hill Road
Stanfordville, NY 12581
(800) 726-3323 or (914) 266-8093;
fax (914) 266-4051;
e-mail: lakehouse@bigfoot.com

Innkeepers: Judy and Rick Kohler
Rooms: 10, including 7 suites, all with private baths, air conditioning, TVs, VCRs, telephones, stereos, coffee makers, robes, and CD players; 7 with mini-refrigerators, wet-bars, balconies or patios, fireplaces, and whirlpool tubs
On the grounds: Parking, lake
Extras: Turndown with truffles; bottled water, soft drinks, appetizer baskets provided in each room; fax, computer, copy machine available
Rates: $125 – $495, including full breakfast; two-night minimum weekends; three-night minimum holiday weekends
Credit cards accepted: MasterCard and Visa
Open: Year-round
Smoking: Non-smoking bed and breakfast
How to get there: From New York City, take the Hudson River Parkway north to the Saw Mill River Parkway north and then follow the Taconic Parkway north. Take the exit marked Red Hook/Pine Plains/Route 199 and follow Route 199 west for .5 mile. Take the first right onto Route 53 south and go 3 1/2 miles. Turn right onto Shelley Hill Road and go exactly .9 mile. Turn onto paved driveway. The Lakehouse Inn is at the end of the road.

When hearts turn to romance, few B&Bs can match the dreamy cocoons Judy and Rick Kohler have created for their guests. Each is so huge and so secluded from one another that they feel like individual cottages sequestered away on private islands.

At first sight the cedar-sided house appears modest and unremarkable; even when we walked along the flying-bridge walkway to the entrance, we were unprepared for the gracious and urbane interior. The house envelops its guests in country charm but also offers luxurious and spacious private retreats. For a total getaway from the fast-paced city, I can't imagine a more relaxing sanctuary.

The living room is decorated with flair in gentle earth tones. The vaulted, rough-sawn pine ceiling and the wall of windows offering unobstructed views of tiny Golden Pond give the room a warm, inviting glow. It's furnished with antiques, Oriental rugs on oak floors, twig furniture, comfortable sofas, piles of magazines and books, and an ornately carved oak English bar on which Victorian flow blue china is displayed. It's surrounded by a wraparound deck with twig furniture overlooking the lake.

Each of the suites seems more amorous, more seductive, and more sybaritic than the next. The Casablanca Suite has its own fireplace laid with logs, ready to be lighted, and a private deck. There's a pink damask sofa on which to watch the flames with a loved one while sipping a glass of chilled wine. The canopy bed is swathed in lace. A TV, VCR, and CD player hide in a pine armoire. In the bath, a Jacuzzi for two has a serene view and is surrounded by a lip holding an array of fat candles. The equally spacious Master Suite, located downstairs, has a private deck offering a view of the lake. Oriental rugs cover oak floors, another lace canopy decorates the bed, fat shutters shield the windows, and the pink-tile bath has another Jacuzzi.

Every possible amenity is provided. As Judy explained, "We're so far out in the country that it's too far to go for a soft drink at a store, so we provide all of that in the room." In addition to soft drinks, the refrigerator is stocked with bottled water, appetizers such as smoked salmon, and even Baby Watson cheesecakes (or perhaps a special treat prepared by Judy) in case someone has a late-night sweet-tooth craving. A snack basket contains candy bars, cookies, potato chips, and more. Luscious truffles are offered at bedside.

In the morning, breakfast is delivered to the room in a covered basket. It may include cheese blintzes or French toast with cream cheese and pecans topped with an apricot sauce or heart-shaped frittatas with croissants. Of course, there will also be fresh fruit and freshly baked breads.

If guests do decide to venture forth, they will find rowboats and paddleboats for use on the lake, and swimming or fishing are also popular. There are hammocks and chaise lounges on each of the decks, hiking trails cut through the 22-acre property, and a VCR library that includes almost 150 selections. Historic mansions, local wineries, and superb restaurants are located nearby.

What's Nearby

Stanfordville is located just outside Rhinebeck. The Old Rhinebeck Aerodrome, filled with vintage airplanes dating from 1908 to 1937, is one of the most interesting and unusual museums in the state. You can even take a ride in an open cockpit biplane. Visit Montgomery Place in nearby Annandale-on-Hudson, a 23-room, 1804 Livingston family mansion on a 434-acre estate, where you can walk nature trails and pick your own apples in season. (See also Millbrook and Rhinebeck.)

Halsey House Bed & Breakfast

258 Halsey Lane
Water Mill, NY 11976
telephone/fax (516) 726-6527

Innkeeper: Jane E. Halsey
Rooms: 3,1 with private bath and the other 2 share, all with ceiling fans and radios; telephones available for all rooms
On the grounds: Parking, lawns for croquet
Extras: Turndown with chocolates and lemon ice water
Rates: $100 – $275, including either Continental or full breakfast and afternoon refreshments; two-night minimum weekends Memorial Day - Labor Day; three-night minimum holiday weekends
Credit cards accepted: MasterCard and Visa
Open: Year-round except Christmas
Smoking: Non-smoking bed and breakfast
How to get there: From New York City take I-495 (the Long Island Expressway) to exit 70 (Manorville) and follow Route 111 south to Highway 27 (Sunrise Highway). Follow Highway 27 (which becomes County Road 39 and then Montauk Hwy.) to Water Mill. Turn right onto Halsey Lane, which is just beyond the Sienna Spiritual Center and before the windmill. The B&B is the tenth house on the left.

The Halsey name is as old as the Hamptons. In fact, the Old Halsey House in Southampton, which dates to 1648, is a museum house recognized as the oldest saltbox in New York State. The Halsey family have been farmers here since 1644, and they still operate one of the finest farmstands in the Hamptons, The Green Thumb. They pride themselves on growing strictly organic produce.

The Halsey House Bed & Breakfast was built by Jane Halsey's grandparents in 1910, and Jane herself was raised just down the road. It's in a rural setting surrounded by fields of corn, potatoes, lettuces, and tranquility, as far removed from the glitz and frenetic "scene" of the Hamptons as it can be. It's a handsome weathered-shingle house with green shutters, white trim, and a broad front porch on which to repose in a white wicker chair while you decide whether to meander down to the beach today or to sit right here with a good book.

The common rooms are filled with interesting antiques that belonged to Jane's grandparents and lively primitive art by a Halsey relative that is for sale. The lustrous fir floors are covered with hooked rugs. In the parlor, there are white walls with blue trim, a formal sofa, and an antique armoire. Pine pocket doors separate the parlor from the paneled dining room, which has an oval pedestal oak table, a pine sideboard, and a transitional chest as well as a handsome floor-to-ceiling built-in cupboard whose shelves are filled with Jane's collection of flow-blue and Staffordshire china. There's a bay window overlooking the side yard and fields. An old-fashioned kitchen with a huge commercial stove is open to guests, and in the guest pantry Jane will have a jar of freshly baked cookies waiting.

There are three guest rooms. One has a private bath, and the other two share. Both bathrooms have been thoroughly updated with tile floors and pedestal sinks. Room #1 is the largest. It is decorated in blue and white Waverly fabrics and has a matelassé spread on a bed with a walnut headboard that was rescued from the attic. Rooms #2 and #3 share a hall bath.

Room #2 has a sage green decor. There's a handmade quilt on the white wooden cottage slat bed. Room #3 is decorated in white wicker.

In the summer, Jane has found that her guests like to be free to follow their own schedules, so she prepares a Continental breakfast of freshly baked muffins and coffee cakes and sets it out on a sideboard. Her guests frequently choose to eat on the front porch. In the winter, however, she prepares a full breakfast of perhaps blueberry pancakes with bacon or French toast with homemade sausage, which she serves in the dining room.

The B&B is on an acre of land that includes a barn and a summer kitchen from which Jane occasionally sells antiques. There are roosters and guinea hens often trotting around. The quiet country lanes near Halsey House are ideal for walking and bicycling, and the village of Water Mill has interesting shops, restaurants, and museums. The Green Thumb farmstand is just up the street. Don't forget to take home some fresh fruit, vegetables, or flowers.

What's Nearby

The Water Mill windmill, a handsomely restored relic, stands in the center of the town green. Down a little side street, you can visit the Water Mill Museum, located in a picturesque, weathered-shingle mill with an operating water wheel. Craft shows and art exhibitions are mounted most of the year, and you can buy cornmeal ground here. Upstairs, there's an interesting museum devoted to the early settlers of the region. (See also Bridgehampton and Southampton.)

Westhampton Country Manor

28 Jagger Lane
Westhampton Beach, NY 11977
(888) 288-5540 or (516) 288-9000;
fax (516) 288-3292;
e-mail: whamptonBB@aol.com

Innkeepers: Susan and Bill Dalton
Rooms: 6, including 1 three-bedroom, two-bath cottage, all with private baths, air conditioning, telephones on private lines, answering machines, and radios
On the grounds: Parking, swimming pool, Har-Tru tennis court, gardens
Extras: Plain-paper fax, copier, computer with modem available; notary public; a cat named Jill; soda, bottled water, beer, and wine in guest refrigerator
Rates: $75 - $195 depending on season, with full breakfast; two-night minimum weekends Memorial Day - Labor Day; three-night minimum holiday weekends; cottage rented $1,200 weekly from May to October
Credit cards accepted: American Express, MasterCard, Visa
Open: Year-round
Smoking: Non-smoking bed and breakfast
How to get there: From New York City take I-495 (the Long Island Expressway) to exit 70 (Manorville) and follow Route 111 south to Highway 27 (Sunrise Highway). Follow Highway 27 to exit 63 and go south on Old Riverhead Road to Highway 27A (Montauk Highway). Turn right (west) onto Montauk Highway and continue for 2 miles. Turn left onto Jagger Lane. The B&B is on the corner of Jagger Lane and South Country Road.

You can almost hear the hoofbeats of the horses and the passengers alighting from the stagecoach to refresh themselves at this former stagecoach stop, located on a quiet country lane. The handsome buff-colored Colonial clapboard house has seen numerous changes since it began life in 1810. In 1865, a wing was added to accommodate the waiting room and office of Dr. Jagger, for whom the nearby street is named. The 2¹/₂ acres still contain a picturesque old green barn and a cottage that also date to this period.

Westhampton Beach has the advantage of being the closest Hampton to New York City, and it is also near magnificent ocean beaches, outstanding restaurants, and peaceful bicycling and walking lanes. When Bill and Susan Dalton sought a lifestyle change after retiring (he as Deputy Commissioner for the New York City Department of Parks and she as a physician's assistant), they knew they wanted to open a B&B. The old homestead and outbuildings had been on the market for some time but were in reasonably good condition.

Today, the manor house is a treasure-chest of antiques and interesting architecture. In the living room, there are oak floors, wainscotted walls, and sofas covered in floral fabrics before a fireplace with a painted wooden mantel. French doors lead to a pretty porch with wicker chairs and a profusion of plants. On the grand piano rest a vase of fresh flowers, a Tiffany-style lamp, and a silver tray holding stemmed glasses and a decanter filled with an evening cordial. The separate TV room is so home-like that you feel comfortable eating popcorn and putting your feet up. A VCR and video library keep guests entertained for hours.

As an added plus, Susan and Bill Dalton have created a B&B in their historic buildings that offers all the amenities a business traveler may need, including a comfortable office with ample desk space, a computer with a modem, a fax, and a copy machine. Shelves of books line one wall. This was once Dr. Jagger's office, and there's a handsome piece of stained glass here that dates to his time.

The guest rooms are equipped with antiques and featherbeds, and all the baths have been updated to reflect the needs of today's travelers. Room #1 has an antique spool bed, while #2 has an iron and brass bed with a pink and green quilt. Room #4 has a green iron bed.

Convivial conversation is assured in the dining room, which has a round table surveyed by a stained-glass chandelier. Susan bakes all her own breakfast scones, muffins, and cinnamon rolls. She also prepares a generous fruit plate and fixes entrées such as Dutch babies or a gourmet French toast made with coarse bread that's soaked overnight in a batter and then placed on top of fresh fruit in a casserole and baked.

There's a 20- x 40-foot heated swimming pool surrounded by a picket fence, a Har-Tru tennis court, and a three-bedroom, two-bath cottage on the property that is rented during the summer months on a weekly basis only.

What's Nearby

Westhampton Beach maintains two splendid ocean beaches (fee to park) with a pavilion offering restrooms, showers, and concession stands. The pretty village Main Street is home to craft and antiques shops as well as restaurants and boutiques. The Quogue Wildlife Refuge in nearby Quogue is a wonderful place to take children. There are nature trails, scores of tame deer and ducks, and a refuge where rescued animals are nursed back to health. (See also Southampton.)

Albergo Allegria

Route 296
Windham, NY 12496
(800) 6-ALBERGO or (518) 734-5560;
fax (518) 734-5570;
e-mail: mail@AlbergoUSA.com
website: http://www.AlbergoUSA.com

Innkeepers: Lenore & Vito Radelich and Marianna & Leslie Leman

Rooms: 21, including 9 suites, all with private baths, TVs, VCRs, and telephones; 7 with balconies or decks; 6 with air conditioning and whirlpool tubs; 5 with fireplaces, irons, and ironing boards; 3 with desks; 2 rooms with wheelchair access; cribs available

On the grounds: Parking, wooden deck overlooking the river, wildflower and herb gardens

Extras: Afternoon tea with homemade cookies, hot chocolate, and spiced cider; turndown with homemade local chocolates; fax, copier, modem hookup for business travelers; one "smiling" Samoyed named Shalom

Rates: $65 – $195, including full breakfast and afternoon refreshments; two-night minimum weekends; three-night minimum holidays

Credit cards accepted: MasterCard and Visa

Open: Year-round

Smoking: Permitted in guest rooms only; designated non-smoking guest rooms

How to get there: From I-87 (the New York State Thruway), take exit 21 and follow Route 23 west for 23 miles to Route 296. At the intersection, turn left (south) and go .1 mile. The B&B is on the left opposite La Griglia restaurant.

The air was crisp, leaves rested in piles beside the road, the mood was expectant. How else could it be when you're coming to a B&B whose name means "the inn of happiness" in Italian? As we turned onto Route 296 in the tiny village, we were surprised to see hundreds of cars parked beside a nearby summer resort. It seems the annual Fire Department fundraising

dinner, which marks the end of the season, was scheduled for that night. This traditional turkey dinner with all the trimmings has been taking place the Monday after Columbus Day weekend for more than 100 years.

Every time I visit Albergo Allegria, some wonderful new improvements have been made. The B&B, which is composed of two 1876 boarding houses joined together, is the creation of Lenore and Vito Radelich, who were the owners of La Griglia, the Italian restaurant across the street for many years. They are now ably assisted in their B&B venture by their daughter Marianna and her husband, Leslie. The B&B sits on 2 acres on the Batavia Kill Creek, where the original Johnny Weismueller Tarzan movie was filmed in the 1920s.

The most recent addition is the conversion of the carriage house into five luxurious suites. Each has gas fireplaces, whirlpool tubs, king-sized beds, and 15-foot ceilings with skylights. They are romantic and spacious. The suites and rooms in the main part of the B&B are decorated in pine and oak. Each of the rooms is named for a month or a season. June has a mini-cathedral ceiling with stained-glass windows, lace curtains, and an oak wardrobe and chest, while Summer has a king-sized bed and an enormous double whirlpool tub in the bath.

The B&B has several cozy sitting areas. The downstairs parlor has a cherry-wood mantel over the fireplace, and this is where afternoon tea is served. Upstairs, there's another parlor with a fireplace and a TV and VCR as well as an extensive video library. A lovely gift shop is located off the lobby.

Breakfast is served in the dining room, which has individual tables and oak chairs with pressed backs. Vito prepares incredible breakfasts. He may fix an Italian frittata or Belgian waffles, served with fresh whipped cream and berries, or spiced French toast.

The B&B offers ski packages and dinner packages in concert with the restaurant across the street as well as quiet-season packages. If your wanderings bring you near Albergo Allegria in October, do plan to attend the turkey dinner.

What's Nearby

Albergo Allegria is located in the Catskill Mountains. Ski Windham is 1 mile away; Hunter Mountain is 7 miles; cross-country skiing takes place adjacent to the B&B. There are tennis and golf facilities next door, and a marvelous restaurant is just across the street. You can take the kids to the Supersonic Speedway Fun Park or the Zoom Flume Water Park in nearby Durham. Farther afield, Woodstock is an artsy village with a past. The famed 1960s rock concert took place near here. The town is still peppered with art galleries and museums, artist studios, and craft shops. Musical events take place in the summer at Byrdcliffe Arts Colony, as do photography exhibits at the Center for Photography.

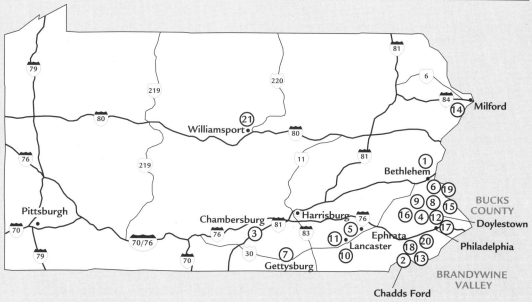

Pennsylvania

Numbers on map refer to towns numbered below.

Sayre Mansion Inn

250 Wyandotte Street
Bethlehem, PA 18015
(610) 882-2100; fax (610) 882-1223

Innkeepers: Norah and John Cappellano; managers, Tom Collins and Jean Fattell
Rooms: 19, including 3 suites, all with private baths, air conditioning, TVs, telephones, and radios; 15 with desks, 2 with fireplaces, 1 with a balcony; 2 rooms with wheelchair access; cribs available
On the grounds: Parking, gardens
Extras: Fax, copier, dataport, mini-refrigerator, VCR, hair dryer, CD player, iron, and ironing board available; meeting room with complete audio/visual equipment; same-day dry cleaning and laundry; access to nearby health club; *The New York Times* and *USA Today* available; complimentary wine, beer, coffee, tea, and snacks on request
Rates: $90 – $135, including Continental breakfast
Credit cards accepted: American Express, Diner's Club, Discover, MasterCard, Visa
Open: Year-round
Smoking: Permitted in 3 rooms; 16 designated non-smoking rooms
How to get there: From Quakertown, take Route 309 north and bear right at the Atlantic Station onto Route 376 north. Continue on Route 376 for about 5.7 miles to a Getty Station on the left. Just after the Getty Station, turn right onto Broadway Avenue and follow the signs toward Route 412 south. Go through the first light; at the stop sign turn left onto Brodhead Avenue. Turn left at the first light onto West 3rd Street. Go straight up the hill (do not bear right) and cross over Wyandotte Street. The Sayre Mansion Inn is on the right.

Located in the heart of Bethlehem, which is mostly known for its steel, lies a distinguished and genteel neighborhood called Fountain Hill. It was once the home of the titans who founded such eminent industries as the Bethlehem Iron Works, which would later be known as Bethlehem Steel, and the Lehigh Valley Railroad. The entire neighborhood is now a National Historic District.

Perhaps the most prominent industrialist of them all was Robert Heysham Sayre, the chief engineer of the Lehigh Valley Railroad and one of the founders of Bethlehem Steel. He built his grand Greek Revival–style mansion high on the hill where he could look down on his railroad and the iron works — just four blocks from Lehigh University, across the street from the handsome Episcopal Church of the Nativity, and near the Fountain Hill Opera House — all institutions Sayre helped to nourish.

The sprawling brick 1858 mansion, which opened as a B&B in 1993, has elegant common rooms with oak floors, elaborate ceiling moldings, oil paintings on the walls, and massive double-hung windows that can be raised to form a doorway to the front veranda. It was restored by Norah and John Cappellano. The B&B is managed by Tom Collins, Norah's brother.

A brass chandelier hangs from the ceiling of the front parlor, which also features a marble fireplace mantel. The dining room has a massive maple table and a wooden mantel over the fireplace. For business travelers, there's a princely conference room on the lower level with stone walls and a vaulted brick ceiling. It's handsomely outfitted with a conference table, chairs, and sophisticated audio/visual equipment. A pantry contains complimentary coffee, sodas, wine, and beer.

There are nineteen guest rooms — most filled with good-quality reproduction pieces, although the suites have fine antiques. All of the baths are spacious and modern, with tile floors and tile tub surrounds. Some have glassed-in showers. Room #3, an interesting garret on the top floor of the mansion, has sloping ceilings and wonderful Gothic-style windows.

Mr. Sayre was a scholarly man who collected fine books. To house them, he built a massive library with an elaborately carved and gilded ceiling. The finest rooms in the B&B are located in this wing. Room #21 includes a substantial section of this amazing ceiling as well as a king-sized bed, an antique armoire, and gilded mirrors. Room #10 is a lovely suite with a living room containing a fireplace, bookshelves filled with books, and a gilded domed ceiling with a crystal chandelier. In the bedroom, there's an antique armoire and an antique carved walnut headboard over the bed.

A Continental breakfast is served in the dining room on black tapestry placemats with old silver and gold-rimmed china. It includes fresh fruit with yogurt, a selection of pastries and breads, cereals, granola, and juices.

What's Nearby — Bethlehem

At the Moravian Museum of Bethlehem, visitors see exhibits that illustrate the ideals, arts, and culture of the early Moravians who settled this area. The National Canal Museum at the Hugh Moore Historical Park in Easton has interactive displays that tell the fascinating story of the building and use of America's interlacing canals. There are also mule-drawn canal boat rides and a visit to a locktender's house. The Bach Choir of Bethlehem offers concerts seasonally that attract a large following. Renninger's Antiques and Farmers Market, an extravaganza that often attracts as many as 1,200 dealers, is located in nearby Denver (near Kutztown). The Nazareth International Speedway is nearby, as is the Lehigh Arts Center.

Wydnor Hall Inn

3612 Old Philadelphia Pike
Bethlehem, PA 18015
(800) 839-0020 or (610) 867-6851;
fax (610) 866-2062

Innkeepers: Charles and Kristina Taylor; manager, Heather Machener

Rooms: 5, including 1 suite, all with private baths, air conditioning, TVs, private line telephones with data-ports, hair dryers, and robes; cribs available

On the grounds: Parking

Extras: Afternoon tea (charge of $12 per person); room service house breakfast and newspaper; custom labeled sparkling water, pressed 100% cotton sheets, heated towel racks, crystal decanters of sherry and brandy; fax available, meeting room

Rates: $75 – $140, including Continental breakfast; full breakfast $8 - $9 additional; two-night minimum weekends May, June, September, and October

Credit cards accepted: American Express, Diner's Club, Discover, MasterCard, Visa

Open: Year-round

Smoking: Non-smoking bed and breakfast

How to get there: From I-78, take exit 21 (Route 412 Hellertown/Bethlehem) and turn left at the end of the ramp onto Route 412 south (this is Main Street, Hellertown). At the 4th traffic light, make a right onto Water Street. In about 1 mile, bear left at the V in the road, then continue 1 mile and turn right at Black River Road. Cross Route 378 at the traffic light. At the stop sign make a left onto Old Philadelphia Pike. Wydnor Hall is .25 mile further on the right.

Bethlehem was settled in 1741 by German immigrants who fled Moravia in current-day Czechoslovakia. The area rapidly became an important agricultural center. The Moravians were ingenious, industrious, and cultured, and several of the early Moravian buildings remain in Bethlehem's historic district.

Wydnor Hall is 3 miles south of Bethlehem. You'll know you've reached the right place when you see the American, Hungarian, and Pennsyl-vania flags gaily hanging at the front door. The handsome 1800s Georgian fieldstone manor house was restored by Charles and Kristina Taylor in 1988. Charles is a retired Bethlehem Steel executive, and Kristina a Hungarian-born artist. Examples of her extraordinary, luminous ceramic pieces will be found on display throughout the B&B, and the oversized cups and saucers she designs are used at breakfast.

The joy of being around this extraordinary

couple is that their sense of curiosity and their desire to keep learning is infectious. Kristina started designing ceramics because she was fascinated by the process. Charles started baking because he loved the French bread he'd eaten in France and he couldn't find anything similar in America. Together, they poured their hearts and souls into this old house to create a B&B to equal the manor house inns they enjoyed so much in Europe. It's a serene and elegant retreat on 2 landscaped acres.

The living room has European oil paintings hanging on creamy ivory walls. A fireplace with a wavy wooden mantel warms the room in winter. A broad selection of books, many of which are leather bound, is available; cut crystal decanters of sherry and brandy sit beside stemmed glasses on a silver tray. Afternoon tea—which includes small sandwiches, light pastries, and a selection of teas—is served every afternoon for an additional charge of $12 per person. Guests generally sit at individual tables draped with heirloom cutwork cloths and eat on either the antique Herend or the Limoges china. The dining room is equally comfortable and inviting, enhanced by two magnificent Waterford crystal chandeliers and Oriental rugs on parquet floors.

The guest rooms are charmingly decorated with antiques and family heirlooms. Beds have handmade quilts and canopies; there are upholstered window seats. The South Room has lacy curtains, drapes made from a quilt, a pretty alcove with a desk, and a window seat. There's a stained-glass window in the bath. The North Suite has a tapestry headboard and a painted blanket chest. The marvelous bath is entered through double doors. It has a black and white tile floor, tall ceilings, a clawfoot tub, and a shower that converts to a steam bath.

Breakfast at Wydnor Hall reflects a European tradition also. Copies of the *Wall Street Journal* or the *International Herald Tribune* are delivered to the room (for an additional charge of $6 for two), or they are available in the dining room, along with coffee, a glass of freshly squeezed orange juice, a selection of seasonal fruit with homemade yogurt, and several of Charles's freshly baked breads such as scones, muffins, or a European crusty roll, along with French fruit preserves. A hot entrée, such as Irish oatmeal pancakes with Swedish lingonberries and maple syrup or an herb and cream cheese omelette with Lancaster County cured bacon, will be prepared for an additional charge.

What's Nearby

See "What's Nearby — Bethlehem," page 195.

The Pennsbury Inn

883 Baltimore Pike
Chadds Ford, PA 19317
(610) 388-1435; fax (610) 388-1436

Innkeepers: Chip Allemann and James Pine
Rooms: 7, all with private baths, air conditioning, TVs, telephones with dataports; 3 rooms with fireplaces, 1 with a balcony
On the grounds: Parking; 8 acres of landscaped grounds, including woodland walking trails; gardens
Extras: Afternoon refreshments; fax and VCR available; two Tibetan terriers named Ying and Yang
Rates: $119 – $225, including full breakfast and afternoon refreshments
Credit cards accepted: American Express, MasterCard, Visa
Open: Year-round
Smoking: Non-smoking bed and breakfast
How to get there: From the NJ Turnpike, take exit 2 (Swedesboro). Take Route 322 west approximately 8 miles to the Commodore Barry Bridge and cross into Pennsylvania. Continue on Route 322 west for approximately 8 more miles to Route 1 (Baltimore Pike). Turn left onto Route 1 and travel south. Go through six traffic lights. The B&B is half a mile after the sixth traffic light on the right across from a large white barn.

In the days when horseback riders and dusty stagecoach travel were the norm, the Old Baltimore Pike (Route 1) was the primary link between Philadelphia and Baltimore. Stone taverns housed and fed travelers on their weary journey. Elegant plantation estates, stone villas, and clapboard mansions were joined by this modern new road.

The original portion of the Pennsbury Inn, which is listed on the National Register of Historic Places, was built of blue granite rubble stone from the Brandywine Valley in 1714. It was originally part of a plantation, then it became an inn, a tavern, a tannery, a stagecoach stop, and eventually the heart of the Brandywine Battlefield during the Revolutionary War. There is some evidence that Lafayette and Daniel Webster once stayed here.

The ingenious inspiration for the restoration of the creamy-white clapboard and brick B&B originated because Chip and Jim wanted a house to showcase the elegant furniture their firm designs. Their store in nearby Hockessin, Delaware, is the retail outlet where the finely crafted pieces from southeast Asia (where designs were heavily influenced by the 18th-century Dutch Colonials) are combined with American and European fabrics. At Pennsbury Inn, the designs are showcased in complete room settings, and all the furniture is for sale.

Guests enter the B&B through the Tavern, which has pine paneled walls and a stucco fireplace flanked by plush red sofas. The TV is hidden behind a cleverly made highboy that appears to hold drawers but instead has a hinged front that slides up to reveal the TV. The Design Room is a blaze of crimson walls, furniture upholstered in red and white toile, and glass-doored cases holding shelves of books. Oil paintings hang on the walls The living room has an enormous arched stone fireplace, a sisal rug, and sofas in rust and green fabrics accented with needlepoint pillows.

The guest rooms are equally elegant. The Winterthur Room, for example, is the one most favored by brides. It has a center Palladian window with a view of the gardens, which include a little waterfall and a pond with koi. The Lafayette Room, located in the portion of the house in which the great French statesman may have stayed, has a private winding staircase, a fireplace, a queen-sized four-poster bed, and window treatments using Pierre Deux toile de Jouy fabric called "Lafayette," which documents the hero's Revolutionary War encounters. The sitting area has glazed yellow-on-yellow walls. In the Daniel Webster Room, there's an original 1749 paneled fireplace mantel and a tiger-maple queen-sized bed.

Breakfast is served in the dining room and also in the living room at a table overlooking the gardens. Fresh flowers dress the tables, which are set with fine china, linens, silver, and crystal. Guest may feast on strawberry pancakes, cinnamon muffins, fresh fruit, and juices. In the afternoon, guests are treated to freshly baked cookies. One time when we were visiting, a batch of coconut macaroons emerged from the oven.

What's Nearby

Longwood Gardens, the magnificent 350-acre horticultural gardens formerly the preserve of Pierre S. duPont, has fantastic displays year-round. The glass-domed conservatories have blooms even on the darkest winter days. Chaddsford Winery is also located nearby, where tastings of excellent white and red wines and a tour of the winery may be had. The Brandywine River Museum, where the Wyeth family paintings are displayed in a Civil War-era grist mill, is within a mile. (See also Mendenhall, Unionville, and West Chester.)

The Ragged Edge Inn

1090 Ragged Edge Road
Chambersburg, PA 17201
(mailing address: 1660 Woodstock Road,
Fayetteville, PA 17222)
(717) 261-1195; fax (717) 263-2118;
e-mail: raggededge@innernet.net

Innkeeper: Darlene Elders
Rooms: 10, including 1 suite, all with private baths, air conditioning, TVs, and radios; 5 with telephones; 4 with Jacuzzis, CD/tape players, irons, and ironing boards; 3 with fireplaces, mini-refrigerators, coffee makers, and desks; 2 with full kitchens and 3 with microwaves; microwave kitchens, refrigerators, and telephones are located on each floor
On the grounds: Parking; on 6.5 acres that include lawns, gardens, and wooded areas
Extras: Fax, computer, and copier available; meeting room; laundry room; dry cleaning pick up and delivery; pantry
Rates: $59 – $179, including full candlelight brunch on weekends and Continental breakfast on weekdays; two-night minimum holiday weekends
Credit cards accepted: American Express, Discover, MasterCard, Visa
Open: Year-round
Smoking: Non-smoking bed and breakfast
How to get there: From I-81, take Pennsylvania exit 6 onto Route 30 east (Lincoln Way). Follow Route 30 toward Gettysburg for 2.5 miles to Ragged Edge Road. Turn left (north) onto Ragged Edge Road. The B&B is 1 mile on the right.

Innkeeper Darlene Elders has a theme for her bed and breakfast, and it goes like this: "If every day were Christmas, our hearts would be filled with loving, caring, giving, and sharing every day — not just at Christmas." So, I had Christmas in June. When I first visited this marvelous B&B, a fully decorated tree graced the grand front-to-back foyer, and others were scattered throughout the B&B — just as they are year-round.

This unique 13,000-square-foot 1900s brick mansion sits on a limestone hilltop surrounded by lawns and gardens. Behind the B&B, there's a 50-foot precipice of ragged rocks that drops to a creek below — giving the B&B its name. Built by Moorhead Kennedy, the president of the Cumberland Valley Railroad and vice president of the Pennsylvania Railroad, the mansion was often the setting for lavish parties. One imagines grand entrances down the three-story chestnut stairway with its elaborately turned spindles while the impressive arched window on the landing provided an impressive backdrop.

Darlene, who is an accountant, purchased

the B&B in 1989 and has been restoring it ever since. Although she opened the B&B with one guest room in 1993, she feels it wasn't until 1997 that she could say the house was complete. Now she's working on the gardens.

The furnishings are as elegant as the setting. In the living room—which has rich mahogany walls, oak floors laid on a diagonal, heavy oak doors, and a fireplace with a marble surround—there are overstuffed mohair sofas and chairs and a lovely mahogany china cabinet filled with Darlene's Christmas collectibles. The butler's pantry now serves as a guest pantry with a microwave, jars of granola and cookies, and a large plate of fresh fruit. On each floor, there's a refrigerator, a microwave oven, and corn for popping.

The guest rooms have lovely antiques as well. The Kennedy Suite, a favorite with honeymooners, has a brass bed, a fireplace flanked by wing chairs, and a bath with marbleized walls, a pedestal sink, and a whirlpool tub. Darlene calls the Ivy Room the "playful honeymoon" room.

The sunny, bright room has a trellis headboard, a hot tub-like whirlpool with a skylight above, and a bath with a real throne and another skylight. The Rose Room has a king-sized bed with iron posts and another fireplace. The lovely bath has a pedestal sink with glass knobs and a whirlpool tub.

During the week there's a Continental help-yourself breakfast, but on weekends Darlene, who learned her terrific cooking style from her father ("I never use a recipe," she says), fixes a fantastic brunch. Guests eat in the dining room, which has a gorgeous handcarved French oak sideboard and table. Every meal is different, so there's no typical menu, but you may be assured that it will be unique. She will start with a whimsy (she calls it a "decadent") — maybe a chocolate pizza. For an entrée she may prepare sherried sausages and eggs over an English muffin with a side dish of herbed potato casserole, but don't count on it. She'll really prepare whatever fits the mood of the day.

What's Nearby

Chambersburg has the dubious distinction of being the only Northern town burned during the Civil War, and it was raided numerous times. Whitetail Ski Resort and Mountain Biking Center offers sports activities year-round, and the Whitetail Fly Fishing School is renowned as one of the best places to learn to fish for trout and smallmouth bass on the East Coast. In addition, there are about five golf courses within a short drive of the B&B. Wilson College is located in Chambersburg, and it is often the site of lectures and concerts, while the Totem Pole Playhouse, in nearby Fayetteville, mounts summer stock productions. A huge antiques mall on Route 30 draws antique hounds from near and far.

Highland Farms

70 East Road
Doylestown, PA 18901
(215) 340-1354

Innkeeper: Mary Schnitzer
Rooms: 4, 2 with private baths and 2 that share a bath, all including air conditioning; telephone with private line available in library
On the grounds: Parking, swimming pool, tennis court, grazing sheep, grape arbor, baby elephant bathtub
Extras: Afternoon canapés and wine; sherry and blackberry brandy at bedside; cat named Nutmeg on premises
Rates: $135 – $195, including full breakfast, afternoon canapés and wine, and evening sherry or brandy; two-night minimum weekends; three-night minimum holiday weekends
Credit cards accepted: MasterCard and Visa
Open: Year-round
Smoking: Non-smoking bed and breakfast
How to get there: From I-78 in New Jersey west, take exit 29 onto I-287 south. Then take exit 13 onto Route 202 south. Follow Route 202 across the Delaware River and continue for about 10 miles to Doylestown. In Doylestown, cross Route 313, then take the second left onto East Road. The B&B is the fourth driveway on the right.

No wonder Oscar Hammerstein wrote such memorable songs! From this hilltop retreat where he and his family lived, he must have experienced many a "beautiful morning." The formal and gracious manor house now gives us reason to warble just as happily, as it's a fantasyland B&B that commemorates Hammerstein's most popular Broadway hits.

Mary Schnitzer has faithfully created a living legacy to the Hammerstein legend. She has done a masterful job of restoring the house, which is listed on the National Register of His-

toric Places, to its former elegance. It's as dramatic as a stage set. The banquet-sized dining room has plum-colored walls and a massive brass chandelier that oversees a Chippendale-style table. An Oriental rug sits on a deep-hued oak floor. In the living room, there's a pastel Savonnerie rug and a lime-wood cabinet built into one wall by Hammerstein's wife, Dorothy. A second-floor library is filled with Hammerstein memorabilia and has a TV/VCR with a video library of his hits. An old wooden sled has been made into a coffee table that's stacked with books about Hammerstein.

One guest room, Carousel, incorporates painted horses on the floor and walls, while another, Oklahoma, has a Southwestern focus that includes an antique oak bed draped with a canopy crocheted by Mary's grandmother. Handpainted magnolias border the ceiling and embellish the corner cupboard. In The King and I, there's a hand-painted fireplace mantel and a bed with a frothy white canopy. Show Boat and Oklahoma share a bath.

Mary goes to great lengths to ensure guests' comfort. Her four-course breakfasts are painstakingly planned, with such treats as grapefruit marinated in blackberry brandy, homemade granola, fresh-baked popovers, mushroom tarts with chive cream, and freshly brewed coffee. In the afternoon she prepares canapés or finger sandwiches to enjoy with wine, lemonade, or iced tea. At night, when guests return to their rooms, they find a silver tray bearing sherry or blackberry brandy and a personal note from their hostess.

The 5-acre grounds contain a tennis court, a pear-shaped swimming pool with a cabana, grazing sheep, and a grape arbor where Henry Fonda was married. A baby elephant's bath is left over from an owner prior to Hammerstein who owned a circus. Flower gardens, terraces, and a wraparound porch complete the picture.

What's Nearby — Doylestown

The James A. Michener Art Museum in Doylestown offers ongoing exhibits for adults and children. See art from the collection of James and Mari Michener and a permanent exhibit that celebrates Michener's contributions to American literature. Next door, the Mercer Museum contains exhibits important to Bucks County, including implements for more than sixty early American trades, such as woodworking and textile manufacturing, as well as Native American tools. The Moravian Pottery and Tile Works in Doylestown was started by Henry Mercer in 1912 to revive Bucks County's 1800s pottery-making industry. The handmade decorated tiles are still being produced and may be purchased at the factory store. There are self-guided tours of the foundry and of the beautiful building that houses it. Fonthill, Henry Mercer's fantastic mansion with 44 rooms, 18 fireplaces, 32 stairwells, and a lavishly embellished interior, was designed by Doylestown's Renaissance man between 1908 and 1910. It's now a National Historic Landmark containing art and decorative arts. It's open to visitors.

The Inn At Fordhook Farm

105 New Britain Road
Doylestown, PA 18901
(215) 345-1766; fax (215) 345-1791

Innkeeper: Carole Burpee; proprietor, Jonathan Burpee
Rooms: 7, including 1 suite and 2 bedrooms in Carriage House, 6 with private baths, all with air conditioning, telephones; 2 with porches; 2 with fireplaces
On the grounds: Gardens, parking, cross-country skiing, croquet, badminton, tobogganing, walking and hiking trails
Extras: Pantry with snacks and freshly baked cookies
Rates: $100 – $200, including full breakfast; two-night minimum weekends from April to December
Credit cards accepted: American Express, MasterCard, Visa
Open: Year-round
Smoking: Non-smoking bed and breakfast
How to get there: From I-78 in New Jersey, take exit 29 onto I-287 south. Then take exit 13 onto Route 202 south. Follow Route 202 across the Delaware River and continue for about 10 miles to Doylestown. In Doylestown, follow State Street (Route 202) south past the hospital and over the Route 611 bypass; watch carefully and turn left at the light onto New Britain Road (next to the gate for Delaware Valley College). The B&B entrance is ¹/4 mile farther on the left through two stone pillars. Follow the drive over the little bridge to the large stone house on the right.

As you sit in W. Atlee Burpee's well-worn study, you can imagine him designing the first Burpee seed catalog; when you stay in the master bedroom, which contains his original furniture, you can almost see him standing at the window in the expectant morning light to see how much his crops have grown; and when you sit in the old living room to read a book from the abundant shelves or to peruse the family albums, you can almost hear the happy laughter of the Burpee children as they assemble for dinner. The estate is now owned by Jonathan Burpee, the grandson of W. Atlee. It's run by Jonathan's wife, Carole.

The Inn at Fordhook Farm is a slice of Americana unlike any other. Like a comfortable pair of slippers, little has changed over the years in the home where three generations of the

Burpee family grew up. Across the back of the house, a tiled terrace is shaded by 200-year-old linden trees and overlooks 60 acres of fields, which slip away from the house, barn, and carriage house in undulating waves. After an afternoon of sightseeing, guests often help themselves to cookies or snacks from the inn's pantry and sit here to enjoy the peaceful quiet.

In the Burpee Room, originally the master bedroom, reached by a stairway directly from the study, there's an old four-poster bed and an antique dresser as well as a wood-burning fireplace and a balcony. Simon's Room has lots of books on shelves and leaded casement windows and another fireplace. The Carriage House has a two-bedroom suite that includes David Burpee's chestnut-paneled library and a Palladian window overlooking the original seed-trial gardens. These are now used as community gardens.

Breakfast is served in the old-world dining room with its beamed ceilings, leaded- and stained-glass windows, and fireplace faced with tiles from the nearby Moravian Tile Works. Breakfast will start with juice and fruit as well as freshly baked pastries. Then, you may be fortunate enough to feast on the inn's famous oatmeal pancakes, which are luscious, thick, and wonderful served with maple syrup. On request, guests may enjoy afternoon tea with lemon bars, tarts, and tea.

What's Nearby

See "What's Nearby — Doylestown," page 203.

Pine Tree Farm
2155 Lower State Road
Doylestown, PA 18901
(215) 348-0632

Innkeepers: Ron and Joy Feigles
Rooms: 3, all with private baths, air conditioning, telephones, hair dryers, and desks
On the grounds: Parking, swimming pool, pond, 16½ acres of lawns, gardens, and nature areas
Extras: Afternoon tea, wine, and cookies in the pantry
Rates: $150 – $170, including breakfast and afternoon refreshments; two-night minimum weekends; three-night minimum holiday weekends
Credit cards accepted: None
Open: Year-round except for Christmas
Smoking: Non-smoking bed and breakfast
How to get there: From I-78 in New Jersey, take exit 29 onto I-287 south. Then take exit 13 onto Route 202 south. Follow Route 202 across the Delaware River and continue for about 10 miles to Doylestown. Stay on Route 202 (do not take the Route 202 Bypass). Go through the first traffic light and bear left at the second traffic light onto Court Street. Pine Tree Farm is approximately 1.25 miles ahead on the left.

I will never forget my first visit to Pine Tree Farm. As I stood beside the handsome stone farmhouse, admiring the clipped lawns beneath the apple and pine trees, I sensed I was not alone. There, in the shade of an apple tree, a pair of deer watched me expectantly, although they soon resumed their feast of fallen apples. It's this sense of calm and peace that Joy and Ron Feigles have created, where humans and wildlife live contentedly side by side, that brings guests back again and again.

Joy and Ron have been welcoming guests to their 1730s fieldstone manor house since 1987, and it's hard to imagine more gracious hosts. Joy has a degree in hotel administration, she's a talented decorator, and, in addition, she loves to cook. Guests are treated as treasured friends at Pine Tree Farm rather than as overnight travelers. While we became acquainted, we had a glass of wine and nibbled on the cheese that had been set out for guests.

The living room, with an abundance of plants, is gracious and charming and overlooks the pool and the gardens. The dining room has a fireplace in the corner. The tiny library, which has another fireplace and stacks of interesting books, is the cozy retreat that I like best. A patchwork cloth in rich velvet colors covers a round table, and puffy love seats face each other in front of the fireplace, which is faced with Mercer tiles. There's a French door that leads to the gardens and to the pond in the distance.

I love the enchanting guest rooms Joy and Ron have created. My favorite is the Pink Room, with its romantic white twig canopy bed draped in a mauve floral chintz. Upstairs a two-room suite has a white iron bed, and a pretty yellow room contains a pine pineapple-post bed and a window seat with views of the pond. The bathroom is stenciled. Each of the rooms has its own personality, but they are all crisp and bright with an abundance of attractive fabrics.

Joy's breakfasts are bountiful and convivial. We started with fresh fruit and homemade granola, a cranberry scone, and coffee cake made from a recipe that Joy's mother had used for years. It's a rich, buttery confection topped with brown sugar and nuts. Joy next served Grand Marnier French toast with maple syrup and German sausage. Other favorite offerings include puffed-apple pancakes and eggs Benedict.

Although we felt removed from all hint of civilization on this low-key estate, we especially appreciate that it's close to the many attractions of Doylestown. There are excellent restaurants nearby as well as antiques shops, boutiques, and museums.

What's Nearby

See "What's Nearby — Doylestown," page 203.

Innkeepers: Glenn and Mildred Wissler
Rooms: 5, all with private baths, air conditioning, and radios; telephone available in living room
On the grounds: Parking, pond with swans and ducks, gardens
Extras: Chocolates at turndown
Rates: $95 – $135, including full breakfast; two-night minimum weekends
Credit cards accepted: Discover, MasterCard, Visa
Open: Year-round
Smoking: Non-smoking bed and breakfast
How to get there: From I-76 take exit 21 and go south on Route 222 for 5 miles to Route 322. Travel west on Route 322. After passing the Family Time Restaurant, take the fifth road on the right (at Pine Tree Motors) onto Clearview Road. The B&B is the first farm on the right.

Clearview Farm Bed & Breakfast

355 Clearview Road
Ephrata, PA 17522
(717) 733-6333

On a rural country lane in the midst of a patchwork of neatly fenced fields, red barns, blue silos, and white houses, Clearview Farm stands out. The handsome limestone farmhouse has a spring-fed pond in its front yard, spacious lawns, brick pathways, and trim gardens, and it sits on a hill offering splendid views across the fields to the distant town. Glenn and Mildred Wissler raised their children here, tilled the land, and tended their 200-acre farm for thirty-nine years before opening it to guests.

When they first purchased the property, they decided they wanted a "modern" house and spent a great deal of effort covering the oak floors with wall-to-wall carpeting and removing the wainscotting from the walls. Over the years, however, they grew to appreciate the craftsmanship of their 1814 house, and when they converted it to a B&B, they restored much of the house's fine old features. Mildred confessed, "Glenn loves a construction project anyway."

Today the living room has a light green carpet and the Victorian sofas and chairs are upholstered in a rainbow of pastel colors. There are an abundance of happy ferns in planters and a bay window with views of the fields. The den has a fireplace, books, and games. In the dining room, there's a rose rug, a brass chandelier, and a beautiful antique Victorian armoire with glass doors revealing the set of Royal Doulton china that's used for breakfast.

The guest rooms contain fine Victorian antiques as well. In the Royal Room, for example, there's an elaborately carved walnut Victorian bed, a Victorian étagère, and marble-topped Victorian tables. In the spacious bath, there's a clawfoot tub and a shower. The Princess Room has a canopy bed with a lacy canopy, a marble-topped Victorian dresser and a Victorian cradle filled with dolls. All the handmade quilts on the beds were made by Mildred. Guests especially appreciate the lovely Victorian chests and colonial drysinks that Glenn used as bases for bathroom sinks.

Breakfast is a lavish repast that will begin with freshly baked muffins or cinnamon rolls, followed by perhaps a ham and cheese soufflé, which itself is followed by raspberry crêpes. The plates are among the prettiest you will see, decorated abundantly with bright edible flowers.

Guests love to meander around the 200-acre farm, which the Wisslers continue to farm.

What's Nearby — Ephrata

The Ephrata Cloister, one of Pennsylvania's most interesting attractions, is located here. Built of stone in a German medieval style in 1732, the Cloister was one of the earliest experiments in communal living. Designed as a retreat for Protestant men and women, it was renowned for its printing and publishing center and for the poetry and music its members produced. Today there are tours of 12 restored buildings, craft demonstrations year-round, and, on summer weekends, a musical drama depicting cloister life. The lovely stone buildings are on beautiful park-like grounds. Nearby you can tour the Pennsylvania Dutch countryside for handmade quilts or attend the famous Kutztown antiques fair. (See also Lancaster and Lititz.)

Innkeeper: Dorothy Graybill

Rooms: 8, including 1 suite, all with private baths, air conditioning, fireplaces, and night shirts; 6 with mini-refrigerators and desks; 3 with whirlpool tubs; telephones available in all rooms; 1 room with wheelchair access

On the grounds: Parking, award-winning dahlia garden, other gardens

Extras: Snacks, including freshly baked cookies, available all day; chamber music piped into rooms; fresh flowers in rooms; guest pets allowed with prior permission; one rabbit named Peter on premises

Rates: $75 – $170, including full breakfast and afternoon refreshments; two-night minimum if stay includes Saturday and on holiday weekends

Credit cards accepted: MasterCard and Visa

Open: Year-round

Smoking: Non-smoking bed and breakfast

How to get there: From I-76, take exit 21 and follow Route 222 south. At the Ephrata exit, turn west onto Route 322 (Main Street) and travel 2.5 miles, passing through the town of Ephrata. After passing the Ephrata Cloister, you will climb a long hill. At the traffic light at the top of the hill, turn left onto Academy Drive and then immediately turn right into the B&B's parking lot. It is on the corner of Academy Drive and Main Street.

Historic Smithton Inn

900 West Main Street
Ephrata, PA 17522
(717) 733-6094

When Dorothy Graybill purchased the Smithton Inn in 1983, she began a personal odyssey that has never stopped. Although the handsome 1763 fieldstone structure had been used as a stagecoach stop and stone tavern from its beginning, Dorothy had quite a different concept for her inn than one reminiscent of the rough and lusty meeting place of its earliest years. At some point during your stay, for example, do not fail to admire the recent additions of raised-stucco murals in the gables on the west wing and the northwest side. Executed by Dorothy's partner, Allen, one depicts the B&B's logo and the other shows the sun, moon, and stars with doves raining love and peace on the earth in the shape of heart raindrops.

Located in the heart of the Pennsylvania Dutch countryside—in an area of Mennonite,

Amish, and Brethren homes and horse-drawn carriages and farm wagons—the inn is a showcase of local crafts and styles. There's a painted chest in the entry; the canopy beds and desks were handmade; the tiles surrounding the whirlpool tubs were glazed locally; there are hand-woven bed canopies and drapes, hand-stitched quilts on the beds, and hand-painted blanket chests on which to place your suitcase. The baths, however, are up-to-date and modern. Slip into one of the handmade nightshirts provided and sit in a leather chair before the room fireplace in the evening and attempt to read a book from your room's collection by candlelight, thus immersing yourself totally in the B&Bs charms.

Dorothy was raised in Lancaster County, and she has a wealth of information about local history. As you sit in the dining room admiring the display of quilts on the wall, the early Pennsylvania redware on the pine sideboard, the gift items on the harvest table, and the folk art on the windowsill, you appreciate Dorothy's dedication to local artistry and crafts.

Breakfast will include juice and fruit as well as perhaps blueberry waffles or apple pancakes. In the special snack area, guests can help themselves to raspberry lemonade or peach iced tea as well as hot tea, cookies, and pretzels.

There are almost an acre of gardens to explore and benches to sit on to absorb their beauty. Don't miss the incredible display of award-winning dahlias, and there's a pond and a fountain as well. Peter, the pet black flop-eared rabbit, lives in a cage in the shade of the summer trees.

What's Nearby

See "What's Nearby — Ephrata," page 209.

Isaac Stover House

845 River Road
Erwinna, PA 18920
(610) 294-8044; fax (610) 294-8132

Innkeeper: Vincent Howe; proprietors, Sally Jessy Raphael and Karl Soderlund
Rooms: 7, 5 with private baths, 2 share one bath, all with air conditioning; telephone available in Tap Room and kitchen; portable telephones available
On the grounds: Parking, gardens, hammock
Extras: Turndown with chocolates, cookies, and port; wine and cheese every afternoon; three cats named Mac, Sam, and Dee on premises
Rates: $125 – $175, including full breakfast, afternoon wine and cheese, and evening cookies and port; two-night minimum, Labor Day weekend through New Year's weekend.
Credit cards accepted: MasterCard and Visa
Open: Year-round
Smoking: Permitted in downstairs common areas only
How to get there: From the New Jersey Turnpike, take exit 14 and then take I-78 west to exit 15 (Clinton/Pittstown). Turn left at the end of the ramp onto Route 513 south and go for 11 miles to the New Jersey town of Frenchtown. Cross the Delaware River on the Frenchtown Bridge and turn left onto Route 32 south. Follow Route 32 for 2 miles. The inn is on the right.

When Sally Jessy Raphael and her husband and manager, Karl Soderlund, purchased the brick Bucks County manor house with its mansard roof in 1987, it was on a whim. But Sally dived in with her characteristic enthusiasm and put together a hodge-podge of rooms that were filled to the brim with old furniture and campy paraphernalia acquired at flea markets and antiques shops.

But that was then, and this is now. In 1995, Sally decided to start over, and this time, acknowledging the stately old house's Federal style, she chose a refined and elegant decor, combining period antiques with personal mementos collected on trips around the world. The transformation included a bright coat of white paint on the exterior trim, a sparkling new kitchen, and guest rooms that are dignified and charming. Located across the street from the Delaware River, many of the rooms have lovely views of the lazy river.

The common rooms, which earlier had seemed dark, are now painted a white-on-white scheme so that the marble fireplaces are featured. The random-width pine floors gleam, uncovered by rugs. Pretty French chairs and love seats in the double parlors are lighted by a crystal chandelier and backed by palms. In the Victorian tap room, the pecan wall panels cast a soft glow. There's a piano along the wall, and a bar, where wine and cheese are served every afternoon, is in the corner.

The guest rooms contain a combination of antiques and period pieces, all accented with rich fabrics and wallpapers. The Bird Room, for example, has an iron bed and fanciful bird wallpaper. The Blue and Cream Room combines moire fabric with French toile wallpaper and has a dark-wood bedroom suite with flowers painted across the drawers and headboard. Sally hand-painted several of the drawers herself. In the Yellow Room an iron canopy bed is covered with a rich tapestry and Pierre Deux paper covers the walls.

Vinny Howe, the innkeeper, is a great cook and justifiably proud of his new kitchen. Guests are invited into the kitchen while he prepares breakfast. In fact, they're invited into the kitchen at any hour of the day. It's just that kind of place. For breakfast he will prepare muffins and breads, fresh fruit and juice, and perhaps an omelet with home fries or eggs Benedict. Sometime (although not often) Sally herself shows up to make her favorite French toast.

The B&B is located on 10 acres and is directly across from the Delaware River, where the old towpath makes a great walking and bicycling trail. For an afternoon of pure relaxation, however, I love to take a book out to the hammock under the evergreen trees and lose myself in a well-told tale.

What's Nearby

Five covered bridges are close enough to the B&B to offer great bicycling destinations. Built between 1832 and 1874, they span a variety of styles. Bucks County River Country is also nearby in Point Pleasant, where canoes, tubes, kayaks, and rafts can be rented for trips down the scenic Delaware River. (See also Kintnersville, New Hope, Ottsville, and Upper Black Eddy.)

Battlefield Bed & Breakfast Inn

2264 Emmitsburg Road
Gettysburg, PA 17325
(717) 334-8804; fax (717) 334-7330

Innkeepers: Charlie and Florence Tarbox
Rooms: 8, including 2 suites, all with private baths and air conditioning; 4 with desks; 2 with fireplaces; cribs available; portable telephone in summer kitchen available
On the grounds: Parking, 46 acres of grounds including two ponds, a creek, and a wildlife preserve; barn, stable, and horses
Extras: Civil War demonstrations; fax, telephone, copy machine available; tea and cookies offered all day
Rates: $75 – $160, including full breakfast; two-night minimum weekends
Credit cards accepted: American Express, Diner's Club, Discover, MasterCard, Visa
Open: Year-round
Smoking: Permitted only in separate vacation house on property
How to get there: From Route 15, take the Steinwehr Avenue exit north toward Gettysburg. The driveway to the B&B is exactly 2.4 miles ahead on the right. Turn into the dirt road at the sign and drive .25 mile to its end.

The battle of Gettysburg was a pivotal turning point in the Civil War. The Confederate and Federal Armies waged a three-day battle on July 1, 2, and 3 of 1863 that resulted in 51,000 American men either losing their lives or being wounded or captured. President Abraham Lincoln's eloquent tribute to these men still rings in our ears. "The brave men, living and dead, who struggled here, have consecrated it (the ground) far above our poor power to add or detract. The world will little note, nor long remember what we say here, but it can never forget what they did here." A visit to Gettysburg, and especially to Battlefield Bed and Breakfast Inn, makes these events come to life.

If you choose to stay at the Battlefield Bed and Breakfast, an 1809 clapboard and stone building tucked away at the end of a dirt road on 46 acres in the heart of the battlefield, you will become totally immersed in the Gettysburg experience. In this quiet and peaceful setting with spacious lawns, stables and horses, a creek, walking trails through a nature preserve where deer and fox live, two ponds with Canada geese, snowy egrets, blue heron, and an abundance of bird feeders, you will be greeted by Charlie or Florence dressed in full Civil War-era attire. Following breakfast every morning you will be given a living history lesson or demonstration. Perhaps Charlie, who seems to live and breathe the Civil War era, will induct you into the infantry and issue you a uniform, or he will demonstrate a cavalry program on one of his horses, or you will play Civil War-era games and sing songs.

The former summer kitchen is now a gathering room with a square grand piano, a television and a VCR, and a huge old cooking fireplace with a racheting system for raising and lowering pots. The parlor has another fireplace and cabinets filled with interesting old china. There's a small gift shop containing books about the Civil War and small artifacts.

The guest rooms are all named for Civil War regiments or soldiers who fought on the property or were engaged in battle from these fields, and each door has a copy of the appropriate regimental flag on the door. In Graham's Battery, there's a braided rug on the floor, a quilt on the bed, an antique oak ice box used as an end table, and a fireplace. In General Merritt's Headquarters, the four-poster bed is covered with another quilt, there's a sitting room, and another fireplace. The baths are simple and functional and have stenciling on the walls. One of the most atmospheric rooms is the 2nd US Dragoons, which has rock walls, a beamed ceiling, an oak bed with a quilt coverlet, and a campaign desk.

A full breakfast is served in the dining room every morning. A typical menu might include freshly baked applesauce/pecan muffins with an apple crumble topping served with whipped cream, followed by apricot cream French toast accompanied by Italian sausage and dilled potatoes, or the menu may include an entrée of cream cheese crêpes with blackberry sauce. Florence garnishes all the plates with colorful edible flowers.

There are miles of trails to hike, and with even a semi-active imagination, the Civil War comes alive as you tramp the fields where the awful battles took place.

What's Nearby — Gettysburg

Gettysburg National Military Park is a 4,000-acre preserve dotted with almost 2,000 military monuments and more than 40 miles of roads. Stop to read the markers or take a tour with a guide. The park is guaranteed to have a lasting impact on both adults and children. Visitors to Gettysburg should plan to stay several days to experience the full historical impact. The only permanent home of Dwight and Mamie Eisenhower is also located here. A visit to their humble farm offers new insights into the life of one of America's most popular presidents.

Innkeepers: Denis and Roberta Sullivan
Rooms: 8, all with private baths, air conditioning, telephones, and radios; 5 with fireplaces; 4 with spa/steam showers; 1 with a Jacuzzi; TVs/VCRs available on request; 1 room with wheelchair access
On the grounds: Parking, large patio, garden
Extras: Chocolates in rooms; tea, cakes, cookies, and sometimes beer and wine available in dining room every afternoon; dinners arranged on request; one chocolate Labrador named "Mousse au Chocolat"; passes provided for nearby Y, which has a pool, exercise equipment, and racquetball
Rates: $78 – $135, including full breakfast; two-night minimum holiday weekends
Credit cards accepted: American Express, Discover, MasterCard, Visa
Open: Year-round except Christmas
Smoking: Non-smoking bed and breakfast
How to get there: From Route 15, take the Baltimore Street exit onto Route 97. Proceed 2.7 miles to the third traffic light. Turn right onto East Middle Street. The Gaslight Inn is at #33, the third house on the right. The parking area is in the rear.

The Gaslight Inn

33 East Middle Street
Gettysburg, PA 17325
(717) 337-9100

In the summer, during the height of the tourist season, the streets of downtown Gettysburg throng with visitors. The small town swells to accommodate the 2.5 million visitors who come annually. If at all possible, time your visit to avoid July and August. I visited Gettysburg one year in January, when the skies were a robin's egg blue and it was possible to drive the entire battlefield circuit at a leisurely pace, with few other cars sharing the road.

The Gaslight Inn, a creamy-colored 1872 brick building, is Gettysburg's most upscale B&B. Guests enter through a wrought iron gate and walk along a brick garden path bordered with tulips and lilies and lighted by a gas lamp.

When Denis and Roberta Sullivan purchased the building in 1994, it was a ramshackle apartment house. Following a total renovation, they opened it as a B&B in 1994. Crisp, fashionable, and stylish, the B&B blends antique and modern effortlessly.

The B&B has double parlors with pale buff-colored walls, Oriental rugs on narrow-strip oak floors, Oriental screens, and elaborate Lincrusta decor along the top of the walls. On the opposite side of the entry, the dining room is enhanced by a Victorian chandelier, stained-glass windows rescued from an old church, an inlaid cherry table, and a lovely china cabinet. Soft music plays throughout the rooms and can even be heard on the porch. A courtyard in the garden (which has a little pond) offers a place to relax in the afternoon or to take a cup of coffee in the morning before heading out to visit the sights. Upstairs, there's another sitting room with shelves stocked with books about the Civil War as well as a TV, VCR, and a video library with Civil War documentaries and movie classics.

The guest rooms are serene oases. The Daisy Room, which is wheelchair accessible, has oak floors and a private brick patio. Upstairs, the Aster and the Sweet William Rooms both have gas fireplaces, handsome brass beds, and porches. The Ivy Room has ivy wallpaper and a bed with a lovely antique French Louis XIV head-board. All the baths are sparkling fresh with tile floors and tub surrounds. The Lily Room has a double Jacuzzi tub, and four of the rooms have double-sized steam spa/showers.

Roberta is a caterer as well as an innkeeper, and one of the first things you'll see when entering the dining room is the array of baked goods on the buffet. There will probably be a hot dish as well as several kinds of cookies, nuts, chocolates, soft drinks, hot coffee or tea, beer, and wine.

Breakfast is served in the dining room at the large cherry table. The meal will always start with six choices of juice, fresh fruit (perhaps a baked apple or a mélange of tropical fruit), and freshly baked breads such as feather-light scones or sticky buns. Roberta will then prepare one of her specialty entrées — perhaps gingerbread waffles with fresh fruit and whipped cream or orange buttermilk pancakes.

What's Nearby

See "What's Nearby — Gettysburg," page 215.

The Old Appleford Inn

218 Carlisle Street
Gettysburg, PA 17325
(800) 275-3373 or (717) 337-1711;
fax (717) 334-6228;
website: http://www.virtualcities.com/pa

Innkeepers: John and Jane Wiley
Rooms: 11, including 1 suite, all with private baths, air conditioning, and radios; 3 with desks; 2 with fireplaces; telephone available in library
On the grounds: Parking, gardens
Extras: Freshly baked cookies, port, and sherry available; chocolates on pillow; fax, hair dryers, iron, and ironing board available; one Golden Retriever named Honeybunch, three cats named Magic, Cassie, and Orie on premises
Rates: $80 –$150, including full breakfast; two-night minimum weekends from April to October and holiday weekends
Credit cards accepted: American Express, Discover, MasterCard, Visa
Open: Year-round
Smoking: Non-smoking bed and breakfast
How to get there: From Route 15, take the York Street exit and travel 3 miles west on Route 30. Turn right at Lincoln Square onto Carlisle Street. The B&B is on the left in just over 2 blocks.

The Old Appleford Inn, which opened in 1984, was Gettysburg's first B&B. Located next to Gettysburg College, the 1867 Italianate Victorian brick mansion is in a quiet residential area of private homes and fraternity houses. It's been owned by John and Jane Wiley, experienced innkeepers who formerly operated a full-service inn in Eagles Mere, Pennsylvania, since 1995. Friendly, helpful, and knowledgeable, they pamper their guests with personalized suggestions for local sightseeing, port and sherry in the evening, and freshly baked cookies on arrival.

Just off the wide entry hall, there's a tall reception desk backed by shelves containing Jane's antique bottle collection. In the living room, there's a grand piano and a fireplace, but the cozy library, which has shelves filled with numerous books about the Civil War, oak tables, and Oriental rugs on oak floors as well as games and puzzles, is the spot where most guests congregate. On the second floor landing, the antique violin collection attracts considerable guest attention, as do the many cross-stitch samplers throughout the inn. There's a sun room, which is filled with pretty white wicker chairs with colorful floral cushions, an abundance of plants, a refrigerator filled with soft drinks, a little TV, and a Kitchen Queen cupboard where hot coffee and tea, a bowl of fresh apples, snacks, and cookies will be found.

The guest rooms are charming, and they all have private baths, although these vary in size and accoutrements. The nicest is the General Pickett, which is also the largest room. It has two bedrooms, both with iron beds, and a terrific bath with a navy blue tile floor, navy towels, and an oak dresser holding the sink. The General Longstreet has an oak bed and an oak dresser with a sink in the room. The bath is small.

Breakfast is served in the formal dining room by candlelight. There's a lovely oak buffet and a corner cupboard filled with Jane's great-grandmother's Haviland china. Guests are seated around an oak table. Following fresh fruit and freshly baked muffins, Jane may serve tomato-basil eggs or cherry crêpes.

The B&B sits on spacious lawns with a pretty garden in back. There are benches spaced among the flower gardens.

What's Nearby

See "What's Nearby — Gettysburg," page 215.

Barley Sheaf Farm

5281 York Road (Route 202)
(mailing address: P.O. Box 10)
Holicong, PA 18928
(215) 794-5104; fax (215) 794-5332;
e-mail: barleysheaf@netreach.net

Innkeepers: Veronika and Peter Süess
Rooms: 12, including 4 suites, all with private baths and air conditioning; 8 with telephones; 4 with desks, patios, and robes; 3 with fireplaces; 1 with a kitchen; 1 suite with wheelchair access
On the grounds: Parking, swimming pool, pastures with grazing sheep, spring-fed pond, walking trails, volleyball, badminton, croquet, horseshoes
Extras: Coffee, tea, and treats in the afternoon; chocolates at turndown; fax available; one Swiss Bernese mountain dog named Barley Boy, one canary named Lovebug
Rates: $105 – $236, including full breakfast; two-night minimum weekends; three-night minimum holiday weekends
Credit cards accepted: American Express, MasterCard, Visa
Open: Year-round
Smoking: Non-smoking bed and breakfast
How to get there: From I-78 in New Jersey, take exit 29 onto I-287 south. Then take exit 13 onto Route 202 south. Follow Route 202 across the Delaware River and continue for about 6 miles. Watch for the B&B sign at a driveway on the left.

When George S. Kaufman, the eminent playwright, was in residence here in the 1920s and 1930s, it was the scene of lively entertainment. He worked on many of his plays here, although *Guys and Dolls* was much later. He probably met with neighbor Oscar Hammerstein on occasion here also.

The pretty farmhouse and outbuildings were converted to a B&B in 1976, making it the first in Bucks County. The original innkeepers, after a long and successful career, sold the property to Peter and Veronika Süess, a Swiss/German couple, in 1994, and the new innkeepers have been fortifying the high standards ever since. Friendly and outgoing, they have particularly concentrated on increasing their corporate business by converting a former outbuilding to a small corporate/executive center and by adding two luxury suites to the barn, one with a woodstove.

The B&B is located on 30 acres that include sweeping lawns, pastures with grazing sheep, walking trails through wooded areas, a pond for fishing, a flower garden, and a swimming pool. At a safe distance, there are hives of bees who produce honey for the B&B. We love the sense of peace and tranquility we feel here. The first sound you'll hear in the morning is a rooster crowing or birds singing merrily in the trees. Barley Boy, a Swiss Bernese mountain dog, will greet you and try to engage you in play. Lovebug, the canary, happily trills a pretty song in the breakfast room.

Guests enter through a reception area and small gift shop. Conversation areas are grouped around the fireplace in the living room and also in the small TV room. There are games, numerous books to choose from, puzzles, and a small table that's set with coffee, tea, and a treat in the afternoon.

The guest rooms vary from those in the main house, which have simple, country decor, to the elegant suites in the barn. They have all been freshly painted in light, soothing colors and decorated with spritely floral fabrics. There are iron beds, sleigh beds, brass beds, and four-posters. Many of the baths have clawfoot tubs. I've always loved the cozy little cottage rooms reached by walking along a stone pathway with beds of waist-high tiger lilies on either side. They have beamed ceilings, brick floors, window seats, and fireplaces.

The multi-level conference center, which is complete with private interview offices, overlooks the pastures of grazing sheep. It seems to me that only congenial decisions could be made in such a relaxed setting.

A full breakfast is served in the sunny brick-floored dining room that's filled with plants and has a wood-burning stove. Guests enjoy chatting around the long tables, and there are views across the lawns to the pool. Breakfast will begin with freshly squeezed orange juice, followed by fruit and freshly baked breakfast breads. The entrée might be a potato-onion frittata or croissant French toast topped with cranberry sauce.

Holicong is in the heart of Bucks County, midway between the museums in Doylestown and the shops and restaurants in New Hope.

What's Nearby

Carousel World, located nearby in Lahaska, features a museum of carousel art, and visitors can ride an antique carousel. The Pearl S. Buck House is located nearby in Dublin. The 1835 stone house was the home of America's first woman to earn the Nobel and Pulitzer Prizes. (See also Doylestown, Mechanicsville, and New Hope.)

The Bucksville House

4501 Durham Road (Route 412)
Kintnersville, PA 18930
telephone/fax (610) 847-8948

Innkeepers: Barbara and Joe Szollosi
Rooms: 5, including 1 suite, all with private baths, air conditioning, and desks; 3 with fireplaces; 1 with a patio; 1 room with wheelchair access
On the grounds: Parking, two ponds, a screened gazebo, herb and flower gardens
Extras: Afternoon refreshments of homemade cookies, tea, and cider; evening carafe of homemade wine; telephone, fax, copier available; one cat named Muffy on premises
Rates: $100 – $150, including full breakfast; two-night minimum weekends; three-night minimum holiday weekends
Credit cards accepted: American Express, Discover, MasterCard, Visa
Open: Year-round
Smoking: Non-smoking bed and breakfast
How to get there: From I-78, take the 1st exit in Pennsylvania (Easton). At the top of the ramp, turn left and then turn left again at the first road onto Cedarville Road. Go 1.5 miles to its end. Turn right onto Easton Road (Route 611) south and go 12 miles to Ferndale. Turn right at the light onto Church Hill Road. Go 1.5 miles to its end. The B&B is on the left on the corner of Durham Road (Route 412).

The handsome creamy-colored stucco house with grey-green shutters has been welcoming travelers for most of its 202 years. In the 1840s it was known as the Bucksville Hotel, and subsequently it became a stagecoach stop. It appears as if wagon wheels were repaired in the room that is now the dining room. During Prohibition, the building served as a speakeasy, and in the 1930s it was a tavern. Barbara and Joe Szollosi, former teachers, restored the gracious building in 1984 and opened it as a B&B.

They did a terrific restoration job. Barbara has been collecting fine antiques for years, and they now grace the rooms of the B&B. In addition, Joe is a craftsman, and he has made numerous reproduction pieces. Guests enter a cozy brick-floored room with an extensive library in pine bookshelves, skylights, a spinning wheel, a Shaker-style bench, and tables for checkers and games. A brilliant red and white quilt hangs on the wall. The large living room has a gracious fireplace with a wood mantel and a lovely secretary, while the den has random-width pine floors, a coal stove, exceptional quilts hanging on the walls, and a collection of old games.

The guest rooms are beautifully furnished with beds with lacy fishnet canopies or pineapple or cannonball posts. There are braided and Oriental rugs on the floors, and three of the rooms have woodburning fireplaces. Barbara has an eagle's eye for gorgeous handmade quilts. Some of the more than seventy exquisite examples that she's purchased at antique auctions cover the beds and hang on the walls. She's supplemented the collection with intricate examples made by a local craftswoman. The baths are finished with wood or tile floors.

The little touches that Barb and Joe have thought of to pamper their guests include a plate of freshly baked cookies and cider in the afternoon and in the evening, a carafe of Joe's homemade wine (there are several nearby commercial wineries to visit also).

The B&B is located on 4 acres that include a spacious brick courtyard with stone and wood benches shaded by a massive maple tree. Neat brick pathways lead to a grape arbor, an herb garden, and a flower garden with azaleas, rhododendrons, perennials, annuals, and bulbs that also includes two ponds. A screened-in gazebo overlooks the gardens.

Breakfast is served in the dining room, which has another fireplace or, in summer, in the gazebo. A typical meal may include Angelic eggs casserole—a cheese dish that contains three cheeses and puffs up like a soufflé—accompanied by ham and freshly made muffins or perhaps orange waffles with bacon and sausage.

What's Nearby

The Bucks County Horse Park & Polo Club is located just around the corner. Guests can ride here if they bring their own horse or watch polo games if they have not. Nockamixon State Park offers plenty of summer fun including a huge swimming and diving pool, hiking and bicycling trails, picnicking areas, and a 7-mile-long lake with canoes, paddleboats, and rowboats for rent. Or, stop at the Antique Hardware Store and Andrew's Furniture and Crafts in Kintnersville for a look at the interesting tools and local crafts. Sand Castle Winery is located nearby.

Lightfarm Bed & Breakfast

2042 Berger Road
Kintnersville, PA 18930
(610) 847-3276; fax (610) 847-2026
website: http://www2.epix.net/~litefarm

Innkeepers: Max and Carol Sempowski
Rooms: 4, including 1 suite, all with private baths, air conditioning, TVs, radios, hair dryers, and desks; telephones and cribs available
On the grounds: Parking, spring-fed pond, hot tub, fields with sheep grazing, nature trails
Extras: Archaeological dig and museum; fax available; turndown with Hershey kiss and special note; pet accommodations available for a fee; six dogs, farm cats, two pot-bellied pigs, flock of sheep on property
Rates: $85 – $160, including full breakfast; two-night minimum in October and on holiday weekends
Credit cards accepted: American Express, MasterCard, Visa
Open: Year-round
Smoking: Non-smoking bed and breakfast
How to get there: From I-78, take the 1st exit in Pennsylvania (Easton). At the top of the ramp, turn left and then turn left again at the first road onto Cedarville Road. Go 1.5 miles to its end. Turn right onto Easton Road (Route 611) south and go 12 miles to Ferndale. Turn right at the light onto Church Hill Road. Go 1.5 miles to its end. Turn right onto Durham Road (Route 412) north. Go 1 mile and look for the B&B sign on the right. Turn right onto Berger Road and continue for .75 mile. The B&B is the second farm on the right.

Travelers who love to immerse themselves in the history of an area will find numerous things to fascinate them at Lightfarm Bed & Breakfast. Although most B&Bs in Bucks County are upscale and toney, Lightfarm offers a refreshing change of pace. Not only will guests learn from the artifacts collected in the archaeological dig on site and displayed in the B&B's museum, they will be treated to extraordinary stenciled walls created by innkeeper Carol Sempowski from old colonial patterns and to colorful handmade log cabin and wedding ring quilts covering the beds, which were also made by Carol.

The museum is located in a stone-walled and beam-ceilinged lower-level room. Archaeology classes from Bucks County Community College are held here. The owners surmise, from the number of highly decorated fragments and shards of Pennsylvania redware and stub-stem pipes that have been found, that an early pottery manufactory may have been located on the farm.

Located on a 92-acre working farm in a rural setting of barns, neatly fenced fields with grazing sheep, wooded areas, and a pond, the 1811 stone farmhouse offers beautiful views of the surrounding farmland. Inside there are wide-plank pine floors and beamed ceilings, and in the original old kitchen, there's a huge fireplace that still has its hinged shutter doors that close in front when it's not in use. The parlor boasts a Baldwin acrosonic piano, a grandfather clock, and an antique highboy. Museum-quality collections of Pennsylvania redware, Hummel figurines, and statues of border collies (the indispensable workhorse of a farm, according to Carol) line the shelves. On the walls, there's a collection of Wallace Nutting painted photographs.

The B&B has four rooms —all with beautiful stenciling in multiple colors. Solomon's Room has wide-plank pine floors, green-colored paneled walls, window seats with views of the fields, and a bed with a fishnet canopy. One of Carol's quilts in green shades is on the bed. John Jacob's Room has a bow-top canopy, walls that are highly stenciled, and a rag rug on the pine floor. Although the baths are neat, modern, and clean, they are not as up-to-date as at most of the B&Bs in this book.

I love to wake to the smell of baking bread, and that lovely aroma wafts up to the guest rooms here as Carol prepares either fruit muffins or zucchini or banana bread in the morning. Breakfast may be taken at leisure, however. It is served in the formal dining room, which has a brass lamp, built-in cupboards, and a maple table. The table is set with linen, silver, and Johnson Brothers Old Britain Castles china. Carol may prepare a double-crust sausage pie with homemade applesauce or perhaps eggs with cream cheese and chives.

Because Lightfarm is still a working farm, Carol and Mike invite guests to help tend the garden and to feed the animals, if they desire. In addition to the two pot-bellied pigs, a flock of sheep, six dogs, and farm cats, there are two peacocks, two American turkeys, and white-crested black Polish chickens on the property. Guests also enjoy meandering along the nature trails that lead to a hollow where deer graze or that skirt Gallows Run Creek and run through the pine forest. For utter relaxation, however, they can just sit in a chair beside the spring-fed pond or loosen kinked muscles in the hot tub on the porch.

What's Nearby

The Crayola Factory at Two Rivers Landing in Easton includes a 2,000-square-foot interactive exhibit area and a tour where you can see Crayola crayons and markers being made. Learn about Crayola history and participate in interactive exhibits. Then visit the Crayola Store, where arts and crafts, gifts, and clothing are sold.

Gardens of Eden B&B

1894 Eden Road
Lancaster, PA 17601
(717) 393-5179; fax (717) 393-7722;
website: http://www.padutchinns.com

Innkeepers: Marilyn and Bill Ebel
Rooms: 4, including 1 cottage, all with private baths, air conditioning, radios, hair dryers, and robes; cottage with fireplace, small kitchen, coffee maker, TV, and porch; 3 rooms with desks; portable phone available
On the grounds: Parking, spacious gardens, walking trails, canoe and rowboat for use on river, fishing, bicycle storage
Extras: Afternoon hot and cold drinks, freshly made cookies or cake; turndown with chocolates; fax available
Rates: $95–$130, including full breakfast; two-night minimum weekends; three-night minimum holiday weekends
Credit cards accepted: MasterCard & Visa
Open: Year-round
Smoking: Permitted outdoors only
How to get there: From I-76, take exit 21 and follow Route 222 south for about 15 miles to Lancaster. Stay in the right lane and exit onto Route 30 east. At the next junction, exit onto Route 23 east toward New Holland. In less than .8 mile, turn right onto Eden Road. In .4 mile, just before the bridge, turn right into the B&B's lane and park below the stone wall.

Seldom do you find a B&B that's so perfectly named. Serendipidously located on Eden Road on a 3¹/₂-acre site that overlooks a waterfall on the Conestoga River, the B&B is surrounded by lush gardens. Lawns and flower beds rise behind the house, offering a perpetual kaleidoscope of color from early spring to late fall. In front, there are terraces and sloping hillsides planted with an abundance of daffodils and wildflowers that end in a grassy space at river's edge. Nature trails hug the river beyond and rise along the slopes behind the inn. Two county bicycle routes pass by. Along with their brochure, Marilyn and Bill Ebel send guests a pamphlet that begins with lines from Robert Browning's famous poem: "The lark's on the wing; The snail's on the thorn; God's in His heaven— All's right with the world!" It lists the many birds (including the brilliant yellow winged-type Baltimore oriole), animals (including white tail deer), and flowers (numbering almost seventy-five, all arranged and named by color) that will be found on the property. Could there be a more peaceful and bucolic place?

The B&B is a lovely 1867 brick Federal manor house with a slate roof, green shutters, and white pillars on either side of the door. The last time I was there a family of tiny Carolina wrens had made their nest in the front door decoration. They were undoubtedly so enchanted with Marilyn's design that they felt right at home. That's not surprising, since Marilyn is an acclaimed floral designer and instructor.

The common rooms are warm and inviting, just like the innkeepers. Burnished white pine floors are covered by Oriental rugs. The gracious living room has a white wooden fireplace mantel, floor-to-ceiling bookcases, and a 1907 Steinway grand piano. Other antiques, such as a tall-case clock made in Reading between 1799 and 1818, share space with a hooked rug made by Marilyn; paintings, photographs, and crafts by local artists; and Marilyn's dried floral arrangements.

In the guest rooms, there are antique beds.

A wise old wooden owl sculpture sits on an old pump just beyond the stone terrace of the two-story Beecher Cottage, which was created from the original summer kitchen. Baskets hang from the ceiling, the fireplace burns logs in winter, a table sits by a paned window offering views of the barn. Upstairs, the bed is covered with another quilt.

The dining room is as welcoming as the rest of the house. Colorful placemats and china grace the Queen Anne-style reproduction table, and pieces of folk art sit on a shelf. An antique brass chandelier oversees the scene. Breakfasts are creative and healthful. There will always be fruit, juice, and muesli as well as either a baked egg dish or maybe waffles served with the Ebels' homemade violet syrup. Plates are decorated with edible flowers and fruit.

The East of Eden Pub, an excellent restaurant, lies on the opposite bank of the river, a short walk across the little bridge.

What's Nearby — Lancaster

To savor the delights of the Amish/Mennonite countryside, stop at the Mennonite Information Center. Guides can be hired to ride in your own car to direct you along the backroads as they describe the farm and religious life of the local families. Or they may take you to less commercial homes where quilts and furniture are made. The Lancaster Central Market is the nation's oldest publicly owned farmers' market. Open Tuesday, Friday, and Saturday starting at 6 A.M., this is the place to buy local produce, meats, bakery and craft items. Visit James Buchanan's home, Wheatland, for an insight into the life of America's 15th president. The American Music Theater opened in Lancaster in the spring of 1997; in the Heritage Center Museum of Lancaster County, there are exhibits that tell the story of the area's rich cultural history and a museum store where the work of current-day quilters, folk artists, and furniture makers can be purchased. (See also Ephrata and Lititz.)

The King's Cottage, A Bed & Breakfast Inn

1049 East King Street (Route 462)
Lancaster, PA 17602
(800) 747-8717 or (717) 397-1017;
fax (717) 397-3447

Innkeepers: Karen and Jim Owens
Rooms: 9, including 1 cottage, all with private baths, air conditioning, and radios; 7 with desks; 2 with telephones and TVs; 3 with porches; 1 with a fireplace and a whirlpool tub; portable telephone available; one room has wheelchair access
On the grounds: Parking; garden with lily and fish pond
Extras: Small gift shop; fax available; turndown with chocolates on the pillow; afternoon tea and evening cordials served in the library
Rates: $100 – $195, including full breakfast; two-night minimum weekends; three-night minimum holiday weekends
Credit cards accepted: Discover, MasterCard, Visa
Open: Year-round
Smoking: Non-smoking bed and breakfast
How to get there: From I-76, take exit 21 and follow Route 222 south for 15 miles to Lancaster. Turn east onto Route 30 and follow this to Route 23 west (Walnut Street) to King Street. Turn right at the end of the exit ramp. At the second light, turn left onto Ranck Avenue. At the second stop sign, turn left onto East Orange Street. Follow East Orange Street for 1 block to Cottage Avenue and turn right. The B&B is the last building on the right, on the corner of East King Street and Cottage Avenue. Turn right into the lane just before the B&B and then turn left into the parking area.

You don't expect to see a golden stucco house with a Spanish tile roof in the heart of Amish/Mennonite country, but here it is. Built in 1913, the house is listed on the National Register of Historic Places. Instead of a strictly Mission-style interior, the house has architectural elements in both Victorian and Art Deco styles. Karen and Jim Owens opened the B&B in 1987.

Guests enter a Florida room with a tile floor

that contains an extensive gift shop that includes quilts, pillows, and books as well as a sitting area with wicker furniture. The living room has a traditional marble fireplace and comfortable sofas. Through a grand doorway flanked by fluted columns, there's a library that includes an Art Deco fireplace and a bay window as well as a TV, VCR, and a video library.

The guest rooms are decorated with a combination of antiques and country pieces. The Princess Room, which has wedgwood blue Waverly fabric, has an antique four-poster cherry bed and a private tile-floored porch overlooking the lily pond and gardens. The bath is large and has a double sink with a marble counter and a clawfoot tub. The Contessa, on the ground floor, also has a private porch as well as a canopied bed with an antique mahogany headboard, a magnificent antique cherry secretary with a bookcase above, and an adjoining bath with a rose-colored marble sink.

The Carriage House, a separate little building entered through a barn door, is the most luxurious accommodation. It has an iron verdigris canopy bed draped with diaphanous white fabric and a purple floral spread on the bed. There's a gas fireplace, an antique armoire, pink walls, and an oak floor. The spacious bath features a tile floor, a Jacuzzi, and a sink in a marble counter.

Breakfast is served in the formal dining room, which has quilts on the walls, built-in Palladian-style china cabinets, a crystal chandelier, and pale green walls with white trim. Two large tables are set with fine linen and china. Karen has an extensive repertoire of breakfast menus. She may fix broiled grapefruit with spicy pear muffins, followed by ham and cheese crêpes with hollandaise sauce. Or, it may be a fresh fruit salad followed by a plum torte with sausage.

Afternoon tea is served in the library. It features such delicacies as King's Delight, a tea cake with a nut crust and a whipped cream and cream cheese filling that's topped with fresh blueberries or strawberries, or Hummingbird cake, a dense banana/coconut/pineapple cake with a coconut frosting. Few guests leave without purchasing one of the B&B's cookbooks. In the evening, the hosts set out cordials in the library.

What's Nearby

See "What's Nearby — Lancaster," page 227.

Innkeepers: Debrah and Werner Mosimann
Rooms: 7, including 1 suite, all with private baths, air conditioning, telephones, balconies, and radios; 2 with desks and Jacuzzis; 1 with TV & VCR; crib available
On the grounds: Parking, on 30 acres with abundant gardens; walking and hiking trails; canoe for use on a small adjacent lake
Extras: Turndown with chocolates on the pillow; afternoon snacks with freshly baked cookies or pastries; two golden retrievers named Heidi and Gretl and cats outside only
Rates: $95 – $150, including full breakfast; lower rates from January through March; two-night minimum weekends, April - January 2nd; three-night minimum holiday weekends
Credit cards accepted: American Express, Discover, MasterCard, Visa
Open: Year-round except December 24 - 26
Smoking: Smoking permitted outdoors only
How to get there: From I-76, take exit 21 and follow Route 222 south to Route 322. Take the Ephrata exit and travel west on Route 322 until it intersects with Route 501 in Brickerville. Turn left onto Route 501 and travel south to the first crossroads, which is Brubaker Valley Road. Turn right and go 1 mile to the lake. Just before the lake, turn right onto Blantz Road. The B&B is the first driveway on the left.

Swiss Woods B&B
500 Blantz Road
Lititz, PA 17543
(800) 594-8018 or (717) 627-3358;
fax (717) 627-3483
e-mail: MREY88A@prodigy.com

Lititz was founded in 1756 by Moravians (Moravia is now part of Czechoslovakia), as was much of the surrounding countryside, and the handsome stone buildings of the village give it the appearance of a Rhine River village. The town is a National Historic District. Swiss Woods B&B is located 3 miles north of Lititz. On a 30-acre hilltop, the grounds are resplendently alive with colorful gardens from early spring when the daffodils create a carpet of yellow to late fall when the maple trees wear their coats of red and orange. There are walking trails through the woods and down to small Speedwell Forge Lake and benches throughout the glorious gardens that offer guests tranquil places to enjoy the many birds, flowers, and animals.

The inn appears to have been plucked directly from a Swiss mountainside, and it's no wonder. Werner Mosimann was raised in Switzerland, and he and Debrah lived there for several years. When they built their B&B in 1984, they fashioned it after the Swiss chalets they loved so much. Although Debrah was raised nearby, her family has a Swiss lineage also. She will point out the mantel in the Anker Stube, the warm common room, that was hand hewn by her father and the wall of sandstones that were cut by Werner. Guests enter through this room, which has rag rugs on pine floors, persimmon and navy colored chairs and sofas, an upright piano, and tables and chairs by the wall of windows that looks out at the gardens.

One of the advantages of building a new B&B is that you can include features that might have been precluded in the transformation of an older building. One of the joys of Swiss Woods is the fact that every room has its own balcony or patio, allowing guests a bird's eye view of the gardens, which Werner, who has a degree in agronomy, tends from morning until night. Naturally, the railings hold planter boxes filled with bright blooms, just as in Switzerland, and the B&B is filled with vases of fresh flowers. Some of the beds are on platforms, others are four-poster cherry beds, but my favorites are the new twisted spindle pine beds. All are covered with feather-light down comforters with pretty chintz-covered duvets. My favorite room is Lake of Geneva, which has a pine bed with massive posts, a balcony with views of Speedwell Forge Lake, and a modern bath with a red and white tile floor, pine cabinets, and a Jacuzzi under a skylight.

Breakfast is served in Anker Stube at tables that overlook the gardens. It will begin with a fresh fruit platter and assorted freshly baked muffins — perhaps a selection of chocolate chip, strawberry, and pecan. This may be followed by a baked egg and cheese dish or by cinnamon raisin French toast stuffed with chocolate and strawberry cream cheese.

There's a little gift shop at the B&B that has beautiful quilts, quilted potholders and pillows, mugs, tote bags, and pretty children's and adult's pinafores in spritely colors. Nearby, there's a guest pantry with a refrigerator, and coffee maker. A jar of chocolate chip cookies or snickerdoodles awaits on the buffet in the Anker Stube every afternoon.

What's Nearby

Visit The Wilbur Chocolate Company's Candy Americana Museum & Store in Lititz for an education about the history of American candy-making. There are demonstrations, displays of antique molds, and candy at discounted prices. Also, visit the Sturgis Pretzel factory, founded in 1861, making it the oldest pretzel bakery in America. (See also Ephrata and Lancaster.)

Stoneymead

3719 Indian Spring Road
(mailing address: P.O. Box 366)
Mechanicsville, PA 18934
(215) 794-8081; fax (215) 794-3054

Innkeepers: Nancy and George Wells
Rooms: 3, including 2 suites, all with private baths, air conditioning, telephones with dataports, TVs, robes, and radios; 2 with fireplaces
On the grounds: Parking; extensive gardens with a pond, stream, and waterfall; bass fishing in the pond
Extras: Afternoon tea with homemade cookies and sometimes small sandwiches or cheese and crackers; standard poodle named Will and Himalayan cat named Teddy on premises
Rates: $100 – $175, including full breakfast; two-night minimum weekends
Credit cards accepted: MasterCard and Visa
Open: February - November
Smoking: Non-smoking bed and breakfast
How to get there: On Route 202 from New Jersey, cross the Delaware River and continue to the fourth light. Turn right (north) onto Street Road and continue to the second stop sign. Turn left onto Mechanicsville Road. Turn right onto Indian Spring Road. The long driveway is about .75 mile on the right.

There's a wonderful joy of discovery when I find an unsung treasure. So, you can imagine my excitement when, after a long day of looking at potential candidates for this book, I drove up the driveway of Stoneymead. Its 53 acres of stone walls, a stream, a pond, and flower-filled gardens (there are more than 15,000 daffodils that bloom in spring) were as lovely as an arboretum. The house, portions of which date to 1790, is composed of four warm buff-colored fieldstone sections with gabled roofs, all tied together in a stately design. A courtyard in front leads to a classic pillared Georgian entry portico. In back, however, the walls are huge arched panes of glass offering spectacular vistas of the gardens.

This idyllic house in its perfect setting is the creation of Nancy Wells, who was raised in Pennsylvania but lived for many years in California. Missing the change of seasons she had enjoyed so much as a child, she and her husband, George, purchased the 1790s house and land in 1981. It had formerly been owned by Broadway actress Zoe Caldwell and her husband, Robert Whitehead, a producer. Bit by bit the grounds and house evolved, and in 1987 it was significantly expanded.

In the tile-floored sun porch, which has

walls of windows and skylights, there are an abundance of happy plants, including many orchids, as well as a fireplace. This room is a wonderful place to relax with a book and watch the little waterfall just outside. The parlor, in the 1790 section, has a beamed ceiling, paneled cupboards on either side of the fireplace, and mullioned windows. A Persian rug covers the oak floors. Afternoon tea is served here or on the porch in the summer.

Two of the guest rooms are located in the oldest section. All the rooms come with interesting histories and excellent tiled private baths. In The Hideaway, a suite on the third floor, Nancy sponged the headboard on the bed and stenciled the bath with tasseled ribbons. The charming sitting room has wicker tables, pretty slipper chairs, a rocker used to rock Nancy when she was a baby, and built-in bookcases filled with books.

The remaining guest room is Laura's Room, an utterly charming suite created for the Wells's daughter. Nancy sponged the entire suite in a Queen Anne rose color. A wall of bookcases in the sitting room contains some of Laura's dolls, toys, and books. A huge Paddington Bear was acquired in London at Fortnum & Masons. Family treasures abound. The elaborate crocheted spreads on the twin beds were made by Nancy's grandmother, a sewing table belonged to another grandmother, and two hooked rugs were made by an aunt.

Breakfast is served in the dining room at a large oak table under a leafy iron chandelier in winter. Huge arched windows provide fantastic views of the gardens. In summer breakfast is served on the terrace. Nancy begins the meal with fresh juice (perhaps apricot) followed by a fruit dish such as baked apples or fresh berries and perhaps a strawberry/rhubarb coffee cake. Possible entrées include eggs goldenrod or gingerbread pancakes served with sausage.

Mechanicsville is in central Bucks County, close to the shopping outlets, antiques shops, and restaurants of Lahaska, midway between Doylestown and New Hope.

What's Nearby

The Buckingham Vineyards, where visitors may tour the winery and sample the wines, is just south in Buckingham Valley. Bucks County Audubon Society is also nearby, where field trips to wildlife sanctuaries and organized stargazing take place throughout the summer. Malmark, Inc.–Bellcraftsmen is in nearby Plumsteadville. This interesting shop makes the beautifully tuned bronze handbells that are used by handbell choirs throughout the world. (See also Doylestown, Holicong, and New Hope.)

Innkeepers: Ole and Patricia Retlev
Rooms: 15, including 2 suites, all with private baths, air conditioning, telephones, and televisions; 11 with private porches or patios; 10 with desks; 8 with fireplaces; 1 room with wheelchair access
On the grounds: Parking; gardens
Extras: Afternoon tea with cookies; fresh flowers in the rooms
Rates: $135 – $225, including Continental breakfast; two-night minimum weekends; three-night minimum major holidays
Credit cards accepted: American Express, Discover, MasterCard, Visa
Open: Year-round
Smoking: Non-smoking bed and breakfast
How to get there: From I-95 in Wilmington, DE, take exit 7 and follow Route 52 north through Greenville and Centerville, crossing the state line into Pennsylvania. Fairville is the first village on Route 52 in Pennsylvania. The B&B is about 1.5 miles beyond the state line.

Fairville Inn

506 Kennett Pike
(mailing address: P.O. Box 219)
Mendenhall, PA 19357
(610) 388-5900; fax (610) 388-5902

Patricia and Ole Retlev have been the innkeepers of this outstanding B&B since 1986, and they never stop working to improve their treasure. The beautiful 1820s Federal-style building with its covered veranda, is located on 3$^1/_2$ acres of luxurious gardens just off a winding country road that is midway between Longwood Gardens and Winterthur Museum and Gardens. As you meander along the picturesque back roads, you understand why three generations of Wyeths have preserved the area on canvas.

The common rooms of the B&B are welcoming and inviting. In the living room, which has a fireplace, a huge copper coffee table holds freshly baked Swedish cookies (in recognition of Ole's heritage) in the afternoon to accompany tea, coffee, or a cold drink. There are colorful bouquets of flowers from the garden on tables.

In the bright breakfast room, guests sit at individual tables, and Patti sets out a buffet of freshly baked scones, muffins, and sticky buns. Patti was raised near here, and she told me that she and her mother go to a farm in southern Delaware to pick tiny, sweet strawberries to make into the luscious jam Patti serves at the inn. A fresh rose adorns each table.

There are five rooms in the main house, each with a canopy or four-poster bed and stylish furnishings. The rooms in the carriage house feature cathedral ceilings, barnwood walls, and fireplaces. Each has a modern bath. They overlook the pond and gardens and have private decks with pots of flowering plants. I watched one morning as hummingbirds sampled the sweet honey of a deep red hibiscus, and I saw a pretty yellow butterfly light on a purple butterfly bush. Two more rooms with fireplaces and decks are located in the barn.

Ole and Patti have done much of the work on their B&B themselves with the help of Patti's father, and Patti sewed all the drapes and bed trimmings herself. I could just imagine her scurrying to find the proper fabrics when she learned that Barbra Streisand would be coming in a few days and the only room available was one she had been planning to redecorate. She told me she spent sixty hours making new window and canopy curtains for the room, and she completed it just in time for Ms. Streisand's visit.

There are several interesting shops and restaurants in nearby Fairville. Buckley's Tavern, an 1817 former stagecoach stop, which has beamed ceilings and paneled walls, has retained much of its early atmosphere. The menu ranges from burgers to chicken and steak.

What's Nearby

Winterthur Museum and Gardens is located only a few miles from the Fairville Inn. The former home of Henry Francis duPont contains America's finest and most complete display of decorative arts and antiques. There are 175 period rooms as well as spectacular gardens that cover much of the almost 1,000-acre estate. Nearby, the Hagley Museum is located on 230 acres that include the first Dupont mills and powder works as well as the original duPont Georgian-style 1803 family mansion. (See also Chadds Ford, Unionville, and West Chester.)

Pine Hill Bed & Breakfast

Pine Hill Farm Road
(mailing address: P.O. Box 1001)
Milford, PA 18337
telephone/fax (717) 296-7395

Innkeepers: Lynn and Bob Patton
Rooms: 5, including 2 suites, all with private baths, air conditioning, and porches or patios; 3 with TVs; 2 with VCRs; telephone available
On the grounds: Parking; 268 acres of forests and fields with two streams and a waterfall; 5 miles of hiking and cross-country trails (map available)
Extras: Private antiques shop; two cats named Flannel and Oxford on premises
Rates: $95 – $120, including full breakfast; two-night minimum Memorial Day through October if stay includes a Friday or Saturday night
Credit cards accepted: Discover, MasterCard, Visa
Open: Year-round except Thanksgiving and Christmas Day
Smoking: Non-smoking bed and breakfast
How to get there: Specific directions given when reservations are made.

Serendipity brought Lynn and Bob Patton to this place and time, but when you hear the story, you know it was meant to be. For years at family gatherings, stories were told about the mountaintop hideaway that had once been a family retreat, but no one knew where it was or if it still existed — eventually it seemed more myth than reality. Then one day the Pattons found a 1930s brochure describing a farm overlooking the Delaware River. Out of curiosity, they drove to see it the next weekend. A caretaker let them come inside, and they recognized much of the old furniture that had played a background role in family pictures. The rest of the story is simple. It was for sale, so they bought it.

That was in 1990, when Bob was still an advertising executive in Manhattan and before they had any intention of living in this remote section of Pennsylvania or of operating a B&B. Since that time, however, they have created a mountaintop aerie on their 268-acre farm that offers the ultimate antidote to stressed-out executives. As deer feed in a meadow and rabbits scurry across a field, life perceptibly slows, and the biggest decision becomes when to schedule the next visit.

To reach the B&B, which is on a private

road about 3 miles north of Milford, you climb and climb, obtaining ever-better vistas of the Delaware River. When you think you can climb no higher, you see the farm and its outbuildings ahead and realize it's at the base of an even higher hill. You'll be greeted warmly by Bob and Lynn in a reception room that contains Bob's collection of old metal advertising boxes and signs. More old advertising pieces are found throughout the B&B as well as beautiful pieces of antique furniture. In the library there are an abundance of books and a great stone fireplace. The dining room, which has a country-fresh ambience, has another fireplace. A large refectory table is presided over by a huge chandelier. A stone terrace off the dining room offers lovely views of the countryside.

There are three guest rooms in the main house and two suites in the former caretaker's cottage. Waverly has a bed with a headboard made from old barn doors and forest green wainscotted walls. All rooms have nice private baths. The suites in the cottage are spacious and have four-poster beds, living rooms with TV/VCR, and handsome baths with beadboard walls. The sun porch has views of the fields as well as an abundance of games.

Breakfast is either served in the dining room or on the stone terrace. Lynn is noted for the special dish she calls "Eggs McLynn," an individual baked egg dish prepared with bacon and topped with cheese. In addition, there are homemade breads (a favorite is the sourdough French bread) and coffee cakes as well as fresh fruit served in a footed dish and juices.

The Pattons have such an abundance of interesting antiques that they have established a shop in the barn just for their guests. Here such treasures as handmade quilts, advertising boxes, old jars and bottles, glassware, and pine furniture are for sale. There are 5 miles of logging trails throughout the property that lead to two streams and a waterfall.

What's Nearby

Grey Towers, the 1890s French château home of Gifford Pinchot, father of the National Park Service, is nearby. Take a guided tour and then walk up the trail to Pinchot Falls. At the northern end of the Delaware Water Gap National Recreation Area, canoes can be rented at the foot of Pine Hill. At The Columns, the museum maintained by the Milford Historical Society, visitors can view the blood-stained flag that was used to cradle President Lincoln's head after he was shot at Ford's Theater in Washington, DC, which reached the area by as circuitous a route as many of the residents.

Mansion Inn

9 South Main Street
New Hope, PA 18938
(215) 862-1231; fax (215) 862-0277;
e-mail: mansion@pil.net

Innkeeper: Diana Smith; proprietors, Dr. Elio Bracco and Keith David

Rooms: 9, including 5 suites, all with private baths, air conditioning, telephones with dataports, TVs, clock/radios, and robes; 5 with fireplaces, whirlpool tubs, and desks; 2 with porches or patios

On the grounds: Swimming pool; gardens with gazebo

Extras: Turndown with fresh cookies, bottled spring water and ice; candy in common rooms; sherry in parlor; early morning coffee tray and newspaper delivered to room door; wine and cheese late Saturday afternoons

Rates: $175 – $300, including full breakfast; two-night minimum weekends; three-night minimum holidays

Credit cards accepted: American Express, MasterCard, Visa

Open: Year-round

Smoking: Non-smoking bed and breakfast

How to get there: From I-78, take Route 202 south. After crossing the Delaware River, exit onto Route 32 south and go to New Hope. At the traffic light at Bridge Street, turn right. Turn left immediately into the first alley to reach the B&B's parking lot.

For years we walked along the streets of New Hope, browsing in the bookstore or in Katy Kane's antique clothing and linen shop, and wishing that someone would restore the unique Victorian mansion with its mansard roof that sits in the heart of the village. It had all the Victorian excesses we love — a porch embellished with gingerbread, a fanciful cupola, and a grapeleaf wrought-iron fence. At last it's happened, and best of all, it's a bed and breakfast that we can all enjoy.

When Dr. Kenneth Leiby decided to sell the house that had long been his home and office, the entire town was concerned about its possi-ble fate. Although it was on the National Register of Historic Places, there was concern that it might be gutted for shops or offices. Not to worry. When Keith David and Dr. Elio Bracco toured the house and talked to Dr. Leiby, they knew what they had to do. And they did it right.

Today the house fairly gleams. It's painted a buttercup yellow with white trim that enhances its carved brackets, arched windows, and wooden cutwork. Inside, Dr. Leiby had carefully preserved doorways and hardware within the walls whenever he made changes, and the new partners, with Dr. Leiby's help, were able to return the house to its original configuration.

The central hall, with its magnificent mahogany staircase and darkly burnished wood floors topped with Oriental rugs, has a drawing room on one side and a double-length living room on the other. Arched mantels echo the arched entryway. A decanter of sherry with stemmed glasses sits on a silver tray on an antique side table.

We were escorted to the Ashby Suite by innkeeper Diana Smith. The pretty blue-and-white room has a carved canopy bed hung with a blue-and-white French fabric that is repeated in the drapes and wallpaper. A Victorian loveseat and chair are covered in the same fabric, and a beautiful silk Persian rug is on the floor. The featherbeds are dressed with starched white Porthault sheets and matelassé spreads. We slept like contented babies. Upstairs, the Windsor Suite contains a magnificent four-poster bed and a pretty sitting area. A fireplace and a two-person whirlpool tub make this a popular honeymoon destination.

The baths offer all the modern amenities we enjoy today. The floors are tile, as are the tub surrounds, and mirrors are liberally placed across the walls. The hosts have thoughtfully provided such extras as bath salts and oils sitting on a glass shelf.

The house is surrounded with flowers that bloom throughout the spring and summer, and there's a pretty private garden with a gazebo in back. A full-sized heated pool is located behind a picket fence.

For breakfast we feasted on a variety of sweet breads, muffins, and fresh fruit attractively displayed on an antique Dutch chest. For entrées Diana will prepare either French toast (perhaps using croissants and raspberries) or an egg dish (perhaps an omelet with tomato chunks).

New Hope is noted for its numerous antiques shops and fine restaurants, and because the crowds are often thick along New Hope's streets in the summer, it's especially nice to have a private place to park the car.

What's Nearby — New Hope

We love to rise early in the morning to take a brisk walk along the tow path that skirts the Pennsylvania side of the Delaware River. To see the Delaware Canal as it once was, take one of the mule-drawn barge rides that originate just down the street in New Hope. In addition, the Bucks County Playhouse, offering an array of live theater, concerts, musicals, and comedies, is just across the street. The Parry Mansion Museum on Main Street has displays of decorative arts from 1775 to 1900. Peddler's Village and Penn's Purchase Factory Stores are just down the street in Lahaska. The complexes include more than 100 shops featuring everything from interesting antiques to factory outlet shops and restaurants. The New Hope Winery is also in Lahaska. It is open for visits and samples. (See also Doylestown, Holicong, and Mechanicsville as well as Lambertville, New Jersey.)

The Whitehall Inn

1370 Pineville Road
New Hope, PA 18938
(888) 37-WHITE or (215) 598-7945
website: http://www.innbook.com

Innkeepers: Mike and Suella Wass
Rooms: 6, including 1 suite, 4 with private baths and 2 that share one bath, all with air conditioning, hair dryers, clocks, and robes; 4 with fireplaces; telephone available on porch
On the grounds: Parking; swimming pool, rose garden, horse stalls and barns; 13 acres of meadows and fields
Extras: Afternoon high tea; sherry in the evening; turndown with special chocolates,
Rates: $140 – $205, including six-course candlelight breakfast and afternoon high tea; two-night minimum weekends; three-night minimum holiday weekends
Credit cards accepted: American Express, Diner's Club, Discover, MasterCard, Visa
Open: Year-round
Smoking: Non-smoking bed and breakfast
How to get there: From Route 202 in New Jersey, cross the Delaware River into Pennsylvania and continue on Route 202 south toward Doylestown for 4.6 miles to Lahaska. Turn left onto Street Road at Peddler's Village and continue to the second intersection (a short distance beyond the railroad tracks) and bear right onto Pineville Road. Proceed for 1.3 miles to the B&B, which will be on the right.

Mike and Suella Wass opened their 1794 house to B&B guests in 1985, and in the interim they've built a very loyal clientele. The setting is as bucolic as seekers of a country atmosphere could ask for — 13 acres of pastureland complete with an old barn, grazing horses, a rose garden, and a swimming pool.

The Wass's have created a B&B that comes as close to re-creating an authentic eighteenth-century ambience as possible without sacrificing all the amenities today's travelers have grown to

expect. Guests enter a small sun room with a profusion of plants, where a table is likely to contain a jigsaw puzzle in progress. The very personal B&B contains numerous items from both Mike's and Suella's families. In the living room, portraits of Mike's ancestors hang over the fireplace mantel. The Shaker cradle nearby was purchased just before their daughter was born. Suella's exquisite needlework hangs on the walls. Other family items include the upright piano on which Suella learned to play as a child and a side table that was handmade by Mike's father. The wavy-paned mullioned windows admit sunshine that creates a glow across the polished wide-plank pine floors; the fireplace has a painted wooden mantel. The entire room seems to be locked in an earlier time.

The bedrooms continue the eighteenth-century mood. There are wide-plank pine floors and elegant antiques throughout. The Gerald McGimsey Room features a canopy bed with an ivory spread; the Albert Hibbs Rooms has a fishnet canopy bed and a fireplace, while the Phineas Kelly Room has an antique brass-and-iron bed and a fireplace. The baths are stashed away in little adjacent rooms. Although four of the rooms have private baths, two share one bath.

The six-course breakfast at Whitehall Inn is an event. Guests assemble at 9:00 A.M. when the doors of the breakfast room are opened to reveal tables set with fine china and Suella's antique sterling silver. Candles are lighted. A collection of antique lanterns rest on a sideboard, and paintings line the walls. The heavenly aroma of the Wass's specially blended and roasted coffee will have encouraged you to rise early. This is accompanied by perhaps freshly squeezed honey tangerine juice, maple cream biscuits, and butter coffee cake. The soup course might be a warm apple-sweet paprika or a chilled peach and sherry. The fruit course could include a warm poached compote of plums, nectarines, and white grapes with orange rind or maybe a cinnamon-crusted baked pear with a cognac-custard sauce. For an entrée guests may be served a spinach tart with toasted pine nuts and parmesan cheese or maybe French toast souffléd with honey and cream and stuffed with a wild strawberry filling. The dessert course may include a special Whitehall chocolate with Jarlsberg cheese.

Afternoon tea, which is served at 4:00 P.M., is equally elaborate. It includes Suella's cream scones with clotted cream as well as finger sandwiches and freshly baked cakes and cookies.

If you rise early in the morning for a walk through the pastures or along the road, you often will see a deer or a flurry of bunnies scampering across your path. These quiet country roads offer flat, traffic-free rides past a countryside that has changed little in a hundred years.

What's Nearby

See "What's Nearby — New Hope," page 239.

Auldridge Mead

523 Geigel Hill Road
Ottsville, PA 18942
(610) 847-5842; fax (610) 847-5664

Innkeeper: Craig Mattoli
Rooms: 5, including 1 suite, 3 with private bath and 2 sharing a bath, all with air conditioning, TVs, and robes; 4 with desks; 2 with hair dryers; 1 with a fireplace; telephone available
On the grounds: Parking, swimming pool, hiking and walking trails, stables for horses, riding trails
Extras: Guest refrigerator supplied with drinks; coffee and newspaper delivered to guest rooms before breakfast; beds dressed with fine cotton sheets, down comforters, and pillows; specially milled soaps; guest pets permitted with prior permission
Rates: $85 – $199, including full breakfast; lower corporate rates available; two-night minimum most weekends
Credit cards accepted: MasterCard and Visa
Open: Year-round
Smoking: Permitted in common areas but not in guest rooms
How to get there: From I-78, take the Hellertown/Bethlehem exit onto Route 412 south. Travel about 12 miles until it intersects with Route 611. Follow Route 611 south for 2.2 miles and turn left onto Tohickon Valley Road at the Mobil Mini-Mart (on the left). Go 1 block to Durham Road and turn left. At the first crossroad, turn right onto Geigel Hill Road. Travel 2 miles to the B&B, which will be on the right.

Tucked away in a section of Bucks County seldom traveled by tourists, Auldridge Mead (which means "old meadow on the ridge") offers many reasons to make the journey. For one thing, innkeeper Craig Mattoli is a current-day Leonardo da Vinci. Is there anything he can't do? Graduating from college as a physicist in the 1970s, he became a Wall Street whiz in the 1980s. Today, however, in addition to his innkeeping duties, he makes exquisite wooden hand-crafted furniture using rare woods that he

personally selects for their coloration and graining. Starting as a designer of twig-style chairs and beds, Craig now makes furniture from polished hardwoods such as walnut, cherry, birch, and apple. He also happens to be a terrific cook (as is his friend, Karyn Coigne, who was a chef at the Four Seasons Hotel in Philadelphia), and there are frequent classes in Italian and French cooking at the B&B.

The B&B is located on top of a hill in a 200+-year-old stone house with a slate roof. A wonderful old stone bank barn with stables often has horses who are boarding. A picturesque stone smoke-and-bake house is a backdrop for a profusion of flowers, and a red granary building houses Craig's furniture workshop. The farm contains a score of fruit trees—including pear, peach, apple, and cherry. Although the complex is merely 4 miles from Route 32 and the Delaware River, it is a winsome rural retreat that's as far removed from the stresses of Wall Street as it can be.

The living room has stone walls, beamed ceilings, and pine floors with a huge braided rug. Craig and Karyn mixed their own buttermilk-based paints to create the crackle finish they desired. A large-screen TV and VCR are located here along with a video library and a CD player and disks. There are six fireplaces in the B&B, and a massive stone example is located here. The dining room has another fireplace.

One of the guest rooms is located on the first floor in the original summer kitchen. The massive old fireplace is still hidden behind shuttered doors painted the original robin's egg blue. There are stone walls, antiques, and a bed handcrafted by Craig of ebony, maple, and mahogany. Two more rooms are located on the second floor, reached up a narrow winding stair. They have beautiful stenciling of hanging bouquets on the walls, beamed ceilings, and quilts on the beds. These rooms share a bright little yellow bath with a clawfoot tub. On the third floor, Craig created a lovely, rustic room with a king-sized twig bed.

A newspaper and coffee is delivered to the door each morning. Breakfast, which is served in the dining room, will include freshly squeezed juice, fresh fruit, and an entrée of perhaps croissant French toast or sour cream pancakes or eggs with foie gras sausage.

One of the joys of staying at Auldridge Mead is that there are fine restaurants, museums, cultural events, and shops within a ten-minute drive, but the peaceful, tranquil countryside surrounding the farm is seldom disturbed by even a passing motorist. Guests are welcome to bring their horses, and Craig will offer stable space and feed (there's a charge) as well as directions to the trails.

What's Nearby

The 611 Market nearby has a marvelous array of trash and treasures. On Tuesdays, antique-lovers in the know head for Rice's Market on Green Hill Road north of Lahaska. The treasures here are renowned. In season you might go to Penn-Vermont Farm to pick fresh berries and fruit. (See also Doylestown, Erwinna, Kintnersville, and Upper Black Eddy.)

The Thomas Bond House

129 South Second Street
Philadelphia, PA 19106
(800) 834-BOND or (215) 923-8523;
fax (215) 923-8504

Innkeeper: Roger Stankay; manager, Thomas Lantry
Rooms: 12, including 2 suites, all with private baths, air conditioning, telephones, TVs, radios, hair dryers, desks, irons, and ironing boards; 3 with whirlpool tubs; 2 with fireplaces
On the grounds: Courtyard/public park adjacent
Extras: Wine and cheese in the evening; freshly baked cookies; swimming and health club available nearby for a fee
Rates: $90 – $160, including Continental breakfast weekdays and full breakfast weekends
Credit cards accepted: American Express, Diner's Club, Discover, MasterCard, Visa
Open: Year-round
Smoking: Non-smoking bed and breakfast
How to get there: From I-95 southbound take exit 17 (I-676/Central Philadelphia). Stay in the right lane until you go down the hill to Callowhill Street, then move to the left lane. Continue straight onto Second Street at the traffic light. The B&B is on the left ¹/2 block beyond Chestnut Street. From I-95 northbound take exit 16 (Washington Avenue/Delaware Avenue). At the end of the ramp, turn left onto Delaware Avenue. Continue north through five lights to Dock Street. Turn left onto Dock Street and go 1 block to Front Street. In 1¹/2 blocks enter Philadelphia Parking Authority Garage and park the car. Walk out the Welcome Park entrance and turn right. The B&B is on the right.

In the eighteenth century, Philadelphia's Second Street was home to the city's leading citizens, and today it is part of the Independence National Historic Park. At the height of the street's popularity, Thomas Bond, a well-known physician and surgeon, occupied a stately brick home on Second Street, separated from the home of William Penn by a garden. When his son got married in 1769, Dr. Bond used his garden to construct a classic Georgian Revival-style home for his son. Today both the elder Bond's home (it's now a parking garage) and that of Penn (it's now a courtyard and park) are gone, but Thomas Bond, Jr.'s, home remains. Over the years it has served as a leather tannery, manufacturing plant, customs brokerage, and a retail shop. The house is on the National Register of

Historic Places and is owned by the National Park Service. It's been a bed and breakfast since 1988.

The parlor appears much as it did when the house was built. There are oil paintings on the wall, a fireplace, and shelves lined with books. An Oriental rug covers the polished floor. At a desk by the window, a family was playing a board game on my last visit. Wine and cheese are laid out every afternoon, and a plate of fresh cookies waits in the evening for guests when they return from dinner or a cultural event.

Across the central hall, the gracious dining room is located on several levels and is appointed with pewter plates and candles. A Continental breakfast is served here during the week, and a bountiful full breakfast is offered on weekends. Popular entrées include peach French toast, a baked dish similar to bread pudding, and baked eggs with three cheeses.

The guest rooms are furnished with Federal reproductions, mostly in Chippendale style. The Dr. Thomas Bond, Jr., room is one of the nicest. It has a canopy rice bed, a working fireplace, and a whirlpool tub. Just above, the Dr. Thomas Bond, Sr., room has a high-poster rice bed, a working fireplace, and another whirlpool tub. In the top-floor Robert Fulton room, there's a pine cannonball bed and a dormer window with a view of the Delaware River. All the baths are modern, although a few are small, and some have the sink in the bedroom. Half the beds are queen-sized, and the rest are double.

The inn is within walking distance of the historic sites of Philadelphia, including Independence Hall and the Liberty Bell. Philadelphia is a great walking town — and a not-so-great bicycling one, due to the numerous cobblestone streets in this section of town. There are excellent restaurants and shops nearby.

What's Nearby

Independence Hall and Congress Hall, which are also part of Independence National Historic Park, are within blocks of the B&B. It is also close to Society Hill and is in the heart of Philadelphia's Old City, where restaurants and shops steeped in Colonial ambience are located.

Liondale Farm

160 East Street Road (Route 926)
(mailing address: P.O. Box 339)
Unionville, PA 19375
(610) 444-7130

Innkeeper: Linda Kaat
Rooms: 4, sharing 2 baths, all with air conditioning, telephones, fireplaces, TVs, VCRs, radios, hair dryers, and desks; cribs available
On the grounds: Parking; gardens; wooded trails, stream, barn, stable and ring for guests who bring their own horses; chicken coop with hens laying fresh eggs
Extras: Tea, wine, beer, cookies in the afternoon; silver tray of cordials in living room; every bathroom amenity you may ever need; well-traveled pets permitted with prior permission; two barn cats
Rates: $125 – $150, including full breakfast
Credit cards accepted: None
Open: Year-round
Smoking: Permitted outside only
How to get there: From I-95 in Wilmington, DE, take exit 7 and follow Route 52 north, crossing the state line into Pennsylvania. After crossing Route 1, turn left (west) onto Route 926. The B&B is 2¹/2 miles from Route 52 on the left.

A long a sleepy little highway in the Brandywine Valley, Liondale Farm sits on 83 acres of pasture, wooded acres, and farmland. The long lane to the farmhouse, which is fronted by a covered veranda, is bordered by majestic evergreen, ash, and copper beech trees interspersed with forsythia and other flowering trees and bushes. Fields of corn, soy beans, and wheat stretch on either side into the distance. To the left, there's a huge barn and stables where guests are invited to bring their horses for a ride in the B&Bs ring or in the fields, and there's also a chicken house where, on my last visit, baby chicks were in an incubator waiting to reach the age when they could produce fresh eggs for the B&B's farm breakfasts. The fields behind the B&B are often used on Sundays by a local pony club for exhibitions.

This idyllic retreat is the newest adventure of experienced innkeeper Linda Kaat, who we have long admired for her creation of the Brandywine's first elegant manor house B&B, Sweetwater Farm. After selling that several years ago and then living abroad, she returned to her roots, where she restored this historic 1770s farmhouse.

Guests enter the spacious living room, which has wide pine floors, tall bookcases, two fireplaces set in paneled walls with interesting built-in cupboards, a plush blue and white sofa, and a wonderful Scottish tall-case clock with ornate brass hands. Fresh flowers fill vases on tables and desks.

The guest rooms are reached by climbing a set of narrow winding stairs at either end of the house. Two rooms are located at each end, each sharing one bath. There are canopy and wicker beds as well as antique desks and antique tables holding vases of fresh flowers. Linda has perfected the art of pampering her guests by thinking of all the little amenities and details that would make their stay memorable. Every room has a telephone and a TV/VCR, and the baths are supplied with silver candlestick lamps, blue willow vases with fresh flowers, silver Revere bowls filled with loofahs, brushes, soaps, and bath salts, and medicine cabinets holding an array of perfumes, cotton balls, Band-aids, and much more.

Breakfast is served in the Colonial-style dining room, which has another woodburning fireplace and a built-in corner china cabinet oddly inserted into a straight wall. The brass chandelier burns candles. Guests are seated at a common table, where the conversation is bound to be fascinating. Linda fixes French toast with strawberry sauce or maple syrup and bacon as well as omelets and other luscious dishes. One morning when I was there, she went next door and picked fresh mushrooms at the mushroom farm for omelets. As soon as her chicks are old enough, she'll make the omelets from farm-fresh eggs.

There are trails to hike through the woods and pastures to roam. The many attractions of the Brandywine Valley lie just beyond the peaceful farm.

What's Nearby

The B&B's 83 acres are backed by Longwood Gardens, and the fields near the B&B are often used in spring and fall for equestrian competitions. The Willowdale Steeplechase & Gold Cup is run nearby, providing exciting viewing of nationally ranked horses leaping over spectacular jumps. There are also carriage parades and family activities. The Brandywine Valley labels itself the "Mushroom Capital of the World." Go to a nearby mushroom farm to pick your own or visit the Mushroom Museum at Phillips Place in nearby Kennett Square. The Franklin Mint Museum is located in nearby Franklin Center on US 1. See heirloom collector dolls and changing art exhibits showcasing the artists featured in Franklin Mint reproductions and view original art by Norman Rockwell and Andrew Wyeth. (See also Chadds Ford, Mendenhall, and West Chester.)

Innkeepers: Bea and Charles Briggs
Rooms: 11, including 1 cottage, all with private baths, air conditioning, radios, and robes; 7 with private porches; 3 with fireplaces, TVs, mini-refrigerators, and desks; 1 with whirlpool tub and CD player; telephones available
On the grounds: Parking; riverside terrace; dock for swimming, boating, canoeing, and fishing
Extras: Turndown with chocolates; afternoon tea with cakes and cookies
Rates: $69 – $250, including full breakfast and afternoon tea; two-night minimum weekends; three-night minimum holiday weekends
Credit cards accepted: MasterCard and Visa
Open: Year-round
Smoking: Non-smoking bed and breakfast
How to get there: From I-78, take exit 15 (Clinton/Pittstown in New Jersey). Go to the light and turn left. Turn left at the end of the ramp onto Route 513 south and go for 11 miles to the New Jersey town of Frenchtown. Cross the Delaware River into Pennsylvania. Turn right onto Route 32 north and go 3 1/2 miles to the B&B, which will be on the right.

Bridgeton House on the Delaware

1525 River Road
Upper Black Eddy, PA 18972
(610) 982-5856;
e-mail: bestinn1@aol.com

Let your imagination run free, just as Bea and Charlie have, and you too can have a unique, one-of-a-kind B&B. At Bridgeton House each room is an exuberant expression of artistic whimsy, but all are melded together into an amusing and original whole. Innkeepers Bea and Charles Briggs, working with Bea's cousin, artist Cheryl Raywood, have created a totally unique B&B.

Taking a circa 1836 terra cotta apartment house with shuttered windows that sits on the Delaware River, Charles, who happens be a master craftsman, created windows, French doors, and porches across the back to provide wonderful views of the river. Bea, who has a terrific decorating eye, coordinated fabrics and furniture, while Cheryl painted bold patterns on walls and ceilings.

Every guestroom is as imaginative as a page from Alice in Wonderland. In the River Suite, for example, red plaid pillows accent the king-size bed. The top half of the walls are painted mustard yellow, while the lower half is a checkerboard of green, blue, and yellow. A bright blue-green chair rail separates the two. Other features include a corner fireplace and a screened porch. Another room has fuchsia and gold walls and a stenciled bath, while a third has a cobalt blue ceiling painted with gold stars. In the baths, Charlie has created polished mahogany cabinets and skirts for the tubs, which contrast with the tile floors and tub surrounds. The beds often have canopies or half-canopies. My favorite room is the cozy Garrett Room, which has pink sponge-painted walls embellished with squiggles, a half-canopy bed, and a romantic porch.

The penthouse suite, on the top floor, however, is stark by contrast. It has white walls, a 12-foot cathedral ceiling, and a fireplace of black-and-white marble. The king-sized bed faces a wall of Palladian-style windows that offer breathtaking views of the river. Charlie created an Art Nouveau hanging bar with stained-glass doors and an enormous bath with a marble floor, a pedestal sink, and a deep tub with a marble surround.

Although the B&B sits close to the road, there is plenty of room in back for car parking, gardens, and a lovely, romantic terrace by the river. Down at the dock, guests can swim and fish, and there are canoes to rent nearby. Guests enter the B&B through a warm and comfortable common room that boasts stacks of books, magazines, games, and jigsaw puzzles.

The breakfast room has walls trimmed with stencils and a gas fireplace. Bea offers a different menu every day. One day it may be a baked pear in a light cream sauce and orange poppy-seed waffles; another, a baked apple with walnuts, oats, and brown sugar, followed by a frittata. Freshly baked breakfast breads include an apple/raisin bread, a lemon tea bread, and a pear bread.

What's Nearby

Take a hammer to Ringing Rocks Park, where the rocks ring like bells when struck. Take a stroll or a bicycle ride along the picturesque 60-mile-long Delaware Canal towpath as it meanders behind old stone houses and gardens adjacent to the Delaware River. Numerous picnic sites offer opportunities to rest and take in the beauty. (See also Erwinna, Kintnersville, and Ottsville in Pennsylvania, and Milford, New Jersey.)

Whitewing Farm Bed & Breakfast

Valley Road (mailing address: RD 6)
West Chester, PA 19382
(610) 388-2664; fax (610) 388-3650

Innkeepers: Ed and Wanda DeSeta
Rooms: 8, including 1 suite, all with private baths, air conditioning, TVs, radios, and desks; 1 with a patio; suite with a fireplace; 2 rooms with wheelchair access; telephone available in den; cribs available
On the grounds: Parking; 10-hole chip and putt golf course; swimming pool; tennis court in 1998
Extras: Afternoon tea including freshly baked cookies; two cocker spaniels named Freckles and Margaret Molly, outside cats, pet cow named Mickey on premises
Rates: $95 – $185, including full breakfast and afternoon tea; two-night minimum weekends April - December
Credit cards accepted: None
Open: Year-round
Smoking: Non-smoking bed and breakfast
How to get there: From I-95 in Wilmington, DE, take exit 7 and follow Route 52 north, crossing the state line into Pennsylvania. Continue on Route 52 for about 6 miles to Valley Road. Turn left onto Valley Road. The driveway to Whitewing Farm is on the right in .75 mile.

Whitewing Farm is one of those secret treasures that's so special you hate to tell anyone about it for fear it may change in some way. Located on 43 acres in the rolling rural countryside of Pennsylvania's Brandywine Valley, it's close to all the popular attractions and yet as far removed spiritually as if it were on another continent. It isn't just that the stream falls from the hillside in a stone-lined trough through a series of waterfalls into the pond or that the stone terraces offer views of the 10-hole pitch and putt golf course or that you can walk down to the pasture to feed Mickey the pet cow, who comes to the fence when he's called to nib-

ble the carrots he loves so much—it's also that Ed and Wanda DeSeta are some of the friendliest and nicest innkeepers you'll ever meet.

The rambling stone main house dates from 1796, but when it became the home of the treasurer of Dupont in the 1940s and 1950s, it took on an entirely updated character. He added the Pine Room, for example, which has beautiful wide-plank oak floors and corduroy-covered sofas before a pine-paneled wall containing a huge cooking fireplace. A pool table fills one end of the large room and gorgeous taxidermy pieces, including a bobcat leaping to catch a grouse and a fox with a fish in its mouth, stand on tables.

Guests enter the B&B through an open kitchen and immediately gravitate to the cookie jar, which is filled daily with a freshly baked offering — perhaps almond and lemon sugar cookies and chocolate buttermilk brownies. A big pine table sits in a bay window, offering a place to sip a cup of tea and gaze at the rolling countryside beyond the swimming pool. The formal living room has another fireplace and a wonderful Winterthur reproduction of a 1700s Rhode Island secretary with shelves above holding a collection of papier-mâché Santa Clauses. In the pine-paneled den, which has another fireplace, there's an Oriental rug on oak floors and shelves filled with books. This is where the telephone is located.

Throughout the B&B, there are huge pots holding cymbidium orchids and flowers. You understand the source, when you visit Nancy's whimsical greenhouse — a rambling structure in which she's painted the walls and cupboards with bouquets of daisies, coneflowers, lilies, and roses. Painted cascades of ivy topple over the doors and windows.

The guest rooms are furnished with nice reproduction pieces and include all the amenities both business and tourist travelers may need. The floors are carpeted, the closets are ample, the wing chairs before the TV are comfortable, and the beds have firm mattresses that assure a restful night's sleep. There are vases of fresh flowers beside the bed and in the bath; a dish of candy sits on a nightstand. The baths have tile floors, marble counters, and showers large enough for two. There's a horsey theme throughout, with horse prints and oils on the walls and a leather statue of a horse in each of the rooms.

Breakfast is served in the formal dining room at a large table set with bright blue placemats. In winter a fire blazes in the fireplace. The meal will start with juice and several freshly baked breakfast breads such as lemon/poppyseed or blueberry/apple. The entrée may include pancakes with raspberry sauce or eggs Benedict.

What's Nearby

Ride the Brandywine Scenic Railroad in West Chester for an excursion beside the Brandywine River or rent a canoe in Northbrook for a lazy ride on the river. Most of all, don't miss a trip to Baldwin's Book Barn, a unique collection of more than 400,000 rare and used books, maps, and prints, located in a historic 1822 stone bank barn on Routes 100 & 52 in West Chester. (See also Chadds Ford, Mendenhall, and Unionville.)

Snyder House Victorian Bed & Breakfast

411 West Fourth Street
Williamsport, PA 17701
(717) 326-0411 or (717) 494-0835;
e-mail: esnyder@csrlink.net

Innkeepers: Elizabeth Snyder-Slothus and Robert Slothus
Rooms: 5, all with private baths, air conditioning, and TVs; 1 with private porch; telephone available
On the grounds: Parking, gardens
Extras: Dinner, catered by next door restaurant, can be served in the room; afternoon tea by request; fresh flowers in all rooms
Rates: $85 – $150, including Continental breakfast; two-night minimum weekends
Credit cards accepted: MasterCard and Visa
Open: Year-round
Smoking: Non-smoking bed and breakfast
How to get there: From I-80, exit onto I-180 and travel toward Williamsport. Take the Downtown/Basin Street exit and stay to the right. Go to the traffic light and turn left onto East Fourth Street. Stay on East Fourth Street through six traffic lights, and you will then enter the Historic District. The B&B is the third mansion on the left.

When Williamsport, which is in north-central Pennsylvania, was the heart of a bustling lumber region, lumber barons built their grand Victorian homes along the street now known as Millionaire's Row. The brick and brownstone double-turret mansion that houses the Snyder House Victorian Bed and Breakfast was built in 1889 as a wedding present for a bride. Lavishly furnished with the finest Victorian pieces of the day, the house and its furnishings have miraculously survived more than 100 years intact. They passed from the original owner to Elizabeth's aunt, who lived here for more than 50 years. Elizabeth and Robert purchased the property in 1989, complete with the furnishings and an attic full of historic treasures.

Elizabeth and Robert seem perfectly melded into the time and place of their Victorian B&B. Elizabeth was raised on a nearby 200-year-old farm, and she continues to maintain her flower and holiday shop, called the Strawberry Basket, there. She lavishly decorates the B&B in dried garlands and is rediscovering floral oil painting. Robert, who is a professor of radiography at Penn College, is also an accomplished pianist, writer, and copy-painter. He frequently entertains guests, especially during Sunday morning breakfasts, with piano pieces.

In the parlor, which is painted a deep green, there's a rose theme. Rose carvings accent the white wooden fireplace mantel, and roses appear in the lovely carpeting. Victorian chairs and loveseats are covered in brocade and tapestry, and there's an electric pump organ and a lavish Victorian chandelier. In the music room/library the walls are painted oxblood, and there's a baby grand piano as well as a mahogany square grand piano. The most unique furnishings, however, are in the dining room, which has creamy ivory walls that serve as a restrained backdrop for the elaborately carved dining room suite, which has been in the house for more than 100 years. The 14-foot table has club claw feet, and the sideboard is intricately carved with fantastical gargoyles. The matching server and china cabinet are equally elaborate. Exuberant stained-glass windows grace both the first and second floor landings.

In the guest rooms, the antique Victorian furniture is also original to the house. The Wittenburg Bridal Suite has a bed with a high walnut Victorian head and foot board, lavishly carved with daisies, ivy, and maple leaves.

There's a matching marble-topped dresser and a marble-topped wash stand. The triple bowed stained-glass windows have hot pink jewels that cast reflections across the walls. The Snyder Anniversary Room also has a high Victorian handcarved headboard, this one embellished with dogwood blossoms. There's a matching full-length cheval mirror, a sitting area filled with antique wicker in the turret, and stained-glass windows with a fleur-de-lis design. Each room has a private bath, and in this one, the clawfoot tub has been marbleized.

No design detail skips Elizabeth's attention. For breakfast, she color-coordinates the food, placemats, and dishes, garnishing the plates with herbs and edible flowers from her gardens. She may prepare baked apples or poached pears with Chambord in the winter, while fresh fruit or berries are served in the growing season. Homemade muffins and breads are accompanied by homemade jams and jellies. The meal is either served from tiered sterling silver servers in the dining room or more informally in the kitchen, which contains a big old-fashioned stove.

What's Nearby

Williamsport is the home of the Little League World Series and the Little League Museum. The World Series, which is held toward the end of August, attracts teams and parents from all over the United States. The Lycoming County Historical Museum contains a wonderful history of the area and includes a diorama depicting the local logging industry, an exhibition of trains, and historical room settings.

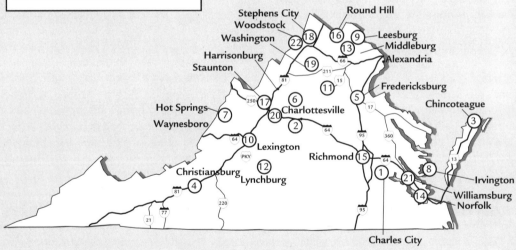

Stephens City
Woodstock
Washington
Harrisonburg
Staunton

Round Hill

Leesburg
Middleburg
Alexandria

Fredericksburg

Chincoteague

Hot Springs
Waynesboro

Charlottesville

Lexington

Christiansburg
Lynchburg

Richmond

Irvington

Williamsburg
Norfolk

Charles City

N

Virginia

Numbers on map refer to towns numbered below.

Edgewood Plantation

4800 John Tyler Memorial Highway (Route 5)
Charles City, VA 23030
(800) 296-3343 or (804) 829-6908;
fax (804) 829-2962

Innkeepers: Julian and Dot Boulware
Rooms: 7, including 2 suites, all with private baths, air conditioning, televisions, VCRs, romantic videos, and radios; 3 with working fireplaces; portable telephones
On the grounds: Parking, swimming pool, gazebo, gardens, gristmill, mill creek, antiques shop, country store
Extras: Turndown with chocolate mints; Victorian high tea; cookies, tea, lemonade, and wine in the afternoon for guests; dog named Jeb Stuart on premises
Rates: $120 – $198, including full breakfast; two-night minimum holiday and special event weekends
Credit cards accepted: American Express, MasterCard, Visa
Open: Year-round
Smoking: Permitted in kitchen and outside only
How to get there: From the north take I-95 to exit 84 and travel south on I-295. Take exit 22A onto Route 5 east (Virginia Scenic Byway). The B&B is on the left in 12.5 miles. From the south take I-95 to exit 46 and travel north on I-295 to exit 22A. Follow directions above.

The peaceful rural countryside of Charles City County has changed little over the years. Plantations with vast tracts of land were built along the James River in close proximity to the Colonial headquarters of Williamsburg, Jamestown, and Yorktown. The current John Tyler Memorial Highway, now a quiet country road, was once the primary link between Williamsburg and Richmond.

Edgewood Plantation, located on 8 acres on this historic highway, is not for everyone. Some will find the vast collection of Victoriana overwhelming. Others, however, will revel in the immersion in the Victorian era.

The house itself is an 1849 Carpenter Gothic, once part of Berkeley Plantation, which is across the street. It has a restrained collection of Victorian wicker on the front porch. Inside, however, every single Victorian table, fireplace mantel, chair, sideboard, dresser, and windowsill, and even the floor space not absolutely needed to put one foot in front of the other, are covered with collections of Victoriana. The kitchen is filled with kitchen queens, tables, chairs, baskets, and stoves covered with Victorian artifacts. There are silver pieces, glassware, brass items, hatboxes, dolls, mannequins dressed in lacy Victorian dresses, fancy hats hanging from a tree, gloves, high-top shoes, fans, and jewelry displayed throughout. Dot Boulware can be blamed — or thanked — for this excess.

The guest rooms have some wonderful Victorian beds that are covered with dolls and lacy pillows. Sarah, for example, has an exceptional 1790s canopy tobacco bed; Victoria has a magnificent carved burled-walnut 1840s headboard; J. E. B. Stuart (who did stop here on his way to Richmond) has an 1818 Empire tester bed with full curtains. A two-bedroom suite on the third floor has iron-and-brass beds and is filled with dolls and doll houses.

On arrival guests are offered tea, wine, cakes, and coffee. Breakfast, which is served in both the dining room and the Tea Room, will include such delicacies as stuffed French toast or banana-and-walnut pancakes, along with fresh fruit and homemade breads.

Edgewood includes a creek, a pool surrounded by a white picket fence, and a gazebo.

It's popular for weddings and receptions. The estate also has a 1725 stone gristmill that ground corn for both the Union and the Confederate armies.

Dot is a friendly, effervescent innkeeper who offers tours of her house daily, and she and Julian sell Victorian antiques and gifts from their country store. She puts on elaborate Victorian tea parties that include sandwiches, scones with clotted cream, pastries, and cakes. She herself is dressed in full Victorian array, and she garbs each guest in a Victorian hat for the occasion. Dot and Julian have lived in the James River plantation area for more than twenty years, and they know all the back roads to take for specialized tours as well as the best restaurants.

What's Nearby — Charles City

Berkeley Plantation, the home of Benjamin Harrison, a signer of the Declaration of Independence, and of President William Henry Harrison, the ninth president of the United States, is located here. It was also the ancestral home of Benjamin Harrison, the twenty-third U.S. president. It is furnished with its original antiques and decor. Shirley, the oldest plantation in Virginia, is nearby. The house is noted for its flying staircase and original portraits, silver, and furniture. Sherwood Forest Plantation was President John Tyler and Julia Gardiner Tyler's home after he left the presidency in 1845. The beautifully restored house is the longest frame house in America and is still occupied by Tyler descendants. Evelynton Plantation, the magnificent Georgian Revival ancestral Ruffin plantation, is also nearby. Belle Air Plantation is noted for its magnificent Jacobean stairway, interior decorative trim, and landscaped grounds. Westover, an elegant plantation built by William Byrd II, the founder of Richmond and Petersburg, is noted for its lovely eighteenth-century gates and its grounds that offer sweeping views of the James River. (See also Williamsburg.)

North Bend Plantation B&B, A James River Plantation

12200 Weyanoke Road
Charles City, VA 23030
(800) 841-1479 or (804) 829-5176;
fax (804) 829-6828

Innkeepers: George and Ridgely Copland
Rooms: 4, including 1 suite, all with private baths, air conditioning, TVs, and desks; telephone available in living room
On the grounds: Parking, swimming pool, bicycles, croquet, horseshoes, volleyball
Extras: Billiard table; refreshments on arrival; turndown with chocolates; complimentary dessert after dinner at local tavern/restaurant; fax available; one black Labrador named Molly on premises
Rates: $120 – $135, including full breakfast, afternoon refreshments, and complimentary dessert; two-night minimum holiday weekends
Credit cards accepted: MasterCard & Visa
Open: Year-round
Smoking: Permitted outdoors only
How to get there: From the north take I-95 to exit 84 and travel south on I-295. Take exit 22A onto Route 5 east (Virginia Scenic Byway). One-half mile after the junction with Route 155, turn right onto Route 619. Travel for $1^1/2$ miles and turn left at the second lane to the B&B. From the south take I-95 to exit 46 and travel north on I-295 to exit 22A. Follow directions above.

Staying at North Bend Plantation is rather like staying within the pages of a history book. Every room in this 1819 Greek Revival–style home, which has been in the same family for most of its 180 years and is on the National Register of Historic Places, has a story to tell. The handsome desk used by Union General Philip Sheridan when he stayed here in 1864 sits in the room named for him. Priceless history books dating to the Civil War tell the story of the battle as it was taking place. A map of the area, pre-

pared for General Sheridan, hangs in the billiards room, which also has a marble-based billiards table.

It was innkeeper George Copland's family who built North Bend Plantation, and it's his family's antique furniture that still fills the rooms. The Harrison/Ruffin families are also prior owners of Berkeley, Westover, and Evelynton plantations, and it's this strong connection to local history that permeates the B&B. George and Ridgely are fonts of historical data, which they are happy to share with their guests.

Although the guest rooms are large and furnished with elegant antiques, this is not a deluxe B&B. Rather, there's a homey, comfortable, lived-in ambience that seems to suit this work in progress. Recent improvements to the white clapboard house with black shutters include a new front porch and a new bath in the Federal Room.

In the Sheridan Room, Edmund Ruffin's magnificent full tester mahogany and burl walnut bed (Ruffin made history when he fired the "shot heard 'round the world," the first shot of the Civil War at Fort Sumter) is dressed with rose-colored bed coverings. The Magnolia Room enjoys a view of a huge old magnolia tree. It has a canopy rice bed and a charming table set with doll dishes and dolls. The Rose Room has a canopy bed with lacy curtains and a huge antique mahogany armoire as well as a gas fireplace.

On the second floor, there's a sun porch with antique wicker and a view of the spacious grounds and swimming pool, but guests also often linger in the Billiards Room or in the living room, where they can peruse through the rare history books and Civil War photographs by Matthew Brady. Tobacco and cotton were probably grown on the plantation's 850 acres originally, but today George grows corn, soybeans, and wheat. Deer will often be seen grazing in the fields.

Breakfast is served in the formal dining room. Lacy white cutwork placemats on the mahogany table are background for fine china, silver, and candles in cutglass holders. Ridgely often serves waffles with her special blackberry syrup, accompanied by bacon or sausage, fresh fruit, and at least two juices.

What's Nearby

See "What's Nearby — Charles City," page 257.

Piney Grove at Southall's Plantation

16920 Southall Plantation Lane
Charles City, VA 23030
(mailing address: P. O. Box 1359,
Williamsburg, VA 23187-1359)
telephone/fax (804) 829-2480

Innkeepers: The Gordineer family; manager, Joan Gordineer
Rooms: 5, including 2 suites, all with private baths, air conditioning, radios, mini-refrigerators, coffee makers, hair dryers, desks, fireplaces, and robes; TVs, irons, and ironing boards available on request; telephone in main house reception hall
On the grounds: Parking; swimming pool, croquet, badminton, volleyball; gardens; barn with farm animals; nature trail; porch swing on veranda
Extras: Mint julep or hot toddy on arrival; Virginia wine or cider in refrigerators; fresh flowers in rooms
Rates: $125 – $160, including full breakfast; two-night minimum holiday weekends
Credit cards accepted: None
Open: Year-round
Smoking: Non-smoking bed and breakfast
How to get there: From the north take I-95 to exit 84 and travel south on I-295. Take exit 22A to Route 5 east (Virginia Scenic Byway). One-half mile after the junction with Route 155, turn left onto Route 615 (watch closely for sign) and continue to the B&B, which will be in 7 miles. From the south take I-95 to exit 46 and travel north on I-295 to exit 22A. Follow remaining directions.

It was a sunny late winter day when we first drove up to Piney Grove. Joan Gordineer was outside pulling weeds in anticipation of spring. As she showed us through her B&B, she said, "For years my family and I dreamed of restoring a period house. When we purchased this modest 1800s plantation house, it had no roof and some of the floor had deteriorated, but otherwise it was intact." The house includes the oldest log structure in Tidewater Virginia, and once inside it's hard to remember that we're actually in the twentieth century. To heighten the sense of an eighteenth-century welcome, Joan brought a hot toddy. Had it been summer, we would have been refreshed by a mint julep. As we sipped, we learned more about this remarkable family.

After the restoration of the main house was complete, the family— consisting of Joan and Joe, her husband; their son Brian (who is a historic preservation specialist) and his wife, Cindy Rae—saw an offer in *Preservation News* that they couldn't resist. The Ladysmith House, a two-story home built in 1857, was for sale for $1 if the new owners would move it. Today it occupies a spot beyond the gardens and contains five guest rooms. The entire property is now on the National Register of Historic Places.

The main house has four common rooms open to inn guests. The Log Room, which has log-and-chink walls and a huge brick fireplace, is used as a breakfast room. The family has dedicated themselves to finding artifacts that have a connection to the house. Old farm implements decorate the walls of the Log Room. In the dining room, which was added to the house in about 1850, there are Piney Grove artifacts and architectural maps. A display of arrowheads found on the property were left by the Chickahominy Indians, who had a settlement here in the seventeenth century. A parlor/library contains Virginia history books, while a reception hall reveals the Gordineer family history.

The appeal of the entire 7-acre property is the concerted attempt to create a B&B that's historically accurate and yet still provides the amenities guests appreciate today. The guest rooms in the Ladysmith House are simple but charming. Although furnished with period antiques and decorated with stencils, pots of garden-fresh flowers, down comforters, and painted floors, each room has a private bath, a fireplace, air conditioning, a radio, a refrigerator stocked with Virginia wine, and a coffee maker. The newest room, located in the original summer kitchen, was created in 1997. It has the same amenities as the other rooms but also has a stone wall, a pierced-tin chandelier, hand-hewn oak beams, a cast-iron stove, and a brass bed covered with a woven coverlet. Antique kitchen accessories decorate the room.

The grounds include a barn that serves as shelter to the resident ponies, goats, chickens, sheep, ducks, and geese. The gardens are gorgeous, and a map describes specimens along a nature trail that meanders through the property. On a slight rise is a freeform pool surrounded by flower gardens and a gazebo.

In the morning we feasted on a plantation breakfast of juice, fresh fruit, Virginia ham, homemade breads, and an egg dish — a cheddar-cheese and egg strata. Another favorite entrée is Joan's Piney Grove Baked French Toast. The meal is served by candlelight on pewter dishes.

What's Nearby

See "What's Nearby — Charles City," page 257.

200 South Street

200 South Street
Charlottesville, VA 22902
(800) 964-7008 or (804) 979-0200;
fax (804) 979-4403;
e-mail: clancyb@cfw.com
website: http://www.southstreetinn.com

Innkeepers: Brendan and Jenny Clancy
Rooms: 20, including 3 suites, all with private baths, air conditioning, telephones with dataports, and radios; 9 with fireplaces; 8 with desks; 6 with Jacuzzis; hair dryers, irons, and ironing boards available; 1 room with wheelchair access; cribs available
On the grounds: Parking; flower beds
Extras: Wine and cheese in the evening; chocolates at turndown; health club available 2 blocks from B&B
Rates: $100 – $200, including Continental breakfast, wine and cheese in the afternoon; two-night minimum weekends in April, May, and September-November
Credit cards accepted: American Express, Diner's Club, MasterCard, Visa
Open: Year-round except Christmas Eve and Christmas Day
Smoking: Non-smoking bed and breakfast
How to get there: From Washington, DC, take I-66 to exit 43 (Gainesville) and follow Route 29 south. In Charlottesville, take the Route 250 bypass east to the third traffic light. Turn right onto McIntire Road. At the second traffic light, turn left onto South Street. Travel ²/₃ block and turn into the driveway on the right between two gateposts. Park in the inn's parking lot and come in the red door in back.

This in-city B&B is located in two gracious townhouses — one yellow brick with white trim, the other yellow clapboard with white trim — on a quiet side street in the city of Charlottesville. Although a secondary line of the railroad runs directly behind the B&B, trains generally do not operate here at night.

The larger building was built in 1856 for Thomas Jefferson's first librarian at the University of Virginia. It is particularly notable for its stunning wraparound veranda and its solid-walnut, two-story serpentine interior stairway. Both buildings are surrounded by wrought-iron fences. They're separated by a driveway to a private parking lot that's entered between brick pillars.

The B&B is now solely owned by Brendan and Jenny Clancy, expatriate New Yorkers, who had been part-owners since 1991, and they've been doing a whirlwind of renovations. The B&B is a sophisticated blend of interesting colors, fabrics, and furnishings.

When I arrived one afternoon, wine and cheese were set out for guests in the library, which overlooks the gardens. This urbane retreat is painted a deep tomato red and has floor-to-ceiling bookcases. A handsome walnut gateleg table is a centerpiece. Breakfast is also served here, or you might prefer to eat on the veranda, which also overlooks the garden. In the summer, this is filled with wicker furniture. A hideaway study is the perfect retreat in which to watch television or just to unwind. Unusual nineteenth-century oil paintings of exotic animals are on display in the main gallery. A front porch, which faces the street, is filled with antique white wicker furniture.

The guest rooms all feature English and Belgian antiques and have an English Country mood. There are canopy beds, gas fireplaces, fantastically carved armoires, and polished, wide-plank yellow pine floors topped with colorful kilims. The baths have tile floors, brass fixtures, and six have Jacuzzis. Room #6, for example, has a canopy bed, a walnut armoire (probably from one of the British channel islands), a carved Victorian desk, and drapes in wedgwood blue and white toile.

Brendan and Jenny serve a Continental breakfast that includes four or five freshly baked breads such as lemon-poppyseed or pumpkin-apple, scones, fresh fruit, and juices. There are a variety of excellent restaurants nearby as well as bicycle trails on which to work off the calories. Downtown Charlottesville has an eclectic, artsy population. There are a variety of art galleries, craft shops, bookstores, and boutiques in the downtown urban mall. In addition, the spectacular Charlottesville Ice Park — offering indoor ice skating, skating lessons, and lots of fun — is a short walk away.

What's Nearby

The primary tourist attraction in the Charlottesville area is Monticello, Thomas Jefferson's stately architectural gem. The building and grounds are meticulously restored, and most of the furniture and household objects were once in the Jefferson family. Many of Jefferson's unusual inventions are on display. Ash Lawn-Highland, the country estate of James Monroe, is nearby also. There are a variety of cultural activities at the University of Virginia throughout the year. (See also Gordonsville and Waynesboro.)

The Watson House Bed & Breakfast and The Inn at Poplar Corner

4240 and 4248 Main Street
(mailing address: P.O. Box 905)
Chincoteague, VA 23336
(800) 336-6787 or (757) 336-6115;
fax (757) 336-5776

Innkeepers: JoAnne and David Snead, Tom and Jacque Derrickson

Rooms: 12, including 4 suites and 2 cottages, all with private baths, air conditioning, radios, and mini-refrigerators; 6 with whirlpool tubs; 1 with a covered balcony; telephone in parlor of both main houses

On the grounds: Parking

Extras: Afternoon refreshments with cakes and cookies; complimentary use of bicycles, beach equipment, and binoculars

Rates: $109 – $149, including full breakfast and afternoon refreshments; two - three night minimum weekends; three - four night minimum holiday weekends

Credit cards accepted: MasterCard and Visa

Open: Mid-March - November

Smoking: Smoking permitted outside only

How to get there: From Route 13, take Route 175 east just south of New Church. Follow this over several bridges and causeways to the drawbridge to Chincoteague. At the traffic light on Main Street, turn left. The B&B is 4 blocks up Main Street on the right.

Chincoteague is a sleepy little village during the winter months, but in the summer the population swells with tourists who come for the vast stretch of beautiful ocean beaches, to eat the fresh local seafood, and to see the wild ponies made famous by Marguerite Henry's book *Misty of Chincoteague*. Chincoteague is the only village of note on both Chincoteague and Assateague Islands. It is located on Virginia's Eastern Shore just below the Maryland border.

When the Derricksons and the Sneads (parents, daughter, and her husband, all with long ties to Chincoteague) renovated The Watson House in 1992, they won a Chincoteague Restoration Award for their sensitive historic revival of this Main Street Victorian, which they painted a buff color with olive trim. But when their establishment was filled almost every night, they purchased two nearby cottages that can each sleep up to eight people. These come with Jacuzzis, washers and dryers, kitchens, cable TVs, telephones, and central air and heat. Still, they had to turn people away. So, in 1995 they built The Inn at Poplar Corner.

Both B&Bs offer broad front verandas and gabled rooflines dripping with gingerbread. It isn't often you see a newly built B&B that fits so perfectly into its environment. Yet The Inn at Poplar Corner, a rose-colored Victorian with white trim, slipped into the surrounding streetscape as neatly as if it had been here as long as its sister property, which harks to 1898. The two B&Bs are just across Poplar Street from one another.

The decor of The Watson House is restrained Victorian. Each of the rooms has its own private bath, although several are quite small. The Inn at Poplar Corner, on the other hand, is much more grand. Each of the large suites has a refrigerator, and the spacious private baths have whirlpool tubs. One of the suites has its own private covered porch. There are parlors in both buildings for relaxation as well as wraparound porches, but the most popular spot is the third-floor sitting room in the Poplar Corner house. It has a reading area with a view of the marshes and of sunsets over Chincoteague Bay.

Both JoAnne and Jacque are wonderful cooks who love to share their recipes with their guests. In fact, few people leave without purchasing a copy of their cookbook, which is filled with interesting and inventive recipes. Breakfast may start with glazed lemon-almond bread and morning rolls, followed by Watson House peaches and cream French toast or a puffed crab roll with cheese sauce.

Afternoon refreshment time is never missed by guests in the know. It may include chocolate eclair cake, a brownie caramel pie, and salted peanut chews, among a myriad of other goodies.

What's Nearby — Chincoteague

The many recreational pleasures of Chincoteague are legendary. The Chincoteague National Wildlife Refuge (operated by the U.S. Fish and Wildlife Service) and the Assateague Island National Seashore offer 37 miles of beaches. Visitors can fish, crab, clam, hike (sightings of wild ponies are frequent), bike, beachcomb for shells, lay on the beach, or bird watch (it's in the prime Atlantic Flyway). Tours with naturalists are also available. On the bay side, it's also possible to water-ski, boat, and canoe. Watch the annual wild pony roundup in July, when the ponies swim the inlet between Assateague and Chincoteague. There's an auction following where the foals are sold. (See also Snow Hill, Maryland.)

The Oaks Victorian Inn

311 East Main Street
Christiansburg, VA 24073
(800) 336-6257 or (540) 381-1500
fax (540) 382-1728; website:
http://www.innbook.com/oaksa.html

Innkeepers: Margaret and Tom Ray
Rooms: 7, all with private baths, air conditioning, telephones with dataports, TVs, radios, stocked mini-refrigerators, desks, hair dryers, and robes; 5 with fireplaces; 2 with Jacuzzis
On the grounds: Parking; perennial gardens, fish pond, fountain; garden gazebo with hot tub
Extras: Complimentary refreshments in mini-refrigerator, decanter of sherry, cookie jar with homemade cookies and fresh fruit in every room; turndown with chocolates; West Highland terrier named Kaile Bonnie Faire and two cats named Princess Mia and Prince on premises
Rates: $115 – $150, including full breakfast; two-night minimum special event weekends at local universities
Credit cards accepted: American Express, Discover, MasterCard, Visa
Open: Year-round except first two weeks in January
Smoking: Non-smoking bed and breakfast
How to get there: From I-81 take exit 114. Turn left if approaching from the south and right if coming from the north, and you will be on Main Street. Continue for approximately 2 miles to fork at Park and Main Streets. Bear right onto Park, then left into The Oaks driveway.

Christiansburg is in the beautiful highlands between the Blue Ridge and the Allegheny Mountains. More than 200 years old, the town was originally an outpost on the old Wilderness Trail, located on the edge of the American frontier. As civilization pushed westward, the town became a lumber and agricultural center, and at one time there were more than twelve fashionable Victorian hotels where guests could stay while "taking the baths" in the local hot springs. Today, it's a major university town since both Virginia Tech and Radford Universities are nearby.

The Oaks, named for the seven magnificent white oak trees that shade the spectacular turrets and porches surrounding this classic Queen Anne Victorian beauty, is a gem by anyone's standards. It sits on a knoll surveying its domain of manicured lawns, boxwood hedges, and flower beds.

Romance pervades the elegant home, which was built by Major William Pierce as a wedding present for his bride, Julia. Together they raised seven children in their home. Nevertheless, by the time Margaret and Tom Ray saw it, the front door had fallen off and the basement was flooded. Today, after a caring and thorough restoration, the house is painted a daffodil yellow with white trim, and it's listed on the National Register of Historic Places.

Visitors first enter the grand entry hall, which has pine woodwork and an imposing staircase with a stunning stained-glass window on the landing. The B&B is furnished throughout with antiques. Here, there's an oak writing desk, a chiming clock, and a piano. The study, a magnet for conversation, has an outstanding Louis XV buffet and a gas fireplace. The parlor, which adjoins it, has multiple windows in a turret and another gas fireplace. In summer, however, guests love to congregate either on the massive wraparound porch with its rockers and wicker chairs or in the gardens in back, which have wrought iron tables and chairs on a brick terrace as well as perennial gardens, a fish pond, and a fountain. Tucked into a garden gazebo, the inviting hot tub offers a romantic starlit retreat.

The guest rooms are equally lovely — each with its own personality. Bonnie Victoria has a lace canopy bed with a crocheted coverlet and an Empire writing desk as well as a gas fireplace. There are adjoining his and hers baths with two showers and a clawfoot tub. Julia Pierce, a room that has five turret windows, has a hand-painted slate fireplace mantel, a cherry chest dating to 1820, and a wonderful $7^1/_2$-foot-tall 1860s Victorian walnut handcarved bed. It's decorated in soft green and peach fabrics. The bath has a Jacuzzi for two as well as a shower and a cherry vanity.

Breakfast is served in the former sun room, which has a fireplace and windows on three sides overlooking the gardens and terrace. A marvelous heavily carved Flemish bookcase with leaded-glass doors holds the B&B's music system. Soft candlelight lends a glow to the lovely antique Dresden china that Tom inherited from his grandmother. The inventive Southern menu varies daily, but it may include cranberry/orange scones accompanied by fresh fruit and juice and followed by light potato pancakes topped with a lemon-dill sauce, sherried mushrooms, and roasted bell peppers.

What's Nearby

Located between the Blue Ridge and the Allegheny Mountains and near the Appalachian Trail, Christiansburg offers limitless opportunities for recreational fun. The New River State Park Bike Trail, The Dixie Caverns, and Chateau Morrisette Winery all present interesting diversions. The Long Way Home Outdoor drama is performed every summer in Radford. At Smithfield Plantation Historic Site, the birthplace of two Virginia governors, costumed guides describe life on the frontier.

Innkeeper: Susan T. Williams
Rooms: 9, including 2 suites, all with private baths, air conditioning, and radios; 7 with desks; 4 with TVs; 3 with mini-refrigerators; 2 with coffee makers; telephone located in front hall
On the grounds: Parking; brick patio shaded by two large magnolia trees
Extras: Fax available; a Belgian sheepdog named Madeline and a Great Pyrenees named Beau on premises
Rates: $95 – $145, including Continental breakfast
Credit cards accepted: American Express, MasterCard, Visa
Open: Year-round
Smoking: Non-smoking bed and breakfast
How to get there: From I-95 take exit 130A onto Route 3 east and travel 3 miles to Fredericksburg. Follow the signs to the Fredericksburg City Visitors Center. The B&B is across the street. It has its own parking lot behind the building, entered from Sophia Street.

Richard Johnston Inn

711 Caroline Street
Fredericksburg, VA 22401
(540) 899-7606

Fredericksburg is a lovely gift from the past. There are more than 350 eighteenth- and nineteenth-century buildings in its 40-block National Historic District. The rosy-brick facades look much as they did when George Washington and James Monroe walked these streets. A visit to the Fredericksburg Visitor Center, which is just across the street, is the first place to stop to pick up several of the excellent walking maps of the town.

Richard Johnston, who was mayor of Fredericksburg in 1809 and 1810, lived in these rosy brick buildings that were built in 1754 and 1780. The B&B is a serene retreat that faithfully re-creates the ambience of the Federal period while offering the amenities we crave today. When we arrived, we were glad the B&B has its own parking lot, as the town teemed with visitors, all vying for parking places on the street.

Susan Williams, proprietor and innkeeper since 1992, has created a lovely and historic spot in which to stay. Most guests enter the B&B via stairs from the courtyard near the parking area. The main floor has 12-foot ceilings, and there's a living room decorated in navy and rose with comfortable wing chairs, a fireplace, and an Oriental rug on the heart pine floors. Guests will find board games, jigsaw puzzles, and playing cards to use on tables in the dining room.

The guest rooms are furnished with lovely antiques and reproductions. My favorite is Room #9, which is located in the original kitchen. It has a brick floor and two antique double-sized beds. Room #11 has a canopy bed with rice-carved posts. Room #4, on the third floor, has a four-poster bed with pineapple-carved posts and a matching dresser, while Room #5, on the second floor, has a spectacu-lar 1830s mahogany plantation-style bed. Two very elegant suites have private entrances off the brick courtyard in back. All the private baths are modern and up-to-date, although several are not en suite but located off the hallway.

A Continental breakfast of freshly baked breads and muffins, fresh fruit, juice, and coffee is served in the dining room at the cherry Duncan Phyfe table. Susan uses fine china, silver, and linens, and she serves the juice in stemmed glasses.

Caroline Street is filled with excellent antiques shops and boutiques; the sidewalks bustle with browsers. Next door to the inn, a charming little shop specializes in teddy bears. Several fine restaurants are located nearby. Merriman's is right next door, and Le Lafayette Restaurant, in a handsome landmarked 1771 Georgian building, is just down the street.

What's Nearby

History lives in Fredericksburg. For one thing, George Washington was born nearby at Ferry Farm, and Fredericksburg contains considerable Washington history. You can visit the Mary Washington House (the home George purchased for his mother in 1772); Kenmore, the beautifully restored and furnished estate of George's sister Betty Washington Lewis; and Rising Sun Tavern, the restored 1760s tavern where Lafayette once stayed that was at one time the residence of Charles Washington, George's youngest brother. In addition, the Fredericksburg and Spotsylvania National Military Park, chronicling the four major Civil War battles that took place over a two-year period here, offers moving insights into the encounters.

Tivoli

9171 Tivoli Drive
Gordonsville, VA 22942
(800) 840-2225 or (540) 832-2225;
fax (540) 832-3691;
e-mail: tivolibnb@aol.com

Innkeepers: Philip and Susie Audibert
Rooms: 4, all with private baths, air conditioning, telephones, radios, desks, and working fireplaces
On the grounds: Parking; gardens; 235 acres with hiking and mountain biking trails
Extras: Fax and copier available; wine, beer, juice, sodas, and liquor available; golden retrievers named Digger and Ben on premises
Rates: $95 – $135, including full breakfast and refreshments; two-night minimum weekends in October and on holidays
Credit cards accepted: Discover, MasterCard, Visa
Open: Mid-February - December
Smoking: Smoking permitted in common rooms if no objection from other guests. No smoking in guest rooms
How to get there: From Washington, DC, take I-66 west to exit 43 (Gainesville). Follow Route 29 south (it becomes Route 15/29) to a point just beyond Culpeper, where the routes split. Follow Route 15 south to Orange. Turn right onto Route 20 south and go 6 miles to Route 231 south. Turn left and follow Route 231 south for 3 miles to the second turnoff to Route 654, which will be on the right. Take the first left off Route 654 onto Tivoli Drive. The B&B is the large house at the top of the hill.

Tivoli, a 24-room brick mansion, is surrounded on three sides by a covered veranda supported by fourteen massive white Corinthian columns. Built in 1903 and surrounded by a 235-acre working cattle ranch with commanding views of the Blue Ridge Mountains, the Colonial Revival house is on the National Register of Historic Places. Called the "quintessential Colonial Revival mansion," there is some evidence to support the theory that it was designed by Stanford White. It was opened as a B&B by innkeepers Phil and Susie

Audibert in 1993. Phil has lived in the area since he was eight years old, and he was the news director of local WJMA radio station in Orange before becoming an innkeeper. He wrote a fascinating book describing many of the interesting people in the area. Copies will be found in each of the guest rooms.

The rooms, which are furnished with priceless antiques and art that have been in Phil's family for many years, are of grand proportions, with 12-foot-tall ceilings on the first floor. In the spectacular 50-by-25-foot Colonial blue and white living room, there's a burl walnut desk, a nineteenth-century linen press, and a Venetian painting that dates to the 1600s. A ballroom contains a 1920s Steinway grand piano and two mammoth crystal chandeliers that still use only candles. French doors from both the living room and the ballroom lead to the porch. There are two more common rooms on the second floor. The Map Room has a large-screen TV with a VCR and a video library. It offers a marvelous view of the entrance gardens.

There are four guest rooms — all filled with lovely antiques and each with a fireplace and an up-to-date bath. The largest is the Gold Room, which has a king-sized bed with an antique Venetian headboard that has a scene painted in muted blues, greens, and gold. In the bath, the original clawfoot tub has survived. The Rose Room has an elaborately carved antique mahogany bed with a curved footboard. There's a lovely mountain view. Throughout the B&B, guests will be enchanted by the portraits of Audibert family members painted by Phil's grandmother, who studied under Baldini in Paris.

Breakfast is served in the grand dining room, which has a double pedestal table. Two massive nautical paintings grace the walls. The meal will consist of freshly baked breads such as apple-carrot muffins and croissants, house-made granola, and a hot entrée such as one of Phil's creative omelets or a crêpe dish — perhaps one filled with fruit and drizzled with an orange curaçao sauce or one that's filled with mushrooms sautéed in sherry, spinach, and Monterey jack.

Do ask Phil and Susie to direct you to the Shenandoah National Park and to hiking and bicycling trails through the fields and forests on their own property.

What's Nearby

Montpelier, the 2,700-acre estate of James Madison, is located nearby. Owned by the National Trust for Historic Preservation, it was opened to the public in 1987. Every November, the Montpelier Hunt Races are held on the steeplechase course on the property. The James Madison Museum in Orange includes personal and presidential correspondence as well as items belonging to his wife, Dolly. Nearby also is Barboursville Vineyards on the estate once owned by former governor of Virginia James Barbour and still containing the ruins of his mansion, which was designed by Thomas Jefferson. (See also Charlottesville.)

King's Victorian Inn
Bed & Breakfast

Route 220
(mailing address: Route 2, Box 622)
Hot Springs, VA 24445
(540) 839-3134

Innkeepers: Liz and Richard King
Rooms: 6, including 1 suite and plus 2 suites in a downtown cottage; 4 with private baths and 2 that share 1 bath; all with radios; 6 with hair dryers; 3 with porches; and 2 with air conditioning, telephones, refrigerators, and coffee makers; telephone for rooms in main house in common area
On the grounds: Parking; gardens
Extras: Afternoon refreshments with cookies; a golden retriever named GiGi on premises
Rates: $85 - $150, including full breakfast; two-night minimum weekends May - October and holidays
Credit cards accepted: None
Open: Year-round except four days at Christmas
Smoking: Smoking permitted on the veranda only
How to get there: From I-81 take exit 222 in Staunton and follow Route 254 west to Buffalo Gap. In Buffalo Gap take Route 42 south to Goshen. From Goshen follow Route 39 west to Warm Springs. At the junction with Route 220, turn south and stay on Route 220 for 4 miles. The B&B will be on the right. Enter the property by driving between two brick columns.

This pristine pearl grey Victorian with white trim was built in 1899, at the height of the Victorian era. It rests on its spacious lawns overlooking one of the Homestead's golf courses. Pretty benches sit under spreading old maple trees, and flower beds spill over with a kaleidoscope of color. Even in the chill of winter when I first spied the house, it was impressive. There are turrets and gables and bays and a veranda that almost encircles the house.

Liz and Richard King (he's with the postal service in Staunton, and she was a nurse) pur-

chased their grand Victorian when it needed considerable work. Built by Dr. Henry S. Pole, a prominent local doctor, the house has also been used as a restaurant, a rooming house, and a leather shop. The Kings have meticulously restored the gracious building, and although they opened the B&B in 1988 with six rooms, they have added to it almost every year. The Ice House, located just behind the main house, contains a two-level suite, and they also have a downtown cottage with two two-bedroom suites.

The wraparound porch of the B&B is furnished with wooden rocking chairs and wicker tables and chairs — the perfect place to sip that final cup of coffee before setting out on a day of hiking or bicycling or "taking the baths" just as the famous, infamous, and not-at-all famous have done for years. But perhaps you'll be so enchanted by the gardens, which have tulips, daffodils, dogwood trees, and forsythia in spring, that you'll wander down to the boxwood garden to watch the birds bathing in the birdbath.

The common rooms of the B&B are decorated with high-quality reproduction furniture. The formal living room is quite elegant with plush sofas before a gas fireplace and a sunny turret area. Another parlor has Victorian loveseats and chairs and a selection of board games and puzzles. Upstairs, there's a Garden Room with white wicker and a TV for guests to enjoy.

The guest rooms on the second floor include Room #4, which has a high rice-carved mahogany bed with a square canopy and a peach Oriental rug on the oak floor. Room #6 has a teal carpet and a powder room with a vanity table. There's a two-bedroom suite on the third floor.

The formal dining room has another turreted sitting area and a non-functional fireplace. There are two mahogany tables — one with claw feet and the other a Queen Anne-style. They are both covered with fine linen, and breakfast is served on Royal Doulton china with sterling silver, unless it's during the holidays, when Liz brings out the Lenox holiday china. Guests feast on fresh juice and fruit, freshly made muffins or coffee cake, and either scrambled eggs with bacon, sausage, or ham, or maybe a French toast dish.

What's Nearby

Hot Springs is nestled into a valley in the heart of the Allegheny Mountains. The hot springs in nearby Warm Springs attracted Native Americans long before white men arrived. The first rustic log inn was built in 1760. The famed Homestead Resort, on 15,000 acres, is within walking distance. There are numerous restaurants, three golf courses, renowned downhill and cross-country ski runs, a ski school, an ice skating rink, a bowling alley, carriage rides, a marvelous spa, and horseback riding. Guests of the B&B can use the Homestead's facilities, but there is an additional charge. The Garth Newel Music Center has concerts throughout the year. Visit the Bacova Guild Factory outlet in Bacova for a variety of silk-screened gifts.

The Hope and Glory Inn

634 King Carter Drive
(mailing address: P.O. Box 425)
Irvington, VA 22480
(800) 497-8228 or (804) 438-6053;
fax (804) 438-5362

Innkeepers: Joyce Barber and Stacey Spanks; manager, Joyce Barber; proprietor, William Westbrook
Rooms: 11, including 1 suite and 4 cottages, all with private baths, air conditioning, and hair dryers; 6 with private patios or porches; all cottages include telephones with dataports; 1 cottage with wheelchair access; telephone on first floor of main house
On the grounds: Parking; bicycles, tennis, gardens, including a moon garden with flowers that bloom at night; private, romantic, fully enclosed outdoor "bathing room" open to the stars
Extras: Coffee, tea, lemonade in the afternoon; wine, cheese, and snacks in the evening; conference facility
Rates: $95–$175, including full breakfast
Credit cards accepted: None
Open: Year-round
Smoking: Smoking permitted outside only
How to get there: From I-95 take exit 126 south of Fredericksburg and follow Route 17 south for about 55 miles to Tappahannock. Then follow Route 360 east for 6 miles to Route 3. Follow Route 3 south for about 40 miles to Kilmarnock. Watch for Irvington Road 200 and turn right toward Irvington. At the Texaco station, turn right onto King Carter Drive and the B&B will be on the right, just beyond the church.

What can I say? Bill Westbrook is an incurable romantic! Born locally and anticipating retirement in 1998, this Minneapolis exec has created an utterly romantic B&B infused with exuberant playfulness and creative artistry. The impressive yellow Victorian building with its crisp white trim faces the street behind a snappy white picket fence. The building began life as a schoolhouse in 1890.

The whimsical decor of the B&B can partly be attributed to the creativity of local folk artist Brad Stephens, who made the folk art pieces and some of the furniture. His art is for sale at the B&B also. The entire B&B looks as if it's been plucked directly from the pages of Mary Emmerling's *New Country Collecting.*

The first floor, which has an open floor plan, is dominated by a grand center stairway. It has a floor painted in bold green and white squares and furniture cleverly arranged in conversation areas. In one corner there's one of Brad's folk art pieces — an armoire that looks like the front of the B&B. On the opposite side of the room, there's a massive fireplace surrounded by sofas and chairs. An oak table with a marble chess board holds pawns created of 1950s salt and pepper shakers.

Upstairs, the floors are also painted, and there's a pretty sitting area with spritely floral fabric on the chairs. The guest rooms have headboards that use "found" architectural elements — a fancifully shingled gable in one; a picket fence in another. Room #5, on the third floor, is a suite that has crackle-painted tables and chairs and a fence post headboard, while in Room #7 the curtains are hung from a birch limb. Each of the bedrooms has a private bath, although several are quite small.

In back of the B&B, there's a lovely brick courtyard with a fountain where breakfast is served in the summer. Several sweet Victorian cottages have been converted to cozy, charming guest rooms also. They each have private brick patios with pretty Victorian garden furniture, kitchens, and painted floors. The largest cottage has been made into a small conference facility, complete with a fireplace and audio/visual equipment.

The pièces de résistance of the B&B, however, are the romantic hideaways tucked away in the garden. In one secluded corner, there's a Moon Garden illuminated by low lights and candles. In another secluded spot, there's an open-air room enclosed by a seven-foot-high stockade fence. Inside, on the brick floor, there's a claw-foot tub, an elegant antique pedestal sink, and an outdoor shower. Fluffy robes hang on a hook and a plethora of fat candles set the mood for this watery rendezvous for two.

For breakfast, either Joyce or Stacey may prepare their own special version of stuffed French toast, using a filling of cream cheese and orange marmalade and topping it with a pecan and orange-flavored syrup. The meal is accompanied by fresh fruit, juices, and perhaps freshly baked orange-poppyseed muffins. Creamy grits will always be offered.

What's Nearby

Sailing and fishing on the Rappahannock River are both popular recreations, and there are numerous bicycle routes to follow along the flat, picturesque country roads. Several golf courses are close. Historic Christ Church, located here, was built in 1732 on the remains of a 1669 church by Robert "King" Carter, the ancestor of eight governors of Virginia and two U.S. presidents as well as Gen. Robert E. Lee. The magnificent brick Greek-cruciform Colonial structure has a swag roof with four hips, aisles paved with slabs of sandstone, and a wine-glass pulpit. The church is almost entirely as it was in 1732. The adjacent Carter Reception Center and Museum contains historical displays about the life of King Carter.

The Norris House Inn

108 Loudoun Street S.W.
Leesburg, VA 20175
(800) 644-1806 or (703) 777-1806;
fax (703) 771-8051
e-mail: jrtp016@prodigy.com

Innkeepers: Pam and Don McMurray
Rooms: 6, each sharing 1 bath, all with air conditioning, desks, and robes; 3 with working fireplaces; telephone in library
On the grounds: .5 acre of gardens; grape arbor; croquet; Stone House Tea Room just across a pathway
Extras: Decanters of port in the library; turndown with handmade chocolates; wine and cheese in the evening on weekends; music throughout common rooms; two cats on premises
Rates: $100–$145, including full breakfast; two-night minimum if Saturday stay included from April-December
Credit cards accepted: American Express, Diner's Club, Discover, MasterCard, Visa
Open: Year-round
Smoking: Smoking permitted outside only
How to get there: From Washington, DC, take I-495 (the Capital Beltway) to Route 267 (Dulles Toll Road), which terminates in Leesburg. Take exit 1A (Leesburg/Warrenton) and follow Route 15 (King Street) through five traffic signals. Turn left onto Loudoun and go 1 1/2 blocks. The B&B will be on the right. Load and unload in front of the B&B, but park in the village garage.

Downtown Leesburg is a picturesque town with narrow streets shaded by oak and elm trees and bordered by brick and stone houses with ivy climbing their walls. The Norris House Inn, a 1760 brick Federal structure with tall windows, has a classic front door flanked by pillars with a fan light above. Its most notable owners were the Norris family, who built many of Leesburg's elegant buildings and who lived in this house for more than 100 years.

Although the building has been operating as a B&B since 1981, it was purchased in 1991 by Pam and Don McMurray, former California marketing whizzes, who came to Virginia while researching their genealogy and never left. They have furnished it with lovely period antiques.

Guests enter a wide center hall flanked on one side by a front parlor, which has a fireplace and an antique china cabinet. Oriental rugs lie on gleaming wide-plank pine floors. On the opposite side, the library has another Colonial fireplace mantel and Eastlake Victorian cherry bookcases filled with books about travel, cooking, architecture, old houses, and antiques.

The guest rooms are lovely. The Norris Room has a four-poster bed with a fishnet canopy. Decorated in pink and blue, it has a Victorian loveseat and a woodburning fireplace. The Old Dominion Room, which is decorated in shades of sage and ivory, has Eastlake Victorian furnishings, including a marvelous Victorian shaving stand. On the walls, there are hunt prints. Each of the rooms shares a modern, large tile bath. In the second-floor hallway, there's a refrigerator stocked with bottled water and juices. A bowl of fresh fruit is nearby.

The gardens are the glory of this winsome B&B. A 40-foot-long screened-in side veranda has wicker chairs. Behind the house lies a lovely lawn bordered by more flower beds and a rock garden. There's a swing under a grape arbor and white iron benches under a magnolia tree.

The Stone House Tea Room, located next door, is in the oldest stone house in Leesburg.

It's also owned by the McMurrays. It has two romantic stone-walled rooms with an English cottage ambience. One room contains a spot where Henry Clay once scratched his name on the wall. Sandy Ruefer, who operates the tearoom, serves a traditional afternoon tea with sandwiches and pastries. She also has a shop where she sells tea cozies, loose tea, and tea accoutrements.

Breakfast is served in the historic dining room of the B&B, which has another woodburning fireplace, a Duncan Phyfe table, and a built-in china cabinet. Elegant linens cover the table, and Pam uses her beautiful Floradora patterned Royal Doulton china and her family antique Rosepoint silver. The meal starts with fresh orange juice and fruit. Then she may serve eggs Virginia, a variation of eggs Benedict, but using steamed fresh asparagus. The Norrises serve a coffee that's freshly roasted in Leesburg. The meal may end with a strawberry pound cake.

What's Nearby

Leesburg, which was founded in 1758, is just two years older than Norris House. It's a lovely Colonial town with interesting walking streets located just 14 miles from Dulles International Airport and 35 miles from Washington, DC. Two interesting early plantations are open for touring — Oatlands, an 1800s brick mansion with white Corinthian columns that was the home of George Carter, and Morven Park, once the mansion of Westmoreland Davis, a governor of Virginia. A bicycle trail that follows the Washington and Old Dominion railroad bed comes right through Leesburg, while the C & O Canal trail is merely 5 miles away. (See Round Hill.)

Innkeeper: Carole Speton
Rooms: 6, including 1 suite, all with private baths and air conditioning; 2 with fireplaces and TVs; 1 with Jacuzzi, porch, mini-refrigerator, and desk; portable telephone in upstairs hallway
On the grounds: Parking; gardens
Extras: Afternoon tea; fax available; one dog named Kumar on premises
Rates: $85 – $145, including full breakfast and afternoon tea; two-night minimum weekends in May and October as well as holiday weekends
Credit cards accepted: MasterCard and Visa
Open: Year-round
Smoking: Non-smoking bed and breakfast
How to get there: From I-81 traveling north, take exit 188B onto Route 60 west. Follow Route 60 through Lexington (it becomes Nelson Street). Turn left onto Borden Road and continue for 1 mile to Brierley Hill, which will be on the left. From I-81 traveling south, take exit 191 onto I-64 west. Continue on I-64 to exit 55 and then follow Route 11 south to Lexington, passing Virginia Military Institute and Washington and Lee University. At Nelson Street (Route 60) turn right and follow it west to Borden Road. Then follow directions above.

Brierley Hill Country Inn

Borden Road
(mailing address: Route 2, Box 21A)
Lexington, VA 24450
(800) 422-4925 or (540) 464-8421;
fax (540) 464-8925;
e-mail: cspeton@cfw.com

When Carole and Barry Speton, who then lived in Vancouver, British Columbia, began visiting their daughter at school in Virginia, they felt an immediate affinity for the area. On each visit they stayed in B&Bs and eventually decided to move here to open their own. So they purchased 8 acres on a sunny hilltop just outside historic Lexington that offered views of the Blue Ridge Mountains and the Shenandoah Valley and built their dream B&B. The blue clapboard English country farmhouse, which has crisp white trim and a spacious veranda, opened for business in 1993.

Guests enter a hall that has an antique oak reception table and an 1850s tall case clock made in Brierley Hill, England, and for which the B&B is named. The Lewes Room is a popular gathering place where a fire glows in the hearth in the winter and spritely Laura Ashley fabrics in the Lewes pattern dress the sofas. In the spacious upstairs hallway, there's a TV for guests to watch.

Each of the guest rooms is named for a flower that grows on the hillsides or in the gardens. The Primrose Room has a magnificent antique brass bed with an elaborate head- and footboard and a floral-covered sofa. The pink-and-white striped wallpaper provides a pretty backdrop for the lacy curtains. The Cowslip Room is done is sunny yellows and has a canopy bed painted dark green. It offers views across the spacious meadows. The Peony Room is also done in yellow. It has a canopy bed painted townhouse ivory and a woodburning fireplace. Oriental rugs rest on oak floors, and there are views of the mountains on three sides. The Rose Suite features a fireplace and a bath with a whirlpool tub as well as a shower.

Afternoon tea is served either in the dining room or in summer, on the veranda. There may be lemonade with cookies and cake or in winter perhaps tea with scones and little sandwiches. Breakfast will be served in the formal dining room, which has a brass chandelier and a fireplace. Crisp English chintz in a rose pattern, candles, and fine crystal enhance the individual tables. A typical menu will include fresh juice and fruit and freshly baked breads such as Carole's apple turnovers or her oat-bran bread. Entrées may feature a wine and cheese baked egg casserole or Grand Marnier French toast. Accompaniments include Virginia lean ham or spicy sausage patties, pan fries, grits, or cornmeal patties with cheese and onions. On selected nights it may be possible to have dinner at the B&B also.

What's Nearby

Lexington is filled with historic sites to visit. Start with a tour of Virginia Military Institute, which was established in 1839, and also of Washington and Lee University. The George C. Marshall Museum (author of the Marshall Plan) is on the VMI campus. You can also tour the Stonewall Jackson House, the home he and his wife purchased when he was an instructor at VMI. The Virginia Horse Center is located on 400 acres just outside Lexington. There are horse shows, auctions, lessons, riding demonstrations, and equestrian art and photography shows. Visitors should also plan a trip to Natural Bridge, a 215-foot-high, 90-foot limestone arch that spans a gorge created by Cedar Creek. It's one of the Seven Natural Wonders of the World and located just east of Lexington. Sound and light shows take place there in the summer.

The Inn at Meander Plantation

James Madison Highway (Route 15)
(mailing address: Route 5, Box 460)
Locust Dale, VA 22948
(800) 385-4936 or
telephone/fax (540) 672-4912

Innkeepers: Suzanne Thomas, Suzie Blanchard, and Bob Blanchard
Rooms: 8, including 2 suites and 3 cottages, all with private baths, air conditioning, telephones, radios, and porches; 5 with fireplaces and dataports; 3 with desks; 2 with TVs; 1 with mini-refrigerator and VCR
On the grounds: Parking; boxwood and perennial gardens, herb gardens, 80 acres of lawns and meadows; croquet, volleyball, hammock; river for fishing, tubing or swimming; four horses on property
Extras: Turndown with chocolates; evening cheese and crackers; afternoon cookies and fruit, coffee, tea, sodas, and juice; exercise room (personal trainer and massages by appointment); fax, computer, printer, copier available; dinner and picnic-basket lunches available by advance request; stable accommodations for horses available; two dogs named Honey and Sara and three cats named Bojo, William, and Little Kitty on premises
Rates: $95 – $195, including full breakfast and afternoon refreshments; two-night minimum holiday weekends
Credit cards accepted: MasterCard and Visa
Open: Year-round
Smoking: Non-smoking bed and breakfast
How to get there: From Washington, DC, take I-66 west to exit 43 (Gainesville). Follow Route 29 south (it becomes Route 15/29) to a point just beyond Culpeper, where the routes split. Follow Route 15 south beyond Culpeper for about 9 miles. The B&B is on the west (right) side of Route 15.

How did a Texas native and a couple from Georgia and Michigan, who met in Chicago, happen to open a B&B together in Virginia, we asked? Well, it's a long story, but they did. It took several years of searching and a tremendous amount of patience and perseverance, but the historic manor house and buildings at a bend in the Robinson River and on an 80-acre

horse farm have developed into one of the finest places in Virginia to stay.

Meander Plantation was originally a 3,000-acre land grant to Col. Joshua Fry, a member of the House of Burgesses and a professor at William and Mary College in Williamsburg. Col. Fry and Peter Jefferson (the father of Thomas) were the first to draw an official map of Virginia

Colony. A French copy of that map now hangs in the living room at Meander Plantation. Col. Fry's son, Henry, built the brick Georgian manor house in 1766. Throughout Henry Fry's lifetime, the dignitaries of the day were entertained here. Thomas Jefferson was a frequent visitor; General Lafayette came often.

Narrowly escaping the hands of developers, the estate was purchased in 1991 by the current team. It had been vacant for many years and needed considerable restoration, but since Suzie had been Historic Preservation Officer of the Chicago suburb of Wilmette, she knew just what to do. They opened the property as a B&B in 1993.

In the main house, which has 11-foot ceilings, guests enter a reception area with a fireplace and a baby grand piano. An arched entry leads to a Georgian living room with another woodburning fireplace and chintz covered sofas. The manor house is joined to the summer kitchen by a covered brick passageway bordered by grand arches. Guests can sit on the two-tiered porch in back and gaze at the Blue Ridge Mountains. Or they can settle into a wooden rocker on the broad front veranda to sip a tall iced tea and watch the bluebirds,

cardinals, and orioles eat from the feeder.

The guest rooms are stunning. The Master Bedroom, decorated in a rich pink, has a four-poster rice bed with a white Battenburg lace duvet over the down comforter, and a woodburning fireplace. The polished heart pine floors have hooked wool rugs. There's a modern tiled bath. The former summer kitchen is now a guest suite. It has a living room with chestnut floors and a bedroom upstairs with a four-poster bed and a woodburning fireplace. Three dependency buildings house charming private rooms with fireplaces.

Breakfast is served in the formal dining room, which is painted a Monticello rose with white trim. It has two antique buffets, a brass chandelier, a woodburning fireplace, and a black slate floor. Suzie fixes terrific meals (she also writes food articles). She may start with a moist Hawaiian bread containing pineapples, bananas, and nuts or with blueberry scones as well as fresh fruit and juice. She may follow this with a quiche of Vidalia onions and sausage, which itself will be followed by her special spicy multi-grain pancakes served with freshly made apple butter and topped with Vermont maple syrup.

What's Nearby

One of the innkeepers will be pleased to make reservations for guests to take horseback riding or hunting lessons at a nearby farm or to take a hot air balloon ride, which can leave right from the B&B's property. For a firsthand history lesson in the Civil War, visits to Brandy Station and Cedar Mountain battlefields are instructive. The Skyline Drive in the Shenandoah National Park is a spectacular drive, especially in the spring when the rhododendrons are in bloom.

Federal Crest Inn
Bed & Breakfast

1101 Federal Street
Lynchburg, VA 24504
(800) 818-6155 or (804) 845-6155;
fax (804) 845-1445; website:
http://www.inmind.com/federalcrest

Innkeepers: Phil and Ann Ripley

Rooms: 5, including 3 suites, all with private baths, air conditioning, radios, and robes; 3 with TVs and fireplaces; 1 with a whirlpool tub; portable telephone on a separate line for guests to use

On the grounds: Parking; gardens

Extras: Mole Hole Gift Shop on premises; Fifties Cafe with jukebox; Eagles Nest Theater with 60" TV; fresh fruit and snack basket in every room; freshly baked snacks and soda on arrival; turndown with mints; meeting space with stage; fax machine available; one dog named Carmel and one cat named Toni on premises

Rates: $85 – $115, including full breakfast and afternoon snacks; two-night minimum weekends in May and October

Credit cards accepted: American Express, Discover, MasterCard, Visa

Open: Year-round

Smoking: Non-smoking bed and breakfast

How to get there: From the Route 29 expressway, take the Main Street (downtown) exit. Continue on Main Street to Eleventh Street. Turn left onto Eleventh Street and go 6 blocks to Federal Street. The B&B is on the left corner of Federal and Eleventh Streets. Continue on Eleventh Street to the parking area behind the B&B.

Just like Rome, Lynchburg is built on seven steep hills affording spectacular views of the surrounding countryside. The town's industrialists and merchants built grand homes on the hilltops, each attempting to outdo the other. Along the streets of the Federal Hill Historic District, where the Federal Crest Inn is located, there are numerous fine nineteenth- and early twentieth-century mansions. Among the finest is this Georgian Revival 8,000-square-foot brick mansion with its tile roof that was built in 1909 for a prominent local lawyer.

Ann and Phil Ripley have created a delight-ful B&B here. Guests enter a foyer with gleaming heart pine floors and pink moire fabric on the walls, a crystal chandelier, and original moldings. The living room has a carved white wood fireplace mantel. Beautiful pocket doors lead to a library, which has the original bookcases with glass doors where the law books were kept. The Ripleys have added a lovely china cabinet filled with pink crystal, and there's also a gas fireplace.

The elegant dining room has paneled walls, a coffered ceiling, and another gas fireplace. One of my favorite rooms, however, is the origi-nal garden room in which the Ripley's have created a cafe with a 1950s theme. There's a tile floor and a great old jukebox complete with hits from the 1950s and 1960s. In addition, a little nook has been set aside as the Mole Hole Gift Shop, where lucky guests can purchase some of Ann's artwork. She's created paintings on damaged roof tiles and paints customized Christmas ornaments. Her original watercolored notecards are also available here.

Another unique room, which the Ripley's call the Eagle's Nest, is found on the third floor. Created originally as the ultimate playroom, it has a stage where the owner's three daughters and two sons could create their own plays. It's now used as a conference facility and has state-of-the-art audio/visual capabilities. High tech business presentations take place here. When not in use for a meeting, it's a terrific place to watch a special event on the 60" TV or a movie from the video collection.

The guest rooms are on the second floor, reached by climbing a grand stairway to an enormous landing. They are named for trees growing on the property. The grandest is Blue Spruce, which has marine blue walls, a mahogany canopy bed dressed with Battenburg lace, and a gas fireplace. The private porch, reached through a Jeffersonian window/door, has a library table, a queen-sized sofa, and a TV set. The terrific bath has a tile floor and a Jacuzzi surrounded by a mural of the Blue Ridge Mountains that was painted by Ann. In the Dogwood Room, an iron canopy bed is swathed in yards of white lace, and there's a white cutwork spread. Pink and white dogwood branches stand in a corner, and there's a handsome gas fireplace and a walnut marble-topped dresser. The tile bath is modern and up-to-date.

Breakfast at Federal Crest is an event. It's served by candlelight with fine sterling silver. The meal begins with "message muffins," fruit muffins (perhaps blueberry) in which a message has been baked. When guests find the message inside their muffin, they read it aloud to the other guests. In addition, guests will be served a fruit cup or maybe a sugar-topped broiled grapefruit followed by Federal Crest egg casserole, a light soufflé dish served with cooked apples and bacon.

What's Nearby — Lynchburg

You can visit Thomas Jefferson's summer home, Poplar Forest, which he considered to be "the best dwelling house in the state, except that of Monticello." It's an extraordinary brick octagonal house with dependencies and landscaping. It was opened to the public recently, as it was in private hands until 1984 and it's still undergoing restoration. In addition, visit Red Hill, a home and plantation where Patrick Henry lived and died.

Lynchburg Mansion Inn

405 Madison Street
Lynchburg, VA 24504
(800) 352-1199 or (804) 528-5400

Innkeepers: Bob and Mauranna Sherman
Rooms: 5, including 2 suites, all with private baths, air conditioning, telephones, TVs, radios, and robes; 4 with desks; 3 with fireplaces; 2 with porches; suites with kitchens
On the grounds: Parking; gardens, gazebo; hot tub
Extras: Turndown with chocolates; newspaper at door in morning; lace bag of potpourri tied to bedposts; two miniature schnauzers named Happy and Krissy in owners' quarters
Rates: $99 – $129, including full breakfast; two-night minimum weekends in May and October as well as holiday and college weekends
Credit cards accepted: American Express, MasterCard, Visa
Open: Year-round
Smoking: Non-smoking bed and breakfast
How to get there: From Route 29 take exit 1 (Main Street/Downtown) and turn west onto Main Street. At Fifth Street, turn left and go 4 blocks. Turn right onto Madison Street. The B&B is on the left on the corner of Fourth and Madison. It's the huge pillared mansion behind a 6-foot-high wrought-iron fence.

Thomas Jefferson considered the Lynchburg area "the most interesting spot in the state," so he built his summer home here. Soon, other dignitaries made it their permanent home. At the time, the primary crop grown on the surrounding plantations was "dark" tobacco, the leaves used for pipe and chewing tobacco. At first, bateaux transported the leaves on rivers and canals to Richmond, but eventually, a web of railroads that passed through Lynchburg contributed to the town's growth.

Lynchburg Mansion Inn, located in the Garland Hill Historic District, where the streets are still paved with brick, is certainly no shy violet. This mansion, sitting proudly behind its 6-foot-high wrought-iron fence and with its grand two-story columns, definitely makes a statement. The 9,000-square-foot pale green stucco Spanish Georgian mansion was built in 1914 by James R. Gilliam, the wealthiest man in Lynchburg. The building was built to impress. There are twenty-two massive columns circling the

105-foot Spanish-tiled veranda. Bob and Mauranna Sherman renovated this jewel and turned it into a B&B in 1990.

The double front doors of the house lead to a noble 50-foot grand hall with majestic cherry columns and wainscotting, oak floors, and a cherry and oak staircase that sweeps upward for three stories. The ceilings on the first floor are 11 feet high, while those on the second floor are 10 feet.

For guest relaxation, there's a living room with overstuffed sofas and chairs and a broad selection of books to read before the fireplace. Upstairs, there's a second-floor sun room filled with plants. In addition, there are gardens to roam, a hot tub to relax in, and a sweeping veranda with wicker furniture where you can listen to the swish of the palm fronds as they sway gently in the breeze.

The entire B&B is furnished with fabulous antiques and original signed artwork. The first floor Veranda Suite, for example, has a bed with a 7-foot-tall burled walnut headboard and a matching dresser as well as a fireplace. In the private solarium, there's a kitchen. The Garden Suite, which is in the original billiards room, has a paneled bedroom with boxed beams and a huge stone fireplace. The Raffles-style bed has Ralph Lauren linens. The French Country room has Victorian fretwork decor and a bed made of light pine and covered with frothy white Battenburg lace. The baths feature a combination of turn-of-the-century accoutrements and twenty-first-century comfort. There are hexagonal tile floors, pedestal sinks, and clawfoot tubs.

Newspapers are delivered to doorways every morning, and coffee and juice are set out on a second-floor table. Breakfast is served in the formal dining room, which has a brass chandelier, oak floors, a fireplace, and a mauve and white rug. The large mahogany table is set with antique German gold-rimmed plates, silver flatware, linens, and crystal. Mauranna may start the meal with a Mediterranean medley consisting of grapes, plums, peaches, figs, sliced dates, and pineapple chunks warmed in fruit juices and then topped with coconut and sliced almonds and garnished with a fresh flower. Entrées may include peach French toast, which is allowed to stand overnight in a caramel custard sauce and baked for an hour in the morning, or a salmon and asparagus quiche.

What's Nearby

See "What's Nearby — Lynchburg," page 283.

The Longbarn

37129 Adams Green Lane
(mailing address: P.O. Box 208)
Middleburg, VA 20118
(540) 687-4137 or (540) 687-3770;
fax (540) 687-4044;
e-mail: thelongbarn@aol.com

Innkeeper: Chiara Langley
Rooms: 3, all with private baths, air conditioning, radios, desks, hair dryers, and robes; guest telephone in the living room
On the grounds: Parking; gardens and fields with gazebo and pond, fishing; tiny chapel for weddings
Extras: Afternoon refreshments of tea, juices, and fresh fruit; mineral water and cookies in room; turn-down with chocolates; fax and VCR available
Rates: $100 – $135, including full breakfast and afternoon tea and snacks; two-night minimum holiday weekends
Credit cards accepted: None
Open: Year-round
Smoking: Non-smoking bed and breakfast
How to get there: From Washington, DC, take I-66 west to exit 57B (just outside Fairfax) and exit onto Route 50. Follow Route 50 west past Aldie. Just before the Middleburg town sign, turn left onto Route 758 (Melmore Place). Turn left onto Route 1040 (Adams Green Lane). At the fourth driveway on the right, turn right. The sign will say "The Longbarn #37129."

The charming village of Middleburg is in the heart of Virginia's hunt country, surrounded by grazing thoroughbred horses in green fields bordered by neatly tended fences. The village itself is filled with mellow buff-colored stone houses resting under massive old trees. Brick sidewalks pass elegant antiques shops, quaint restaurants, and old stagecoach taverns.

When Chiara Langley, an effervescent Italian lady from Emilia Romagna and her husband, Rolland (known as Landy), moved east from San Francisco in 1989, they lived initially in Washington, DC. One day, however, Chiara saw a tiny ad for a barn in the Virginia countryside. She fell in love with the setting, the barn (which had already been converted to a house), and the grounds and outbuildings, so the couple bought it for their home. Although they had not intended to turn the barn into a B&B, Chiara's sister owns the acclaimed inn, Villa Gaidello, in Castelfranco, Italy, and eventually they decided to become innkeepers themselves.

Because of the open space of the original barn, the Langley's were able to create lovely large rooms. The living room, for example, which has warm barnwood walls and a fireplace at one end, has a U-shaped loft surrounding it. Upstairs, there's a huge dining galleria filled with the Langley's beautiful collection of late 1800s European and American paintings interspersed with terra cotta sculptures. The table is a magnificent inlaid mahogany George V piece. It's illuminated by a delicate gold and mauve Murano chandelier. A massive new deck just off the loft offers views of the 8-acre property— including gardens, the dairy barn, the corn crib chapel, the cattle shoot, the hen house, and the serene pasturelands. On the other side of the house, a "white blossom path" leads to the wild duck pond with its waterside gazebo.

There are three large and gorgeous guest rooms, and all have excellent private baths. The Garden Room, on the first floor, overlooks the gardens. In the spaces between the windows, Chiara's friend Misia, an artist from Italy, painted the missing segments on the wall in trompe l'oeil. The bed is covered with floral chintz, and there's a wicker armoire. There are two rooms upstairs. The Blue Room has a bed with a blue iron headboard dressed in Laura Ashley fabrics and an elegant bombé chest. Misia painted trompe l'oeil drapes on the wall. In the Lab Room, which contains Chiara's microscope from her days as a medical researcher, there's a handmade floral quilt on the bed and many colorful watercolors on the walls.

Breakfast and afternoon tea are served in a little room Chiara calls the dinette, just off her marvelous kitchen. She serves fresh or baked local fruit, a large selection of freshly baked breads, cheeses, and either a quiche with sausage or a European-style egg, a soft-boiled egg served in an egg cup and accompanied by toast in a toast server.

If you come to The Longbarn once, you're sure to come again and again, for as Chiara says, "The Longbarn is a magic and serene island in the modern ocean of stress."

What's Nearby

Middleburg is in the heart of Virginia's horse country, where the picturesque countryside is dotted with thoroughbred horses grazing in fields beyond neat fences. Horses and hounds take precedence here, and it's interesting to watch one of the spectacular steeplechase races or fox hunts (the locals pack a picnic lunch) that take place in spring and fall. Chiara will be pleased to make arrangements for guests to ride at one of the nearby stables. In addition, there are boundless antiques shops nearby. Bicycling along the country roads is a popular pastime, as is visiting nearby Piedmont Winery.(See also Round Hill.)

Page House Inn

323 Fairfax Avenue
Norfolk, VA 23507
(800) 599-7659 or (757) 625-5033;
fax (757) 623-9451;
e-mail: innkeeper@pagehouseinn.com

Innkeepers: Stephanie DeBelardino and Ezio DeBelardino
Rooms: 7, including 2 suites, all with private baths, air conditioning, telephones with dataports, TVs, radios, and robes; 5 with desks; 3 with fireplaces
On the grounds: Parking; side yard
Extras: Afternoon cappuccino and freshly baked cookies on arrival; soft drinks, juices, snacks, fruit, candy in common rooms throughout the day and night; fax/copier available; two Boston terriers named Charlie and Tootsie on premises
Rates: $90 – $175, including Continental breakfast, afternoon refreshments, and snacks; two-night minimum weekends from April through October and holidays
Credit cards accepted: MasterCard and Visa
Open: Year-round
Smoking: Non-smoking bed and breakfast
How to get there: From I-64, take the I-264 exit to downtown Norfolk. Continue on I-264 to exit 9 (Waterside Drive). Continue on Waterside (the name of the street will change to Boush) to Olney Road. Turn left onto Olney. Go 2 blocks and turn left onto Mowbray Arch. In 1 block turn right onto Fairfax. The B&B is the first building on the left. The parking area is behind the B&B.

In 1940 the authors of the WPA guide to Virginia described Norfolk as "a fusion of land and sea, of boats and brick houses, of civilians and sailors." Little has changed that dichotomy over the years. Still the home of the largest naval base in the world, Norfolk probably does have more sailors than civilians. Travelers who stay at Page House Inn have the good fortune to be staying in historic Ghent, a waterside neighborhood built between 1892 and 1912 and filled with wonderful old mansions.

When Stephanie, who plays an active role in the Virginia Innkeeper's Association, and Ezio, who is a retired contractor, first spied their dream B&B, it was in the last throes of devastation: condemned and ready for demolition. But they could see the beauty beyond the damage. Ezio worked his magic slowly but resolutely until all the woodwork was restored and the oak floors were polished to a soft glow. Then Stephanie called her aunt, who is a decorator, and together they combined family antiques and newly purchased items to create an elegant but comfortable B&B.

On a recent afternoon visit, Stephanie

opened the polished oak door to reveal a wide hallway with a sweeping stairway that climbs three stories. She invited us into the formal parlor with its marine blue walls, handsome floral window coverings, oil paintings, and puffy sofas before the fireplace. Soon steaming cups of cappuccino and a plate of luscious cookies were placed before us. As we nibbled and sipped, we looked at photographs of the restoration.

Other common areas for guest enjoyment include an informal parlor on the opposite side of the entrance hall that has a fireplace with an oak mantel and plaid sofas. Oak tables and chairs here provide a place to play a variety of supplied games or to complete a jigsaw puzzle. There's also a roof garden off the second-floor hallway with an iron swing and tables and chairs for spending a few relaxing minutes with that last cup of coffee before heading out to see the sights.

Our room for the night was a wonderful suite called Miss Diane. It has a navy blue carpet throughout and blue and white drapes and wall coverings. The bedroom has a white iron bed before a gas fireplace. There's a foyer with a table and chairs and a parlor with another fireplace and sofas and chairs covered in a blue and white fabric. The beautifully restored bath has a clawfoot tub. The newest room, created on the first floor in 1997, has a fireplace and a fabulous bath that includes a private hot tub for two as well as a huge shower that converts to steam. Some rooms even have wet bars, refrigerators, and VCRs. The ultimate romantic accommodation, however, is called Boat and Breakfast. One couple, or two couples traveling together, can stay overnight aboard the *Bianca,* a 43-foot nauticat built in Finland and moored just down the street.

Breakfast for B&B guests is served in the formal dining room, or, with advance notice, it can be served by candlelight on a table in the guest's room. Stephanie offers a Continental "plus" breakfast that will include fresh fruits and poached or baked fruit along with freshly baked sourdough bread and cream scones.

What's Nearby

The Chrysler Museum of Art is just across the street from The Page House Inn. There you'll see one of the finest collections of Tiffany glass in any museum in the world as well as Art Nouveau furniture, photography, paintings, and decorative art. Nauticus, The National Maritime Center, has such diverse nautical exhibits as the Naval Museum, interactive virtual-reality flight simulators, and tours of visiting ships in the harbor. The Norfolk Naval Base, home port of more than 100 naval vessels, is the largest naval installation in the world. Tours are offered throughout the year.

The Emmanuel Hutzler House

2036 Monument Avenue
Richmond, VA 23220
(804) 353-6900; fax (804) 355-5053;
e-mail: be.our.guest@bensonhouse.com
website: http://www.bensonhouse.com

Innkeepers: Lyn Benson and John Richardson
Rooms: 4, including 2 suites, all with private baths, air conditioning, telephones, TVs, radios, coffee makers, hair dryers, irons, and ironing boards; 3 with desks; 2 with fireplaces and whirlpool tubs
On the grounds: Parking
Extras: Fruit juices, coffee, sodas available all day
Rates: $89 – $145, including full breakfast; two-night minimum holiday and special event weekends
Credit cards accepted: American Express, Diner's Club, Discover, MasterCard, Visa
Open: Year-round except December 24th - 31st
Smoking: Non-smoking bed and breakfast
How to get there: From I-95, follow signs for I-64 (Petersburg/I-64 east/Norfolk/Williamsburg (not I-295). Take exit 78 and turn right onto Boulevard and follow it for 1 mile to Broad Street. Turn left onto Broad and go approximately .5 mile past the Science Museum. Turn right onto Meadow and go 2 blocks; then turn right onto Monument. The B&B is on the corner of Monument and Allison. You can unload in front, but overnight parking is in the rear.

Be sure to ask Lyn and John to show you pictures of the renovation of their magnificent B&B on Richmond's grandest boulevard. At one point it seemed to be nothing but structural members. Lyn and John stripped all the mahogany on the first floor themselves, including the walls of paneling and the intricate stair spindles. The painstaking work of restoration has paid off handsomely, as today the beige brick 1914 townhouse glows with warmth and vitality.

Located in Richmond's finest neighborhood,

Monument Avenue is a broad boulevard with a grassy median incorporating magnificent statues of illustrious figures from Richmond's history. Among the most noteworthy is that of Jefferson Davis, which portrays the Confederate president as if giving a speech. He's backed by a huge semicircle of classical columns. Stonewall Jackson, J .E. B. Stuart, and Robert E. Lee are astride their horses. The most recent addition is a statue of tennis great Arthur Ashe, who was born here.

On entering The Emmanuel Hutzler House,

guests find themselves in a grand 8,000-square-foot mansion with an entry hall dominated by a sweeping mahogany stairway. The staircase has the unusual distinction of rising in half-steps instead of full because the original owner had a bad leg. To the right, a handsome living room is enclosed in mahogany paneling that includes a coffered ceiling, boxed beams, and bookcases on either side of the fireplace. An elegant French tapestry hangs above. Richmond history books sit on the large coffee table, illuminated with natural light from the bay of leaded-glass windows. TC, the friendly inn cat, loves to stretch out here on one of the damask sofas to bask in the warmth from the fireplace.

There are four spacious guest rooms on the second floor, and all are equipped with modern baths. My favorite is Marion's Room, which has watermelon-toned walls, a brass-and-iron bed, and an antique English desk. Henrietta's Room has hunter green walls, a decorative tiled fireplace, a bed with a cherry chairback headboard, and a Chippendale love seat. Isaac's Room has a four-poster bed. The Robinette Suite has a marble fireplace, a four-poster bed, and a cherry Sheraton dresser. The tiled bath includes a Jacuzzi and a separate shower.

Breakfast is served in the formal dining room on a massive common table that's overseen by a handsome pier mirror. It will include fresh fruit, cereals, muffins or breads, and a hot dish such as French toast with bacon or scrambled eggs with sausage and fried Virginia apples.

The small parking lot is just outside the back door. When you come in, you leave your keys so that John can move your car if someone needs to leave before you do.

What's Nearby

Richmond is a beautiful and resilient Southern city with a proud heritage and significant architecture. The city was the site of the treason trial of Aaron Burr (presided over by John Marshall). Capital of the Confederacy from 1841–1845, it is now the capital of Virginia and has one of the most impressive capitol buildings, partly designed by Thomas Jefferson, of any state. Other interesting sites to see are the Confederate Museum, the Edgar Allan Poe Shrine (he spent much of his boyhood here); St. John's Church, where Patrick Henry gave his famous "Give me Liberty or Give me Death" speech; and Shockoe Slip and Shockoe Bottom, the oldest sections of Richmond, which now contain upscale restaurants and shops.

Poor House Farm B&B

35304 Poor House Lane
Round Hill, VA 20141
(540) 554-2511; fax (540) 554-8512

Innkeeper: Dottie Mace
Rooms: 4, including 1 cottage, all with private baths, air conditioning, radios, desks, fireplaces, robes, irons, and ironing boards; 2 with telephones, TVs, VCRs, and CD players; 1 with porch, mini-refrigerator, coffee maker, and hair dryer; cribs available
On the grounds: Parking; on 12 acres with gardens, hiking trails, and pond; fishing
Extras: Wine, cheese, and crackers in afternoon; turn-down with chocolates and sometimes warm cookies; fresh flowers in the rooms; pitcher of ice water in room; fax available; picnic lunches packed for guests; one dog named Bentley and two cats named Charlie and Muffy on premises
Rates: $95 – $145, including full breakfast and afternoon refreshments; two-night minimum weekends in May and October
Credit cards accepted: American Express, MasterCard, Visa
Open: Year-round
Smoking: Non-smoking bed and breakfast
How to get there: From Washington, DC, take I-66 west to exit 57B (just outside Fairfax) and exit onto Route 50. Follow Route 50 west to 2.5 miles beyond the village of Middleburg. Turn right onto Route 611 (St. Louis Road) and go 6.5 miles. Turn left onto Route 630 (Unison Road) and continue for .5 mile. Turn right onto Route 700 (Wood Trail Lane) and go .25 mile. Turn left onto Route 756 (Poor House Lane) and travel .5 mile. The B&B is .5 mile on the right.

Dottie Mace traveled the world with her late husband, Fred, when he was in the U.S. Navy, but eventually they settled down on this peaceful farm close to Middleburg in the heart of the horsey fox-hunting and steeplechase countryside. They purchased this 1814 pre–Civil War plantation, which had at one time been the Loudoun County Home for the Indigent, in 1986. By that time, it had been abandoned for more than forty years and had no electricity or plumbing. After four years of renovations, and using savvy decorating skills, they opened their B&B in 1991 — an elegant and refined upscale retreat that is a far cry from the home that housed the indigents. Although Fred passed away in 1996, Dottie has continued to improve and add to the B&B.

In the brick Colonial estate house, which has

a broad porch on the south side and light green shutters and roof, there's a gorgeous living room with oak floors topped with kilims and the original painted fireplace mantel. A massive oak hunt table occupies one wall, and two built-in china hutches contain sets of antique dishes. Watercolors of English gardens decorate the walls. A library is located near the kitchen. It has walls lined with bookshelves and a fireplace. Hunt pictures and duck decoys add a masculine touch.

There's a broad veranda, which has wicker furniture with striped and floral cushions and an abundance of flowers and hanging baskets. Several birdhouses (one is called "Nest and Breakfast") keep guests entertained. From this vantage point, guests look out over the lush flower gardens, the old slave quarter cottages, and down to the farm pond.

There are three rooms in the main house, each with a fireplace, a featherbed, and a full bath. The Unison Room has a four-poster bed and a sitting room. Dark woods are used as well as cream and burgundy floral fabrics. The bath has a wooden floor and a clawfoot tub with a hand-held shower. The Jefferson Room is decorat-ed in an elegant green and yellow Waverly fabric and has another canopy bed. The guest room on the third floor has an iron-and-brass bed and a sparkling new tiled bath. In addition, the former plantation summer kitchen, located in a brick building near the main house, has been converted to the the Cook House Cottage. It has a living room with a massive brick fireplace, as well as a dining area and a small kitchen. The upstairs bedroom has a pencil post bed.

Breakfast is served either in the dining area, which is part of the living room, or on the veranda. In either case, the tables are set with colorful linens and pretty china and silver. Dottie starts the meal with fresh fruit or berries, depending on what's in season, accompanied by scones and popovers. For an entrée, she may prepare French toast stuffed with cream cheese and topped with maple syrup and nutmeg. In the afternoon, she prepares a snack — maybe whoopie pies or scones or popovers.

The Poor House Farm is an ideal retreat from the stresses of the corporate and government world. It's a place to put things in perspective; to contemplate what's truly important in life.

What's Nearby

This is the heart of horse country. You'll pass fields of grazing horses on your way to the B&B. The Piedmont Hunt Club, which is headquartered nearby, passes through the property about four times a year. Dottie recommends a stable just around the corner for horseback riding, and a local couple nearby have been offering hot air balloon rides for more than twenty-five years. Meredith, Piedmont, and Swedenburg wineries are all within an easy drive. (See also Middleburg.)

The Sampson Eagon Inn

238 East Beverley Street
Staunton, VA 24401
(800) 597-9722;
telephone/fax (540) 886-8200

Innkeepers: Frank and Laura Mattingly
Rooms: 5, including 2 suites, all with private baths, air conditioning, telephones with dataports, TVs, VCRs, radios, desks, magnifying mirrors in all bathrooms, irons, and ironing boards; 4 with decorative fireplaces; 2 with CD players
On the grounds: Parking; gardens with benches
Extras: Snacks such as fruit, mineral water, coffee, sodas available 24 hours; fax and copier available; fresh flowers in rooms; one cairn terrier, Jeepers Creepers, on premises
Rates: $89 – $110, including full breakfast; two-night minimum weekends, April - November
Credit cards accepted: American Express, MasterCard, Visa
Open: Year-round
Smoking: Non-smoking bed and breakfast
How to get there: From I-81 take exit 222 and follow Route 250 west to Staunton. Turn right onto Route 11 (Coalter Street) and continue past the traffic light. The B&B is on the left, at the corner of Coalter and Beverley Streets.

It's hard to describe such perfection. It isn't just that Laura and Frank Mattingly have completed a superb restoration of their 1840s Greek Revival mansion in the Gospel Hill Historic District, and it isn't just that they've filled it with gorgeous American Federal and Empire antiques from their outstanding collection. Nor is it the fact that these friendly, knowledgeable innkeepers have included all the guest amenities one could imagine for absolute guest comfort. It's the combination of all their expertise and

thoughtfulness that makes this B&B stand out above the rest.

The handsome creamy-colored house with its columned portico sits behind a stone wall across the street from the home in which Woodrow Wilson was born. The Mattinglys have a passion for history and historic preservation that shows in the restoration of the polished pine floors and moldings that surround the 12-foot-ceilings on the main floor. The moldings particularly stand out against the peach-colored walls in the parlor, which has been furnished with an 1840s butler's desk, fine American and English oil paintings, and an Oriental rug.

The guest rooms are named for people who lived in the house, and each room is furnished in the period of its namesake. The Kayser Room, for example, harks to the mid-1800s when the Kayser family owned the house. It has a magnificent carved New York State four-poster Empire canopy bed draped with creamy damask and accented with teal blue. There's a two-tier crystal chandelier and an ornate fireplace mantel with columns carved to match the bed. The mantel is topped by a late Victorian pier mirror. (Alas, although each room once had a working fireplace, none are currently functional.) The Holt Room is furnished in Colonial Revival style, reflecting the taste of the Holt family, who lived here in the 1920s. The fireplace is surrounded by blue-and-white Delft tiles; the four poster mahogany bed and a matching highboy date to the 1930s. The room is lavishly swagged in cream-and-blue French toile. Thoroughly modern bathrooms include pedestal sinks, and in Tam's Suite the original brass-and-glass towel bars remain.

The dining room is one of the most memorable rooms in the house. It is furnished with a mid-nineteenth-century Duncan Phyfe pedestal table, a Sheraton sideboard, and Chippendale chairs that date to the 1760s. Breakfast is served on antique Royal Doulton china accompanied by family sterling silver and Waterford crystal glasses. Laura's specialty breakfast is Grand Marnier soufflé pancakes, which she serves with a strawberry sauce, country sausages, and freshly baked breads or muffins.

A side garden is filled with flowers in summer that guests may enjoy while sitting on benches in their midst or from a slightly loftier perch on the side porch, which has a swing for two.

What's Nearby

The Woodrow Wilson Birthplace and Museum is across the street. Although Wilson only lived here in his infancy, the excellent museum traces his life as a professor and president of Princeton University as well as through his presidency. The Museum of American Frontier Culture offers excellent living history exhibits of life on the frontier, including costumed guides who demonstrate farming, crafts, and domestic chores. Staunton is in the Shenandoah Valley, tucked between the Shenandoah Mountains and the Blue Ridge Mountains, close to both the Blue Ridge Parkway and the Skyline Drive. (See also Waynesboro.)

The Inn at Vaucluse Springs
140 Vaucluse Spring Lane
Stephens City, VA 22655
(800) 869-0525 or (540) 869-0200;
fax (540) 869-9546

Innkeepers: Mike and Karen Caplanis; Neil and Barry Myers
Rooms: 12, including 2 suites and 2 cottages, all with private baths, air conditioning, and fireplaces; 11 with whirlpool tubs; 7 with desks; 4 with private porches; 1 with wheelchair access; telephone in alcove near keeping room
On the grounds: Parking; swimming pool, gardens, 103 acres of pastures and open land; trout stream for fishing; cross-country skiing when adequate snow
Extras: Afternoon refreshments; fax and limited word-processing available; meeting room; newspapers available; a Gordon setter named Miss MacIntosh and a cat named Toby on premises
Rates: $125 – $190, including full breakfast; two-night minimum weekends mid-April through mid-June and mid-September through mid-November
Credit cards accepted: MasterCard & Visa
Open: Year-round
Smoking: Non-smoking bed and breakfast
How to get there: From Washington, DC, take I-66 west to its end and exit onto I-81 north. Take exit 302 (the first exit) off I-81 and turn left onto Route 627, traveling west toward Middletown. Continue to the end of Route 627 and turn right (north) onto Route 11. Drive 2 miles on Route 11 and turn left onto Route 638 (Vaucluse Road). Drive .75 mile and turn left onto Vaucluse Spring Lane.

When John Chumley had his art studio and gallery here, the tumble of buildings may have been as dynamic as they are today, but it's doubtful they were any more picturesque. Anchored by Vaucluse Spring Pond, the 103 acres that now comprise The Inn at Vaucluse Springs has a fascinating history that begins even before the Chumley family lived here.

The grand brick Federal manor house that sits on a distant hill was built by Strother Jones on land he purchased from his father, Gabriel Jones, known as the Valley Lawyer, in about 1785. The Civil War impoverished the Jones family, however, and they lost Vaucluse, which was named after the Vaucluse region of France. By the time the Caplanis and Myers families discovered the property, the manor house had been abandoned for some 100 years and only the chimney was left of Mr.

Jones's original law office.

Restored and decorated in a sophisticated style, the inn now consists of B&B rooms in the Chumley Homeplace as well as in Chumley's former gallery. Throughout the B&B there are Chumley prints on the walls (he painted realistic scenes of the Shenandoah Valley), and all rooms have beds dressed in brilliant Ralph Lauren-type designer fabrics, gas fireplaces, and (all except one) whirlpool tubs in modern bathrooms. We love the two-level Mill House Studio, which has its own stone terrace beside the mill pond, a gas fireplace in the living room, an upstairs bedroom with an enchanting view, and the soothing sound of water rushing through the mill race to lull guests to sleep.

The keeping room in the Chumley Homeplace—which has walnut log and chink walls, exposed beams, a large stone fireplace, tufted oxblood leather and natural-wicker furniture, and Oriental rugs on polished heart pine floors—offers a cozy and inviting spot to read or talk to other guests. The B&B telephone is in an alcove. A sun porch overlooks the millpond.

Breakfast is served in a bright stone-floored enclosed terrace with a beamed ceiling, exposed posts, a tile floor, and mullioned windows on three sides. Karen and Neil may start the meal with lemon-poppyseed muffins followed by Mike's dramatic six-fruit muesli, which is layered with whipped cream in a parfait glass. Next comes a quiche Shenandoah accompanied by applewood-smoked trout or maybe banana-pecan pancakes with cider-glazed sausages and fans of bananas and strawberrys.

The manor house, which has 11-foot-tall ceilings and 10-foot-tall windows, was undergoing a sensational renovation on my last visit. Neil told me it will have a reception room and a library for guests to relax in and also two dining rooms. They expect to have this ready late in 1997.

There's a lovely heated swimming pool surrounded by a stone wall in front of the gallery building. At times the gallery is used for small meetings or conferences. The pastures are often populated with Holstein cows.

What's Nearby

Do not leave the area without picking up a bag of Route 11 Potato Chips, natural chips made just up the road in Middletown that are the best chips you'll ever eat (you can watch them being made, too). Belle Grove Plantation, a National Trust property, is a beautiful restored 1700s stone mansion that should be included on any visit to the area. Thomas Jefferson influenced its design. Other scenic diversions include Fort Valley with its Woodstock tower for spectacular vistas and the State Arboretum of Virginia, which has the most extensive boxwood collection in North America. You can drive a circular route through its 170 acres.

Middleton Inn

176 Main Street
(mailing address: P.O. Box 254)
Washington, VA 22747
(800) 816-8157 or (540) 675-2020;
fax (540) 675-1050;
e-mail: middlein@shentel.net

Innkeeper: Mary Ann Kuhn
Rooms: 5, including 1 cottage, all with private baths, air conditioning, telephones, TVs, hair dryers, porches or balconies, fireplaces, robes, CD players, irons, and ironing boards; 2 with desks; 1 with a Jacuzzi, stereo, mini-refrigerator, and coffee maker
On the grounds: Parking; gardens; open fields, barn, stables, paddocks, horses
Extras: Afternoon tea and cookies; wine and cheese in the evening; port and chocolates at turndown; fax available; four dogs named Prince Charles, Lady Carolina, Hannah, and Gauge on premises; three horses named Star, Wallabee, and Gambler in stables; five outside cats
Rates: $235 – $345, including full breakfast; two-night minimum weekends in October and on holiday weekends
Credit cards accepted: American Express, MasterCard, Visa
Open: Year-round
Smoking: Non-smoking bed and breakfast
How to get there: From Washington, DC, take I-66 west to exit 43A (Gainesville). Follow Route 29 south for 12 miles into Warrenton and turn right onto Route 211 west. Go 23 miles and turn right at the sign for the Washington Business District. Turn left at the stop sign onto Main Street and go 2 blocks. The B&B is on the left.

We love the rural quiet of "Little Washington." The cluster of old houses and the clutch of shops, the old post office and library belie the sophistication beneath the surface. To all outward appearances this is a rural farm village that's changed little since the nineteenth century. But we all know better.

Middleton Inn was created in 1995 by Mary Ann Kuhn, a former *Washington Post* reporter and producer for CBS-TV news. On a 1996 trip through Virginia, I heard persistent reports about her terrific new B&B, so I couldn't wait to see it for myself. I was not disappointed.

The 1850s brick Federal manor house sits on a 6-acre knoll just outside the town. It was built originally by Middleton Miller, who designed uniforms for the Confederate Army — thus the name.

The B&B is a dream. Mary Ann proudly greeted me in the spacious center hall and took me to the living room, where wine and cheese were set out for her guests. (In summer guests relax in the afternoon on one of the spacious porches.) The living room has sunny daffodil yellow walls, plaid sofas, and a creamy marble fireplace. Oil paintings and sporting prints of foxhounds, horses, and hunters line the walls. The focal point, however, is a magnificent, carved rosewood, square grand pianoforte from the 1830s with a bust of George Bush on its polished surface.

Mary Ann showed me to the Hunt Room, a spacious room with hunter green walls, a beautiful antique carved four-poster bed with its own steps to reach it, an antique Empire bureau, a French-horn chandelier, and a fireplace. The marble bath is exquisite, with a tiny soaking tub and a full shower. All of the rooms have working fireplaces and either a porch or a veranda.

For those who want total privacy, a charming guest cottage is located nearby. It also has a fireplace, and the living room holds shelves of interesting books. Upstairs, a loft bedroom has a sleigh bed and the marble bath contains a Jacuzzi.

For dinner I treated myself to a marvelous meal at The Inn at Little Washington, where the impressive food never disappoints. When I returned, I found a decanter of port and delicious chocolates awaiting me.

The next morning I awoke to the tantalizing smell of hot-from-the-oven muffins. In the elegantly dressed dining room, we savored fresh fruit and eggs Benedict. Mary Ann prepares them with smoked trout instead of Canadian bacon, and they were delicious. On other days she might fix raspberry pancakes.

What's Nearby — Washington

Come in the spring or fall to watch the Virginia foxhunting or steeplechase events. Little Washington Theater has performances of plays, readings, and concerts that take place year-round. The Skyline Drive and the Appalachian Trail follow the crest of the mountains in Shenandoah National Park. Spectacular vistas from both the drive and the trail are awarded to travelers, especially in the spring when the rhododendrons are in bloom. You can pick your own strawberries, raspberries, apples, and peaches at nearby farms or visit Oasis Vineyards, Naked Mountain Vineyard & Winery, and Linden Vineyards & Orchards to sample the local wines. Come in December and select your Christmas tree from a local tree farm.

Sycamore Hill House and Gardens

110 Menefee Mountain Lane
Washington, VA 22747
(540) 675-3046

Innkeepers: Kerri and Stephen Wagner
Rooms: 3, all with private baths, air conditioning, and hair dryers; 2 with radios; 1 with TV, desk, robes, and CD player; guest telephone on a separate line in the living room
On the grounds: Parking; extensive flower gardens; 52 acres on a mountain top; 65-foot veranda with spectacular views
Extras: Turndown with mints and brandy; chocolate chip cookies in guest rooms on arrival; fresh flowers in guest rooms; one huge white shaggy dog named Mollie Bean, one white cat named Zippy, and one calico cat named Pansy on premises but not on guest floor
Rates: $100 – $200, including full breakfast; two-night minimum holiday weekends and all weekends in spring and fall
Credit cards accepted: MasterCard and Visa
Open: February - December
Smoking: Non-smoking bed and breakfast
How to get there: From Washington, DC, take I-66 west for 23 miles to exit 43A (Gainesville). Follow Route 29 south for 12 miles into Warrenton and turn right onto Route 211 west. Go 23 miles and turn right at the sign for the Washington Business District. Immediately turn right again onto Route 638. Follow this road past the library to the white pillars and turn left. The B&B is about 1 mile up the hill.

As you wind higher and higher up Menefee Mountain, you pass beyond the pine trees and meadows, where perhaps you'll see deer grazing or a red fox dart across a field (this is also a National Wildlife Habitat).

Wrapping the Virginia fieldstone house, which sits on 52 acres at 1,043 feet, in a kaleidoscope of hues, gardens delight the eye. You become so enchanted by the bluebirds flitting into their special houses, the hummingbirds sampling the nectar in their red garden, and the beds of more than fifty varieties of flowers—including roses, daffodils, zinnias, and more than 2,000 iris—that you don't even notice the view. It's only after you enter the house that you become aware of it — that overwhelming, top-of-the-world view that stretches across the south side of the house, looking directly across at the Blue Ridge Mountains.

Many B&Bs have wraparound porches; this one has a wraparound view. The bowed windows above a 65-foot projecting veranda furnished with Kennedy rockers seem to reach out and bring the outside in. And the gardens don't stop at the front door, either. Stretching down the hillside are dogwood and redbud trees, a vegetable and herb garden, and a perennial bed filled with peonies, columbines, and day lilies. Inside there are pots of orchids, African violets, ivy, and spectacular clivias, which have brilliant orange flowers in the spring.

The gardens are the creation of Kerri Wagner, who has been adding to them ever since she and her husband, internationally acclaimed illustrator Stephen Wagner, purchased the house in 1987. Steve's original art, some of which he executed as covers for Time-Life Books, *National Geographic*, and others, decorate the walls of this extraordinary B&B. Be sure to pull yourself away from the view long enough to study his work. The B&B is decorated in a smart contemporary style — blond oak floors are covered by Oriental rugs. In winter, a huge stone fireplace warms the living room.

The three guest rooms are on the same level as the common rooms. The Master Bedroom has a 6-foot picture window with a fantastic view across the valley. In a private setting at one end of the house, it has a high four-poster pineapple-post pine bed dressed in a beautiful Amish quilt in shades of pale green and rose, and it also has a dressing room and a private bath. The Peach Room and Wicker Room are at the opposite side of the house. The Peach Room has a brass bed and built-in cases of books. It has views that stretch out in three directions and an in-room bath. The Wicker Room, which also has a view, is furnished with white wicker. It has soft grey walls and contains light pink accent pieces. It has a bath just across the hallway.

Breakfast is served on glass-topped tables in the dining room. Kerri prepares a vegetarian menu that includes a marvelous array of fresh fruit and home-baked breads such as cinnamon raisin bread or country biscuits. She may fix a cinnamon-apple puff (rather like a soufflé) for an entrée or perhaps scalloped eggs, a combination of eggs, scallions, and cheese.

What's Nearby

See "What's Nearby — Washington," page 299.

The Iris Inn

191 Chinquapin Drive
Waynesboro, VA 22980
(540) 943-1991; fax: (540) 943-7770;
e-mail: irisinn@cfw.com

Innkeepers: Wayne and Iris Karl
Rooms: 9, including 2 suites, all with private baths, air conditioning, telephones with dataports, TVs, radios, mini-refrigerators, hair dryers, robes, CD players; 8 with decks or patios; 6 with desks; 3 with VCRs and whirlpool tubs; 2 with fireplaces, coffee makers, irons, and ironing boards; 3 rooms with wheelchair access
On the grounds: Parking; gardens with more than 3,000 iris; 20 acres of grounds; observation tower; hot tub
Extras: Treadmills and bicycles in suites; freshly baked cookies available at all times; beverages at check-in; small conference room
Rates: $80 – $140, including full breakfast; two-night minimum weekends
Credit cards accepted: American Express, MasterCard, Visa
Open: Year-round
Smoking: Non-smoking bed and breakfast
How to get there: From I-64, take exit 96 (Waynesboro-Lyndhurst) and go south on Route 624 toward Lyndhurst. Take an immediate left onto Chinquapin Drive. The driveway to the B&B is approximately .3 mile up the hill on the left.

The Iris Inn is appropriately named for two reasons: a brilliant display of iris covers the bank beside the driveway leading to this hilltop aerie, and Iris Karl, along with her husband, Wayne, is one of the innkeepers.

This unique B&B was built by the Karls in 1992 after they had been unable to find an existing B&B to buy. The cedar and brick building, with its arched entrance, has decks or balconies off each of its guest rooms except one, offering woodsy vistas of trees, birds at numerous feeders, and gardens. Sitting on 21 acres, the architecturally dramatic original structure is now complemented by a new building, which was completed in 1997. It contains two suites and a small conference/meeting facility. A three-story tower includes a tree-top cupola with views of the Shenandoah Valley, and there's a hot tub on the first-floor deck that offers evening sunset views over the valley.

The great room of the main building continues to be the focal point of the B&B. At one end, a fieldstone fireplace soars to the 20-foot cathedral ceiling. On another wall, a mural, painted by wildlife artist Joan Henley, includes gentle deer, fearless rabbits, bold raccoons, statuesque herons, bluebirds and robins, chipmunks and squirrels, and a carpet of flowers. In a loft overlooking the room, there's a library, a piano, and easy chairs offering views of the real fields of wildflowers, trees, mountains, and the Shenandoah Valley — a panorama that lies just beyond the windows. It's in the midst of a designated "forever wild" area. Filled with sunlight that streams in the walls of windows, the great room is where guests gather to read, to converse, and to eat breakfast every morning.

The guest rooms have woodland themes as well. Each is identified by a handpainted sign framed and hung by a rope. In the Bird Room, which has wallpaper featuring birds and bird watercolors on the walls, there's a pineapple post pine bed and a lovely pine armoire, while the Duck Room, which is wheelchair accessible, has a bed with an oak headboard and a sitting area with a wicker sofa. The private baths have hand-painted tiles that reflect the room's theme as well. The newest suites have fireplaces, private decks, lofts reached by spiral stairways, canopy beds, kitchens, and baths with whirlpool tubs. Joan painted woodland creatures on the furniture here. In one room there's a squirrel painted on a dresser drawer who is waiting to crawl inside to retrieve his acorns, which are painted inside.

Iris prepares a full breakfast that will start with fresh fruit and freshly baked breads such as apple-nut muffins and coffee cake. The entrée may feature an egg strata with browned potatoes and bacon.

What's Nearby

Waynesboro is the home of the P. Buckley Moss Museum, a museum devoted to the work of one of America's most celebrated living artists. See her charming watercolors, etchings, and prints of Amish and Mennonite families, farms, and buildings. Virginia Metalcrafters is also headquartered in Waynesboro. Visitors to the factory can watch as molten brass is poured into sand molds. Trivets, candlesticks, sconces, chandeliers, and much more can be purchased in the shop. The Skyline Drive, the Blue Ridge Parkway, and the Appalachian Trail are just 3 miles east of the B&B. (See also Charlottesville and Staunton.)

Innkeepers: Carol, Jim, and Bróna Malecha
Rooms: 9, including 2 suites, all with private baths, air conditioning, and radios; 3 with desks; 2 with fireplaces and tape players; cribs available; guest telephones located on second and third floors of the main house and there is also a portable telephone
On the grounds: Parking
Extras: Refreshments in afternoon; sherry and nuts in evening; fax, iron, and ironing board available
Rates: $95 – $175, including full breakfast; two-night minimum holiday weekends and all weekends in April, October, and December
Credit cards accepted: MasterCard and Visa
Open: Year-round
Smoking: Non-smoking bed and breakfast
How to get there: From I-64, take exit 242A (Busch Gardens) onto Route 199. Follow Route 199 for 5 miles. Turn right onto Route 5/Route 31 east (Jamestown Road). Go 1.2 miles. The Cedars will be on the right. The parking lot is behind the B&B.

Cedars Bed & Breakfast

616 Jamestown Road
Williamsburg, VA 23185
(800) 296-3591 or (757) 229-3591;
fax (757) 229-0756

The Cedars has been welcoming guests since the 1930s, but when Carol, Jim, and Bróna Malecha purchased it in 1993, they transformed it into a bed and breakfast of the 1990s. Located just across the street from the College of William and Mary and within walking distance of Merchant Square and Colonial Williamsburg, the Cedars is a great choice in its location, style, and friendliness.

Carol greeted me in the gracious Colonial sitting room of her home, where guests often relax in the evening before the fireplace. The soul of the inn, however, is the handsome, tile-floored tavern porch. An all-season room filled with sunlight, plants, and flowers, it has eighteenth-century, scallop-legged tables set with novelty candles in hurricanes. Tea, hot chocolate, and soft drinks are set out in the afternoon. In the evening this is a favorite place to read, play cards, or enjoy one of the many board games.

We were staying in the George Washington Suite, located on the first floor. It's a beauty. The high ceilings give dimension to the carved mahogany canopy bed and antique armoire. A sunny sitting room contains a lovely antique writing desk, and the tile-floored bath has a tile shower.

Most of the guest rooms are located upstairs, where a decanter of sherry and a dish of macadamia nuts await on a table on the landing so that guests can help themselves to a snack before or after dinner. The Plantation Room has an arched bed with a fishnet canopy and a bow-front dresser, while the Christopher Wren Room, on the top floor, has windows on three sides, a four-poster bed draped in a plum floral fabric, and a dormer window with a window seat. A charming brick carriage house behind the main house was most recently renovated to provide two additional rooms. The Lord Botetourt Room has a slanted ceiling, a pine wardrobe, and a corner gas fireplace as well as a modern white-tiled bath.

Carol's hobby is food and wine, so breakfast here is one of those "don't miss" affairs. She sets out an assortment of items on a hand-hewn huntboard on the tavern porch. The array is astounding and includes some of the most inventive breakfast items I've encountered. There will always be an assortment of freshly baked breads (perhaps cranberry muffins or monkey bread) as well as a tray of fresh fruit. In addition, she might create an oatmeal-pudding entrée. This unusual dish is made with oatmeal, eggs, milk, cottage cheese, nutmeg, and cinnamon. Brandied raisins and maple syrup are served on the side. Another specialty is a mushroom egg puff or a sausage-and-apple casserole. To accompany the entrée, there will be Virginia ham biscuits or perhaps baked or poached fruit. You definitely will not go away hungry.

What's Nearby — Williamsburg

Walk along the restored streets and visit the numerous shops where candles, hats, shoes, and furniture are made. Take a tour of the Governor's Palace, the Capitol, Raleigh Tavern, Bassett Hall, the George Wythe House, the Abby Aldrich Rockefeller Folk Art Center, and the DeWitt Wallace Decorative Arts Gallery. Eat in the reconstructed taverns operated by the Colonial Williamsburg Foundation. Other nearby attractions include Jamestown Settlement, the first English settlement in America; Carter's Grove Plantation; and Busch Gardens, a 360-acre family amusement park adjacent to the Anheuser-Busch brewery, which also offers tours. (See also Charles City, Virginia.)

Liberty Rose
Bed & Breakfast Inn

1022 Jamestown Road
Williamsburg, VA 23185
(800) 545-1825 or (757) 253-1260;
website: http://www.libertyrose.com

Innkeepers: Brad and Sandra Hirz
Rooms: 4, including 2 suites, all with private baths, air conditioning, telephones, TVs, radios, hair dryers, robes, irons, and ironing boards; 2 with fireplaces and desks
On the grounds: Parking; gardens; swings in 100-year-old trees
Extras: Freshly baked chocolate chip cookies on arrival; soft drinks and juice always available; afternoon tea and snacks; turndown with a long-stemmed papersilk rose on the pillow
Rates: $125 – $225, including full breakfast; two-night minimum May - October and in December; three-night minimum some holidays and on weekends May - October and in December
Credit cards accepted: American Express, Master-Card, Visa
Open: Year-round
Smoking: Non-smoking bed and breakfast
How to get there: From I-64, take exit 242A (Busch Gardens) onto Route 199. Follow Route 199 for 5 miles. Turn right onto Route 5/Route 31 east (Jamestown Road). Go .5 mile to the B&B, which will be on the left. Watch for the long white picket fence and drive between the brick entrance pillars.

If you feel as if you've been in a Colonial time warp in Williamsburg, the Liberty Rose will be a welcome change. Definitely not Colonial in ambience, the B&B has an eclectic style that might best be described as Southern Victorian. One thing is for sure, however: Each guest room is a thoroughly romantic retreat — a couple's paradise.

The Liberty Rose is located about a mile from Colonial Williamsburg on the way to Jamestown. On a hill surrounded by venerable beech, oak, and poplar trees, the slate-roofed clapboard house offers a serene and relaxing retreat after visiting the numerous local historic sites.

Sandi and Brad Hirz have owned Liberty

Rose since 1987. Warm and gracious, Sandi is the perfect hostess. In addition to her bed and breakfast, she is also an interior designer and a wedding consultant. She greeted us and immediately offered a plate of freshly baked chocolate chip cookies. Who could resist?

There's a grand Victorian parlor with a fireplace and a piano for the use of all the guests as well as a pretty and sunny morning porch that overlooks the gardens. This opens to a bluestone courtyard that is surrounded by lush flower beds.

The guest rooms at Liberty Rose are a reflection of Sandi's imaginative design ideas. Rose Victoria, for example, where we were staying, has an elaborate cherry French canopy bed swagged in fringed and tasseled bed curtains. It has red damask wall coverings, a tin ceiling, and ivory woodwork. A television is hidden in an exquisite French antique walnut armoire. The bath is incredible. One wall was taken from a Victorian turn-of-the-century townhouse that was torn down. There's an oversized clawfoot tub (the perfect size for two-person bubble baths) and a red marble shower.

Suite Williamsburg contains a massive carved ball-and-claw tester bed with curtains and valences in copper silk stripes and a bed cover in a rose-colored jacquard fabric. A working fireplace and a bath that contains cherry paneling, a clawfoot tub, and a black Italian-tile shower make this a popular sanctuary for honeymooners. The television in this room is cleverly concealed in a swiveled box painted to look like an elaborate doll mansion. Magnolia Peach and Savannah Lace contain similarly romantic decor. The elaborate rosewood tobacco-post bed in Savannah Lace is incredible.

Breakfast is either served on the morning porch or in the courtyard. Sandi is a great cook. One day she fixed a breakfast that included French toast stuffed with cream cheese and marmalade and topped with fresh strawberries. Alongside, she served eggs and bacon. Another day she filled a croissant with thickly sliced Virginia ham, Swiss cheese, and honey mustard, and heated it. This was served with country-fried potatoes, fresh fruit, and freshly baked muffins. She also makes Granny Smith apple-fritter hotcakes topped with roasted pecans. With this she serves scrambled eggs with cheese-and-sausage patties.

What's Nearby

See "What's Nearby — Williamsburg," page 305.

Innkeepers: Ellen and Ed Markel, Jr.
Rooms: 12, all with private baths, air conditioning, and radios; 9 with telephones, hair dryers, and porches; 7 with fireplaces; 1 room with wheelchair access; crib available; guest telephone in living room
On the grounds: Parking; 5 acres of lawns and gardens with views of river and mountains; herb garden; fishing on the river; horseshoes
Extras: Lemonade, tea, or cider and cookies in the afternoon; soft drinks in refrigerator at all times; conference room; a golden retriever named Holly on premises
Rates: $90 – $115, including full breakfast; two-night minimum holiday weekends and spring and fall weekends
Credit cards accepted: MasterCard, Visa
Open: Year-round except Christmas and two weeks in January
Smoking: Non-smoking bed and breakfast
How to get there: From I-81, take exit 283 to Route 11 south. Follow Route 11 for 2 miles south of Woodstock. The B&B is on the left side of the road at the junction with Route 672 (Chapman Landing Road).

The Inn at Narrow Passage

Route 11 South
(mailing address: P.O. Box 608)
Woodstock, VA 22664
(800) 459-8002 or (540) 459-8000;
fax (540) 459-8001;
e-mail marnpass@shentel.net
website: www.shentel.net/narrowpassageinn

Historic Route 11 follows the trail forged by post riders and stagecoach drivers along the Great Wagon Road that led through the Shenandoah River valley, which is tucked between two rugged mountain ranges. The road eventually took travelers to the western frontier through the mountains at the Cumberland Gap in the southwest corner of Virginia. The route is still dotted with old stagecoach taverns and wayside stops, and the rustic, atmospheric Inn at Narrow Passage is one of the most engaging. It sits on a

5-acre plot that overlooks the Shenandoah River.

The oldest section of the B&B, which has thick log-and-chink walls that could withstand attack from Indians, was built in 1740. At this spot in the road, the trail snaked through a limestone ridge so narrow that there was only room for passage of one wagon at a time, making the journey quite dangerous. Travelers were often subjected to Indian attacks here. In 1862 during the Civil War, Stonewall Jackson made the B&B his headquarters while he conducted his

Valley Campaign.

Ellen and Ed Markel have done an excellent job of retaining the rustic, old-fashioned mood while giving us all the modern comforts we enjoy today. They added a wing to the original B&B constructed in such a harmonious style that all parts seamlessly blend together.

Guests have a number of options for relaxation. The original log living room has exposed beams, log walls, wide-plank pine floors, and a huge limestone fireplace. Plaid sofas and wing chairs and Early American tables and chests are arranged in conversation areas. In the newer wing, the Markels used old pine flooring and paneling to create a gathering room that's hard to distinguish from its neighbor, which is 250 years older. A broad porch across the back has white cedar rockers where guests can sit in the afternoon with a cool drink to watch the lazy passage of the Shenandoah River against the outline of the Massanutten Mountains just beyond the B&B's lawns and gardens.

The guest rooms are furnished with Early American reproduction pieces. Room #8, for example, has a hand-made pine bed with a fishnet canopy and a brick fireplace. Room #S-2 is spacious and comfortable. It also has a pine bed with a fishnet canopy and a fireplace as well as hand-crafted pine chests with shafts of wheat carved into the doors. Every room has a private, modern bath. The new section also contains a handsome conference room that's ideal for small meetings.

Breakfast is served in the Colonial-style dining room, which has wood-plank pine floors, pine paneling, and another stone fireplace. There are beamed ceilings, tin chandeliers, Windsor tables and chairs, and mullioned windows dressed with country-cotton ball-fringed curtains. Ellen serves a bevy of fruits and breads, including perhaps a cherry-almond or a cinnamon-walnut coffee cake. The entrée may consist of bacon, eggs, and hashbrowns or French toast with sausage and apples — hearty fare well-suited to the many visitors who come here to hike, fish, or bicycle.

What's Nearby

The foothills of the Massanutten Mountains harbor several spectacular caverns. The Luray Caverns contain beautiful caves with eerie formations. The caves and tunnels are lit with colored lights and dramatized with music. Other nearby caverns include the Endless Caverns and the Shenandoah Caverns. Climb to the top of the Massanutten Tower to see the seven bends of the Shenandoah River winding like a giant snake below; then sample the river's recreational fare by fishing or hiking along its banks.

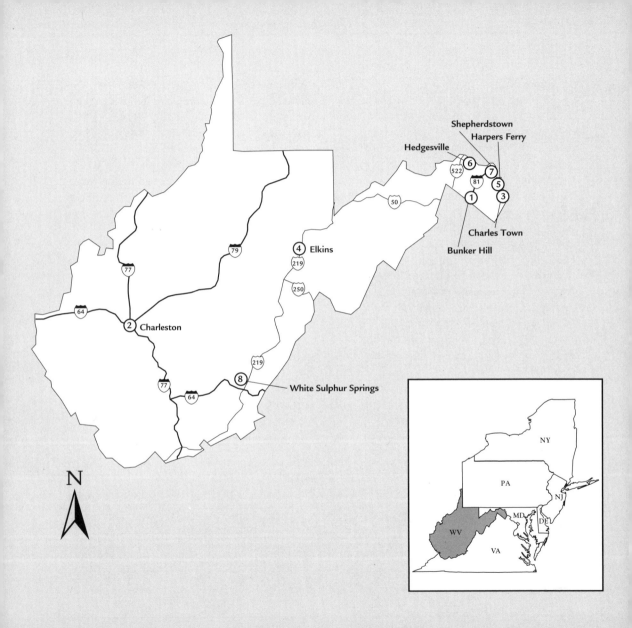

Shepherdstown

Harpers Ferry

Hedgesville

522

6

81

7

5

3

1

Charles Town

Bunker Hill

50

4 Elkins

219

79

250

77

64

2 Charleston

219

8 White Sulphur Springs

77

64

N

NY

PA

NJ

MD

DE

WV

VA

West Virginia

Numbers on map refer to towns numbered below.

Edgewood Manor B&B

Route 11, Rural Route 2, Box 329
(mailing address: P.O. Box 509)
Bunker Hill, WV 25413
(304) 229-9353; fax (304) 229-9359;
e-mail: edgewood@intrepid.net
website: http://wwweb.com/www/
EDGEWOOD

Innkeepers: Sharon and John Feldt and Birdie Lamkin
Rooms: 6, including 1 suite, 4 with private baths and 2 that share a bath, and all with air conditioning and robes; 3 with fireplaces; 2 with desks; telephone in library, although there are jacks in every room and a portable telephone as well
On the grounds: Parking; 52 acres with gardens, a pond, and wooded areas; croquet, horseshoes, badminton
Extras: Snacks including cookies or brownies, tea, coffee, cappuccino, and lemonade; turndown with chocolate candies, warm cookies, and hot chocolate; afternoon tea, including scones, finger sandwiches, and desserts, available with reservations (extra charge); a picnic lunch for two prepared April through September with advance notice (extra charge); fax, telephone, copier, computer with Internet access available; gift shop; two cats named Fat Boy and Muffin, in owners quarters only
Rates: $85 – $145, including full breakfast; two-night minimum holiday and special-event weekends
Credit cards accepted: American Express, Discover, MasterCard, Visa
Open: Year-round
Smoking: Non-smoking bed and breakfast
How to get there: From I-81, take West Virginia exit marked Whitehall/Route 11 and follow Route 11 north. The B&B is about 3.5 miles ahead on the left. You will see the B&B sign beside a Civil War monument.

West Virginia contains many Civil War reminders, but few buildings have witnessed as many historical events as Edgewood Manor. General Stonewall Jackson headquartered here; General Robert E. Lee and his troops camped here; the Civil War battle of Bunker Hill was fought here; John Boyd, who was raised here, was accused of spying and arrested here; and General James Pettigrew drew his last breath here.

When the 1839 brick mansion was pur-

chased by John and Sharon Feldt and Sharon's mother Birdie Lamkin in 1995, it needed considerable work. In the process of doing the repairs, John, an attorney, and Sharon and Birdie, both educators, conducted extensive historical research. Today their guests enjoy the fruit of their work, and the building is on the National Register of Historic Places.

The Civil War seems to come alive at Edgewood. There's a library with a cozy fireplace sur-

BUNKER HILL, WEST VIRGINIA

rounded by a wooden mantel and an extensive collection of Civil War books on the bookshelves. The music room has another fireplace and an 1839 pianoforte. The Tuscarora Brass Band, of which Mr. Feldt is director and whose members play with period saxhorns, is headquartered here. There's a parlor with a fireplace and an 1810 carved Virginia sofa that is original to the house. In a cupboard, the innkeepers display their scone mix, lemon and lime curd, and apple butter, which is for sale.

The guest rooms are beautifully furnished. One is dedicated to General Pettigrew and contains a fireplace, an elegant leaded crystal chandelier, a bed dressed in a burgundy quilt with a crocheted ecru coverlet and a fishnet canopy as well as maps, artifacts, and a portrait of the General. The Texas Room celebrates the Feldt and Lamkin heritage, as the trio were all raised in that state. The theme features bluebonnets (the Texas state flower) and the yellow rose of Texas, and there are books and magazines about Texas. This room has twin wicker beds dressed in yellow and blue fabrics. All the baths have tile floors and new fixtures.

A light breakfast of homemade muffins, juices, fresh fruits, and coffee or tea is set out on the upstairs porch in warm weather, which is furnished with wicker chairs, a dining table, and a porch swing. Guests can sit here overlooking the rose garden and fountain before starting out for a day of sightseeing.

For those who enjoy a larger breakfast, it is served in the formal dining room, which has an elegant mahogany pedestal table and sideboard and a grandfather clock in the corner. Sharon and Birdie own twelve sets of china, so it's always fun to see which pieces they will use. The meal may start with baked apples or pears accompanied by homemade peach muffins or honey oatmeal bread. The entrée may be a spinach quiche or perhaps a Texas scramble, a dish that began as a mistake and has become a best-request item. Every afternoon high tea is served, with freshly baked scones, finger sandwiches, dipped fruits, and pastries.

The grounds of Edgewood Plantation include a stone-lined pond filled with koi and surrounded by day lilies, a stream, and a carriage path to a secret bower.

What's Nearby

People come from miles around to visit the Bunker Hill Antiques Mall, which is located just down the lane from the B&B in an old brick three-story mill. There are more than 200 dealers, and the facility is open seven days a week. Bunker Hill is close to Winchester, Virginia, where the Victorian cottage that served as Stonewall Jackson's headquarters in the winter of 1861–1862 is filled with maps, photographs, and memorabilia. (See also Charles Town.)

The Brass Pineapple

1611 Virginia Street East
Charleston, WV 25311
(800) CALL WVA;
telephone/fax (304) 344-0748

Innkeeper: Sue Pepper
Rooms: 7, including 1 suite, all with air conditioning, private line telephones with dataports and voice mail, TVs, VCRs, radios, hair dryers, desks, and robes; 1 with mini-refrigerator and CD player
On the grounds: Parking; rose garden
Extras: Afternoon tea with pastries, fresh fruit, cheese or tea sandwiches; turndown with chocolates or milk and cookies; snack basket and sherry in hallway; gift shop; exercise room with treadmill, stationery bike, and weights; fax, copier, available; bicycles provided for touring historic area
Rates: $75 – $115, including full breakfast and afternoon tea; two-night minimum on special-event weekends
Credit cards accepted: American Express, Diner's Club, MasterCard, Visa
Open: Year-round except major holidays
Smoking: Non-smoking bed and breakfast
How to get there: From I-64 take exit 99 (Greenbrier Street), turn left onto Greenbrier Street, and continue to the Kanawha River. Turn right onto Kanawha Boulevard, go 1 block and turn right onto Elizabeth Street, go 1 more block and turn right onto Virginia Street. The B&B is in the middle of the block on the right. Park behind the B&B.

The Brass Pineapple is located in the historic district of Charleston, near the beautiful and impressive, 293-foot-high gold-domed state capitol building, which was designed in 1921 by Cass Gilbert, architect of the U.S. Supreme Court Building in Washington, DC, and the Woolworth Building in New York City. Overshadowed by two massive oak trees, the house was built in 1910 by real estate developer, E. C. Bauer. Nothing but the best would do. He incorporated Italian tile, oak paneling, and exquisite stained- and leaded-glass windows into the design that combines both Art Nouveau and Victorian elements.

When Sue Pepper first saw the house, it had long-before been converted to apartments. The oak paneling had been painted white, spacious rooms had been dissected, and the lower portion of the grand stairway had been removed to make room for a bathroom. Today, however, the golden paneling gleams, the rooms are spacious and inviting, there are Oriental rugs on polished oak floors, and, thanks to the discovery of the original stairway balustrades in the basement, the stairs once again climb grandly upward from the entry hall.

The formal parlor, which has an oak floor with an Oriental rug, a Victorian chandelier, and antique Victorian furniture, is an inviting place to sit. A covered veranda in front, which has a hexagonal tile floor and black wrought iron tables and chairs, is a summer outdoor living room. Hanging baskets of flowers and candles are lighted in the evening, giving it a romantic, dreamy effect. Sue has a gift shop in the entrance foyer featuring West Virginia items, and an exercise room is located on the lower level.

The guest rooms are charming and original. The English Gentleman is furnished with a beautiful antique walnut carved Victorian bedroom set that includes a bed with a high headboard and footboard and a marble-topped dresser that contains a sink. The masculine room is paneled in elegant raised walnut and has marble baseboards. An oak Morris chair sits beside the decorative fireplace. In the Hearts & Flowers Bridal Suite, there's a king-sized white iron-and-brass bed and a separate sitting room with a TV, VCR, and a video library stocked with romantic movies. The newest room, Charleston Manor, has an iron bed with frothy white coverings and an antique desk and dresser.

Breakfast and afternoon tea are served in the formal dining room, which has richly grained tiger oak wainscoting, an oak floor with an Oriental carpet, and a crystal chandelier. Golden-toned stained glass in the bay of windows gives the room a warm and sunny feeling. Sue has an extensive breakfast repertoire. Solicitous of her guest's wishes, she offers an option of a Continental or a full breakfast. There will always be fresh or cooked fruits, such as vanilla scented pears or cinnamon fried apples, fruit breads such as banana walnut or blueberry streusel muffins, and perhaps hot oatmeal or cold cereals. This may be supplemented by a sausage-and-egg casserole or chocolate waffles.

Sue supplies bicycles to pedal through the historic district and over to see the capitol grounds.

What's Nearby

Charleston is located on the Kanawha River, where there are jogging trails that border the river and sternwheeler cruises. You may wish to visit Sunrise Museum and Science Hall, the 1890s mansion and gardens of Governor William MacCorkle. Located on 16 acres, it includes a science hall, planetarium, nature trails, gardens, and a furnished mansion, Torquilstone. The state capitol houses a cultural center, a craft shop, and a theater as well as the West Virginia State Museum, where West Virginia's history is traced from the earliest Native American inhabitants to the twentieth century. And it's free!

The Carriage Inn

417 East Washington Street
Charles Town, WV 25414
(800) 867-9830 or (304) 728-8003;
fax (304) 728-2976;
e-mail: carriage@intrepid.net
website: http://www.carriage inn.com

Innkeepers: Al and Kay Standish
Rooms: 6, including 2 suites, all with private baths, air conditioning, and radios; 4 with fireplaces; 2 with televisions and 1 with a mini-refrigerator; telephone located in main hall at reservation desk
On the grounds: Parking; gardens
Extras: Coffee or tea available all day
Rates: $75 – $155, including full breakfast; two-night minimum weekends in October and winter holiday weekends
Credit cards accepted: MasterCard and Visa
Open: Year-round
Smoking: Non-smoking bed and breakfast
How to get there: From Washington, DC, take I-270 north to Frederick, Maryland, and then take Route 340 west. In about 20 miles you will cross the Potomac River Bridge into Virginia. Proceed for 2 more miles on Route 340 to the Shenandoah River Bridge to West Virginia. Continue on Route 340 to Charles Town. In Charles Town, Route 340 becomes Route 51 and Washington Street. The B&B will be on the left on the corner of East Washington and Seminary Streets. You will pass it before reaching the downtown section.

The handsome grey brick 1836 mansion sits proudly on an acre of manicured lawn behind a black wrought-iron fence. Black shutters frame the windows, and a broad porch with four fluted columns creates a grand entrance. Located near the Charles Town Races, the B&B is an easy walk from town.

You'll undoubtedly be greeted by the friendly innkeeper, Kay Standish, who is justifiably proud of her B&B. She and her husband, Al, have owned the B&B since 1996, and they've furnished it with many lovely family antiques. The attractive parlor has high ceilings, a gas fireplace, a piano, and family antiques that include a lovely old desk. Oriental rugs cover the narrow-board oak floors. Be sure to read the yellowed old newspaper accounts of the nearby battles hanging on the walls. On the opposite side of the entry, the dining room is in what was the original east parlor. This is where General Ulysses S. Grant and General Philip Sheridan met to discuss their Shenandoah Valley strategy in 1864 during the Civil War. Another sitting room is located upstairs, where there's a refrigerator for guests to use as well as a TV.

The guest rooms are appealing. In the Green Room, there's a four-poster bed with a fishnet canopy and a gas fireplace, while in the Porch Room, there's both a canopy bed and a gas fireplace as well as a sitting porch furnished with a TV. Were I to choose a favorite (which is difficult), I believe it would be either the Blue Room, which has large windows that fill the room with light and a very high four-poster rice bed, or the Rose Room, which has a four-poster maple bed with a fishnet canopy. Both these rooms have sunken baths with steep steps that may be difficult for some people to negotiate.

The Carriage House has been converted into a lovely suite, which is a nice place for families to stay. There are light pink sponged walls and a sitting area with a fireplace. Upstairs there's a bedroom decorated in green and yellow that contains a pretty brass bed.

Breakfast is served in the formal dining room, which has another fireplace. A beautiful 1890s family silver coffee and tea set stands on the buffet. Kay uses her family sterling flatware and lovely ivory Lenox with a gold rim to serve breakfast. Come prepared to have a scrumptious meal. Cooking has long been one of Kay's favorite activities. She's received awards in cooking contests, and her recipes have been featured in newspaper articles. A typical breakfast may include orange juice, sliced kiwi with strawberry puree, a breakfast cheese pie with strawberry and peach slices accompanied by Canadian bacon, and double-chocolate banana muffins. Refills of Starbucks coffee are encouraged while guests become acquainted around the table.

What's Nearby — Charles Town

Charles Town is noted for several unusual attractions. The Charles Town Races, a thoroughbred race track, has been open since 1933. There are live races Wednesday, Friday, Saturday, and Sunday, and simulcast races the rest of the week. Charles Town is also the place where abolitionist John Brown was tried and hung for treason in 1859. You can visit the Jefferson County Courthouse where the trial took place and also see where he was executed. There are historical markers identifying other Civil War events throughout the town. At the Old Opera House, live theatrical performances take place year-round. (See also Harpers Ferry and Shepherdstown.)

The Cottonwood Inn
Mill Lane
(mailing address: Route 2, Box 61-S)
Charles Town, WV 25414
(800) 868-1188 or (304) 725-3371;
fax (304) 728-4763;
e-mail: travels@mydestination
website: http://www.mydestination.com/
cottonwood

Innkeepers: Joe and Barbara Sobol
Rooms: 7, all with private baths, air conditioning, and desks; 6 with TVs; telephone located in living room
On the grounds: Parking; on 6 acres with walking trails and a stream crossed by a wooden bridge; large picnic pavilion
Extras: Cold drinks or hot cider in afternoon; fax and computer with limited Internet access available; two dachshunds named Saide and Higgins and two cats named Spot and Shadow in owners' quarters
Rates: $65 – $120, including full breakfast; two-night minimum holiday weekends
Credit cards accepted: American Express, MasterCard, Visa
Open: Year-round
Smoking: Non-smoking bed and breakfast
How to get there: From I-81, take exit 12 (Charles Town/Martinsburg) onto Route 51 and travel east toward Charles Town. At the junction with Route 9, take Route 9 east toward Leesburg. About 1 mile after crossing Route 340, turn south onto Kabletown Road. Go 3.2 miles to Mill Lane and turn right. The B&B's driveway is .2 mile straight ahead.

If you prefer your B&Bs to be quiet retreats from the noise of horns and sirens and from the rush and bustle of city life, then you must come to The Cottonwood Inn. Tucked away on 6 acres in a remote setting of ponds and streams and gardens and lawns, this heavenly spot is at the end of a peaceful lane. As you cross the little bridge across Bullskin Run and see the pristine farmhouse beyond, you know you're in for a treat. Joe and Barbara Sobol have owned the

B&B since 1994 and have made many improvements to the established property.

The 1840s white-trimmed yellow brick farmhouse is fronted by a broad porch just made for relaxation. Sit here in a rocker or on the porch swing in the cool of a summer evening and listen to the rush of the stream, the chirp of the crickets, and the breeze through the cottonwoods, and watch the fireflies dance through the night. Wake in the morning to the joyous sound of the birds.

The B&B has a warm and comfortable ambience. One thing you'll notice immediately are the extraordinary quilts throughout. There's one with an intricate pattern by an award-winning artist in the entry hall, and another in the living room. A cozy reading area and a brick fireplace in the living room invite perusal through the bookshelves, while the piano will appeal to musically talented guests.

The guest rooms are charming, with various nooks and crannies that add to their interest. Room #1 has a four-poster pine bed and green walls, while Room #2 contains a sleigh bed, natural pine floors, a fireplace, and plank walls. Room #3 has a brick wall and a four-poster maple bed as well as a bath with a clawfoot tub, while Room #4 has a beamed ceiling and a pedestal sink in the bath.

Breakfast is served in the breakfast room, which was the original farmhouse kitchen. The huge cooking fireplace can still be stoked up on cold winter days, and the beamed ceiling and plank walls give the room a warm glow. Barbara prepares a breakfast that begins with fresh fruit and juice and perhaps an apple-cherry coffee cake. For an entrée she may fix a potato-cheese casserole and smoked turkey puffed pastry.

In addition to running the B&B, Joe and Barbara are video experts. They own a company called Destination Images, and they write and produce video tours of European country destinations, specializing in driving tours beyond the cities. They invite their guests into the studio to see how they make, edit, and produce the videos — a fascinating experience.

What's Nearby

See "What's Nearby — Charles Town," page 317.

Innkeepers: Connie and Paul Garnett
Rooms: 5, 3 with private baths and radios; 1 with a Jacuzzi
On the grounds: Parking; gardens
Extras: Dog named Boo and cat named Tuxedo on premises
Rates: $55 – $75, including full breakfast; three-night minimum during Forest Festival, six-night minimum during Augusta Heritage Festival
Credit cards accepted: None
Open: Year-round
Smoking: Non-smoking bed and breakfast
How to get there: From I-79, take exit 99 (Weston/Buckhannon) and travel east on Route 33 into Elkins, where Route 33 is called Randolph Avenue. Turn left at the Iron Horse Statue onto Sycamore Street. The B&B is in 1 long block on the right — on the corner of Sycamore and Buffalo Streets.

The Warfield House Bed & Breakfast

318 Buffalo Street
Elkins, WV 26241
(888) 636-4555; fax (304) 636-1457;
website: http://www.222.virtualcities.com

The Warfield House, a grand 1901 late-Victorian beauty, boasts spectacular stained glass, elaborate moldings and woodwork, a sweeping stairway with carved spindles, and a dramatic terra cotta fireplace wall that has elaborate ornamentation. Prosperity came to the formerly rural town of Elkins, whose economy was based on coal and timber, via the railroad. When owners of the railroad Senator Henry Gassaway Davis and his son-in-law Senator Stephen Elkins made the town the main hub, the quiet little village blossomed into a full-fledged town, and elaborate mansions soon lined the streets. This particular mansion was built by Harry Warfield, the president of the Elkins National Bank.

When Connie and Paul Garnett purchased the building in 1995, however, it had fallen on rough times. They have meticulously polished the rich oak and cherry woodwork, and the oak floors gleam. Paul and Connie are both cellists who met while playing with the Georgetown Symphony. Paul now has a computer business, and Connie is a full-time innkeeper.

The yellow shingled house with its pristine white trim has a broad 70-foot wraparound porch filled with inviting furniture. Green wicker chairs have pretty floral cushions, and there are an abundance of tables and a green porch swing. Beyond the entry hall, where you can admire the ornate stairway and the fantastic stained-glass windows on the landing, there's a parlor with a piano and oak moldings and a pocket door leading to the living room, which has the most spectacular terra cotta fireplace, walls of bookshelves, cherry moldings, an elegant Oriental rug on the polished oak floor, and a patchwork quilt on a table.

Connie and Paul have turned the former butler's pantry into a guest pantry. It's complete with a microwave, a guest refrigerator, a coffee maker, and shelves filled with glasses and cups. It seems as if there's nothing they've forgotten in their efforts to make their guests comfortable.

The guest rooms are spacious and inviting — each with its own personality. I would have to say my favorite is the Maple Room, which has a marvelous maple quarterposter bed draped in lace and a curly maple French armoire as well as a yel-low painted corner cupboard. At present, this room shares a bath with the Pine Room, but there are plans to give it its own. The Walnut Room has an elaborate Victorian walnut bed and a private bath with a shower, while the Pine Room has white iron beds covered with metlasse spreads and wicker chairs. The oddest room in the house is the hallway bathroom for the Pine Room. Instead of harmonizing with the rest of the Victorian house, this bath is a study in Art Deco. There are shiny black walls and blue fixtures.

Breakfast is served in the formal dining room, which has an oak table, oak pressed-back chairs, oak wainscotting, and a built-in oak china cabinet. Lace curtains cover the windows in the bay. The full breakfast will start with fresh fruit and juice as well as home-baked cinnamon rolls or fruit starburst roll-ups and an entrée of Dutch apple pancakes or French toast stuffed with cream cheese, ricotta cheese, and jam.

What's Nearby

Elkins is located in the Monongahela National Forest, an unspoiled wilderness of 908,000 acres that includes rivers and streams for fishing, forests and plateaux for bird watching, rock climbing, hiking, rafting, canoeing, and camping. Davis and Elkins College is located across Sycamore Street from the B&B, and this is where the famed Augusta Heritage Festival—a five-week celebration of the music, dance, folklore, and crafts of Appalachia—takes place. You can learn and participate in such varied activities as bead embroidery, twig furniture construction, playing the fiddle, or clog dancing. In the 1.5-acre Elkins City Park, just across Buffalo Street, there are tennis courts, horseshoes, and every Wednesday night local fiddlers gather for "Pickin' in the Park," an impromptu fiddle fest.

Harpers Ferry Guest House

800 Washington Street
(mailing address: P.O. Box 1079)
Harpers Ferry, WV 25425
(304) 535-6955

Innkeepers: Al and Allison Alsdorf
Rooms: 3, all with private baths, air conditioning, TVs, coffee makers, and desks; 1 room with wheelchair access
On the grounds: Parking; gardens
Rates: $63 – $90, including full breakfast
Credit cards accepted: None
Open: Year-round
Smoking: Non-smoking bed and breakfast
How to get there: From Washington, DC, take I-270 north to Frederick, Maryland, and then take Route 340 south. In about 20 miles you will cross the Potomac River Bridge into Virginia. Proceed for 2 more miles on Route 340 to the Shenandoah River Bridge to West Virginia. About 200 yards after crossing the Shenandoah bridge, turn right onto Union Street and continue for a little over a quarter mile to Washington Street. Turn right onto Washington. The B&B is 1 block up the hill on the corner of Washington and Jackson Streets.

Harpers Ferry is located at the intersection of two powerful rivers, the Potomac and the Shenandoah, and at the juncture of Maryland, Virginia, and West Virginia. Picturesque and European in appearance, the village seems poised for an artist's canvas or a photographer's film. Built on a steep hill, the village grew after Robert Harper established a ferry across the river at this point. Eventually, mills powered by the fierce waterpower were built along the riverbanks. Even today, narrow streets made more for riders on horseback than those in cars climb the impossibly steep hills, making you very glad to have a place behind your B&B in which to park. The lower village has been beautifully restored by the National Park Service, and there are lovely trails along the riverfront and throughout the village.

The Harpers Ferry Guest House strikes the perfect balance between a casual place for hikers and bicyclists to relax and an upscale spot for those visiting the town for its cultural activities. Each of the rooms is spacious and attractively decorated, and the baths are fresh and sparkling clean.

On my first visit to Harpers Ferry Guest House, I was greeted by a hiker who had started walking the 2,160-mile Appalachian Trail at its start in Georgia. Now, some 965 miles later, he welcomed the comfort of this relaxed B&B. With no pretensions, this very neat and very clean B&B, which is located across the street from the Appalachian Trail Conference headquarters, even has a place in the basement for hikers to stow and repack their gear.

Al and Allison built the grey clapboard B&B, which has white trim, in 1993. The style is vaguely Victorian. While Al continues to work for Lockheed, Allison, who formerly ran a diner in the Hudson River Valley, handles the innkeeping duties. There's a living room with pine furniture and a handsome brick fireplace. Polished yellow pine floors gleam, covered by braided rugs. Lovely quilts hang on the walls. The couple fix breakfast in a large open kitchen, which overlooks an oak table in the eating area "so guests can see me make all my mistakes," Al jovially told me. A typical morning breakfast will include fresh juice and fruit, a vegetable omelet accompanied by homefries or French toast with stuffed mushrooms. Homemade muffins might be of the blueberry, raisin bran, or poppyseed variety.

There is one guest room on the main floor. The Lincoln Room, which is wheelchair accessible, has twin beds and a shower in the bath. There are two guest rooms upstairs, each with yellow pine floors and tall ceilings. In the Lee Room, there's a queen four-poster bed covered with quilts. In a little alcove, there's a table with a coffee maker; a TV and a desk are in the room. The Jackson Room has a four-poster cherry bed with a canopy top and a colorful quilt covering it. The spacious bath includes all the amenities.

Were I to hike the length of the Appalachian Trail (which I've always imagined I'd do some day), this is the kind of B&B in which I'd like to stay each night.

What's Nearby

Harpers Ferry National Historical Park is the scene of the confrontation between abolitionist John Brown and troops led by Robert E. Lee. The National Park Service has completed an extraordinarily fine restoration of the mellow brick buildings in the Lower Town, where you can walk along streets lined with preserved shops, buildings, and houses. The recreational possibilities of the area are limitless. There's rafting and canoeing in the Shenandoah River. Alongside the old Chesapeake and Ohio Canal, which passes through Harpers Ferry, there's now a hiking and bicycling trail that stretches from Washington, DC, to Cumberland, Maryland. Harpers Ferry is the headquarters of The Appalachian Trail Conference, and the trail marches through here also. (See also Charles Town and Shepherdstown.)

The Farmhouse on Tomahawk Run

1 Tomahawk Run Place
Hedgesville, WV 25427
telephone/fax (304) 754-7350
website: http://www.travelwv.com

Innkeepers: Judy and Hugh Erskine
Rooms: 5, including 1 suite, all with air conditioning and radios; 4 with porches; 1 with coffee makers, desks, and hair dryers; 4 with dataport capabilities; 1 room with wheelchair access; telephone in great room
On the grounds: Parking; on 280 acres with walking paths through the hills, woods, and meadows; flower gardens, patio with arbor and benches; stone spring house
Extras: Turndown with chocolates; afternoon tea with homemade fruit breads
Rates: $75 – $140, including full breakfast; two-night minimum holiday weekends
Credit cards accepted: Discover
Open: Mid-February to mid-January
Smoking: Non-smoking bed and breakfast
How to get there: From I-81, take exit 16 west and follow Route 9 for 6 miles (2 miles beyond the Hedgesville traffic light) to Route 7 (Tomahawk Road). Turn left and go 2.5 miles on Tomahawk Road. Turn right between the Tomahawk Christian Church and the Tomahawk Valley Store onto Tomahawk Run Place. Go .5 mile to the B&B, which will be on the left.

In a very rural setting, this lovely B&B is a welcome surprise. When Judy Erskine inherited the overgrown 280-acre farm with its dilapidated farmhouse and stone springhouse, she had fond memories of coming here as a child. The land was first granted to Israel Robinson in 1740 by Lord Fairfax, who was then British Proprietor of the area. Judy is a direct descendant of Robinson's, so this land has been in her family for more than 250 years — surely one of the longest of any English land grant in the United States. The house and buildings are now on the National Register of Historic Places.

Judy and her husband Hugh began their restoration odyssey in 1991 and were ready to open the doors to guests by 1994. When comparing the pictures of the farmhouse before the restoration with the finished B&B, you marvel at their vision.

Guests enter a wide stone hallway that contains a weasel — a yarn winder that emits a "pop" when it has finished a skein — initiating the old saying "pop goes the weasel." Hugh is retired from the U.S. government, but while he was an active employee, the couple lived all over the world. Many of the decorative items and the furniture in the B&B were collected in their travels. In addition, Hugh's grandfather was a missionary to Japan, and the magnificent carved dining room table and black walnut buffet are his legacy. A quilt that hangs over the upstairs stair railing was made by Judy's grandmother.

At the end of the hallway, in a new wing, a gathering room has been created. It has an oak floor, tall ceilings, and a massive fieldstone fireplace. A regimental drum serves as a table. Beyond the French doors, there's a wraparound porch with a West Virginia mahogany floor and a hot tub. The view of the meadows, the old privy, the stone spring house (it still encloses the spring, which is in the shape of a tomahawk, giving the entire area its name), and the woods beyond is peaceful and still. The quiet is interrupted only by the songs of the birds that flit from birdhouse to birdhouse.

Hester's Room, which is located on the first floor and is wheelchair accessible, is presided over by a stern picture of its namesake, an ancestor of Judy's. There's a four-poster bed with blue bed coverings and a very pretty new bathroom with a tile floor and a shower. There are two more guest rooms upstairs, and each has its own wide porch. They are decorated with lovely quilts or cutwork duvets and interesting furniture, such as a chest made from the house's attic floorboards that now contains a sink. The baths are absolutely top quality. The two rooms in the Carriage House are ideal for a family. There is a kitchen and a living room with a gas fireplace as well as two bedrooms and two baths. French doors off the living room open onto a large deck, and one of the bedrooms has a private balcony.

Breakfast is served in the dining room on the Japanese table (and also in a smaller room if the B&B is full). A typical meal may include a fresh fruit cup or a baked apple, homemade muffins (perhaps blueberry-yogurt or cranberry-apple), and a main course of maybe a cheese strata with roasted rosemary potatoes, Canadian bacon, and homemade Colonial bread toast or black walnut pancakes (from the B&Bs trees) with fresh local sausage and maple or blueberry syrup.

What's Nearby

Hedgesville is located between Berkeley Springs and Martinsburg. In Martinsburg, the Boarman Arts Center specializes in the work of West Virginia artists. Come here to purchase original art. People come from miles around to go to the extensive outlet mall located in a converted woolen mill in Martinsburg. In Berkeley Springs you can bathe in the warm mineral waters at Berkeley Springs State Park. Massages and heat treatments can accompany a therapeutic bath. Cacapon Resort State Park is a 6,000-acre preserve with a lake for swimming, fishing, and boating; an 18-hole golf course; hiking trails; and horseback riding.

Thomas Shepherd Inn

300 West German Street
(mailing address: P.O. Box 1162)
Shepherdstown, WV 25443
(304) 876-3715; fax (304) 876-1386;
e-mail: mrg@intrepid.net
website:
http://www.intrepid.net/thomas.shepherd

Innkeeper: Margaret Perry
Rooms: 7, all with private baths and air conditioning; guest telephone upstairs in library and downstairs in sitting room.
On the grounds: Parking; gardens
Extras: Sherry in the evening; fax, meeting room available; two Lhasa apsos, Walter and Vernonica, on premises
Rates: $85 – $125, including full breakfast; two-night minimum all holiday weekends and also if stay includes Saturday from April to Thanksgiving
Credit cards accepted: American Express, Discover, MasterCard, Visa
Open: Year-round
Smoking: Smoking on porch only
How to get there: From I-81, take exit 16 onto Route 9 east and follow signs to Route 45. In Martinsburg take Route 45 east to Shepherdstown. Route 45 becomes West German Street in Shepherdstown. The B&B is at the intersection of West German and Duke Streets in the center of town.

Shepherdstown, which was founded in 1727 by German settlers, is the oldest town in West Virginia, but it wasn't until Thomas Shepherd arrived in 1734 that the town began to grow. The entire town is a historic district and listed on the National Register of Historic Places. The B&B, a creamy-colored brick Federal building with green shutters, was built in 1868 to house the parsonage of the Lutheran Church. It was converted to a B&B in 1984, and Margaret Perry purchased it in 1990.

Margaret is a friendly, outgoing innkeeper who is a font of information about Shepherdstown. You might sit in the lovely back garden where her adorable Lhasa apsos play while she tells you about the best access points to the C&O Canal bicycle path or the Appalachian Trail. And she will certainly fill you in about the town's newest restaurants, galleries, and shops.

The B&B is appropriately furnished in a Colonial style. Guests can relax in a formal living room, which has wide-plank pine floors covered with Oriental rugs, green-checked sofas, and cranberry-colored wing chairs before a fireplace. A decanter of sherry and glasses sit here. The extensive gift shop in the dining room reflects Margaret's varied interests. It includes cookbooks, flower seeds, jams, and bags of potpourri. There's also a library on the second floor that has a TV, VCR, video library, and a selection of books. Off the library, there's a covered tree-top porch that is complete with white rockers, a braided rug, and a romantic trellis-work wall. An array of flowering plants flourish here.

The guest rooms are simply decorated with comfortable Colonial furnishings that include canopy and poster beds and other antiques. The nicest rooms are Room #2, which has a sleigh bed and a new bath, and Room #7, which has a sitting area with a non-functional fireplace, a bedroom with a lovely Victorian half-tester bed,

and a nice bath. It's all decorated in Laura Ashley fabrics. Although each of the rooms has a private bath, several are very tiny, and Room #3 has a bath across the hallway.

Margaret has a culinary background, and she loves to cook. She serves breakfast in two small and cozy dining rooms. One has a handsome brass chandelier, polished pine floors, a pretty corner cupboard where segments of the gift shop repose, and a fireplace mantel. Guests eat on antique tables that seat six. She may include blueberry sour cream muffins, juice, fresh fruit, and strawberry pancakes with maple-flavored sausage and Vermont maple syrup. The repast is served by candlelight on china that is coordinated with the linens and using stemmed glasses. Every plate is garnished with bright edible flowers and herbs.

What's Nearby

A walking tour of historic Shepherdstown will take you past buildings dating to 1790. Visit the Historic Shepherdstown Museum and the Rumsey Steamboat Museum to learn more about the village. In recent years, Shepherdstown has developed an artsy following. There are upscale art galleries, craft shops, restaurants, clothing boutiques, and antiques shops along the streets. (See also Charles Town and Harpers Ferry, West Virginia, as well as Sharpsburg, Maryland.)

Innkeepers: Anne Carberry and Cliff Parrish
Rooms: 6, including 1 suite and 1 cabin, all with private baths, air conditioning, and radios; 5 with fireplaces; 1 with a Jacuzzi; telephones on request
On the grounds: Parking; gardens; basketball area
Extras: Coffee/tea and newspaper delivered to room; complimentary soft drinks
Rates: $80 – $120; including full breakfast
Credit cards accepted: MasterCard and Visa
Open: Year-round
Smoking: Smoking on covered porch only
How to get there: From I-64 traveling west, take exit 181. Travel west on Route 60 for .8 mile. The B&B is on the right adjacent to Castle Drive. From I-64 traveling east, take exit 175 and travel east on Route 60 for 4 miles. The B&B is on the left.

The James Wylie House

208 East Main Street
White Sulphur Springs, WV 24986
(304) 536-9444; fax (304) 536-2345

The three-story red brick Georgian Colonial-style house that enfolds the James Wylie House B&B was built in 1819. When the main house was discovered by the B&B's former owners, however, it had been abandoned and had graffiti and bird nests for decor. Behind the main house, a small 1794 log cabin had a river rock fireplace that threatened to collapse, and the foot-wide log walls had lost their chinking. Carefully restored, it was converted to a B&B in 1988, and it's now listed on the National Register of Historic Places.

The B&B has been under the care of Anne Carberry and Cliff Parrish since 1996. Cliff was born in England (you can't miss the accent) but previously lived in the Pacific Northwest, where he was a noted expert court witness about real estate values.

The B&B has glossy wide-plank oak floors covered with Oriental rugs, brass chandeliers, and elegant antiques. There are two living rooms — a quiet one with a Victorian sofa, a decorative fireplace mantel (although the B&B has eight fireplaces, none are functional), and a piano. It has blue walls with white trim. The other room is decorated in plum and green colors and has comfortable chairs for watching the TV or a movie on the VCR. The B&B is located on an acre of lawns and flower gardens. Guests will often while away an evening sitting on the front porch with its green wrought-iron tables and chairs.

The bedrooms are charming and very pretty. Every room has a fireplace mantel. One room is painted cobalt blue with white trim and has a blue and white duvet over the verdigris iron bed. There's an Oriental rug on the floor and an unusual pine wardrobe. Another room has a pencil-post bed and a floral duvet. Every room has its own bath, and one even has a Jacuzzi. The atmospheric old log cabin has log and chink interior construction. There's a sitting area with a beautiful working river rock fireplace as well as a kitchen and an eating area on the first floor. Upstairs, the bedroom includes a clawfoot tub, while the bath has a shower.

Breakfast is served in the formal dining room, which has a pine floor. Guests eat at a pine table with oak chairs. A plum-colored tablecloth is a dramatic backdrop for the white china and the incredible meal. Both Cliff and Anne are gourmet cooks. A typical menu might include freshly squeezed grapefruit juice, served with French toast stuffed with apples, bananas, and raisins and topped with an Amaretto sauce, accompanied by a cheese and sausage omelet. Or, perhaps they will fix crêpes filled with strawberries and topped with clotted cream, which Cliff has prepared himself, accompanied by ham and Irish potato cakes. Is there a cookbook on the way? The couple will prepare dinner for guests by special arrangement.

What's Nearby

White Sulphur Springs is the home of The Greenbrier, the grandest of the grand resorts. B&B guests can use the sports facilities, but there is a steep fee to do so. There is a mind-boggling array of things to do. You can golf on a variety of courses, eat in five different restaurants, and drink in six bars (three with entertainment), go horseback riding, play tennis, bowl, trap and skeet shoot, shop in some very posh shops, go ice skating or sleigh riding, or become a new you in the full-service spa. Or, take the tour of the fascinating catacombs that were designed during the Cold War to become the nerve center for the president and Congress of the United States in case of an attack. In the nearby 9,300-acre Greenbrier State Forest, you can fish, swim, hike, and work out on a fitness trail.

Indexes

Alphabetical Index to B&Bs

B&Bs Especially Suited to Children

Delaware

Maryland

B&Bs in or Near Cities

B&Bs by the Ocean

B&Bs on the Delmarva Penninsula